BLACK
POLITICS
IN
CONSERVATIVE
AMERICA

BLACK
POLITICS
IN
CONSERVATIVE
AMERICA

MARCUS D. POHLMANN

Longman
New York & London

Black Politics in Conservative America

Longman, 95 Church Street, White Plains, N.Y. 10601
A division of Addison-Wesley Publishing Co., Inc.

Associated companies:
Longman Group Ltd., London
Longman Cheshire Pty., Melbourne
Longman Paul Pty., Auckland
Copp Clark Pitman, Toronto

Executive editor: David J. Estrin
Production editor: Halley Gatenby
Text design adaptation: Jill Francis Wood
Cover design and illustration: Kevin C. Kall
Text art: K & S Graphics
Production supervisor: Kathleen Ryan

Library of Congress Cataloging-in-Publication Data

Pohlmann, Marcus D., 1950-
    Black politics in conservative America / Marcus D. Pohlmann.
      p.   cm.
    Bibliography: p.
    Includes index.
    ISBN 0-582-28684-0
    1. Afro-Americans—Politics and government.   2. Conservatism—
United States.   3. United States—Politics and government.
I. Title.
E185.615.P544   1990
323.1′196073—dc19   88-34375
                                                                   CIP

ABCDEFGHIJ-DO-99 98 97 96 95 94 93 92 91 90

This book is dedicated to Barbara Pohlmann
with love and appreciation

Contents

Acknowledgments

I wish to express my appreciation to a great many colleagues and students who have contributed to the evolution of this book. George Galster, Ken Goings, James Jennings, and Diane Pinderhughes have been a tremendous help in providing insightful criticisms of the entire manuscript. Bob Blair, Dan Calhoun, Thomas Dye, David England, Edward Greenberg, Ken Hoover, Randy Kesserling, David Levenbach, and Frank Miller contributed useful suggestions at a number of differnet stages. Walt Vanderbush made an invaluable contribution to the section on the educational system. I also wish to thank my many students over the years, especially those in my Black Politics courses. I appreciate the confidence and support both of my editor, David Estrin, and of the Rhodes College Faculty Development Committee, which granted me generous financial assistance. Cullen Weeden and Jean Shunk were extremely helpful in typing drafts, while both Steve Beckham and Grant Whittle did a terrific job verifying quotations and references. Justin Pohlman was patient, understanding, and loving far beyond his years. I want to acknowledge Charles V. Hamilton in particular, not only for inspiring me in this field but also for providing a model of a social scientist who is at one and the same time analytical, compassionate, and dedicated to the cause of human liberation.

PART ONE

Studying Race and Politics in America

CHAPTER ONE

Introduction

John and Sharon Williams are both 30-year-old high school graduates. They work 40 hours every week, 50 weeks out of every year, in order to support themselves and their two children. They have been told since grade school that if they work hard they will get ahead, own a nice house in the suburbs, and possibly even own their own company some day. That is the American dream, and they both were raised to believe in it.

But John and Sharon are black. If the market value of the goods and services they produce is $12 each hour, or $2,000 per month, their paychecks should reflect that. But they do not. Instead, John and Sharon receive approximately $320 less per month because of the color of their skin. An additional $800 goes to government in the form of various taxes so that government can provide their nation with a variety of services. Finally, some $200 a month goes to a small group of wealthy individuals in what is categorized in Chapter 5 as a form of tribute for the privilege of living and working in the nation these individuals own. That leaves John and Sharon with approximately $680 every month ($158 per week) with which to pay the landlord, make car payments, buy food and clothing, and pay other miscellaneous expenses for a family of four.

For John and Sharon Williams, a black couple in America—the land of opportunity—this may well be all there is ever going to be.

Their country is steeped in the rhetoric of "democracy" and "equal opportunity," and its government collects hundreds of billions of dollars a year in taxes from men and women like John and Sharon at least in part to help make that dream a reality. Why, then, does the game turn out so unevenly, decade after decade? For example, why does the average black family continue to earn 40 percent less than the average white family? Why do a small number of white men continue to own the controlling shares of virtually all of the nation's major corporations, facilitating their annual collection of billions of dollars from everyone else? Do John and Sharon really believe that members of this white elite are more talented, hard-working, or lucky than they are? Or do they simply believe that without white racism, there would be free and open competition for those elite positions? If they believe neither of those, why have such consistent results not driven John and Sharon to oppose the present political-economic arrangement more actively?

To begin to answer such questions, it is useful to look first at the American political economy. In doing so, there are clear indications that this system was designed to impede rather than facilitate fundamental change. Instead of providing mechanisms by which the less privileged majority can forge a future with fewer impediments to equal political and economic opportunity, the system described in these chapters can do little other than help reinforce the inequitable status quo. That status quo embodies a history of individual and institutionalized racism that has left black Americans far behind from the start.

Consider the analogy of a marathon between two equally skilled and motivated contestants. One runner has easy access to the best training facilities, coaches, and nourishment available. She trains full time, eats well, and arrives at the starting line in peak condition. The other runner, through no fault of her own, cannot gain access to those resources and is forced to train after a hard day's work and on weekends. The rules of the race are the same for both runners once they arrive at the starting blocks, but in fact the race is anything but fair, and the result is all but preordained.

FOCUS

Black people are not like other ethnic groups in American society. To begin with, blacks came to these shores, not as immigrants seeking a better life, but as slaves intended for use as forced laborers. The racist ideology erected to justify slavery served after the Civil War to keep blacks oppressed and subservient. . . . Businessmen, infected by their own racist dogma, preferred to import foreign labor. With the advent of the civil rights movement, the monolithic structure of racism began to show cracks, but then it was already too late. Black people were to enjoy the unfortunate distinction of being among the first surplus products of an advanced American technology and economic system.[1]

It is important to recognize at the outset that the black experience in the United States is unique, and thus analogies between that experience and those of other "immigrant" groups must be drawn with great caution. The original black population of this country consisted of people who were wrested from their homelands by force and ultimately sold into slavery. Their labor soon became integral to the agricultural economy of the American South, and, consequently, structures arose to protect that arrangement, including social and religious rationalizations for white supremacy and laws prohibiting educating slaves or harboring them if they ran away. Almost two centuries after the initiation of slavery in the United States, slaves were legally emancipated in the aftermath of a bloody civil war, rapidly elevated to a degree of power during Reconstruction, and then abandoned to the vengeance of their former masters with the collapse of Reconstruction. Night riders, lynchings, and sharecropper peonage pushed many blacks to move north in what came to be known as the Great Migration. But unlike the white immigrants who had preceded them into the northern cities, these new arrivals were soon to witness, among other things, the nearly complete disappearance of the political party machine as an assimilation agent, a decline in blue-collar jobs, and a continuing exodus of middle-class taxpayers.

The purpose of this book is twofold:

1. to analyze major problems black Americans face in 20th-century America and the related political and economic structures, with the ultimate goal of

developing a policy agenda for implementation once political power has been achieved

2. to scrutinize black political experiences over the course of U.S. history in order to develop political tactics for achieving policy changes

Internal differences in class, sex, and region have existed throughout the history of black Americans. In this book, however, I will focus on a number of interests common to virtually all blacks, without losing sight of separable and occasionally conflicting interests within black America. In addition, I will suggest that a number of the problems addressed are not unique to blacks. In particular, the development of the postindustrial economy—discussed at greater length in Chapter 2—has created a variety of socioeconomic dilemmas for middle-, working-, and lower-class whites as well. Ultimately, that reality only adds credence to the book's conclusions.

Finally, note that this book is not primarily a historical analysis of black involvement in the American political system, focusing on events like the Amenia Conference and political entities like the Congressional Black Caucus. To treat those developments as central would be to employ the traditional approach of taking the overall system as a given and focusing on the political process within it. A number of history and political science texts already do that quite adequately. Instead, in this study I will broaden the scope of analysis, putting primary focus on underlying political and economic structures. Specifically, the socioeconomic results for black Americans are scrutinized; I then work back to see if, and in what ways, basic political and economic structures have contributed to those results —and if they have contributed, how they can be changed.

CENTRAL HYPOTHESES

The central hypotheses of this book are as follows:

1. The American political and economic systems are intricately intertwined, particularly in the postindustrial era.
2. There is an economic class structure in the United States, and virtually all of black America is left out of the ranks of the dominant class.
3. The American government serves to reinforce the economic class structure.
4. The education system, the mass media, and possibly even the church are important socializing agents that function to suppress the consciousness of the non-owning class.
5. The resulting political-economic system, which primarily serves the interests of the white owning elite, must be altered if justice is to be achieved.

The analysis will begin with a historical overview of blacks' positions in American society in general and in the U.S. class structure in particular. It will then present an adaptation of Charles V. Hamilton's "conduit colonialism" model[2] in order to demonstrate how America's liberal governmental policies within a capitalist economy have come to reinforce the subordinate economic positions of the black middle, working, and lower classes. Thus, even as government assistance has helped propel the American gross national product and stock market, the American dream has continued to be an American nightmare for far too many American blacks. Why have political efforts not succeeded in redirecting the thrust of this government policy? Specific political arenas will be examined to reveal their inherently conservative functions. Finally, the alternatives section will argue for a tightly organized political coalition of disinherited groups, employing a diversified and multifront strategy with goals that include altering both the political and economic structures that have long helped to perpetuate their position. Such a development is extremely important for all these groups; focusing on black Americans, it is particularly vital if the vestiges of slavery are finally to be eradicated and justice finally attained.

Before proceeding, it is important to pause and consider what is being meant by the word *justice*. Would justice have been achieved if class inequities remained, stripped of their racial component? In other words, is the ultimate goal simply to see blacks assimilate effectively into the class structure that now exists? From this author's perspective, the answer to that is no. The goal is not to see blacks, or any other group, assimilate into a system that allows some status differences and mobility but also a considerable degree of unnecessary insecurity and pain. To opt for a less hierarchical political-economic system, however, does entail a trade-off. It would mean taking a system that allows a few to succeed in exploitive positions and trading it for a less exploitive system with fewer extremes of wealth and power. That flies in the face of many fundamental beliefs long held in America. But when the American dream for a few amounts to an American nightmare for far more and American insomnia for many of the rest, there can be no "justice." It is time for a fundamental change in the political economic structures, so that blacks—and all other citizens currently excluded from the American dream—can find justice and dignity in a system based not on exploitation but on a fair distribution of wealth and power.

Nevertheless, it is clear that such structural alterations are necessary, but not sufficient, to achieve racial justice in America. Racism would continue to stall progressive change even if major structural alterations could be implemented immediately. Racist individuals in positions of power will continue to find ways to discriminate. Yet these structural changes will still accomplish two very important ends. First, they will help clear the way for far more equal economic and political opportunity if and when racism diminishes. Second, they will take some of the sting out of existing racism by forcibly providing more equity for most black Americans.

CHAPTER OVERVIEW

Chapter 2: Theoretical Context

The mainstream political science approach to studying politics is to separate the political and economic systems and to focus on the political behavior of individuals and groups in a sort of empirical vacuum. Chapter 2 sets out a different theoretical approach, however, one that underlies the analysis throughout the remainder of the book. In particular, it allows for a broader focus that encompasses critical links between the political and economic systems. As a case in point, the chapter concludes by turning to the political realities evolving in today's "postindustrial" economy, and that overview makes quite clear the integral connection between political and economic structures, the limits of the mainstream theoretical approach, and the need for the theoretical synthesis developed in the chapter.

Chapters 3–5 will outline race and class structures within which black Americans have been forced to operate, while Chapters 6–8 will discuss the ways in which basic governmental institutions function to impede fundamental challenge to those structures.

Chapter 3: Blacks in American Society

Chapter 3 adds basic historical context. In begins by outlining some of the central events in the political history of black Americans, culminating with major victories in the Congress and the Supreme Court of the United States. It then turns to measures of actual political, social, and economic progress. In particular, it looks at trends in black educational attainment, occupations, unemployment, income, poverty, housing conditions, health conditions, neighborhood pollution, crime rates, and casualties in the nation's wars. It concludes by looking at differing black and white perceptions of these trends, especially in light of busing and affirmative action efforts to attack enduring forms of discrimination.

Chapter 4: The Class Structure

Chapter 4 focuses on the economic class structure that underlies the political process. In particular, it looks at the concentration of wealth in the United States—a concentration that has been growing even greater thanks to some of the largest mergers in the history of the country. It then describes the concentrated ownership of those assets, focusing on the extremely small proportion held by black Americans. Blacks, for example, hold only about 2 percent of the nation's capital stock; and although they also own 3 percent of the businesses, most all of those businesses are very small and vulnerable and operate on the margins of the economy. Lacking anything resembling a proportionate share of the nation's wealth, blacks—like most whites—are left dependent on the decisions of a small white owning class.

Chapter 5: Functions of a Welfare State

To demonstrate how the functioning of the American political-economic system has reinforced the underlying economic class structure, Chapter 5 endeavors to estimate the amount of money that has been transferred each year from the black and white middle and working classes to the investment portfolios of the small white owning class. This transference takes a variety of forms, such as private-sector profits from transactions with government and nongovernment consumers and direct transfers from government in the form of grants and credit subsidies.

Then, as capital becomes continually more mobile thanks to the transportation and communications technologies of the postindustrial period, the venture capitalists end up in an even stronger position to extract ever larger shares of the nation's income. For example, employees as well as federal, state, and local governments are warned, "Either grant us the concessions we ask, or we will invest our capital elsewhere." Thus the dominant position of the owning class becomes increasingly more secure, while those beneath them have actually been experiencing a real-dollar income decline.

Instead of increasing interracial and interclass solidarity among the non-owners, however, some clear polarization has grown out of their frustrations. This appears to be due in large part to both misperceptions and an underlying faith in the enduring myth of economic fairness and interclass mobility in America.

And why have governmental officials fostered these inequities rather than rectifying them?

Chapter 6: The Judicial Arena

Insulated somewhat from the electoral reach of the majority, the federal judicial process has often proved to be the most promising governmental avenue by which oppressed minorities could seek protection and assistance. This has certainly been true at a number of junctures in the history of black Americans, at least as long as the redress sought did not pose a serious challenge to the historic maldistribution of property. Nevertheless, even within those confines, major judicial victories are normally very slow in coming and can be stalled or even reversed in implementation or by subsequent court decisions.

Chapter 7: The Electoral Arena

At the founding of this nation, the electoral system was not designed to empower the masses—suffrage was generally limited to propertied white males, and the United States Senate was to be elected by state legislators. Those restrictions have since been eliminated, but a number of others continue to institutionalize race and class inequities. For example, the practice of privately funding virtually all political campaigns certainly puts the less privileged at a participatory disadvantage, and requiring presidential candidates to gain 15 percent of a state's primary election vote in order to receive any of that state's delegates to the Democratic party's national nominating convention clearly works to the disadvantage of black Democrats.

The party system as a whole is no less obstructive. A variety of rules and practices have impeded the path of third-party challenges to the inherently conservative two-party system—for instance, the winner-take-all, single-member-district arrangement, petitioning laws, the Campaign Finance Act, interpretations of the equal-time provision, and even a history of overt and covert police harassment of a number of them. As for the two major parties, they tend to be moderate and nonideological due to the very nature of a two-party system, and their decentralization and lack of patronage and nomination control have left them incapable of organizing and disciplining their mass and governmental memberships anyway.

Given an electoral system without a number of strong ideologically distinct political parties to educate and lead public opinion, it should not be surprising that many Americans hold uninformed and internally contradictory attitudes and that voting turnout is lower than virtually anywhere else in the world. It should come as even less of a surprise that, as Chapter 10 will indicate, black Americans are becoming increasingly distrustful of the entire system's ability to respond to their needs. They have done everything right. They are geographically concentrated in strategic locations and, controlling for socioeconomic status, turn out at a higher rate than whites. And they have voted as a cohesive bloc for the majority party virtually ever since the Emancipation Proclamation. Unfortunately, for reasons such as those just outlined, the electoral system is simply incapable of providing the means to achieve fundamental change.

Chapter 8: The Legislative Arena

Congress, the presidency, and the bureaucracy are intricately intertwined in the process of writing, passing, and executing federal laws. Thus they combine to form the legislative arena. Like its judicial and electoral counterparts, this arena is conservative by design. Beyond the unrepresentative demographics of its members, its rules and procedures make fundamental change extremely difficult to accomplish.

As a result, although blacks have achieved passage of some major pieces of legislation, those gains have come very sporadically, at a very high cost, and have proved difficult to sustain. Nonetheless, there have been a few hopeful signs. The growth of the Congressional Black Caucus has been a particularly significant development, as has the increasing black presence at the top and bottom levels of the executive bureaucracy.

Chapter 9: The Information Arena

Chapter 9 addresses why the information presented in the previous chapters is not more readily apparent, giving rise to rebellions against both race and class structures as well as the political system that reinforces them. The information arena discussed in Chapter 9 is seen as including the educational system, the mass media, and components of the black church. Each is seen as impeding consciousness of the realities in some significant ways, while helping to sustain a dominant culture that poses no real threat to these structural relationships.

Chapter 10: Shaping the Future

The book will conclude with the argument that a fundamental altering of basic economic and political structures will have to occur if blacks are ever to escape the vestiges of slavery. To that end, they must be prepared to join a tightly organized coalition of disinherited groups, comparable to Jesse Jackson's concept of a "rainbow coalition." Then, with the numbers and discipline to command attention, they must proceed on a variety of fronts, from education to voting to lobbying to litigation to the crisis-stimulating direct action that seems to be necessary in order to move the inherently conservative political system of the United States. The details of such a movement cannot be prescribed; they must arise naturally and dynamically from the real-life experiences and circumstances of real people.

TERMINOLOGY

The central argument presented in *Black Politics in Conservative America* is that not only does individual racism persist, but the historical effects of such racism have been institutionalized in the conservative American political economy. To make that case, it is first important to define "racism," "conservatism," and the ideological foundations on which the American political economy has been built.

Racism

Individual *prejudice* is defined as

> any set of beliefs that organic, genetically transmitted differences (whether real or imagined) between human groups are intrinsically associated with the presence or absence of certain socially relevant abilities or characteristics, hence that such differences are a legitimate basis for invidious distinctions between groups socially defined as races.[3]

Individual *racism* entails adding discriminatory actions to those prejudicial beliefs. When such racism gets incorporated into basic societal institutions, this is called "institutional racism."[4] Of the various institutions that serve to reinforce racism in America, one of the most basic is the nation's conservative political ideology.

The American Political Ideology

As any political community attempts to cope with an ever-changing environment, it must apply political power in order to achieve certain of its goals. The setting of these goals and the application of this power are guided by a set of societal beliefs, or a collective "ideology." Phillip Converse defines *ideology* as a logically coherent set of principles explaining political reality and justifying political preferences.[5] Kenneth and Patricia Dolbeare define it as the integration of political beliefs into a relatively coherent picture of "(1) how the present social, economic, and political order operates, (2) why this is so and whether it is good or bad, and (3) what should be done about it, if anything."[6] An ideology, then, becomes the value prism through which the world is viewed, as well as a set of guiding principles that help people make judgments about that world.

Ideology thus intervenes between so-called "objective" conditions and events and the people who perceive and evaluate them. It is a socially generated and transmitted screen that is consistent with . . . the deeper cultural values and way of thinking characteristic of people in a given society.[7]

In terms of public policy, ideology is crucial, for it guides the choice as to which problems are to be tackled and which options seriously considered—the political agenda. And as E. E. Schattschneider argues, the "definition of alternatives is the supreme instrument of power."[8]

Just what are the primary tenets of the political ideology that has served to filter America's view of reality, justify its goals, and ultimately shape its political output by structuring the political agenda at the input end of its political process? First, it is essential to note three key political values on which that ideology has been constructed: individualism, materialism, and limited government.

Individualism. Individualism appears to be the most fundamental of America's dominant values. The individual is viewed as the revered center of the political universe. Tied to this is a belief that human beings are competitive by nature. Accordingly, only by recognizing that fact and promoting this competition can either self-fulfillment or social progress be achieved. Individuals are also seen to be endowed with the inalienable rights to life, liberty, and the sanctity of private property, and these are not to be confiscated without full "due process of law," under which all individuals are to receive equal treatment. In addition, individuals are to be guaranteed the right to participate in the creation of these laws, the majority of equal citizens is to prevail, and each person is to be free to express dissent.

Materialism. Materialism is a value closely related to what is often termed the "Protestant work ethic." The assumption is that salvation is achieved by working hard, using one's talents and opportunities, and ultimately attaining worldly possessions as a measure of those efforts. Thus the society comes to place considerable value on consumption, to respect choices based on profitability, and to measure a person's achievement and worth by his or her accumulation of wealth. C. B. MacPherson also notes that, in the process, people come to see and treat themselves as commodities, selling themselves for a wage.[9]

Limited Government. To begin with, government is seen as having no inherent authority. As a collectivist enterprise with coercive potential, its sphere of operation is to be tightly circumscribed by the authority granted it by the individual members of the community and by the inalienable rights of those individuals. Primarily, it is to facilitate and referee competition between individuals as they jockey for positions of relative affluence. Beyond this function, government is generally expected to keep its hands off ("laissez-faire"). In a system where private profit and private consumption reign supreme, public spending, whether for schools, highways, or hospitals, is viewed with much more suspicion than are private investments, even if the latter are directed into rather banal consumer items.

Conservatism

The more general ideology that structures these values into both an experiential prism and a judgmental road map can be called either conservatism or "classical liberalism." It begins with a belief that the greatest good for the greatest number will emerge in both the economic and political marketplaces if competition in those arenas can be kept as unimpeded as possible. Individuals should be allowed to compete freely and openly: economic merchants competing for buyers and political candidates competing for voters. Because governmental regulation is limited, all compete economically as everyone strives for that ultimate symbol of success and salvation, material wealth.

Conservatives are less confident than their modern liberal counterparts that human beings are rational, perfectable, and capable of cooperating for mutual improvement. Thus conservatives put more faith in the economic marketplace than in government. The market provides an ideal arena in which the interests of insecure and competitive individuals can clash, leading to the best approximation of the "social good."

Adam Smith argued that the surest route to social good is when every individual

> neither intends to promote the public interest, nor knows how much he is promoting it. . . . He intends only his own gain, and he is in this, as in many other cases, led by an invisible hand to promote an end which was no part of his intention.[10]

Government, then, is to play a strictly limited role. It is to referee economic interactions and to protect competitive individuals from threatening each others lives, liberty, and private property.

John Locke, a conservative by today's standards, spoke of the primary interest he saw drawing people together into a society: "the mutual preservation of their lives, liberties, and estates which I call by the general name, property."[11]

Thus, in the final analysis, conservatism advocates a very minimal use of government. Its primary purpose is to facilitate an environment that will allow individuals the maximum amount of freedom while still protecting people and their property from other people.[12]

The general rules that are to govern the competition—such as laissez-faire and survival of the fittest—come to be viewed as natural, inevitable, and self-evident. Inasmuch as the ideology is taken as dogma, approval becomes unquestioned, and opponents come to be viewed as mentally or morally deficient.

The Political Result

It should come as no surprise that the prevailing political-economic philosophies of 18th- and 19th-century America are reflected in the fundamental procedures and laws of the land. As will be discussed in detail in Part Three, clashing interests were built into the governmental process, so that it would move slowly and deliberately if and when it should ever decide to move beyond its policing functions. Consequently, legislation has always been much easier to block than to pass.

The great security against a gradual concentration [of power] . . . consists in giving to those who administer each department the necessary constitutional means and personal motives to resist encroachments of the others. . . . Ambition must be made to counteract ambition. . . . If men were angels, no government would be necessary. If angels were to govern men, neither external nor internal controls on government would be necessary. In framing the government which is to be administered by men over men, the great difficulty lies in this: You must first enable the government to control the governed, and in the next place oblige it to control itself.[13]

What happens if a group finds itself needing more than a limited government to help erase the legacy of enslavement and subsequent discrimination? Limiting government would seem to promote the prevailing interests, not the aspiring ones. This certainly has been the case for black Americans (as documented in Chapter 3).

However, slavery aside for a moment, why is that true for blacks when it did not seem to be so for earlier white ethnic immigrants who also were forced to start at the bottom and face discrimination within the confines of limited government?

Most obvious is the difference in skin color. Educated white ethnics who had acquired the necessary middle-class mannerisms could occasionally change their names, addresses, and hair color and "pass" as a member of a more socially acceptable ethnic group. For blacks, by contrast, skin color generally precludes passing as members of higher-status white groups.

In addition, as mentioned earlier, the urban political machine was declining. Thus in many cities, urban blacks were left to try to assimilate without the degree of assistance ward bosses and precinct captains had been able to lend to their white immigrant counterparts. Progressive era reforms and historical events had come together to wound these institutions fatally just as in-migrating blacks needed them most.

Possibly of greatest importance, however, is the fact the nature of the economy has changed in some extremely significant ways. In particular, primary-sector jobs in labor-intensive industries are no longer providing nearly as many bottom rungs to the economic ladder. Instead of beginning work for union scale on an industrial assembly line with clear career ladders for skill development and promotion, today's aspiring workers are far more likely to begin as part-time employees in nonunionized service positions, stocking shelves at discount stores, for example, or bagging hamburgers at fast-food restaurants. This economic change is discussed further in Chapter 2.

Nonetheless, despite these historical inequities, polls continue to show considerable black allegiance to the dominant conservative ideology.

NOTES

1. Robert Allen, *Black Awakening in Capitalist America: An Analytical History* (Garden City, N.Y.: Anchor/Doubleday, 1969), p. 51.
2. Charles V. Hamilton, "Conduit Colonialism and Public Policy," *Black World* (October 1972).
3. Pierre L. van den Berghe, *Race and Racism* (New York: Wiley, 1967), p. 11.

4. Charles V. Hamilton and Stokely Carmichael, *Black Power* (New York: Random House, 1967), p. 4.
5. Phillip Converse, "The Nature of Belief Systems in Mass Publics," in David Apter (ed.), *Ideology and Discontent* (New York: Free Press, 1964).
6. Kenneth Dolbeare and Patricia Dolbeare, *American Ideologies* (Boston: Houghton Mifflin, 1976), pp. 2–3.
7. Ibid., p. 3.
8. E. E. Schattschneider, *The Semi-sovereign People* (New York: Holt, Rinehart and Winston, 1960), p. 68.
9. C. B. MacPherson, *The Political Theory of Possessive Individualism* (New York: Oxford University Press, 1973).
10. Adam Smith, *The Wealth of Nations* (New York: Modern Library, 1969), p. 423.
11. Sir Ernest Barker, *Social Contract: Essays by Locke, Hume, and Rousseau* (London: Oxford University Press, 1960), p. 73.
12. For further references on American conservatism, see Milton Friedman, *Capitalism and Freedom* (Chicago: University of Chicago Press, 1962); Friedrich Hayek, *The Road to Serfdom* (Chicago: University of Chicago Press, 1944); Clinton Rossiter, *Conservativism in America* (New York: Vintage, 1962).
13. James Madison in Clinton Rossiter (ed.), *The Federalist Papers* (New York: New American Library, 1961), p. 322.

CHAPTER TWO

Theoretical Context

Much political science analysis has been built on two fundamental bases: pluralism and systems theory. These approaches, however, have often left the discipline incapable of explaining adequately the interrelationship of racism, biases inherent in the United States' political economy, and the socioeconomic position of black Americans as a group. For example, where black politics has been considered at all, the emphasis generally has been on subjects like how race affects electoral preferences rather than on the harsh reality that blacks have remained in a consistently inferior economic position whether the president was Lyndon Johnson or Ronald Reagan and whether the Congress was dominated by Democrats or Republicans. The aim of this chapter is to outline a theoretical framework that allows systematic analysis of the political, social, and economic structures that appear to have served as barriers to the type of meaningful political change discussed in Chapter 1.

PLURALISM

Pluralism involves analyzing political conflict as it is organized around interest groups. Yet, using a traditional pluralist approach to the analysis of politics, blacks as a whole are not recognized as a meaningful political interest group appropriate to study. In addition, the possibility of institutionalized barriers to effective black participation is not considered either. Such myopia springs from key presuppositions concerning what constitutes an empirically relevant interest group and how the political process actually functions. Consequently, the entire concept of black politics is alien to this approach. An overview of the traditional pluralist approach follows.

Interests

Interests are defined as needs people are aware that they have. Thus the word *need* tends to become valuable as a political science concept only when used as a verb, that is, once that person has decided that he or she "needs" something. It is seen as having little empirical value in its noun form, as when the person has a "need" for indoor plumbing whether aware of it or not. The latter are avoided or discounted in traditional pluralist theory because they involve the analyst in projecting a need onto someone else, which is seen as entailing too much chance

15

for observer bias. Thus when a black person writes a letter to an elected official requesting something, that is an expressed political interest appropriate to study. When that same person is laid off work because his or her company has moved overseas, that person's need for government protection from such arbitrary abandonment is not deemed to be an appropriate subject for "value-neutral" behavioral analysis. Why? Because the analyst has projected a need onto that unemployed worker and has thus become more of an advocate than a purely detached observer.

Interest Groups

Political interest groups are comprised of people sharing commonly felt needs who interact for the purpose of affecting public policy. Pluralist beacon David B. Truman defines them this way:

> Interest group refers to any group that, on the basis of one or more shared attitudes, makes certain claims upon other groups in the society for the establishment, maintenance, or enhancement of forms of behavior that are implied by the shared attitudes.[1]

By that definition, black Americans—despite a common heritage of oppression—do not have a common interest appropriate to study. They would not have such an interest until it could be shown that all black people had at least one conscious purpose in common.

In addition, they are not an empirically relevant group either. Truman puts it this way:

> The significance of a . . . group in producing similar attitudes and behaviors among its members lies, not in their physical resemblance or in their proximity, . . . but in the characteristic relationships among them. These interactions, or relationships, because they have a certain character and frequency, give the group its molding and guiding powers. . . . A minimum frequency of interaction is, of course, necessary before a group in this sense can be said to exist.[2]

Truman is arguing that in order to be an interest group, all members must not only be conscious of a commonly held opinion but must also get together on a regular basis for the purpose of promoting that shared interest. If that is not the case, they are not an interest group appropriate for study as such.

Power Resources

Power resources available to the various political interest groups—time, money, prestige, contacts, media access, and the right to vote and petition elected representatives—are clearly distributed in an uneven fashion. Nevertheless, such uneven distribution is not seen by traditional pluralists as a structural bias worthy of analysis in its own right. First, they argue that those with the largest accumulation of power resources do not automatically have the most political power; for example, candidates who raise the largest amounts of money do not always win their elections. Strategy and circumstances are also important, and the resource-wealthy cannot monopolize these. Second, because everyone has access to at least some power resources, pluralists see any group as capable of becoming competitive if it can effectively pool an adequate number of such resources; for example, the poor can use their numbers to generate a substantial voting bloc and their spare time to swamp officials with messages.

Openness

The political system is considered to be "open" because of the variety of input channels available to interest groups. Not only do all participants have at least some of the resources necessary to compete, but the political process has so many access points that all voices will be heard if they just speak up. For example, there are elections, thousands of officials to contact, and newspaper columns devoted to letters to the editor, not to mention the constitutionally protected "right of the people peaceably to assemble and to petition the government for a redress of grievances."

Government

Government is seen as a relatively unbiased arbiter, refereeing the competition between conflicting groups according to neutral rules. Elected officials will either strive to determine and implement the expressed needs of their constituencies, or they will soon find themselves looking for alternative employment. Therefore, even if these officials are virtually all well-to-do white males, they still can and will respond fairly, for example, to black females who head households—if those black women effectively pool their resources.

Elections

As one might expect, any notion of an abstract "public interest" is discounted. Its existence would require unanimous consent. Nevertheless, traditional pluralists see elections as an important means for determining the "collective wish" at any one point in time, recording the outcome of the political competition between individual groups.

Equilibrium

In the end, it is argued that diverse groups flock to the political process to do battle over scarce public resources. That conflict creates disequilibrium within the political system, and it is then up to the elected officials to find a compromise that will appease the various groups and return the system to equilibrium.

Overall, then, traditional pluralists are arguing that the dispersion of power resources and the multiple opportunities for influencing government guarantee that the system will be relatively open to all. Therefore, political scientists need not concern themselves with the possibility that the rules of the game include some and exclude others in any really significant way. If the rules were stacked in that manner, it might make some sense to explore why categories of people, identifiable by nothing other than their consistent deprivation, so regularly fail to receive the prizes bestowed by the political-economic system. But if it is assumed that the system is open and that all people are basically aware of their own interests, the researcher need only focus on the government's efforts to appease organized groups seeking government favor. Therefore, drawing on such pluralist propositions, systems theory concerns itself only with that type of expressed political conflict.[3]

SYSTEMS THEORY

Gabriel Almond and G. Bingham Powell define a system as possessing two distinctive characteristics: (1) separate and distinguishable components (differentiation) and (2) interaction among those components in order to perform certain functions (integration).[4]

A political system, then, would be a set of differentiated units interacting to perform certain political functions, as when the Congress and the president interact to provide for national defense, assist the poor, or regulate interstate commerce. David Easton pictures it as in Figure 2.1. Inputs include popular support (e.g., recognizing the laws as legitimate and obeying them) and popular demands (e.g., the American Medical Association lobbying against national health insurance). Conversion ultimately amounts to public policymaking, where political actors (e.g., the president and the Congress) respond to various inputs by converting them into policies. Outputs are these authoritative decisions themselves (e.g., a decision not to pass national health insurance legislation). Feedback amounts to public reaction to these outputs. That reaction may be positive, settling the matter,

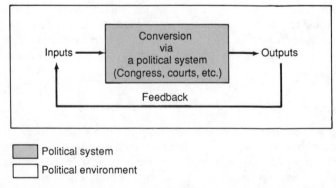

Political system

Political environment

Figure 2.1. David Easton's Political System Model. (From *The Political System* by David Easton. University of Chicago Press. Copyright 1953, © 1971 by David Easton. All rights reserved.)

or it could be negative, leading to further inputs on the issue or a decline in support of the government officials in power and possibly the political system itself.[5]

These bare bones of Easton's model provide a widely accepted picture of how a political system operates. However, this only scratches the surface of what constitutes a political phenomenon. A more searching question is, What is to be included in the category "politics"? And the obvious corollary is, What is and is not public policy and thus is or is not appropriate for a political scientist to analyze?

Easton suggests that politics, or public policymaking, occurs when political officials make authoritative policies for an entire political community.[6] It seems simple, but to appreciate the ambiguities that still remain, consider which of the following acts constitute public policy by this definition.

1. The president of the United States imposes trade sanctions on South Africa.
2. Congress passes the Voting Rights Act.
3. An official at the Board of Elections scrutinizes the nomination petitions of black candidates more closely than those of white candidates.
4. The federal government does not seriously consider a substantial compensatory payment to former slaves following the Civil War.
5. The board of directors of General Motors Corporation decides that the auto company will increase its manufacturing abroad instead of in Detroit, a decision with serious implications for thousands of black American workers.

The decisions of the president and the Congress would seem to qualify inasmuch as these are representatives elected to positions of public authority who make authoritative decisions for the political community. By the same logic, the Board of Elections employee has been delegated public authority by elected officials. But what about the last two cases?

Peter Bachrach and Morton Baratz carefully develop the argument that the alternatives government decides against or will not even consider are often every bit as political and important as ultimate decisions to act.[7] The federal government's decision not even to seriously consider compensating former slaves would thus be viewed as an important public policy affecting a large majority of the black political community. It is simply a negative output rather than a positive one, and it may reflect underlying structural biases.

As for the final example, the decisions made in the boardrooms of General Motors, Exxon, the Chase Manhattan Bank, and USX—or at the executive meetings of the United Auto Workers, the Teamsters, or the United Mine Workers, for that matter—often are policies that significantly affect large segments of the black political community. They may also be authoritative in the sense that the public accepts these organizations' prerogatives to make such decisions; yet they are not particularly open to much direct popular input.

In summary, systems theory defines the political system as institutions such as the legislative body, chief executive, and bureaucracy interacting to process inputs and emit outputs in a way that will enable them to maintain adequate support from the citizenry. Nonetheless, strict adherence to a combination of traditional pluralism and systems theory leaves the researcher incapable of addressing the type of important policy-related questions raised by the preceding examples 4 and 5. Consider three concrete cases in point that focus on potential structural biases stemming from the interrelationship between America's political and economic systems.

Case 1: Class and Political Participation

Income is distributed quite unevenly in the United States (see Table 2.1). For example, families in the top quintile make nearly as much money as the other 80 percent of the families combined, and this distribution has remained remarkably consistent over time. In addition, many of the families in the lower 80 percent were only able to achieve the incomes they had by virtue of having two or three wage earners or by receiving cash grants from governmental public assistance programs.[8] Thus there appear to be obvious income classes in the United States, and those classes have distinct interests in the degree to which government does or does not reinforce this economic inequality.

In terms of the black community, 40 percent of all black families and a majority of all black children fall into the bottom fifth, a reality that has generally been this bad or worse since slavery. Thus one might reasonably expect to see a rather large group of low-income black Americans becoming quite active politically in an attempt to alter a system that permits—and possibly even reinforces—such a maldistribution of income. Yet, as Lester Milbraith and M. L. Goel conclude,

> it is almost universally true that the more prosperous persons are more likely to participate in politics than the less prosperous. . . . [And] the relationship between income and unconventional political participation is similar to the relationship between SES and conventional political participation.[9]

What do such developments indicate about the political system in America?

A traditional analyst could be expected to argue as follows. If economic injustices are befalling large segments of the population, little precludes these people from seeking political redress by actively participating in the input

TABLE 2.1 FAMILY INCOME AS A PERCENTAGE OF NATIONAL INCOME, 1947–1985

Population Quintile	1947	1950	1955	1960	1965	1970	1975	1980	1985
Top fifth	43	43	42	41	41	41	41	42	43
Second fifth	23	23	23	24	24	24	24	24	24
Third fifth	17	17	18	18	18	18	18	18	17
Fourth fifth	12	12	12	12	12	12	12	11	11
Bottom fifth	5	5	5	5	5	5	5	5	5

Source: U.S. Department of Commerce, Bureau of the Census, Current Population Reports, and unpublished data.

processes. How can one begin to suggest that the entire system may be structurally biased simply because the conversion process is not responding to interests some analysts claim people have? If these people really felt that certain governmental actions were in their best interests, they would at least be attempting to use the input channels available in order to bring about such policies. For the political analyst to venture into the realm of interest inference is to run an unnecessary risk of introducing bias into the analysis and its conclusions. If political participation is unimpeded, and especially if no single elite dominates these open competitions, there is what can reasonably be viewed as a political system capable of adequately reflecting the community's various political interests.

But what if, no matter how open the procedures, the political race is fixed from the start, making the winners and losers pretty much preordained?

Although technically open to every citizen, the input process certainly does appear to be more open to some than to others. For example, as Milbraith and Goel and numerous other analysts of American political participation have concluded, the poor spend more time eking out a living, leaving less time for politics.[10] Lesser status also makes them less likely to have direct contact with the decision makers, while lower income leaves them less money with which to purchase special consideration by making large campaign contributions. In addition, the dominant American political value system may well be leading the vast majority of American wage earners to accept their subordinate economic position as being a politically irremediable economic injustice. Thus the political system may be far more likely to reproduce, rather than rectify, the inequalities of the economic structure on which it is built. Simply to ignore the possibility of such structural biases seems empirically myopic.

Case 2: Urban Renewal

Under urban renewal, homes in and near the central business district are razed and their predominantly low-income minority residents displaced. The land is then sold below market value to venture capitalists. Meanwhile, the displaced poor are often never relocated. Between 1949 and 1961, some 126,000 housing units were destroyed, displacing 113,000 families and 36,000 individuals, yet only 28,000 new housing units were built in their stead.[11]

Analyzing such an issue so as better to understand who has how much political power in a community, most traditional analysts would once again begin with the proposition that to minimize the introduction of the researcher's own values into a study, there must first be an assumption that people are the best judges of their own political interests. Peoples' political activity, or lack thereof, can thus be seen as a reasonably accurate reflection of those interests. Consequently, the results of a relatively unimpeded competition in the political process again provides an acceptable reflection of the various political interests in that community.

For example, a city council is chosen by means of the standard American electoral process. The council confronts the issue of urban renewal. It proceeds to hold public hearings on the question of whether to raze an inhabited slum block to make way for the erection of a new corporate headquarters. After the hearings, the council votes to raze the neighborhood. Traditional analysts would then approach this political decision by first assuming that the council has effectively refereed a relatively fair competition between various interests in the city. If the procedures are judged to be physically unimpeded, it is assumed that the process was open enough so as not to exclude any interest group from the outset.

But what if the majority of the council members are local business operators or are otherwise beholden to local business owners, either because of their large campaign contributions or the importance of their investments to the community? Is it not possible that the final council decision might primarily be a reflection of narrow elite interests rather than broader interests in the community as a whole? And if such elitism is occurring in most of the city's public policymaking arenas, just how open is the political process in this community?

Nonetheless, to address such questions of structural bias requires some objective determination of peoples' interests, and that is an analytical jump traditional analysts are generally unwilling to make.

Case 3: Poletown

Consider the 3,500 lower-income residents of Detroit's half-white, half-black Poletown neighborhood. In 1980, General Motors threatened to locate 6,000 jobs elsewhere if already ailing Detroit would not raze 1,176 Poletown homes so that a new $600 million Cadillac plant could be built there. The city of Detroit had little choice. A number of residents became concerned, however, and formed the Poletown Area Revitalization Task Force. They appealed to the mayor, the city council, and the courts, to no avail. With the help of hundreds of millions of dollars in public subsidies, 465 acres were to be razed, on which sat 1,176 homes, 100 small businesses, 16 churches, 2 schools, and a hospital; in return, GM promised 3,000 jobs, "economics permitting."

Detroit's black mayor, Coleman Young, author of the $700 million subsidy plan that the Michigan Environmental Review Board termed "incomplete, indefensible, and misleading," summarized it thus: "Jobs are our economic base, the key to our survival and future prosperity." He also termed a court ruling that rejected the Poletown Neighborhood Council's final effort to block the plan a "significant victory" for the city of Detroit. Nonetheless, in actuality, the city government was spending hundreds of millions of dollars out of its very limited budget and destroying an entire functioning neighborhood without a legally binding guarantee of even one job from General Motors.[12]

The most important lesson in case 3, in terms of the relationship between politics and the underlying economic structures, is that in the Poletown debate, the only realistic alternatives for the city of Detroit concerned how many concessions to make to General Motors. The muncipal government ultimately used eminent domain to condemn and destroy an entire neighborhood. No one, for example, seriously considered using eminent domain to condemn GM property in Detroit and seize it "for the public good." Why did this not occur? To begin with, the latter type of governmental seizure simply falls outside the present realm of acceptability as established by the dominant political culture in the United States. Beyond that, many local investors could have invested their money elsewhere, literally "freezing out" the economy of Detroit in retaliation. In addition, by withholding capital investments, the owners of capital outside the city would be capable of damaging the economies of both the state of Michigan and the entire United States, if necessary, until such "destabilizing" public policy was "righted."

MARXIAN THEORY

> In the social production of their life, men enter into definite relations . . . of production which correspond to a definite stage of development of their material productive forces. The sum total of these relations of production constitutes the economic structure of society, the real foundation, on which rises a legal and political superstructure and to which correspond definite forms of social consciousness.[13]

Karl Marx hypothesized that societal institutions such as the political system inevitably function to reinforce underlying economic class relationships. Thus if a society is organized under a capitalistic economic system—one in which a small owning class controls business capital and uses it first and foremost to attempt to make profits for itself while everyone else receives wages for working for the owners—the political system will function to help maintain the domination of the capitalist class over the subordinate mass of working people.

Marx's argument can be outlined in the following seven propositions:

1. The evolution and structure of any society arise from the dominant method of economic production, be it feudalistic, capitalistic, or socialistic. In other words, the historical development of a society's social and political relationships—its "superstructure"—reflect and reinforce the domination and subordination existing in the economy.

2. Production under capitalism is accomplished when the owners of the means of production engage workers in wage contracts. As a consequence, human labor becomes a commodity to be bought and sold in the marketplace. When owners sell the resulting products for more than they paid workers to produce them, providing themselves with a return on invested capital, they are seen to be exploiting the workers by not allowing them to realize the full market value of their work.

3. Products are then distributed via the marketplace, according to the principle of supply and demand. Thus production comes to be determined by the potential profitability of any given product, and consumption is based on one's ability to pay and not necessarily by one's needs.

4. Capitalistic enterprises must continue to expand in order to survive in a competitive marketplace. This requires a relentless search for cheaper labor and materials, the production of as many potentially profitable items as possible, and the cultivation of every conceivable market for those products. All of this is done without concern for the actual needs of society.

5. Owners and non-owners end up competing for scarce resources.
6. Paradoxes arise: resources are depleted; industrialization under capitalism has made people both interdependent and at the same time competitive with one another; a maldistribution of wealth and products leaves mansions at one end of town and slums at the other; division of labor and subordination in the workplace mutilate peoples' creative potential and leave them alienated from their work and thus from themselves.
7. The non-owning classes are increasingly likely to become more aware of their common plight, as well as more united and better organized; however, revolution does not occur immediately or automatically. Cultural, social, and political institutions and values continue to reflect and reinforce the maldistribution of wealth and power in the society; some examples are privately funded electoral campaigns and privately owned means of mass communication (the media) and beliefs that poverty results from one's own inadequacies, that human beings are naturally individualistic and greedy, or that blacks are genetically inferior.[14]

An analogy often used to help explain the relationship between capitalism's political and economic systems is that of a coiled spring. Think of a large and powerful spring being held down by the force of a person's hand. The spring symbolizes the inherent tension in the underlying economic class relations —workers against owners. If the repressing hand—symbolizing superstructural devices—begins to weaken, at some point the spring will be unleashed. That release would represent the class tensions being forcefully resolved as the working class throws off the yoke of the capitalist class.

Two very important premises are in operation here. Marx is suggesting, first of all, that a class structure is inevitable under capitalism. Specifically, there will not only be a small owning class and a large non-owning class, but there will also be societal barriers that all but preclude anyone from crossing those class lines. One is highly likely to remain in the class in which one is born, regardless of talent or hard work. Second, if this class structure exists, it will possess inherent conflict. By this he means that it is in the best interest of the members of the working class to control the means of production themselves, rather than to work for a small class of owners. Should the workers become aware of this, political conflict will occur, and the political system may no longer be able to keep the workers from seizing a more proportionate share of control over the means of production.[15]

AN ALTERNATIVE THEORETICAL APPROACH

At this point, it is important to return to the Eastonian model. If analysis is to occur wholly within Easton's original schema, it will be difficult to consider underlying economic structures and their relationship to politics. Easton, however grudgingly, limits his definition of a political system to the operation of the conversion mechanisms, and he proceeds to differentiate his political system from his political environment. Yet Marx is claiming that the political system is intricately intertwined with the economic system, functioning primarily to reflect and reinforce an underlying economic class structure. Consequently, rather than simply ignoring that possibility, *political environment* will be defined to include people's relations to the productive apparatus, and *political system* will be defined to include the entire political environment. This is shown in Figure 2.2. Such a revision of Easton's model allows analysis of any authoritative decision or nondecision that significantly affects the black community, as well as analysis of possible structural impediments to effective black political input into those decisions.

To complete this theoretical discussion and begin to understand more fully the link between the political and economic systems in late 20th-century America, it is instructive to note how the development of a postindustrial economy has affected the distribution of power. Such a discussion should make quite clear why it is empirical folly to try to analyze the political system separate from its economic context.

THE POSTINDUSTRIAL POLITICAL ECONOMY

After World War II, technological changes in transportation, communications, and automation made it possible for increasingly centralized and internationally dominant American corporations to search the United States and abroad for more attractive industrial environments. However, they did not immediately take advantage of these opportunities, striking instead a truce with American labor unions and continuing to make sizable profits by virtue of their international position of superiority. As late as 1960, there was virtually no Third World production of manufactured goods for export; yet, in the face of mounting international competition from Japan and Western Europe in particular, the economic downturn of the mid-1970s seems to have set off what Barry Bluestone and Bennett Harrison have called the "hypermobility of [U.S.] capital."[16] Since that time, many U.S.-based multinational corporations have launched aggressive searches for production settings that provide cheaper and more abundant resources,

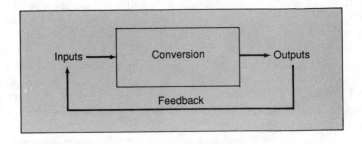

Political system (which includes the political environment)

Figure 2.2. David Easton's Political System Model, Revised

less expensive and more pliant labor, and a high degree of political stability.[17] Furthermore, some of the last remaining legal impediments to such mobility have recently been removed by National Labor Relations Board (NLRB) and federal court decisions.[18]

The resulting shifts in capital have come in a variety of ways. The overt physical relocation of an entire plant is relatively rare. Less drastic and more common are such techniques as redirecting profits and depreciation allowances, gradually relocating pieces of physical capital, laying off workers while contracting out their work to cheaper plants, and, of course, shutdowns or bankruptcy.[19]

Regardless of the form they take, such private decisions have an enormous impact on individual citizens, neighborhoods, and the governments involved.

In terms of impact on individuals, take Chicago's South Works as an example. Of the thousands of workers laid off between 1978 and 1984, fully 50 percent were finding it impossible to obtain adequate alternative employment. For black workers, that figure was 60 percent. Combining the unemployed and the reemployed, average household income dropped from $22,000 to $12,500; 11 percent were evicted from their homes; one-quarter felt compelled to find cheaper residences; and an additional one-third were behind on their mortgage or rent payments.[20]

Beyond losses of income, however, other individual and neighborhood problems can be found in the wake of such layoffs. Neighborhoods deteriorate. Property values plummet. Community networks gradually disintegrate. Health worsens when medical insurance has been severed. Retirement plans are curtailed. And suicide rates soar to 30 times the national average. Dr. M. Harvey Brenner found that for every 1 percent increase in national unemployment, there is a corresponding increase of 650 murders, 920 suicides, 4,000 admissions to state mental institutions, 3,300 admissions to state or federal prisons, and 37,000 deaths (27,000 from cardiovascular problems); furthermore, child abuse is three times greater in families where the breadwinner is unemployed. Brenner also found corresponding increases in automobile accidents, infant deaths, and cigarette smoking and other forms of drug abuse. He concluded that if unemployment was classified by the Public Health Service instead of the Labor Department, it would be considered a "killer disease."[21]

In terms of politics, the increasing mobility of capital has significant implications for government policy. For example, the nation, state, or locality is well aware that departing firms will also take with them their share of the tax base, and the new unemployed will no longer be available as a tax source. This revenue loss has obvious implications for the level of services that can continue to be offered to the population as a whole, just when the need for social services will have increased as a result of the layoffs. To remain solvent, therefore, the government would be forced either to raise taxes or to cut service levels, both of which are likely to drive away even more taxpayers.

As a result of this understanding, consider the following syllogism:

1. In all political systems, a healthy economy must be government's top priority if jobs and taxes are to be generated.

2. Under capitalism, a healthy economy depends on the profitability of private corporations.

3. Therefore, governments in capitalist societies must do what is necessary to maintain the profitability of their private corporations.

New York City mayor Ed Koch put it this way: "The main job of municipal government is to create a climate in which private business can expand in the city to provide jobs and profit."[22]

The requisites of corporate profitability become the ultimate parameters circumscribing the political decisions of any government operating in a postindustrial capitalist economy. And even though many non-owners of capital may gain material benefits from a healthy economy, the process precludes any serious challenge to the basic structure of ownership and power. In the postindustrial era, if a government responds to the interests of non-owners by implementing fundamentally redistributive public policies, this drives private-sector capital to more favorable locations. Such interests, therefore, must generally be ignored or, at best, occasionally placated.

Yet virtually ignoring all this potential power, the standard political science approach used in testing for the distribution of political power is to try to correlate group voting, campaign contributions, lobbying efforts, and the like with the decisions of public officials. The results have tended to be mixed. This has led to the general conclusion that the corporate elite—normally hypothesized to be the most likely candidate for the position of power elite—are often just another special-interest group, for they do not appear noticeably more likely to "win" contested decisions.[23] This approach ignores, however, the critical economic role of the large corporate interests and the political power it entails.

With the health of a government unit dependent on the profitability of its private corporations, the corporate elite seldom have to lift a political finger, for the priority of their interests is inherent in capitalism, especially postindustrial capitalism. As capital becomes increasingly more mobile, this corporate power will most likely increase accordingly.[24]

SUMMARY

The standard political science approach is to focus on the political behavior of individuals and groups within the existing political apparatus using variants of systems theory. The political and economic structures get separated, and political activity is analyzed in an empirical vacuum of sorts. The justification is contained in a corresponding theory called pluralism, which, as traditionally applied, presumes enough openness in the political system that the analyst need not be concerned about structural biases favoring some groups of people over others.

Yet there is considerable empirical myopia inherent in that traditional theoretical approach. In its place, a different theoretical context, suggested here, would integrate pluralist theory, systems theory, and Marxian theory. This would allow for a broader focus encompassing potential links between the political and economic systems.

Finally, an overview of the postindustrial economy sets the stage for the subsequent analysis of black politics, making clear the integral connection between political and economic structures, the limits of the traditional theoretical approach, and the need to synthesize the three theories discussed. The study that follows will consider black Americans as a political interest group with common objective interests, and it will attempt to test the political process for structural impediments to meaningful black participation and impact.

NOTES

1. David B. Truman, *The Governmental Process: Political Interests and Public Opinion* (New York: Knopf, 1971), p. 33.
2. Ibid., p. 24.
3. For a defense of the position described in the text, see Robert Dahl's articles in the *American Political Science Review* (June 1958; June 1966). For other well-known samples of traditional pluralist thinking, see Arthur Bentley, *The Process of Government* (Chicago: University of Chicago Press, 1908); Earl Latham, "The Group Basis of Politics," *American Political Science Review* (June 1952); Robert Dahl, *Pluralist Democracy in the United States* (Chicago: Rand McNally, 1967): Truman, *The Governmental Process*; Nelson Polsby, *Community Power and Political Theory* (New Haven, Conn.: Yale University Press, 1980).

   For critical analysis of traditional pluralism, see Robert Dahl and Charles Lindbloom, *Politics, Economics, and Welfare* (Chicago: University of Chicago Press, 1976); Charles Lindbloom, *Politics and Markets* (New York: Basic Books, 1977); Robert Dahl, *Dilemmas of Pluralist Democracy* (New Haven, Conn.: Yale University Press, 1982); Michael Parenti, "Power and Pluralism," *Journal of Politics* (August 1970); John Manley, "Neo-pluralism," *American Political Science Review* (June 1983); Kenneth Dollbeare and Murray Edelman, *American Politics* (Lexington, Mass.: Heath, 1981), pp. 40–41.
4. Gabriel Almond and G. Bingham Powell, *Comparative Politics: A Developmental Approach* (Boston: Little, Brown, 1966).
5. David Easton, *The Political System* (New York: Knopf, 1953); David Easton, *A Framework for Political Analysis* (Englewood Cliffs, N.J.: Prentice-Hall, 1965).
6. Ibid.
7. Peter Bachrach and Morton Baratz, "Two Faces of Power," *American Political Science Review* (December 1962); Peter Bachrach and Morton Baratz, "Decisions and Nondecisions: An Analytical Framework," *American Political Science Review* (September 1963).
8. Lester Thurow, *Zero-Sum Society* (New York: Basic Books, 1980); George Sternlieb and James Hughes, *Income and Jobs: USA* (New Brunswick, N.J.: Center for Urban Policy Research, 1984).
9. Lester Millbraith and M. L. Goel, *Political Participation* (Chicago: Rand McNally, 1977), pp. 96–97. Also see Sidney Verba and Norman Nie, *Participation in America* (New York: Harper & Row, 1972), pt. 1 and chap. 20.
10. For example, see Milbraith and Goel, *Political Participation*, p. 97.
11. For a more detailed discussion, see the National Commission on Urban Problems, *Building the American City* (New York: Praeger, 1969), p. 153; Martin Anderson, *The Federal Bulldozer* (Cambridge, Mass.: MIT Press, 1964); Bernard Frieden and Marshall Kaplan, *The Politics of Neglect* (Cambridge, Mass.: MIT Press, 1975); Susan Fainstein et

al., *Restructuring the City* (White Plains, N.Y.: Longman, 1983); Nancy Kleniewski, "From Industrial to Corporate City: The Role of Urban Renewal," in William Tabb and Larry Sawers (eds.), *Marxism and the Metropolis* (New York: Oxford University Press, 1978); Dennis Judd, *The Politics of American Cities* (Boston: Little, Brown, 1984), pp. 273–274.

12. Quotes and information from *New York Times*, September 15, 1980; December 10, 1980.

13. Karl Marx, preface to "A Contribution to the Critique of Political Economy," as quoted in Robert Tucker (ed.), *The Marx-Engels Reader* (New York: Norton, 1978), p. 4.

14. This outline was drawn from summaries presented in David Gordon (ed.), *Problems in Political Economy* (Lexington, Mass.: Heath, 1977), pp. 3–10; Kenneth Dolbeare and Patricia Dolbeare, *American Ideologies* (Boston: Houghton, Mifflin, 1976), chap. 8; and Tabb and Sawers, *Marxism and the Metropolis*, pp. 3–17. This synthesis originally appeared in Marcus Pohlmann, *Political Power in the Postindustrial City* (Millwood, N.Y.: Associated Faculties Press, 1986).

   For more detailed discussion of Marx's theory of the state and its relationship to capitalism's economic class system, see Karl Marx and Frederick Engels, *Articles from the Nene Rheinische*, tr. S. Rvazanskava, ed. B. Isaacs (Moscow: Progress Publishers, 1964); D. Easton and K. H. Guddat, *Writings of the Young Karl Marx on Philosophy and Society* (Garden City, N.Y.: Doubleday, 1967); Karl Marx, preface to "Contribution to the Critique," Karl Marx, *Die Grundrisse*, tr. Martin Nicolaus (Baltimore: Penguin, 1973); and Karl Marx and Frederick Engels, *The German Ideology*, tr. and ed. S. Rvazanskava (Moscow: Progress Publishers, 1964). For good secondary discussions of these views, see David McLellan, *The Thought of Karl Marx* (New York: Harper & Row, 1971) chaps. 4, 6; John McMurtry, *The Structure of Marx's World View* (Princeton, N.J.: Princeton University Press, 1978), chaps. 3, 4.

15. See Karl Marx, *The Poverty of Philosophy*, ed. Frederick Engels (Moscow: Progress Publishers, 1966); Karl Marx, *Grundrisse*; Karl Marx, *Das Kapital*, ed. Frederick Engels (Moscow: Progress Publishers, 1965), esp. vols. 1, 3, 4.

   For summaries of Marx's overall thinking, see McLellan, *The Thought of Karl Marx*; Tucker, *The Marx-Engels Reader*. For examples of this perspective as applied to the U.S. national government, see Ira Katznelson and Mark Kesselman, *The Politics of Power* (Orlando, Fla.: Harcourt Brace Jovanovich, 1987); Edward Greenberg, *The American Political System* (Boston: Little, Brown, 1983); Dolbeare and Edelman, *American Politics*; Michael Parenti, *Democracy for the Few* (New York: St. Martin's Press, 1983).

16. Barry Bluestone and Bennett Harrison, *The Deindustrialization of America* (New York: Basic Books, 1982).

17. For a fuller discussion of this phenomenon, see ibid.; William Goldsmith, "Bringing the Third World Home," in Larry Sawers and William Tabb (eds.), *Sunbelt/Snowbelt* (New York: Oxford University Press, 1984); Michael Storper and Richard Walker, "The Spatial Division of Labor," in Sawers and Tabb, *Sunbelt/Snowbelt*, pp. 19–22; Raymond Vernon, *Storm over the Multinationals* (Cambridge, Mass.: Harvard University Press, 1977); Ernest Mandel, *Late Capitalism* (London: New Left Books, 1975); F. Froebel et al., *The New International Division of Labour* (Cambridge: Cambridge University Press, 1980).

18. *New York Times*, January 25, 1984; April 11, 1984.

19. Bennett Harrison and Barry Bluestone, "The Incidence and Regulation of Plant Closings," in Sawers and Tabb, *Sunbelt/Snowbelt*, pp. 368–402.

20. *New York Times*, October 31, 1984.

21. Douglas Fraser et al., *Economic Dislocations: Plant Closings, Plant Relocations, and Plant Conversion*, report prepared for the U.S. Congress, Joint Economic Committee (Washington, D.C., 1979), p. 1; *Chicago Tribune*, April 23, 1983; July 8, 1984. Also see articles by Duane Hagan, Dennis Ahlburg, and Morton Shapiro in *Hospital and*

Community Psychiatry (May 1983); and Bluestone and Harrison, Deindustrialization of America.

22. New York Times, March 4, 1978.

23. For a classic example, see Robert Dahl, Who Governs? (New Haven, Conn.: Yale University Press, 1961). For a comparable piece of empiricism built on entirely different ideological premises, see Lynda Ann Ewen, Corporate Power and Urban Crisis in Detroit (Princeton, N.J.: Princeton University Press, 1978).

24. For more discussion of this subject, see Kenneth Newton, "Feeble Governments and Private Power," in Louis Masotti and Robert Lineberry (eds.), The New Urban Politics (Cambridge, Mass.: Ballinger, 1976); Paul Peterson, City Limits (Chicago: University of Chicago Press, 1981); Alfred Watkins, The Practice of Urban Economics (Beverly Hills, Calif.: Sage, 1980); Barry Bluestone and Bennett Harrison, Capital and Communities (Washington, D.C.: Progressive Alliance, 1980); William Tabb, "Economic Democracy and Regional Restructuring: An Internationalization Perspective," in Sawers and Tabb, Sunbelt/Snowbelt, pp. 403–416.

PART TWO

Blacks and the American Political Economy

CHAPTER THREE

Blacks in American Society

Emancipation elevated [the black man] only to the position of semi-dependent man, not to that of an equal and independent being.

Harold Cruse[1]

Caught in a spider's web of individual and institutionalized racism, black Americans have pursued power for centuries in an attempt to become free and equal participants in the American political and economic systems. They have often disagreed among themselves about the most appropriate goals and strategies for dealing with specific, day-to-day crises, and some of that disagreement has been grounded in fundamentally different values and world views. But solidarity resides in one simple fact: they share the overriding experience of being black in the United States of America.

To provide a historical context for an analysis of institutionalized racism in America, major events in black political history will be outlined, as will measures of political, social, and economic progress.

MAJOR EVENTS IN BLACK POLITICAL HISTORY

The following timeline should facilitate quick review at the outset and easy reference while reading the chapters that follow.

Needless to say, however, the political efforts of numerous black individuals and organizations mark the years between these developments; for example, the work of the National Association for the Advancement of Colored People (NAACP) in pursuing school integration prior to the 1954 U.S. Supreme Court decision in *Brown v. Board of Education*. The strengths and limits of those specific activities, both within and outside the formal political process, are discussed in detail in Chapters 6–10.

Beyond that, the outline certainly does not include all the major events in the political history of black Americans, and it is in no way intended as a substitute for a full black history text like John Hope Franklin's *From Slavery to Freedom*. Nonetheless, it does touch on a number of the most important political events as an overview for the purposes of this book.[2]

1619   The first 20 *black indentured servants* arrive (Jamestown, Virginia).

1637   The first American-based slave ship, *The Desire*, begins its ghoulish work of caging and transporting black Africans for sale in the New World.

1641   *Slavery* begins to be sanctioned by American law.

1688   About this time, German Mennonites join British-born residents and others in pressing for the *abolition* of slavery.

1776   The *Declaration of Independence* is proclaimed, but it is stripped of Jeffersons' antislavery rhetoric by adamant representatives of southern states.

1776   The *Articles of Confederation* extend citizenship to "free inhabitants," although an effort to limit it to "free white inhabitants" is defeated. Nevertheless, a number of states require blacks to register upon entry and limit their stay, while the State Department will issue "travelling papers" but not passports for those free blacks wishing to spend time abroad.

1787   The *United States Constitution* is drafted, with each slave to count as three-fifths of a person for the purpose of determining a state's taxation and representation. The specific criteria for citizenship are left to the states, and Delaware is the only state banning the importation of slaves at this time. However, Article 1, Section 9, does allow the Congress to outlaw U.S. participation in international slave trading after 1808.

1789   *Revolutionary America* finds 92 percent of its roughly 750,000 blacks still enslaved. Free blacks comprise about 2 percent of the national population, and very few of them are allowed to vote.

1793   The *Fugitive Slave Act*, upheld by the Supreme Court in 1842, requires the federal government to assist in returning runaway slaves.

1793   The *10th Amendment* lays the legal groundwork for claims of "states' rights."

1796   Richard Allen founds the African Methodist Episcopal Zion Church, as many free blacks begin to form *black churches*—a practice that expands considerably after the Civil War and leads to an infrastructure that has proved politically useful to the present day.

1800   *Slaves* number over one million, reside almost exclusively in the South, face rape and brutal physical punishments at the hands of their slave masters, and are bound by slave codes that strictly limit their rights (to own property, learn to read, etc.). Meanwhile, approximately 60,000 *free blacks* reside about equally in the North and South, and a few of them even own slaves. Nevertheless, their rights have been eroding since the Revolution, and many live in fear of being enslaved themselves as a result of kidnapping or judicial reversal of their status.

1807   Congress rules that there is to be *no further importation of slaves*, although this only increases the domestic slave trade, and the law is so loosely enforced that some 250,000 slaves are still imported after its passage.

1817   Although never very successful, the *American Colonization Society* works to assist blacks in returning to Africa. In part, it helps provide a safety valve for ridding the nation of black "troublemakers."

1819   With the addition of states such as Alabama, Louisiana, and Mississippi, cotton is now "king," and slave labor is in higher demand than ever. The *Missouri Compromise* represents a truce between slaveholders and abolitionists, setting up a boundary line to govern whether newly admitted states are to be slave or free.

1829   Free black David Walker begins publishing *Walker's Appeal*, which calls for blacks to rise up against slavery, using violence if necessary. Soon there are some *50 black abolitionist groups*.

1831   As *slave resistance* escalates, Nat Turner leads a major slave revolt in Virginia. In just two days, approximately 70 slaves rise up and execute about that many whites. Other forms of resistance include arson, sabotage, work slowdowns, running away, and suicide.

1831   With the number of slaves topping the 2 million mark, white reformer William Lloyd Garrison uses his publication, *The Liberator*, to press for the immediate and total end of slavery. Calling primarily for nonviolent passive resistance, the *white abolition movement* is beginning to become a force. A variety of tactics are being pursued, including the formation of the Liberty party.

1834   As black presence increases in northern cities, racism flourishes. In one of the worst *racial riots* of the 1830s and 1840s, white mobs storm black neighborhoods in Philadelphia.

1838   *Frederick Douglass* escapes his enslavement, ultimately to become an important national leader and spokesperson for his race. Besides using his publication, *The North Star*, to press for an end to slavery and later an antilynching law, he also advises presidents and voluntarily recruits blacks for the Union army as the Civil War erupts.

1850   J. W. Loguen, Harriet Tubman, and others organize and operate the *Underground Railroad*, by this time helping roughly 1,000 blacks a year to escape slavery.

1850   The *Compromise of 1850* allows California to be admitted as a free state and ends slavery in Washington, D.C., in return for stricter enforcement of the Fugitive Slave Act. In response, the first serious talk of secession begins in Alabama, Georgia, Mississippi, and South Carolina.

1852   The novel *Uncle Tom's Cabin* dramatizes some of the abject cruelty imposed by slavery.

1853   *Sojourner Truth* rises to speak at the Fourth National Womens' Rights Convention. Posing the question "Ain't I a woman?" and fending off racist jeers, she speaks clearly of what it is to be black and female in the land of the free and the home of the brave.

1853   The National Council of Colored People is formed, conducting some of the many *black political conventions* prior to the Civil War.

1854   The *Kansas-Nebraska Act* nullifies the Missouri Compromise, allowing states to decide the slavery issue for themselves. This leads to some bloody intrastate warfare.

1855   Wilberforce University is founded as an extension of the African Methodist Episcopal Church, and it reflects the growing effort on the part of blacks to provide *education for black children.*

1857   In *Dred Scott v. Sanford,* the U.S. Supreme Court explicitly declares that the now nearly 4 million slaves are property of their masters and not citizens; thus they have no standing to sue, they have no constitutional rights, and their owners' possession of them is protected by the due process clause of the Fifth Amendment. The decision also challenges the federal government's right to regulate slavery in the "territories."

1859   *In the North,* only six states allow blacks to vote; black public schools are generally segregated and inferior; certain states preclude black testimony if a white is a party in the legal case; some states bar black immigration altogether; and so on.

1859   *John Brown* unsuccessfully leads 22 men in a raid on a federal arsenal in Harpers Ferry, Virginia. The goal was to use the captured weapons to help set off a general slave revolt across the South.

1860   The *Civil War* begins following the election of Abraham Lincoln and the Confederate attack on Fort Sumter.

1861   *Federal Confiscation Acts* allow for the expropriation and freeing of slaves, except in loyal border states where even the Fugitive Slave Act is to continue to be enforced.

1863   The *Emancipation Proclamation* is declared for all but the 800,000 slaves in loyal states, although no material compensation is ever forthcoming for the 246 years of forced labor.

1865   The *13th Amendment* constitutionally abolishes slavery.

1865   The *Freedmen's Bureau* is created to provide former slaves with education and relief assistance as well as to dispose of abandoned property.

1865   President *Abraham Lincoln is assassinated.*

1865   In Savannah, Georgia, General Sherman expropriates 30 miles of southern coastline and grants it to former slaves as an exclusive black settlement. Allotted 40 acres per family, some 40,000 blacks quickly move there. Within months, however, President Andrew Johnson has returned it all to its Confederate owners. Consequently, there and throughout the South, recently freed blacks find themselves *propertyless* and thus forced into virtual peonage at the hands of former slave masters.

1866   Reactionary *race riots* resume with a vengeance. In Memphis, a white rampage leaves 46 blacks and 2 white sympathizers dead, 5 black women raped, and 90 homes, 12 schools, and 2 churches burned.

1867   The Reconstruction Act evades beleaguered President Andrew Johnson and imposes *radical Reconstruction* on the South, disenfranchising the bulk of whites as state constitutions are rewritten. Governance is then left to blacks, anti-Confederate whites, and northern "carpetbaggers."

1867   The *Union League* serves as the southern arm of the Republican party.

1867   The Ku Klux Klan is born, one of a number of *violent reactionary white organizations.*

1868   The *14th Amendment* requires states to guarantee "equal protection" under their laws and not to deprive their citizens of life, liberty, or property without providing "due process of law."

1869   The *National Negro Labor Union* is formed, as blacks are generally excluded from the early white labor movement—a practice that would continue well into the 20th century.

1870   The *15th Amendment* bars states from denying anyone the right to vote because of race.

1872   The *Amnesty Act* reinstates citizenship across the old Confederacy, except for the very most prominent Confederate officials.

1874   The *Democratic party*, based in the South, wins control of the House of Representatives and makes significant gains in the Senate.

1875   A *Civil Rights Act* outlaws racial segregation in public accommodations and the military; however, it, along with other such legislation passed since 1866, is soon struck down by the U.S. Supreme Court.

1876   *Reconstruction officially ends*, as President Rutherford Hayes trades it for enough southern votes in the House to win an extremely close presidential election over Samuel Tilden. Northern troops will no longer remain in the South to protect the rights of former slaves, although that protection has been less than adequate for some time.

1880   The U.S. Supreme Court, in *Stander v. West Virginia*, declares all-white juries to be unconstitutional if written into state law or the result of overt discriminatory acts.

1884   The U.S. Supreme Court, in *Ex parte Yarborough*, affirms a federal law against interfering with a person's right to vote in federal elections.

1895   *Booker T. Washington*, in his Atlanta Exposition Address, lays out the philosophy that underlies his founding of Tuskegee Institute. Southern blacks were urged to "cast down their buckets where they were," remaining in the South and learning farm, mechanical, and domestic skills before worrying about equal political rights in the larger society.

1896   In *Plessy v. Ferguson*, the U.S. Supreme Court declares that legal separation of the races is not a violation of blacks' constitutional rights. "Separate but equal" is equal.

1900   By this time, all southern states have changed their laws and constitutions in order to create the *legal disenfranchisement and segregation* of blacks, 90 percent of whom still reside in the South. In terms of voting, a combination of grandfather clauses, literacy tests, poll taxes, all-white Democratic primaries, administrative discrimination, and outright violence or threats thereof have succeeded in disenfranchising over 95 percent of all southern black voters.

1900   Some of the first *direct action* begins to appear as blacks boycott segregated streetcars in more than 25 cities over the following six years. Although peaceful by intent, some violent confrontations do occur.

1905   W. E. B. Du Bois, Monroe Trotter, and other black leaders organize the *Niagra Movement,* designed to press for equal rights and black solidarity. This movement gives rise to a number of black political conferences including a major one in Amenia, New York, in 1916.

1909   Growing out of the Niagra Movement, the *NAACP* is founded to press for black rights by means of lobbying and court cases. W. E. B. Du Bois edits its official publication, *The Crisis.*

1914   Marcus Garvey founds the *Universal Negro Improvement Association* in Jamaica and soon brings it to the United States. It is grounded in the principles of black pride and a separatism that ultimately involves renewed efforts to help blacks return to Africa.

1915   The U.S. Supreme Court, siding with the NAACP, declares the *grandfather clause unconstitutional* (*Guinn and Beal v. United States*). No longer is it to be more difficult for blacks to vote simply because their grandfathers were not registered.

1915   Some 3,600 blacks have been the victims of *lynch mobs* since 1884.

1915   Spawned by acts of violence, the mechanization of southern agriculture, and industrial job opportunities in the North, the first major wave of the *Great Migration* has begun, and migrating blacks are assisted in their adjustment by the National Urban League and a variety of black newspapers. By 1970, some 6.5 million blacks will have migrated to the North, resulting in half of the black population residing there.

1917   *Racial rioting* occurs in East St. Louis, and it is typical of such rioting at the time, with mobs of angry whites storming black ghettos in retaliation for an alleged incident.

1920   The *19th Amendment* legally enfranchises half the black population —women.

1921   An *antilynching bill* is finally introduced in the Congress, but it is stopped by a filibuster in the Senate.

1925   A. Philip Randolph founds the Brotherhood of Sleeping Car Porters and Maids, a *black labor union* created in the face of continuing racial discrimination on the part of white unions. Such segregation would persist for another three decades.

1929   The *Great Depression* hits blacks particularly hard, leaving them three to four times as likely as other Americans to be receiving public assistance. Yet they even face some discrimination in the relief lines.

1930   The *Black Muslim Movement* emerges in Detroit, later to rise to national prominence under the leadership of Elijah Muhammad and Malcolm X. Its goal is a self-sufficent black nation within the United States, emphasizing self-discipline, thrift, industriousness, pooled resources, and self-defense under Muslim religious beliefs.

1931   For the first of four times, a group of black youths—later to be called the *Scottsboro Boys*—are convicted of raping a white woman. Two of those convictions are ultimately overturned by the U.S. Supreme Court, including the 1932 decision of *Powell v. Alabama,* in which the Sixth Amendment's "right to counsel" was held to be required at the state level too.

1934   The newly created Federal Housing Administration openly sanctions *racial segregation in housing* for its first 10 years of existence.

1936   The *shift of black voters* to the national Democratic party, first noticeable in 1928, is cemented as Franklin Roosevelt receives a majority of black votes.

1936   The *National Negro Congress* emerges as an umbrella organization for the civil rights struggle, which would include the formation of groups such as the Southern Conference for Human Welfare.

1941   Despite the beginning of U.S. involvement in World War II, A. Philip Randolph *threatens a huge, all-black march on Washington* to protest racial discrimination. He ultimately calls it off in return for the establishment of the Fair Employment Practices Commission, although that commission can only investigate and make recommendations concerning training and employment in government defense industries, and it all but disappears after the war.

1941   In *United States v. Classic,* the U.S. Supreme Court rules that the federal government can step in and regulate primary elections, as they are an "integral part" of the right to vote.

1942   The Congress of Racial Equality (*CORE*) is formed and is soon organizing freedom rides, sit-ins, boycotts, rent strikes, and other nonviolent direct actions as a way of challenging continuing racial discrimination.

1943   The Detroit riots are some of the most destructive of a series of *black ghetto revolts,* including a major one in Harlem in 1935.

1945   In *Screws v. United States,* the U.S. Supreme Court affirms that a Georgia sheriff by the name of Screws violated a black man's 14th Amendment rights by taking his life without "due process of law." The man was beaten to death after being arrested for stealing a tire.

1948   The *Democratic party reaches out to blacks* with a series of moves, including President Truman's creation of a federal Commission on Civil Rights, his executive order calling for "fair employment practices" in the federal government, and the desegregation of the military after decades of distinguished black service in separate regiments. In addition, the party adopts a civil rights plank at its presidential nominating convention, prompting a number of southern delegates to bolt and form the State's Rights party, nearly costing Truman the election.

1948   The U.S. Supreme Court, in *Shelley v. Kramer,* strikes down clauses in housing contracts that forbid resale of the property to blacks.

1954   In *Brown v. Board of Education,* the U.S. Supreme Court reverses its 1896 decision and strikes down "separate but equal" as "inherently unequal." (Unfortunately, the case would be brought again 32 years later as school segregation continued in Topeka.)

1955   Martin Luther King, Jr., helps organize the successful *Montgomery Bus Boycott.*

1956   The Federal Bureau of Investigation (FBI) launches its "counter-intelligence program"—code name: *COINTELPRO.* Conducted until 1971, a major purpose is to disrupt allegedly "dangerous" black organizations ranging from the militant Black Panthers to the very moderate National Urban League.

1957   Out of King's Montgomery Improvement Association is formed the Southern Christian Leadership Council (*SCLC*) to continue to organize direct action against racial discrimination in the South.

1957   Federal troops are sent to Little Rock, Arkansas, to assist in the *forceful desegregation* of its schools.

1960   Black students sit at a segregated lunch counter in Greensboro, North Carolina, touching off a wave of such *sit-ins* across the South. Ultimately, even their arrests and convictions are struck down by the U.S. Supreme Court.

1960   The Student Nonviolent Coordinating Committee (*SNCC*) is formed as the student arm of the SCLC, and it functions until ideological rifts tear it apart seven years later.

1961   NAACP founder *W. E. B. Du Bois,* now a member of the American Communist party, renounces his U.S. citizenship and moves to Ghana.

1961   *School segregation* persists, and South Carolina, Alabama, Georgia, Mississippi, and Louisiana still do not have a single integrated public school.

1962   Federalized National Guardsmen escort James Meredith as he becomes the first black student to enter the University of Mississippi. *School desegregation in the South* is beginning to develop momentum.

1963   With more than 200,000 in attendance and capped by Martin Luther King's famous "I Have a Dream" speech, the *March on Washington* is probably the most dramatic of a number of nonviolent protest marches that have been occurring across the South and are beginning to appear in the North as well.

1963   As the world watches black churches being bombed and the dogs and fire hoses being turned on peaceful black protesters, President John Kennedy warns of *impending federal action.* Civil rights activist Medgar Evers is gunned down the day of that speech, and the president will join him within two months.

1964   The *24th Amendment* to the United States Constitution bans poll taxes in federal elections.

1964   The last and most comprehensive of the *Civil Rights Acts* is passed by Congress, directly involving the federal government in the enforcement of black civil rights, especially in the South.

1965   A large *ghetto revolt* erupts in the Watts section of Los Angeles, one of 164 such outbreaks to occur between 1962 and 1968. These revolts leave more than 100 people dead, thousands wounded, thousands more arrested, and hundreds of millions of dollars' worth of property damage.

1965   Congress passes the first of the *Voting Rights Acts,* involving the federal government even further in forcing stubborn states to allow blacks the right to vote.

1965   President Lyndon Baines Johnson declares a *War on Poverty,* which ultimately leads to the creation of a host of federal programs, including Head Start, VISTA, the Job Corps, and Legal Aid. He also creates the Council on Equal Opportunity.

1965   Black Muslim leader *Malcolm X,* articulate spokesperson for the black underclass, is assassinated.

1966   The term *black power* is coined by Stokely Carmichael and Charles V. Hamilton and is first spoken by Carmichael and CORE's Floyd McKissick. Black Power Conferences begin in Newark and spread to other large cities during the next two years.

1966   The *Black Panther party* emerges, in large part to defend black communities against racist violence. Militant *black workers' movements* are also developing, among them the League of Revolutionary Black Workers (Detroit), the Black Panther Caucus of the Fremont GM Plant (California), and the United Black Brotherhood (New Jersey).

1966   The U.S. Supreme Court's decision in *Harper v. Virginia Board of Elections* eliminates poll taxes in state elections as well.

1968   A "tent city" is erected as part of the *Poor Peoples' March on Washington;* this protest is ultimately dispersed by police force.

1968   *Martin Luther King, Jr.,* is assassinated.

1968   As federal troops guard the Capitol building from the rioting that has erupted following the King assassination, the Congress is inside passing the *Fair Housing Act.* It will bar racial discrimination in the sale or rental of private residences.

1969   The Black Economic Development Conference writes a *Black Manifesto,* which calls for reparations among other things.

1971   In *Swann v. Charlotte*, the U.S. Supreme Court rules that busing is a legitimate tool for fighting school segregation, though it is later limited to exclude busing across city-suburb boundaries.

1972   The first *National Black Political Convention* is held the same year that *Shirley Chisholm* becomes the first black candidate to mount a formidable campaign for the office of president of the United States.

1973   James Coleman, whose famous 1968 study helped justify the imposition of busing to improve black educational performance, now concludes that busing is failing because of the "*white flight*" it has helped to generate.

1974   In *San Antonio v. Rodriguez*, the U.S. Supreme Court determines that heavy reliance on neighborhood property taxes is not a discriminatory way to fund public schools, despite tremendous disparities in neighborhood wealth. Although a few individual states have found otherwise and introduced a more redistributive method of school funding, the Supreme Court decision still has serious implications for people living in low-income areas.

1978   *University of California v. Bakke* is the first of a series of Supreme Court decisions clarifying the scope of allowable "affirmative action." The court seems to be saying that race is a legitimate criterion to consider in admission, hiring, firing, and promotion decisions, but rigid quotas are not to be employed unless there is evidence of previous discrimination by that institution or a "clear state need" can be demonstrated. Later decisions will exempt legitimate seniority systems from such affirmative action.

1979   Jesse Jackson launches his *PUSH for Excellence.*

1980   The census confirms *black majorities in large cities* such as Baltimore, Detroit, Newark, and Washington, D.C., and impending majorities in Chicago, Cleveland, Memphis, Philadelphia, and St. Louis.

1980   *Ronald Reagan* is elected president of the United States, with major implications for the enforcement of civil rights laws. For example, not only does his administration all but cease to enforce affirmative action regulations, but it even argues against them in federal court.

1980   *Ghetto unrest* in Miami includes beatings, maimings, burning, looting, and sniper fire, leaving 18 dead, more than 200 seriously wounded, 750 arrested, and more than $100 million in property damage. Smaller incidents occur in Witchita, Chattanooga, and Orlando.

1981   Blacks and laborites join in a massive *March on Washington*, as they do again two years later.

1984   The U.S. Supreme Court, in *Grove City College v. Bell*, declares that the federal government cannot cut financial aid to an entire institution when only one of its branches has violated federal guidelines. The decision poses dilemmas for federal enforcement of a variety of civil rights provisions.

1986   In *Batson v. Kentucky*, the Supreme Court determines that prosecutors cannot use their preemptory challenges to exclude black jurists simply because they feel that blacks are less likely to convict other blacks.

1988   The Congress passes the *Civil Rights Restoration Act* over President Reagan's veto. Its primary purpose is to undo the damage done by the 1984 *Grove City* decision by allowing entire institutions to be denied federal assistance if any of their parts is found to be discriminating.

MEASURES OF PROGRESS

After more than two centuries, the institution of slavery was finally abolished by a civil war. Nonetheless, the legacy of slavery endured. Integration and equal justice met opposition at every turn, and it was nearly another century before even the legal foundations of this discrimination began to be dismantled. Decades of struggle for civil rights did, however, finally begin to succeed following World War II. The right to register and vote came to be enforced directly by the U.S. Department of Justice. Schools were forcibly desegregated. Housing discrimination was outlawed. And not only were employers barred from discriminating openly, but many were compelled to search for qualified black applicants when positions were available. Yet such legal gains have scarcely begun to eradicate centuries of racism and subsequent racial inequities.

Education

An area of marked gains has been education. For example, whereas more than 80 percent of all black Americans were completely illiterate in 1870, very few are today.[3] In addition, the racial differentials in school years completed and college enrollment have been reduced considerably. The black high school dropout rate, for instance, had been reduced to 17 percent by 1985, only slightly higher than the corresponding white rate.[4]

Nevertheless, such progress masks some serious underlying problems. Due largely to the property tax method of public school funding, the historically poorer black community is often left with inferior elementary and secondary educational institutions—clearly a form of institutionalized racism. Test scores indicate that although they are in school and passing from grade to grade, black students are often model years behind their white counterparts in actual knowledge.[5] Nearly one-half of all black teenagers have serious problems in terms of literacy,[6] and although the gap has narrowed slightly in recent years, average black SAT scores remain some 100 points behind those of whites in both the verbal and mathematics categories.[7] At the college level, nearly half of the more than one million black students attend predominantly black institutions; a third are in two-year schools;[8] and blacks are still badly underrepresented in graduate and professional programs.[9] Most alarming of all is the fact that racial gaps in virtually all of these areas have grown significantly since 1977. By 1985, for instance, some 76 percent of white adults had graduated from high school, while the figure was only 60 percent for blacks, and whites were nearly twice as likely to have graduated from college.[10]

Economics

Although college-educated blacks and younger two-parent black families are now doing nearly as well as or better than comparable whites in terms of the economic indicators discussed here, the story is not nearly as encouraging for the large majority of black males who are not fortunate enough to have a college education.[11] Black women, by contrast, have begun to approach income parity with white women, but both are in a clearly inferior economic position vis-à-vis men, especially white men.[12] Furthermore, these inferior positions are reinforced by institutions such as seniority systems, not to mention the "old boy networks" used for passing along job opportunities. The results can be seen in the overall black population's absolute and relative levels of skills, unemployment, income, and poverty.

Occupation. Whereas a sizable majority of whites held either white-collar or blue-collar jobs in the still largely industrial economy of 1940, only about one-third of all blacks did. Instead, most blacks were employed on farms or at the lower levels of the service sector, often as household workers.[13] These jobs reflected a bygone era. Much has changed since, but the occupational position of black Americans has continued to lag. The economy has gone from labor-intensive to capital-intensive manufacturing and thus from manufacturing-related employment to jobs in the professions, technical fields, and services. Whites have made that transition: over 80 percent of them now hold either white-collar or service positions. Blacks have not: a majority of blacks now hold blue-collar positions, and a disproportionate share of their white-collar employment is in sales and clerical positions rather than in management, technical trades, or the professions.[14] In many ways, black Americans seem to be locked at least a generation or more behind whites, left to assume the jobs whites discard, left to be laid off at disproportionate rates, left on the back of the bus of economic change.

Consistent with all of that, blacks do indeed find themselves underrepresented in the managerial and professional ranks. In the mid-1980s, although blacks comprised nearly 12 percent of the U.S. population, only 6 percent of accountants, auditors, and managers were black, 5 percent of computer systems analysts and scientists, 4 percent of engineers and college professors, and 3 percent of architects, lawyers, judges, dentists, and physicians.[15] But even that does not tell the whole story, for they are even further underrepresented in the nation's top private-sector institutions. For example, blacks make up only 2 percent of the lawyers in the top 100 law firms.[16] No Fortune 500 company is headed by a black.[17] Beyond that, a disproportionate number of black managers and professionals are employed directly or indirectly by government—an especially precarious position in times of government retrenchment.

Unemployment. One obvious result of this poor timing can be seen in the unemployment figures. Whereas the black unemployment rate became approximately the same as the white unemployment rate in the 1930s and 1940s, economic changes and the return of white soldiers from the war left them behind once again following World War II. Since that time, the black unemployment rate has been roughly twice the white rate across virtually every major category of educational attainment and occupation. And as nationwide unemployment stagnated at recession levels after the mid-1970s, black Americans fell even further behind. For example, they had become more than $2\frac{1}{2}$ times as likely to be unemployed by 1988. One in eight could not find work that year, according to the conservative estimates of the U.S. Bureau of Labor Statistics, and the figure has been far worse for the burgeoning number of black teenagers, whose official unemployment rate has consistently exceeded 30 percent for more than a decade.[18] Recent unofficial estimates indicate that as many as one-half of all black males are presently unemployed, no longer looking for work, or unaccounted for.[19] The situation is somewhat better for black women, but they generally remain locked in clerical and domestic positions that offer minimal wages and virtually no skill development, benefits, or advancement.[20]

Income. While official black unemployment seems to have become fixed at roughly twice the white rate, black family income has remained at only slightly more than one-half of white income during this same period. As a group, black families made 51 percent of what white families took home in 1947. That figure grew to 63 percent by the end of the reform-oriented 1960s, but it was back down to 56 percent by 1987.[21]

Granted, there has been some segmentation within the black community. Black high school dropouts, for instance, have been falling farther behind their white counterparts,[22] while, by contrast, black males between 25 and 34 years of age, as a group, have succeeded in narrowing the racial income gap. For example, whereas that group earned 49 percent of what their white counterparts earned in 1940, they were making 84 percent by 1984[23]—a trend that seems directly related to their increased number of school years completed. In addition, comparable gains can be seen in the median incomes of black working couples. Taking a family income of $31,500 (1984 dollars) to represent the middle class, the proportion of blacks in that group has increased 12-fold over the past 30 years, and relatively speaking, whereas whites were more than five times as likely to be in that category in the early 1950s, they are only about twice as likely to be there today.[24] Even more impressive is the fact that college-educated black couples are presently outearning comparable white couples.[25]

There are, however, a number of reasons not to be overly optimistic about this apparent trend toward black "middle-classification." First of all, federal affirmative action policies clearly helped accelerate this progress, and the Reagan administration's battle to turn the clock back on such efforts has made it clear that what the federal government giveth, the federal government can cease to provide. That same principle underlies concern about the fact that nearly one in four blacks works for government, where antidiscrimination laws and affirmative action have been more easily enforced.[26] In 1980, for instance, a majority of black male college graduates held jobs tied to federal government spending, and black professional women seemed to be comparably reliant on government employment.[27] Yet such government employment, a major avenue for acquiring middle-income positions, is also very vulnerable to a national change of mood. Between 1980 and 1986, for example, the number of blacks holding policymaking and managerial positions in the federal government declined from 44 percent to 20 percent.[28]

In addition, sizable barriers are developing to inhibit the advancement of those who have remained underprivileged despite these new, somewhat tenuous opportunities. To begin with, whereas more than three-quarters of all black Americans lived in the rural South at the dawn of the 20th century, nearly half of them have since migrated to the urbanized North. This leaves a sizable share of the black population residing in declining industrial cities, lacking the kind of economic opportunities that growing industries afforded their underskilled white predecessors. Last, but certainly not least, whereas 28 percent of black families were headed by a female in 1969, that figure jumped to 40 percent by 1978. Today, nearly one-half of all black children are growing up in fatherless households, a reality made far worse by the close correlation between female-headed households and poverty.[29]

Poverty. In terms of poverty, both the absolute and relative figures have improved, but they are still discouraging. Whereas 55 percent of all blacks were officially "poor" in 1959, a growing economy and a federal "war on poverty" helped reduce that figure to 32 percent by 1969. There is also increasing agreement that this figure has been reduced even further if transfers in kind such as food stamps, Medicaid, and housing subsidies are included as income. However, this trend seems to have stopped, if not begun to reverse; more than one-third of all black Americans were categorized as poor in the mid-1980s, and more than one-half of all black children under the age of 6 found themselves in families living below the poverty line. In relative terms, blacks have remained three times more likely to be poor since World War II, and the median income of poor black families is some 20 percent lower than for poor white families.[30] Thus, the black population as a whole is no longer making absolute gains in this area and has not made any relative ones in the entire postwar period.

Housing

Using occupied living units lacking some or all plumbing as an indicator of substandard housing, blacks have made some progress in recent years but still remain well behind their white counterparts. In 1940, for example, some three-quarters of all black housing fell into that category, twice the white average. Forty years later, less than 6 percent of all black housing fit that description, but that was still more than three times the white average.[31] Thus their absolute position improved considerably, but they fell farther behind relative to whites.

Health

Although infant and maternal mortality have been reduced considerably as medicine has advanced in the course of this century, black rates have remained two to three times higher than whites' and are still a disgrace by international standards. There is also a sizable black-white differential in rates of contracting tuberculosis, cancer, and a number of other diseases, and the black mortality rate for most diseases is considerably higher, especially for hypertension among black males. Lastly, although life expectancy has increased faster for blacks in the 20th century, it still lags behind white life expectancy; the average newborn black male can expect to live only 61 years.[32]

Pollution

The large majority of hazardous waste dumps are located near predominantly black neighborhoods.[33]

Crime

Blacks were 33 percent more likely than whites to be victims of rape, robbery, or assault in 1982 and six times more likely to be murdered.[34] One in 21 black males will be murdered.[35]

War

Blacks are also more likely to serve as cannon fodder in the nation's wars. For example, 23 percent of the soldiers killed in the Vietnam War were black, nearly 13,000 young black men—double the ratio of blacks to the population in general.[36]

Overall, then, there has been some progress in a number of areas. This is particularly true today for well-educated blacks. Political activism ranging from voting to violent protest has occasionally led to gains despite the racism institutionalized in America's conservative political and economic systems. Nonetheless, the United States of America continues to harbor considerable racial inequality, and much of the progress in wiping out the vestiges of slavery appears to have dissipated in the 1980s—another example of the regression that seems inevitable unless more equality can be institutionalized.

In particular, the 1980s have witnessed a relaxation of efforts designed specifically to address institutionalized racism, such as busing and affirmative action.

The concept of neighborhood schools, for example, does not appear racist on its face. Students attending schools in the neighborhoods in which they live, and those schools being funded by assessing the parents and neighbors of those children, would appear to be a racially neutral policy. However, if years of racial discrimination have seriously constrained where most blacks are likely to live, neighborhoods will remain segregated, as will their schools. On top of that, years of racial discrimination have also left blacks in some of the poorest neighborhoods in town; there are fewer taxable assets in those areas and consequently fewer tax dollars with which to fund their schools. Thus recognizing that a dogged allegiance to the neighborhood school concept would only help perpetuate long-existing inequalities, the practice of busing was implemented to try to break the grip of this institutionalized racism. Yet the belief in equal opportunity—a truly fair marathon—has apparently not been enough to create a strong national commitment to desegregating schools on the basis of race and class.

Now consider seniority rules for promotion and retention. Once again, such rules appear racially neutral on their face. The longer a person has worked for a particular employer, the more benefits and protection he or she accrues. But after facing years of overt and covert discrimination, much of it effectively sanctioned by law, blacks are just beginning to have legally protected access to many previously unreachable positions. Nevertheless, seniority rules require that the last hired be the first fired. Consequently, it is very difficult to advance in an economy that experiences periodic slumps. To break that bottleneck, affirmative action was legally established. Yet the 1980s witnessed the chief law enforcement agent in the country, Attorney General Edward Meese, arguing that such practices discriminated against whites with more seniority, and similar arguments were being made by William Bradford Reynolds, head of the Civil Rights Division of the Justice Department.

None of this is surprising, however, when one turns to the public opinion polls. Blacks and whites seem to be seeing two very different realities.

PERCEPTIONS OF PROGRESS

Perceptions of these trends and developments vary considerably across the American population. Particularly striking are the differing perceptions of whites and blacks. Here are some typical polling results from recent years.[37]

1978: *Do blacks have equal job opportunities?*
Whites: 73% yes   Blacks: 38% yes

1980: *Did blacks' quality of life improve in the 1970s?*
Whites: 75% yes   Blacks: 45% yes

1981: *Is there a need for any more busing?*
Whites: 17% yes   Blacks: 60% yes

1984: *Has Ronald Reagan been fair to America's poor?*
Whites: 50% yes   Blacks: 17% yes

1988: *Do blacks receive equal treatment in the justice system?*
Whites: 61% yes   Blacks: 20% yes

The majority of the white population seems to see quite different black circumstances than the large majority of blacks who are actually living in them. Thus, although there is certainly no denying some important gains, many more appear to exist primarily in the minds of white people.

PREJUDICE AND RACISM TODAY

To finish setting the context, it is important to assess contemporary levels and trends in white prejudice and racism. To do that, however, it is first essential to review previously discussed definitions of those terms. For the purposes of this analysis, individual *prejudice* is defined as prejudging people on the basis of a group to which they belong rather than on their individual merits. Individual *racism* involves adding discriminatory actions to those prejudicial beliefs. Thus, believing blacks to be inferior workers is prejudice, but refusing to hire a black applicant on the basis of that prejudgment is racism.

White Prejudice

Over the course of recent years, George Gallup asked the following questions to a cross-section of American whites and obtained the yes responses indicated:[38]

> *Do you disapprove of marriage between whites and non-whites?*
> 1968: 84% (est.)   1983: 56%

> *If your party nominated a generally well qualified man for President and he happened to be a black, would you refuse to vote for him?*
> 1958: 64% (est.)   1983: 18%

In February 1979, *Newsweek* ran the results of attitudinal polls Lou Harris had been taking since 1963.[39] White Americans agreed with the following statements as indicated:

> *Blacks are inferior to white people.*
> 1963: 31%   1978: 15%

> *Blacks care less for the family than whites.*
> 1963: 31%   1978: 18%

> *Blacks have less native intelligence than whites.*
> 1963: 39%   1978: 25%

> *Blacks breed crime.*
> 1963: 35%   1978: 29%

> *Blacks are more violent than whites.*
> 1967: 42%   1978: 34%

> *Blacks want to live off the handout.*
> 1963: 41%   1978: 36%

> *Blacks tend to have less ambition than whites.*
> 1963: 66%   1978: 49%

In an absolute sense, it is disturbing that more than one in three whites still believes that blacks "want to live off the handout" and are "more violent" than whites, while a virtual majority of whites still oppose interracial marriages and believe that blacks have "less ambition."

Nevertheless, the trends in polling results are clear. Whites are becoming less prejudiced. Or are they? At the very least it is clear that whites have become less willing to display their racial prejudices publicly. However, it has also become less "socially acceptable" to admit them. One is left to wonder just how many whites, safe behind closed doors and in like-minded company, still hold many of the views of this rather candid "middle American."

> The thing that bothers me about the Negro people is this: they're not like the rest of us. . . . If you ask me, they're slow, that's what I think. They're out for a good time. They want things made easy for them. . . . They actually want relief. They think they're entitled to it! . . . They want all they can get—for free. They don't really like to work. They do work, alot of them, I know. But it's against their wish I believe. They seem to have the idea that they're entitled to something from the rest of us. That's the big thing with them: they've suffered and we should cry our heads off and give them the country, lock, stock, and barrel because we've been bad to them. . . . Pity is for the weak, my grandfather used to tell us kids that. But your niggers, alot of them want pity; and they get it. . . . People are afraid to speak out, say certain things, because they know they'll be called "prejudiced," and in fact they are not at all that; they are letting the chips fall where they do.[40]

Racism

Underlying prejudicial beliefs are quite readily apparent in a host of white literature, including *The Races of Men* by Robert Know, *The Inequality of the Human Race* by J. A. De Gobineau, *Types of Mankind* by J. C. Nott and G. R. Glidden, *The Origin of Races* by Carleton Coon, and more recently in the writings of William Shockley and Arthur Jensen. When those beliefs have gotten translated into action, this phenomenon has proved even more dangerous. Focusing on the American experience, this has included the imposition of slavery, the brutal crushing of Native Americans, and a variety of imperialistic foreign policies in China, the Philippines, and other nonwhite developing countries.

In the United States, racist acts have plagued black Americans well beyond the Emancipation Proclamation. They have included the less visible institutionalized and individual practices that created and perpetuate the caste system reflected in the socioeconomic data in this chapter. Yet, for reasons that have included intimidation and vengeance, they have often been quite overt and highly visible, for example, night riders, lynchings, and the storming of black neighborhoods by white mobs. Although somewhat less frequent, these blatantly violent acts continue and in many ways simply represent the tip of a very large iceberg of prejudice and racism.

Mobile, Alabama (March 1981)
A black man, accused of killing a white police officer, is set free because of a mistrial. Two admitted Klan members seek revenge by randomly abducting a 19-year-old black youth. They beat him with a tree limb as he pleads for his life, and when he is finally beaten into submission, they strangle him, cut his throat three times, tie a rope around his neck, and hang him from a tree to demonstrate "Klan strength in Alabama."[41]

Steubenville, Ohio (April 1981)

Another 19-year-old black male is murdered in an apparent act of racist violence. In this instance, the youth is shot in the head for allegedly dating a white girl.[42]

Detroit, Michigan (May 1981)

For over two years a black woman is harassed by a group of whites for choosing to live in a predominantly white neighborhood. They throw baseballs through her windows and paint KKK insignias on her garage. Then three whites, aged 19–23, throw a pipe bomb through her bathroom window. When she attempts to throw it back outside, it explodes and leaves her maimed.[43]

Baltimore, Maryland (June 1981)

A black Morgan State University student gets into an argument with a white woman employee where he works. Following the incident, he is attacked by eight whites who beat him with pool sticks. He suffers a broken left arm, contusions, and swelling of the brain.[44]

Brooklyn, New York (June 1982)

Three middle-aged black transit workers finish their shift at midnight. They stop to buy a snack on their way home. When emerging from the store, they are harassed by a number of whites. When their car fails to start, the group of whites swells. Amid chants of "niggers go home," the car is smashed with blunt objects. Two of the transit workers flee, but the driver is pulled from the car and beaten to death.[45]

Boston, Massachusetts (June 1982)

A black woman moves into the white neighborhood of Dorchester. As she walks to and from her home, she endures racial taunts, stone throwing, and hard shoves. Finally, a gasoline bomb is hurled through her window.[46]

Chicago, Illinois (November 1984)

A black family moves into an all-white enclave called The Island, next to Cicero and Oak Park. Approximately a dozen whites, armed with guns, spend an entire night hurling bricks, bottles, pipes, and tire irons through their windows. Unable to call police because phone service has not yet been installed, the family huddles behind their furniture until they are able to flee down a back alley at daybreak. Throughout the nightlong attack, no neighbors came to their rescue, while police cars apparently cruised past on three different occasions and did nothing to stop it.[47]

Philadelphia, Pennsylvania (November 1985)

A black family and an interracial couple move into the predominantly white area of Elmwood. Vandalism begins almost immediately, and it culminates in 400 whites congregating outside their homes and chanting for them to leave.[48]

Queens, New York (December 1986)

At approximately midnight, faced with near freezing temperatures, three black men leave their stalled car to seek shelter. As they walk through the all-white Howard Beach area, three white youths shout racial slurs at them, words are exchanged, and gestures are exchanged shortly thereafter at a pizza parlor. The white youths then proceed to a party and round up eight friends, saying, "There's some niggers in the pizza parlor—let's go kill them." Armed with bats and sticks, they chase and beat the black men; one flees onto a highway and is struck dead by a car.[49]

Peekskill, New York (November 1987)
A black insurance adjuster is confronted by three bat- and pipe-wielding white men on the outskirts of town. He is chased until he is finally rescued by a passing motorist. Five days later, his family's home is firebombed.[50]

Staten Island, New York (June 1988)
A 24-year-old black man is walking home from his job at a Burger King restaurant when a carload of white youths begin shouting racial slurs. The youths then get out of the car, circle the black man, and beat him with a stick and a baseball bat until he is able to break free and run for safety in a nearby pizza shop.[51]

SUMMARY

The political history of black Americans has led to some impressive victories in the Congress and the U.S. Supreme Court, but inequities persist. Trends in black educational attainment, occupations, unemployment, income, poverty, housing conditions, health conditions, neighborhood pollution, crime rates, and casualties in the nation's wars are not encouraging overall. In addition, blacks and whites perceive black progress differently, particularly as the divisive policies of busing and affirmative action have been employed to attack forms of institutionalized discrimination. Prejudice and racism clearly linger in the white community.

NOTES

1. Harold Cruse, *Rebellion or Revolution?* (New York: Morrow, 1968), pp. 76–77.
2. The ensuing historical timeline has benefited significantly from reference sources such as Robert Allen, *Black Awakening in Capitalist America: An Analytical History* (Garden City, N.Y.: Anchor/Doubleday, 1969); Albert Blaustein and Robert Zangrando, *Civil Rights and the Black American* (New York: Washington Square Press, 1968); John Hope Franklin, *From Slavery to Freedom: A History of Negro Americans* (New York: Knopf, 1980); Charles V. Hamilton, *The Black Experience in American Politics* (New York: Putnam, 1973); Manning Marable, *How Capitalism Underdeveloped Black America* (Boston: South End Press, 1983); Howard Zinn, *A People's History of the United States* (New York: Harper & Row, 1980).
3. Department of Commerce, Bureau of the Census, *Statistical Abstracts of the United States* (Washington, D.C.: GPO, various years); Department of Commerce, Bureau of the Census, Current Population Reports, P-23, No. 80, *The Social and Economic Status of the Black Population in the United States: A Historical Overview, 1790–1978* (Washington, D.C.: GPO, 1978); Department of Education, Office of Civil Rights, periodic reports (Washington, D.C.: GPO, various years); American Council of Education Reports (Washington, D.C.: American Council of Education, various years).
4. *New York Times*, May 11, 1988.
5. *New York Times*, September 19, 1985.
6. See note 3.
7. *New York Times*, September 23, 1987; September 20, 1988; September 21, 1988.
8. *New York Times*, February 1, 1984; works cited in note 3.
9. *New York Times*, November 5, 1987.
10. *New York Times*, November 18, 1987; December 3, 1987.

11. Department of Commerce, Bureau of the Census, *Money Income of Families: Aggregate, Mean and Per Capita, by Family Characteristics* (Washington, D.C.: GPO, various years); *New York Times*, June 2, 1981; August 7, 1985; Erik Wright, "Race, Class, and Income Inequality," *American Journal of Sociology* (May 1978).

12. Department of Commerce, *Statistical Abstracts*; Department of Commerce, *Social and Economic Status*; Equal Employment Opportunity Commission Reports (Washington, D.C.: GPO, various years); Department of Labor, Bureau of Labor Statistics, annual reports (Washington, D.C.: GPO, various years).

13. Ibid.

14. Ibid.

15. Ibid.

16. George Davis and Glegg Watson, *Black Life in Corporate America: Swimming in the Mainstream* (Garden City, N.Y.: Doubleday, 1985); *New York Times*, July 14, 1987.

17. Ibid.

18. Department of Labor, Bureau of Labor Statistics, annual reports.

19. *New York Times*, May 11, 1984.

20. See note 12.

21. Department of Commerce, *Statistical Abstracts*; Department of Commerce, *Money Income of Families*; *Christian Science Monitor*, October 18, 1988.

22. *New York Times*, June 2, 1981.

23. James D. Smith and Finis Welch, *Closing the Gap* (Santa Monica, Calif.: Rand, 1986).

24. Ibid.; National Urban League, *The State of Black America, 1987* (New York: National Urban League, 1987).

25. Department of Commerce, Bureau of the Census, *Current Population Reports*, Series P-20, No. 366 (Washington, D.C.: GPO, 1981), pp. 182, 184.

26. See note 12.

27. Richard McGahey, "Industrial Policy," *Review of Black Political Economy* (Summer-Fall 1984), pp. 85–96; *Memphis Commercial Appeal*, June 22, 1987, p. B4.

28. *New York Times*, July 14, 1987.

29. Department of Commerce, *Statistical Abstracts*; Department of Commerce, *Social and Economic Status*; *New York Times*, May 11, 1984; January 26, 1987; William J. Wilson, *The Truly Disadvantaged* (Chicago: University of Chicago Press, 1987).

30. National Urban League, *State of Black America*, pp. 53–56, 135.

31. Department of Commerce, *Statistical Abstracts*; Department of Commerce, *Social and Economic Status*.

32. Department of Health and Human Services, National Center for Health Statistics.

33. *New York Times*, December 28, 1983; April 16, 1987.

34. Department of Justice, Bureau of Justice Statistics, *Crime Victimization in the United States* (Washington, D.C.: GPO, various years).

35. National Association for the Advancement of Colored People (NAACP), *The Crisis* (March 1986), p. 26.

36. Department of Defense figures.

37. 1978, 1980, and 1981 polls conducted by George Gallup; 1984 poll by NBC; 1988 polls by Lou Harris and Media General-Associated Press. Also see Howard Schuman et al., *Racial Attitudes in America* (Cambridge, Mass.: Harvard University Press, 1985).

38. George Gallup, Jr., *The Gallup Poll: Public Opinion* (Wilmington, Del.: Scholarly Resources, Inc., annual series). Also see Schuman, *Racial Attitudes*.

39. *Newsweek*, February 26, 1979, p. 48. Also see Schuman, *Racial Attitudes*.

40. Interview in Robert Coles and Jon Erickson, *The Middle Americans* (Boston: Little, Brown, 1971), pp. 9–10.

41. *New York Times*, February 2, 1984.

42. Marable, *How Capitalism Underdeveloped Black America*, p. 241.

43. Ibid., pp. 240–241.

44. Ibid., p. 240.
45. *New York Times*, June 23, 1982; March 4, 1983.
46. *New York Times*, June 2, 1982.
47. *New York Times*, November 18, 1984.
48. *New York Times*, December 1, 1985.
49. *New York Times*, December 24, 1986; January 5, 1987; September 23, 1987.
50. *New York Times*, December 14, 1987.
51. *New York Times*, June 23, 1988.

CHAPTER FOUR

The Class Structure

"America belongs to the white man." That statement is nearly correct. But to be even more accurate we should say, "America belongs to a very small number of white men." They are the tiny fraction of the population that owns the bulk of the nation's property, corporate stock, and financial accounts.

This chapter focuses on the economic class structure that underlies the political process. In particular, it looks at the concentration of corporate capital in the United States, a concentration that has increased due to some of the largest mergers in the history of the country. It then describes the concentrated ownership of those assets, focusing on the extremely small proportion held by black Americans. Failing to own any significant share of the nation's corporate capital, blacks are left dependent on the decisions of a white owning class.

THE CONCEPT OF CLASS

A central focus here and throughout the book is the relationship between economic classes. "Economics" describes how a society's goods and services are produced and distributed. "Economic classes" refer to the subgroupings within a society that delineate that society's most basic power relationships.

For example, under a "capitalistic" economic arrangement like the one in the United States, most goods and services are produced by privately owned companies and distributed according to people's ability to pay. The owners of these companies, referred to as capitalists, directly or indirectly hire others to work for them and pay those workers a wage. That wage, however, is not set at the full market value of what the workers produce. Instead, the capitalist sells the fruits of the workers' labors for more than the workers are paid and thus extracts a "profit" in the bargain.

The end result in terms of power is that the workers are dependent on the capitalist for their very livelihoods. And out of that dependence comes subordination. In the final analysis, it is the owner's company, and the owner's interest in maximization of profits is ultimately the interest that controls the workers. Workers' needs to the contrary must be subordinated, or the workers risk losing their livelihood.

Such subordination also has implications for self-expression and security. By having control over decisions as to what is to be produced and how it is to be produced, one's work provides an opportunity for self-expression. By contrast, when one must work exclusively to maximize the owner's profits, those opportunities are reduced, and there is a tendency to become alienated from the work and ultimately from oneself.[1] In addition, there is little personal security without the cushion of accumulated wealth, and one can become destitute virtually overnight due to a lay-off, extended illness, or large medical bills.[2]

These economic class relationships become an economic class "structure" when the boundary lines between the classes begin to harden. In other words, in the capitalist context, this would be true when there becomes almost no likelihood that one can move from the non-owning class to the owning class or vice versa. The evidence, then, is in the intergenerational reproduction of existing class positions. One is born, lives, and dies a member of the non-owning class, for example, as does one's children, grandchildren, and so on. That results in large part because class positions are inherited. For example, one inherits one's parents' values, connections, wealth, and other attributes. Thus it becomes highly unlikely that a member of the owning class will slip to the non-owning class, regardless of abilities, efforts, and value of his or her skills to the society. Non-owners are similarly likely to remain non-owners no matter how talented and productive they are. Where such is true, a class structure can be said to exist.

At this juncture, it is important to address two additional points: the number of meaningful class groupings to be found in contemporary capitalist societies and how to categorize the self-employed.

First of all, are there normally more than two economic classes within a capitalist economic system today? Using a Kroger grocery as an example, beyond the obvious class distinction between the major stockholders of the company and those who work there, is there not also a significant difference between the store manager and the checkout clerks? Clearly, the former does have a degree of power over the latter. However, that manager has been hired to maximize profits for Kroger stockholders. Thus decisional leeway is limited, and the manager's personal interests are subordinated to those of the company's owners in virtually the very same way the clerks' are. These employees are playing different roles, but the bottom line is the same for both. They must do what they can to turn acceptable profits for those who own the institution. And if they fail, they lose their jobs. This distinction, or lack thereof, will be explored further at the end of this chapter when discussing the contemporary separation of ownership and management.

The second phenomenon, self-employed workers, is conceptually more troublesome. The proportion of the American population that is self-employed, with no non–family members working for them, has shrunk steadily since the nation began and is now less than 8 percent.[3] Yet this is still a sizable number of people, and as a group they remain difficult to categorize. They are clearly not capitalists, as they are not extracting profits from the labor of others. By the same token, they are not really workers either, as they are not having their labor exploited by a capitalist. Thus they end up as a group in between, but in fact they can be seen as a small-scale glimpse of a socialist-type economic arrangement in which all would control the businesses within which they labored.

DISTRIBUTION OF OWNERSHIP

> Widespread accumulation inevitably turns into accumulation by the few. . . . Accumulation, which means, under the rule of private property, concentration of capital in a few hands, is a necessary consequence when capitalists are left free to follow their natural course.[4]

Corporate Concentration

Just how concentrated is the ownership of capital in the United States? There are more than 16 million private businesses in the United States, and together they make more than $8 trillion in sales every year. Greater than 90 percent of those sales, however, are made by corporations,[5] which number fewer than 3 million. And if the focus is narrowed to the approximately 200,000 manufacturing corporations, one gets an even clearer idea of just how concentrated the American means of production has become.

The top 500 manufacturers (0.25 percent of all such corporations) presently employ more than 70 percent of the nation's industrial work force and possess more than 70 percent of its manufacturing assets. Even more revealing, however, are the details presented in Figure 4.1. The 200 largest manufacturers—roughly 0.1 percent of all such corporations—possess more than 60 percent of the nation's

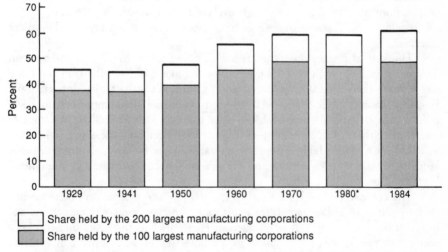

☐ Share held by the 200 largest manufacturing corporations

▨ Share held by the 100 largest manufacturing corporations

*This slight decline is in large part a result of a 1975 definitional change, which excluded foreign assets.

Figure 4.1. Share of Manufacturing Assets, 1929–1984 (Sources: 1929 and 1941 from Senate Subcommittee on Antitrust and Monopoly, "Economic Concentration" [Washington, D.C.: GPO, 1979], p. 173; remainder from U.S. Department of Commerce, Bureau of the Census, *Statistical Abstracts of the United States, 1986* [Washington, D.C.: GPO, 1986], p. 524)

TABLE 4.1 *FORTUNE'S* TOP 10 INDUSTRIAL CORPORATIONS, 1960–1985 (by sales)

	1960	1970	1980	1985
1.	General Motors	General Motors	Exxon*	Exxon
2.	Standard Oil (N.J.)	Standard Oil (N.J.)	General Motors	General Motors
3.	Ford	Ford	Mobil	Mobil
4.	General Electric	General Electric	IBM	Ford
5.	U.S. Steel	IBM	Ford	Texaco
6.	Mobil	Chrysler	Texaco	IBM
7.	Gulf	Mobil	Standard Oil (Calif.)	Du Pont
8.	Texaco	Texaco	Gulf	AT&T
9.	Chrysler	ITT	Standard Oil (Ind.)	General Electric
10.	Swift	Gulf	General Electric	Standard Oil (Calif.)

*Formerly Standard Oil (N.J.). *Source:* Fortune *(July 1960, May 1970, May 1980, May 1985).*

manufacturing assets, while the top 100 alone control nearly one-half of the manufacturing capital. This concentration has grown significantly over the course of this century.

Who are the very largest of these industrial giants? Table 4.1 indicates both who they are and just how stable their ranks have been in the 1970s and 1980s. The lists have consistently been dominated by essentially the same oil companies and automobile manufacturers. It should also be remembered that many of these corporations have become increasingly diversified conglomerates. A number of the oil companies, for example, have bought up much of the nation's coal and uranium reserves.

The size of these firms is impressive. For example, in 1985 the American Telephone & Telegraph (AT&T) ledger looked like this: $40 billion in corporate assets, more than 365,000 employees, and $33 billion worth of sales. International Business Machines (IBM) had $43 billion in assets, 395,000 employees, and $46 billion in sales. And General Motors topped them all with $52 billion in corporate assets, more than 748,000 employees in some four dozen countries, and $84 billion worth of sales. These budget figures are rivaled in size by only a handful of other large multinational corporations and the governments of countries like the United States and the Soviet Union.

The companies that have risen to the top produce the nation's most needed primary products: energy, steel, transportation vehicles, and communications and information equipment. Their production is essential to the economic independence and prosperity of the nation as a whole, not to mention the number of individual Americans whose jobs derive either directly or indirectly from one of these basic manufacturing industries.

Such tight concentration, mammoth size, and strategic importance are not limited to manufacturing either. For example, 33 corporations out of 67,000 (0.05 percent) own half of the nation's transportation, communications, and utility assets. In insurance, the top 10 insurers hold nearly 60 percent of all insurance assets; two, Prudential and Metropolitan, alone possess one-quarter of them.

Combining manufacturers and nonmanufacturers, then, the top 6 percent of America's nonfinancial corporations control more than 90 percent of the nation's nonfinancial corporate assets.[6] From a global perspective, more than one-half of the world's 300 largest corporations are based in the United States, meaning that these largest of American firms also control a hefty proportion of the entire world's corporate capital.

Beyond that, such concentration has been increasing rapidly in the 1980s due to a plethora of corporate mergers. Economist Frederic Scherer points out that there was a proliferation of mergers in the years 1887–1904, 1916–1929, and 1945–1968. Projecting the historical trend, the present growth in the number of mergers should last well into the 1990s, leading to significantly more corporate concentration.[7]

Not only are corporate assets highly concentrated, but these individual corporations often have what are called interlocking directorates, and they have also been engaging in what are termed joint ventures.

A direct interlock exists when a member of the board of directors of one corporation also sits on the board of another corporation. An indirect interlock exists when two corporations each have a director on a third board. In a comprehensive analysis of the phenomenon, the Senate Subcommittee on Intergovernmental Affairs found either direct or indirect interlocks between nearly all of America's largest corporations. John de Butts, for instance, was not only chairman of the board of American Telephone & Telegraph but was also a board member of fellow corporate giants such as General Motors, Citicorp Bank, and United States Steel (now USX).[8]

There has also been a recent tendency toward joint ventures between major international firms. For example, the American Motor Company (AMC) and France's Renault Corporation combined efforts to produce the Alliance automobile. Political scientist Edward Greenberg found the world's 20 largest oil companies involved in some 2,000 such joint operations.[9] In many industries, the list is long and getting longer. This trend could lead to a slower growth in the size of individual multinational corporations, but in the end it simply adds a new dimension to the interlocking phenomenon.

In many ways, the center of this interlocking web of corporate control is the American financial community.

Of the 10 domestic corporations with the most assets, 8 are banks, led by BankAmerica ($151 billion in 1984), Citicorp ($118 billion), and Chase-Manhattan ($87 billion). Within the American banking community, 50 out of 17,700 banks (less than 0.3 percent) hold roughly two-thirds of all bank assets.

In terms of domestic lending, 220 of them do virtually all of it. Nine banks, for example, make over one-quarter of all commercial and industrial loans, including 90 percent of the loans to the petroleum and natural gas industries, three-quarters of those for machine and metal production, and two-thirds of those to the chemical and rubber industries.[10]

Beyond sheer size and monopolization of lending, a number of these banks also held the controlling shares of other giant corporations, which means that their stockholdings are large enough to allow them to dominate decision making in those other companies. For example, five of these banks—Chase, Citicorp, Morgan Guaranty Trust, Bankers Trust, and the Bank of New York—held controlling shares in three-quarters of the top 324 American-based corporations in 1969.[11] Economists Robert Fitch and John Oppenheimer conclude that "to a considerable extent these five banks actually constitute a unified money cartel."[12] As a specific example, Chase, controlled by the Rockefeller family, has held or continues to hold controlling shares in both CBS and NBC, Union Carbide, General Electric, United Airlines, Safeway, and American Telephone & Telegraph.[13]

Actually, there appear to be some 15 industrial-banking complexes so tightly interlocked that they virtually act as single economic entities.[14] Four of the most important are detailed in Table 4.2.

By the early 1980s, Thomas Dye concluded that as few as 7,000 people managed the majority of the nation's resources.[15] At the same time, a Senate study concluded that 15 financial institutions effectively controlled virtually all major corporations.[16] Thus the number of key decision makers may be even smaller than Dye and others have suggested.

Obviously, a relatively small number of very large corporations control the bulk of America's corporate assets. If it can be shown that ownership of these corporations is spread broadly across the American citizenry, those findings will not be nearly so significant. Unfortunately, such is simply not the case.

Concentration of Ownership

Black Americans

"A lot of times, when I'm working, I become as despondent as hell and I feel like crying. I'm not a man, none of us are men! I don't own anything."[17]

To begin with, black Americans own virtually none of the nation's corporate assets. That leaves them almost totally subordinate to the interests of a white owning class. But before documenting that, it is important to remember the historical context within which this reality has developed.

During slavery, millions of blacks were denied the right to own property for 2½ centuries. During that period, even free blacks faced a dual wagè system and other forms of racial discrimination that made it quite difficullt for them to accumulate wealth. Following emancipation, after the promised reparation of "forty acres and a mule" never materialized, black accumulation of wealth continued to be retarded by the nature of available employment. Little could be saved while working as a sharecropper, domestic servant, or leased convict, and employment and wage discrimination continued to plague blacks who attempted to work outside those situations. Many blacks moved to the industrializing North in search of the economic opportunities enjoyed by white immigrants for decades. Later, legally sanctioned discrimination finally began to be struck down. However, it was too little too late, as the American political and economic systems were undergoing fundamental changes that would seriously reduce the number of bottom rungs on

TABLE 4.2 INDUSTRIAL-BANKING COMPLEXES AS IDENTIFIED BY INTERLOCKING DIRECTORATES, 1983

Rockefeller-Morgan Group	Chicago Group	Mellon Group	California Group
American Telephone & Telegraph	Borg-Warner	Alcoa Aluminum	BankAmerica
Borden	Commonwealth Edison	Carborundum Company	Getty Oil
Chase-Manhattan Bank	Continental Illinois	Gulf Oil	North American Rockwell
Chemical Bank	First Chicago Corp.	Mellon National Bank	Security Pacific National Bank
Consolidated Edison	Illinois Central	Pittsburgh Plate Glass	Southern California Edison
Continental Oil	Inland Steel	Westinghouse	Union Oil of California
Equitable Life Insurance	International Harvester		Western Bancorporation
General Electric	Sears-Roebuck		
General Foods	Standard Oil of Indiana		
General Motors			
International Paper			
Metropolitan Life			
Morgan Guaranty Bank			
New York Life			
Procter & Gamble			
Scott Paper			
Southern Pacific			
United States Steel (USX)			

Sources: Michael Patrick Allen, "Economic Interest Groups and the Corporate Elite Structure," Social Science Quarterly, 58 (March 1978), pp. 608–609; Peter Dooley, "The Interlocking Directorate," American Economic Review, 59 (June 1969), pp. 320–321; Thomas Dye, Who's Running America? (Englewood Cliffs, N.J.: Prentice-Hall, 1983); Edward Greenberg, The American Political System (Cambridge, Mass.: Winthrop, 1977).

the ladder of upward mobility. In particular, the urban political machine was declining as the assimilating agent it once was for white ethnics, and rapid growth in technology was allowing mechanization of much of the manual and semiskilled work in unionized industries that had been providing decent wages, benefits, and opportunities for skill development and advancement.[18]

It should come as little surprise that significant disparities have developed between the accumulated wealth of whites and the accumulated wealth of blacks. In 1984, for example, the median white household possessed wealth worth $39,135; the figure was only $3,397 for the median black household.[19]

In absolute terms, the same 1984 governmental study found only 0.5 percent of all black households to have accumulated over $250,000 worth of wealth, while more than 30 percent either owned nothing or owed more than they owned. Where wealth had been successfully accumulated, it most often simply reflected a small amount of equity in a house or automobile. Only 5 percent of black households held any corporate stock or mutal funds at all, and the median holding was only

$2,777—most likely small Individual Retirement Accounts (IRAs). The mean holding was only $2,813, which indicates little variation in size of holdings and extremely few very large accumulations.[20]

From a different perspective, blacks hold only about 2 percent of the nation's capital stock. And although they did own 3 percent of the businesses in 1977, those businesses received only 0.2 percent of all gross receipts. Only 16 percent had even one paid employee, less than 2 percent had more than five on the payroll, and less than 0.2 percent (333 firms) employed more than 50 people. As telling as anything is the fact that 94 percent were sole proprietorships, most of which operated on capital drawn from the owner's personal savings or borrowed from friends. Black-owned businesses have been primarily restaurants, car dealerships, laundries, funeral parlors, gas stations, barber shops, hair salons, shoe repair shops, neighborhood grocery stores, and other service-producing enterprises, most of which are small and operate on the economic margin; more than three-fourths of them go bankrupt within three years of opening.[21]

In urban ghettos, for example, blacks comprise nearly 75 percent of the population but own only 20 to 40 percent of the businesses.[22] And, as Frank Davis has pointed out, high population densities and the resulting scarcity of land are among a number of factors that help guarantee that these will remain small-scale, low-profit, financially precarious enterprises.[23]

In the South, black-owned businesses decreased by nearly one-half with the demise of Jim Crow laws in the 1950s and 1960s.

Table 4-3 lists the most successful contemporary black businesses. Although impressive given the historical obstacles they had to overcome, such firms are a mere drop in the very large bucket of American corporate capital. For example, while General Motors was making $102 billion in sales, only one black-owned business in the entire country had sales exceeding even $1 billion. And although TLC Beatrice had enough annual sales to have put it among the Fortune 500, the second largest black-owned firm, Johnson Publishing, would have had to more than double its sales in order to have entered the ranks of the nation's top 500 manufacturers. And if the sales of the top 100 black firms had been combined, they would still have ranked only 110th—far lower yet when nonmanufacturers are added to the list.

TABLE 4.3 *BLACK ENTERPRISE* MAGAZINE'S TOP SIX BLACK BUSINESSES, 1987 (by sales)

1. TLC Beatrice International Holdings (food processing and distribution)	$1.8 billion
2. Johnson Publishing Company (*Ebony, Jet, Fashion Fair Cosmetics*, etc.)	202 million
3. Philadelphia Coca-Cola Bottling Company	166 million
4. H. J. Russell (construction, development, etc.)	142 million
5. Motown Industries	100 million
6. Soft Sheen Products	81 million

Source: Adapted from Black Enterprise Magazine, May 9, 1988.

Overall, then, blacks owned little of the nation's corporate capital as of the late 1970s, and as a group they have made virtually no gains since. However, such inequality of ownership is not a uniquely racial phenomenon; it exists to nearly the same extent in the American society as a whole. And even though white non-owners do not face the double-edged sword of race and class oppression, they still share with their black counterparts a parallel position in the economic class structure.

Americans in General

"The inequality of wealth holding today resembles what it was on the eve of the Declaration of Independence."[24]

Compiled from a variety of sources, some of the best available data suggests that less than 20 percent of Americans have ever directly owned any stock. Of even more importance is the fact that a far smaller number of them have held nearly all the shares.[25]

The last complete federal survey of stock ownership was conducted by the Federal Reserve Board in 1962. What it found was that the richest 1 percent of U.S. adults owned nearly two-thirds of all stock, the richest 5 percent held 86 percent, and the richest 20 percent held 97 percent. That, of course, left 3 percent of the stock to be owned by the other 80 percent.

Estimates compiled by economists using publicly available estate tax returns help to put black and white ownership figures into historical perspective. The proportion of all stock held by the top 1 percent of the American adult population seemed to peak shortly after World War II. By conservative estimates, this small group still holds more than 50 percent of all corporate stock and has done so since at least 1922. The top 5 percent of American families has continued to hold at least two-thirds of all the stock.[26] Other estimates place these figures even higher.[27]

As for the stock this elite group does not hold, much of it is owned in relatively small amounts, and the size of these shares has shrunk dramatically. Nationwide, for example, the median shareholding was $6,200 in 1985, less than one-third of what it was as recently as a decade earlier, and a growing amount of this investment is tied up in small, tax-sheltered retirement accounts.[28]

In terms of control, which is the essence of ownership, stockholders theoretically have the ultimate say as to the running of the corporations in which they have invested. This role, however, tends to end up in the hands of a small number of the very largest stockholders.

To begin with, an increasing number of corporations do not even operate by a one-share, one-vote principle. A small group of dominant stockholders own "management shares" that may, for example, allow them 10 votes per share. The ordinary shareholder, in contrast, would only be allowed one vote per share or in some cases none at all.[29] Henry Ford II, for instance, was able to control 40 percent of Ford Motor Company's voting rights while owning only 12 percent of the stock.[30]

But even where there is a one-vote-per-share rule, the vote of the stockholders is still proportionately weighted according to the number of shares owned. Therefore, those with the largest accumulation of shares can still dominate, especially because smaller stockholders simply do not band together to counterbalance such power.

Taking the next step and identifying precisely who the dominant shareholders are is much more difficult. Companies are not free with their lists of stockholders. Large shareholders are not generally willing to publicize their precise holdings. And even if this information were readily available, one would still have to track down the roots of all the foundations, holding companies, and trust funds, not to mention names that have changed through marriage, and so on.[31] From the best evidence available, however, one can still get a relatively clear indication of both who these people are and how little has changed over the years.

America's corporate landscape has long been the domain of large family empires. Robert Sheehan found that either individuals or members of a single family held controlling shares in nearly 150 of the nation's largest 500 corporations. He also found that 70 of the family-named companies on this list were still controlled by their founding families.[32]

The Du Ponts, for example, had controlling shares in 10 of the country's biggest corporations, including General Motors, Coca-Cola, Boeing, and Penn Central; and more than one million people were employed in Du Pont–controlled firms. They also controlled 8 of the 40 largest defense contractors, grossing more than $15 billion during the Vietnam War alone.[33]

The Rockefellers held over $300 billion worth of corporate stock, including controlling shares in five of the nation's largest oil companies (headed by Exxon) and four of its largest banks (headed by Chase Manhattan).[34]

The Mellon family also remains significant. They hold controlling shares in such corporate giants as Alcoa and Carborundum.[35]

Beyond all that, William Domhoff warns that even though a good many family corporations have broken up and their stock has been sold on the open market, this has only added to the concentrated control of the wealthiest corporate elites. He reasons that where three families each had their own companies before, now all three may well own stock in each other's companies, giving "the upper class an even greater community of interest than they had in the past when they were bitterly involved in protecting their standing by maintaining their individual companies."[36]

Thus it appears just as true today as when C. Wright Mills wrote in the 1950s that "the idea of a really wide distribution of economic ownership is a cultivated illusion: at the very most, 0.2 or 0.3 percent of the adult population own the bulk, the payoff shares, of the corporate world."[37]

Beyond their domination of individual firms, however, these white corporate elites also have numerous opportunities to get together in groups, facilitating a more collective exertion of power. For example, they regularly cross paths in trade associations, social clubs, ad hoc groups, political action committees, public and private forums, and the boards of various profit-making and nonprofit organizations.

Before moving on, four relatively recent developments warrant brief atten-tion. First of all, institutions of various types directly possess an ever-greater proportion of all stock held. Second, in what Peter Drucker has termed "the unseen revolution,"[38] the proportion of all stock held by public and private pension funds has increased steadily as well. Third, there has been a sizable infusion of foreign capital into the United States. And fourth, there continues to be considerable discussion about the alleged separation between those who own and the profes-sional managers who actually operate these corporations. Nonetheless, closer analysis of these trends suggests that they have not fundamentally altered the class structure.

Institutional Investments. Besides wealthy individuals, large institutions have become important investors. They currently do 50 to 80 percent of all trading on the New York Stock Exchange.[39] This is not a cross section of American institutions: Large banks and insurance companies comprise the overwhelming majority of the institutions involved in stock ownership.[40]

More important, the primary purpose of such institutional investment is to serve the economic interests of the holders of stock in the particular investing company. Thus these institutional investments actually represent investments for individuals, and, consequently, it is not so important that institutions are pur-chasing more and more of the available stock. The important question is who owns the controlling shares of the investing company's stock, and this, we have seen, is apt to be concentrated in a small number of hands. Thus institutional, as opposed to individual, investment does not alter the class structure significantly.

Pension Funds. Pension funds differ in that their ownership is widely dispersed across a large number of pensioners. These funds now exceed $600 billion and hold some 18 percent of all corporate stock.[41] Yet, for a variety of reasons, this has not translated into significantly more economic clout for the nonwealthy.

Less than one-half of the American work force is covered by such funds. In addition, those who are union members have the more substantial pension accounts, but union membership has been declining rapidly to the point where less than one out of every five American workers is unionized today. And even those who belong to the unionized group are destined to have very small individual shares in their union's pension stockholdings; their shares are often voted for them by union appointees; and such investments are often governed by governmental regulations that limit the investment discretion of the trustees. In addition, as the number of stockholders increases while the relative size of their shares decreases, the little dispersal that is taking place may well be strengthening the hands of the major corporate elites by further diluting the remainder of the ownership pool.[42]

Peter Drucker's alarm over "pension fund socialism" in America seems premature.[43] Nevertheless, should organizations like the AFL-CIO ever succeed in fully politicizing their control over such funds, a significant power shift could be in the offing.

Foreign Capital. Although it is difficult to gather reliable data on the amount foreign capitalists have invested in this country, the Federal Reserve Board estimated foreign holdings to be 2 percent of corporate stock in 1965 and 5 percent by 1983.[44] These foreign investments help explain why a smaller share of all domestic corporate stock is presently held by the top 5 percent of Americans. Yet that American owning class still owns the overwhelming majority of all domestic stock, and ownership by foreign capitalists in no way enhances the economic position of the other 95 percent of Americans.

In addition, one should be very careful not to interpret the overall decline in the proportion of stock held by the American owning class to suggest a decline in their economic well being. Although they do indeed own less of the nation's stock, their share of all national wealth has remained relatively steady at more than 40 percent throughout the period under review.[45] Thus the members of the domestic owning class have been more inclined to choose investments other than stock in recent years.

Ownership versus Management. The fourth phenomenon is a development occurring in the upper echelons of this corporate structure that has been labeled the "bureaucratization" of corporate decision making. In the larger corporations, stockholders choose a board of directors that then chooses a set of managers to make the day-to-day decisions for that company. If ultimate concern is with the political power that is inherent in capital ownership, is this power actually shifting from a small group of owners to a larger, fundamentally different group of non-owning managerial elites?

First of all, the managerial cadre has been found to be the largest single group in the stockholding population, and a greater proportion of this group holds stock than in any other group.[46] Approximately 10 of the nation's largest 100 industries are essentially manager-owned,[47] and nearly one-half of the managers of these top corporations each hold at least $1 million worth of stock in their own companies.[48]

This results, at least in part, because these top executives may draw as much as one-half of their salaries in stock bonuses and stock options.[49] Besides helping to guarantee that the managers will have vested interests in the profitability of their companies, such arrangements serve to shelter the executives' incomes. In 1984, for instance, Ford chairman Philip Caldwell received over 60 percent of his $4 million remuneration in the form of stock. Chrysler chairman Lee Iacocca received $4.3 million worth of stock that same year as part of a total compensation package valued at $5.5 million.[50]

Yet most obvious is the fact that any manager's career may well rest on the figures found on the bottom line of the company ledger, for without impressive profits, stock prices will decline, borrowing will become more difficult, less capital will be available for innovation and new investment, and so on—all of which will seriously hamper the attainment of any secondary goals the manager might have. It should come as no surprise, then, that Edward S. Mason found the rate of profit to be virtually the same whether a corporation was run by stockholders or managers.[51]

No matter who is at the helm, the corporate ship seems to sail first and foremost for profits, the ultimate interest of the shareholders and the managers. And even if their interests do occasionally diverge in any given company, the managerial elite is simply not large enough, different enough in motivation, or separate enough from ownership itself to alter the size or nature of the small owning class in any significant way.[52]

SUMMARY

Personal wealth may be the only truly stable measure of self-sufficiency in a capitalist economic system like that of the United States. The accumulation of wealth serves as a buffer in times of adversity (disability, temporary loss of income, etc.) and also guarantees that class position can be handed down from generation to generation (through money for college, funds for private entrepreneurship, etc.). Personal wealth also allows greater opportunities for self-fulfilling work, and most important, it is usually accompanied by increased economic and political power.

In the United States, wealth is highly concentrated in the hands of a small owning class, which is almost exclusively white. All others—especially blacks—are left in varying states of insecurity, dependence, subordination, and alienation, and their positions of non-ownership, like those of ownership, tend to be handed down from generation to generation.

NOTES

1. See David McLellan, *The Thought of Karl Marx* (New York: Harper & Row, 1971), pp. 105–121.
2. See Ferdinand Lundberg, *The Rich and the Super-rich* (Secaucus, N.J.: Lyle Stuart, 1968), p. 29; James N. Morgan, "Panel Study on Income Dynamics," dissertation, University of Michigan, 1977; *New York Times*, July 10, 1977.
3. Michael Reich, "The Development of the U.S. Labor Force," in Richard Edwards (ed.), *The Capitalist System* (Englewood Cliffs, N.J.: Prentice-Hall, 1978), p. 180; U.S. Department of Commerce, Bureau of the Census, *Current Population Reports*, Series P-60.
4. Karl Marx, "Profit of Capital," in J. B. Bottomore (ed.), *Karl Marx: Early Writings* (London: Watts, 1963), p. 91.
5. A *corporation* is a legal entity characterized by joint stock ownership and a continuous legal identity of its own that relieves the stock owners of financial liability. For further explanation, see Paul Samuelson and William Nordhaus, *Economics* (New York: McGraw-Hill, 1985), pp. 438–445.
6. Charles Anderson, *The Political Economy of Social Class* (Englewood Cliffs, N.J.: Prentice-Hall, 1974), p. 211. For a look at corporate mergers in historical perspective, see Frederic Scherer, *Industrial Market Structure and Economic Performance* (Chicago: Rand McNally, 1980): Samuel Reid, *The New Industrial Order* (New York: McGraw-Hill, 1976).
7. Scherer, *Industrial Market Structure*, pp. 119–123; *New York Times*, August 5, 1981.
8. *New York Times*, April 23, 1978. Also see Edward Greenberg, *Capitalism and the American Political Ideal* (New York: Sharpe, 1985), pp. 120–121; Peter Dooley, "The Interlocking Directorate," *American Economic Review* (June 1969), pp. 314–323.
9. Greenberg, *Capitalism*, p. 121.

10. Thomas Dye, *Who's Running America?* (Englewood Cliffs, N.J.: Prentice-Hall, 1983); Richard Barnet and Ronald Muller, "The Negative Effects of Multinational Corporations," in David Mermelstein (ed.), *The Economic Crisis Reader* (New York: Random House, 1975), pp. 154–155.
11. Michael Parenti, *Democracy for the Few* (New York: St. Martin's Press, 1983), p. 12.
12. Quoted in James O'Connor, "Who Rules the Corporations?" *Socialist Revolution* (February 1971), pt. 1, p. 99.
13. Lundberg, *The Rich and the Super-rich*, pp. 144ff; Robert Lampman, *The Share of Top Wealth-holders in National Wealth* (Princeton, N.J.: Princeton University Press, 1962); U.S. Congress, Senate, Committee on Governmental Operations, *Disclosure of Corporate Ownership*, 93d Congr., 1st sess., December 27, 1973 (Washington, D.C.: GPO, 1974), p. 22; David Kotz, "Finance Capital and Corporate Control," in Edwards, *Capitalist System.*
14. Dooley, "Interlocking Directorate."
15. Dye, *Who's Running America?* p. 189.
16. Study by E. Winslow Turner for the U.S. Senate Committee on Governmental Affairs, as reported in the *New York Times*, February 5, 1981. Also see Beth Mintz and Michael Schwartz, "The Structure of Power in American Business," paper presented at the annual meeting of the American Political Science Association, Washington, D.C., September 3, 1977.
17. Harlem resident quoted in Kenneth Clark, *The Dark Ghetto* (New York: Harper & Row, 1965), p. 1.
18. For a more detailed discussion of this postindustrial phenomenon, see Marcus Pohlmann, *Political Power in the Postindustrial City* (Millwood, N.Y.: Associated Faculties Press, 1986).
19. U.S. Department of Commerce, Bureau of the Census, *Household Wealth and Assets Ownership, 1984* (Washington, D.C.: GPO, 1985).
20. Ibid. Also see, for example, Abram Harris, *The Negro as Capitalist* (New York: Haskell, 1936); Timothy Bates, *Black Capitalism* (New York: Praeger, 1973); Roger Ransom and Richard Sutch, *One Kind of Freedom* (Cambridge: Cambridge University Press, 1977).
21. *New York Times*, July 26, 1981. Also see U.S. Department of Commerce, Bureau of the Census, *Survey of Minority-owned Business Enterprises* (Washington, D.C.: GPO, 1979).
22. Firdaus Jhabvala, "The Economic Situation of Black People" and "A Critique of Reformist Solutions to Discrimination," in David Gordon (ed.), *Problems in Political Economy* (Lexington, Mass.: Heath, 1977): *Black Enterprise* (June 1975); James Blackwell, *The Black Community* (New York: Dodd, Mead, 1975), pp. 167–168; National Urban League, *Full Employment as a National Goal* (New York: National Urban League, 1974), p. 55; National Urban League, *State of Black America* (New York: National Urban League, 1978), p. 13; Karl Flaming et al., "Black Powerlessness in Policy-making Positions," *Sociological Quarterly* (Winter 1972); *New York Times*, July 26, 1981.
23. Frank Davis, *The Economics of Black Community Development* (Chicago: Markham, 1972), pp. 72–78, 104.
24. Peter Lindert and Jeffrey Williamson, "Long-Term Trends in American Wealth Inequality," University of Wisconsin's Research Institute on Poverty, Discussion Paper No. 472, 1977, p. 3.
25. New York Stock Exchangee Survey (November 1983), as reported in the *New York Times*, December 1, 1983; Gabriel Kolko, *Wealth and Power in America* (New York: Praeger, 1962), p. 51; James D. Smith and Stephen D. Franklin, "The Concentration of Wealth, 1922–1969," *American Economic Review* (May 1974), p. 164; Edward Greenberg, *The American Political System* (Boston: Little, Brown, 1983), p. 36; Neil Jacoby, *Corporate Powers and Social Responsibility* (New York: Macmillan, 1973), pp. 36–37. The reference is to direct ownership, although a large number of people

indirectly hold shares through banks, insurance companies, and pension funds. Most of the latter group have not controlled these shares in a way that has threatened the dominant power of those who directly hold large individual holdings.

26. Figures for the top 1 percent of Americans from Smith and Franklin. "Concentration of Personal Wealth"; figures for the top 5 percent estimated by taking Smith and Franklin's calculation for the top 1 percent in 1962 and dividing it by a calculation for the top 5 percent from Federal Reserve Bulletin, *Survey of Financial Characteristics of Consumers* (1962), pp. 110–114. The resulting ratio was then applied to Smith and Franklin's other figures to attain the corresponding estimates for the top 5 percent, extrapolated for the years skipped over in the Smith and Franklin article. A 1983 estimate was derived by using dividends reported in 1983 tax returns (see Internal Revenue Service, *Personal Wealth and Statistics of Income Bulletin*, Summer 1983), and extrapolated. Final estimates for the proportion of stock held by the top 5 percent of American adults ranged from a high of 81 percent in 1972 to a low of 59 percent in 1976:

Year	%	Year	%	Year	%
1965	78	1972	81	1979	61
1966	77	1973	75	1980	61
1967	76	1974	69	1981	62
1968	75	1975	64	1982	62
1969	74	1976	59	1983	63
1970	77	1977	60	1984	63
1971	79	1978	60		

Stock is defined as common and preferred issues in domestic and foreign firms, certificates or shares of building and loan and savings and loan associations, federal land bank stocks, accrued dividends, and other investments reporting equity in an enterprise, as well as stock held in trust (though understated).

27. For example, Keith Butters et al., *Effect of Taxation on Investments by Individuals* (Cambridge, Mass.: Riverside Press, 1953), p. 400; Parenti, *Democracy for the Few*, pp. 11–12.

28. *Christian Science Monitor*, December 6, 1985.

29. *New York Times*, March 19, 1985; July 15, 1985; December 17, 1986.

30. Lee Iacocca, *Iacocca: An Autobiography*, (New York: Bantam, 1984), p. 110.

31. William Domhoff, "The Study of State and Ruling Class in Corporate America: New Directions," paper presented at the annual meeting of the American Political Science Association, Washington, D.C., September 3, 1977, provides a good example of how family stock control can be hidden. His research focuses on the Weyerhaeuser lumber company.

32. Robert Sheehan, "Proprietors in the World of Big Business," *Fortune* (June 15, 1967), pp. 178, 182.

33. Gerald Zilg, *Du Pont: Behind the Nylon Curtain* (Englewood Cliffs, N.J.: Prentice-Hall, 1974).

34. Peter Collier and David Horowitz, *Rockefellers: An American Dynasty* (New York: Holt, Rinehart and Winston, 1976); Dye, *Who's Running America?*, pp. 45–46.

35. Dye, *Who's Running America?*, pp. 45–46.

36. William Domhoff, *Who Rules America?* (Englewood Cliffs, N.J.: Prentice-Hall, 1967), p. 40.

37. C. Wright Mills, *The Power Elite* (New York: Oxford University Press, 1956), p. 122. We have focused on publicly traded corporate stock, but there is no evidence that including privately held or nontraded stock would dilute the concentration of ownership.

38. Peter Drucker, *The Unseen Revolution* (New York: Harper & Row, 1976).
39. *Christian Science Monitor*, December 6, 1985.
40. Committee on Governmental Operations, "Corporate Ownership and Control," 94th Cong., 2d sess., November 1976 (Washington, D.C.: GPO, 1977); *New York Times*, January 22, 1978.
41. Federal Reserve Board, *Flow of Fund Accounts, Assets, and Liabilities* (Washington, D.C.: GPO, 1984). The 1983 figure, including all stock held by a combination of public and private pension funds, is up from 5 percent in 1965.
42. For supporting evidence, see Gayle B. Thompson, "Pension Coverage and Benefits: Findings from the Retirement History Society," U.S. Department of Health, Education and Welfare, Social Security Administration, *Social Security Bulletin* (February 1978); U.S. Congress, Senate Committee on Labor and Public Welfare, "Welfare and Pension Plans Investigation," 84th Cong., 2d sess., 1956 (Washington, D.C.: GPO, 1956), pp. 11–14; *New York Times*, February 24, 1978.
43. Drucker, *Unseen Revolution.*
44. *U.S. News and World Report*, August 18, 1977; Federal Reserve Board, *Flow of Fund Accounts*; *New York Times*, March 30, 1987. Also see Martin Tolchin and Susan Tolchin, *Buying into America* (New York: Times Books, 1987).
45. Estimates derived from 1969 figures compiled by the Internal Revenue Service in their *Supplemental Statistics of Income Bulletin* (Washington, D.C.: GPO, 1983). Figures for the share of wealth held by the top 1 percent of American adults were divided by those for the top 5 percent, and the resulting ratio was applied to 1965 and 1972 estimates of the share held by the top 1 percent in those years (Lampman, *Share of Top Wealth-holders*; James D. Smith and Staunton K. Calvert, "Estimating the Wealth of Top Wealth-holders from Estate Tax Returns," *Proceedings of the American Statistical Association* [1965]; unpublished estimates by James D. Smith, the Urban Institute, and Pennsylvania State University) and to 1976 and 1982 estimates of the share held by the top 1 percent in those years (Internal Revenue Service, *Supplemental Statistics of Income Bulletin* [1976, 1982]). Resulting estimates for the proportion of the nation's wealth possessed by the top 5 percent of American adults: 1965, 48%; 1969, 42%; 1972, 44%; 1976, 44%; 1982, 42%.

   Wealth is defined as all corporate stock, trusts, bonds, savings, life insurance, and real estate, less liabilities.
46. Kolko, *Wealth and Power*, p. 67. Kolko also details directors as managers (pp. 60–61) and as owners of large blocks of stock (pp. 61–65). Also see Mills, *Power Elite*, pp. 121–122; D. Villarejo, "Stock Ownership and the Control of Corporations," *New University Thought* (Fall 1961), pp. 33–77, (Winter 1962), pp. 45–65; Paul Blumberg, "Another Day, Another $3,000," in Mark J. Green et al. (eds.), *The Big Business Reader* (New York: Pilgrim Press, 1983), pp. 316–332; *Wall Street Journal*, April 18, 1978.
47. Sheehan, "Proprietors," p. 12.
48. Jeremy Larner, "The Effect of Management Control on the Profits of Large Corporations," in Maurice Zeitlin (ed.), *American Society Inc.* (Chicago: Rand McNally, 1970), pp. 251–262. Also see Kolko, *Wealth and Power*, p. 67; Paul Baran and Paul Sweezy, *Monopoly Capital* (New York: Monthly Review Press, 1966), pp. 34–35; Edward S. Herman, *Corporate Control, Corporate Power* (New York: Cambridge University Press, 1981).
49. Ira Katznelson and Mark Kesselman, *The Politics of Power* (Orlando, Fla.: Harcourt Brace Jovanovich, 1979), p. 79. Also see Ralph Miliband, *The State in Capitalist Society* (New York: Basic Books, 1969), pp. 35–36; Herman, *Corporate Control, Corporate Power.*
50. *New York Times*, April 13, 1985.
51. Edward S. Mason, "Corporation," *International Encyclopedia of the Social Sciences*, vol. 3 (1968), pp. 396–403.

52. For a more complete critique of the owner-management separation thesis, on both conceptual and empirical grounds, see Maurice Zeitlin, "Corporate Ownership and Control," *American Journal of Sociology*, (March 1974), pp. 1073–1119. Also see Miliband's critique of Galbraith in *The Socialist Register* (1968); Herman, *Corporate Control, Corporate Power*.

CHAPTER FIVE

Functions of
a Welfare State

In the fall of 1972, Charles V. Hamilton published an article titled "Conduit Colonialism and Public Policy" in which he set out a model that had four basic components: taxpayers, government, welfare recipients, and "welfare beneficiaries"—wealthy individuals who make sizable profits selling goods and services to the welfare-receiving poor. A primary point was to show how governmental welfare programs caused their recipients to function as channels for transferring money from the paychecks of the average taxpayer to the pockets of a group of wealthy elites. This pass-through occurred when the recipients paid inflated amounts of taxpayer-provided money to the welfare beneficiaries: the landlords, doctors, pharmacists, and other vendors who served them. Consequently, the recipient was a "conduit" and was being "colonized" in the process—left dependent on others for subsistence and at the same time absorbing much of the wrath of the average taxpayer.[1]

By using an extended version of Hamilton's "conduit colonialism" model, this chapter attempts to estimate the degree to which America's liberal-capitalist political economy functions to enrich an "owning class" at the expense of the rest of American society. This runs directly contrary to a prevalent contemporary notion that if the rich are allowed to get richer, almost everybody else will benefit by virtue of a "trickle-down" effect (or "supply-side economics").[2] But whereas Hamilton focused on the systemic functions of the poor as welfare recipients, this study extends his model to focus on the systemic functions of the black and white middle and working classes as well.

In particular, the chapter attempts to estimate the amount of money that has been transferred from the black and white middle and working classes to the bank accounts of the small white owning class over the period from 1965 to 1984. This transfer takes a variety of forms, among them private-sector profits from sales to governmental and nongovernmental consumers and direct transfers from government in the form of grants and credit subsidies.

The chapter concludes that the rich are getting richer and the poor poorer in the United States. That will come as no real surprise to more than three-quarters of the American public, who are already convinced of that.[3] The chapter also concludes that average Americans, black and white, pay a sizable share of their paychecks to government each year and are not pleased about having that hard-earned money go to many of the present welfare recipients. Somewhat less obvious is that a significant portion of those paychecks also goes to the owners of corporate capital, as a sort of "tribute" for the privilege of living in the country they own, and that government, welfare recipients, and this owning class interrelate to create that reality. The documentation and explanation of how that happens will be the primary focus of this chapter.

Where is the opposition to this arrangement? The last section of the chapter presents evidence that suggests that much middle- and working-class anger is diverted toward the poor. In addition, many in the exploited population are coopted by their faith in a mythology that holds out the hope of interclass mobility as a reward for talent, hard work, and frugality.

Before beginning, however, three methodological notes are in order.

First of all, this particular time period (1965–1984) was chosen for study in part because people living in "poverty" were not regularly singled out for separate analysis by the U.S. Census Bureau prior to 1965. Beyond that, the period encompasses both economic slumps and booms as well as significant variations in governmental taxing and spending orientations.

Second, there is no denying that the operation of the economic system is a dynamic process. Corporate profits, for example, generally are not hoarded away in the vaults of the owning class. Instead, they are often spun back into the economy in the form of investments, bonuses, and the like. What this chapter provides are year-end snapshots of this process, and when viewed over time, these year-end snapshots should provide a reasonable indication of which class groupings have been gaining and which losing in the course of this dynamic arrangement.

Third, some of the definitions used have been dictated by data availability; for example, the *owning class* is defined in this chapter as the top 5 percent of American families[4] in terms of income (Chapter 4 used an estimate of the wealth held by the top 5 percent of all adults). The best definition might have been the top 1 percent of wealthholders, but not enough data was available on that small group. Also, some of the developments are analyzed over slightly different time periods; for example, tax payments are measured only through 1983, the most recent comparable data available at the time the book was written. Despite these inconsistencies, this chapter should provide some telling indications.

THE CONCEPTUAL MODEL

The primary components of my adaptation of Charles V. Hamilton's model are presented in Figure 5.1.

Government

In domestic policymaking, it can be argued that government (meaning federal, state, and local levels combined), as an institution, has come to play three basic roles. Economists call them allocation, stabilization, and redistribution. *Allocation* is the provision of maintenance, or "housekeeping," services. These include police

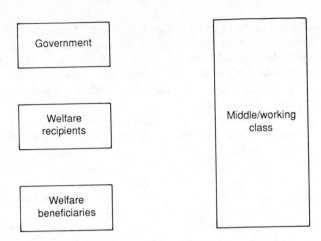

Figure 5.1. Welfare State Capitalism: The Participants

and fire protection, educating the young, and keeping the streets and highways paved. *Stabilization* involves government using fiscal and monetary policies to help maintain a healthy, growing economy. If successful, these actions help secure adequate numbers of jobs, goods, and services for an ever-increasing American population. Finally, through *redistribution*, government attempts to compensate people who suffer significant economic hardship in the course of this process. It does so by using tax revenues to provide assistance in such forms as Aid to Families with Dependent Children (AFDC) when the breadwinner of a family is unable to work or to earn enough money to provide the family with the essentials of life. Other examples are job training for people who lack marketable skills and unemployment compensation for workers who lose their jobs because their employers shifted production patterns or location in order to operate more efficiently.

Economist James O'Connor collapses these three categories into two and calls them the *accumulation* and *legitimation* functions. Government assists the process of capital accumulation by attempting to guarantee an adequate supply of venture capital and productive labor so that the owners of capital can and will invest in ways that will lead to stable economic growth—for example, by providing tax breaks and subsidies to corporations ("social investment"), teachers to educate the corporate work force, road crews to help minimize corporations' transportation costs, police to protect corporate property, and so on ("social consumption"). In legitimation, government compensates people who become economically dislocated, so that the necessary level of social harmony can be maintained, as by providing maintenance services and social-welfare programs ("social expenditures"). As the ownership of capital becomes more concentrated, the capitalist class can coerce the government into socializing even more of the costs of capital accumulation and production, while the benefits remain largely private. This, however, requires that the government also spend more and more on social expenditures in order to retain legitimacy with the non-owners. Thus the role of government continues to expand, and it essentially stabilizes a system that smiles most favorably on the owning class.[5]

The Owning Class (Hamilton's "Welfare Beneficiaries")

A glance at the income distribution in the United States shows how pointed is the income pyramid, how broad its base. . . . If we made an income pyramid out of a child's blocks, with each layer portraying $1000 of income, the peak would be far higher than Mt. Everest, but most people would be within a few feet of the ground.[6]

The owning class consists of the people highest off the ground, in the income pyramid or the even steeper wealth pyramid. These are the white people who assume the chore of accumulating the bulk of the nation's wealth and, ideally, in the process create relatively stable patterns of capital investment. Their discretion in the latter regard adds considerable economic and political power to the personal and family security their wealth provides.[7]

As defined here, this group makes up the top 5 percent of American families in terms of income, which in 1984 meant incomes exceeding $73,200. Each of these families generally had assets of at least $200,000, held stock valued in excess of $50,000, and received more than one-quarter of their incomes from business investments. As a group, they have consistently owned more than two-thirds of the nation's stock.[8] Less than 1 percent of all black families have ever fallen into this category; thus, for empirical convenience, these black families have been included in the middle- and working-class grouping.[9] (See Chapter 4 for a more detailed discussion of the concentration of wealth in America.)

Besides wages, gifts, and inheritance, the owning class derives its income from at least three other sources: the work of their employees, direct government aid, and indirect government aid. To begin with, they make profits from investments of their capital by charging more for products and services than employees are paid to produce and distribute them.[10] Direct government aid includes government subsidies like low-interest loans and tax abatements and profits derived from contracts with government for building things like highways, bombers, housing, and other durable goods. Indirect government aid is the profit realized when selling goods and services to the publicly subsidized indigent (called "welfare recipients" from here on).

Welfare Recipients (Lower Class)

In Brooklyn's grimy Bedford Stuyvesant ghetto, a welfare mother surveys her $195-a-month tenement apartment, an unheated, vermin-ridden urban swamp. The bathroom ceiling and sink drip water on the cracked linoleum floor. There are no lights, no locks on the doors.[11]

If they are aware of its availability and not too proud to accept it, most indigent Americans are eligible to receive relief provisions from the state. Those opting to receive such assistance comprise roughly 10 percent of the U.S. population. Meanwhile, as Herbert Gans and others have pointed out, they and the eligibles not receiving this aid—roughly another 10 percent of Americans[12]—perform a number of economic functions. They serve the system, for example, in the following roles:[13]

1. *Marginal work force.* As long as relief payments are kept low enough, the able-bodied indigent are often compelled to accept virtually any job at any wage at any time. This adds a dimension of elasticity to work force supply as demand for labor periodically rises and falls.[14]

2. *"Dirty workers."* This segment of the population is also compelled to do even the most undesirable jobs.

3. *"Rejects" market.* Given their low incomes, even after welfare assistance, they are more likely to purchase unmarketable items such as damaged merchandise, stale food and beverages, out-of-style clothing, deteriorating housing and automobiles, and the like.

4. *Pawns.* At home, they have been driven from their neighborhoods in order to make way for urban renewal, new highways, hospitals, and universities. They also have provided a disproportionate number of the foot soldiers who have fought and died in America's wars abroad.

5. *Steppingstones.* Their low status allows other groups, often only slightly better off, to feel superior and thus better about their own circumstances.

6. *Clients.* The programs that are designed to help them also provide jobs for the educated unemployed and underemployed, especially surplus administrators.

7. *Lightning rods.* They are an easily visible and vulnerable target for the wrath of the "middle and working class," members of which often feel overworked, underpaid, and overtaxed.

8. *Conduits.* They allow the capitalist class to squeeze venture capital out of the paychecks of the middle and working class. This is accomplished when government transfers money to welfare recipients, who in turn use it to purchase goods and services. The welfare recipients derive elements of their subsistence from these payments, while an often substantial portion of this relief dollar gets passed along to the owning class as profit from these transactions. For example, the landlord of a welfare hotel charges $500 a month for a rundown efficiency apartment; the tenant gets barely subsistence-level shelter, and the landlord makes a sizable profit.[15]

Beyond those economic functions, whether rural or urban, young or old, married or single, migrant or stationary, black, white, or red, the indigent also have much else in common. They live in almost constant fear of crime. They remain rather hopelessly in debt—often to unscrupulous loan sharks. A growing number have become homeless, with estimates ranging from 250,000 to 3 million. And an increasing number are also hungry.

After a trip to West Africa, *Time* correspondent Robert Wurmstedt concluded:

> The poverty in the black and Puerto Rican neighborhoods on the West Side of Chicago is worse than any poverty I saw in West Africa. . . . [The poor of West Africa] do not live in constant fear of violence, vermin, and fire. You don't find the same sense of desperation and hopelessness you find in the American ghetto. [16]

In addition, although the large majority of the able-bodied indigent are employed at least part of the year, the shift to a postindustrial economy has severely limited many of their escape routes. Instead of full-time unionized factory positions with decent wages, benefits, and opportunities for advancement, they are far more likely to end up working at part-time, low-wage service jobs, without benefits and with very little opportunity to advance. [17] For indigent blacks in particular, this is doubly distressing. As William Julius Wilson put it, "It's as though racism, having put the black underclass in its economic place, stepped aside to watch technological change finish the job." [18]

For the purposes of analysis, this group (the "lower class") has been defined as the bottom 20 percent of American families in terms of income, those who have generally been eligible to receive one or more forms of public assistance from the welfare state. [19] Their 1984 incomes were less than $12,489, and they owned virtually no assets whatsoever. Forty percent of all black families, and a majority of black children, fell into this category.

Middle- and Working-Class (MC/WC) Work Force and Tax Base

The 75 percent of American families between the extremes, including 60 percent of America's black families, constitute the "middle and working class." Their incomes fell between $12,489 and $73,200 in 1984, increasingly requiring the paychecks of at least two wage earners in each family in order to remain in that category.

The members of this group also find themselves caught in an economic predicament. They work in either the private or public sector to produce the nation's goods and services. Most are employees of the owning class, working for a wage that is less than the market value of what they produce. In addition, taxation deprives them of a significant portion of their incomes, while billions of dollars of their tax payments end up in the hands of the owning class.

What is left for those who work for a living? If the average tax rate is applied to the median family income, that median family is left with an income below what the Bureau of Labor Statistics estimates it will cost such a family to meet an "intermediate budget" for food, shelter, clothing, transportation, and personal and medical care. [20] Without a cushion of wealth to fall back on if times get significantly worse, these middle- and working-class people find themselves economically vulnerable. A five-year University of Michigan study, for example, concluded that 7 out of 10 American families have at least an even chance of spending some years of their lives in "economic distress," most likely the result of the family losing the paycheck of one of its breadwinners. [21]

Much of this should become clearer by examining the "welfare state capitalism" model of Figure 5.1 as applied to the United States. The model contains seven junctures where money is transferred from one group of participants to another: private-sector corporate profits; personal taxes; direct subsidies, contract profits, interest profits (corporate subsidies); public assistance; and conduit capitalism. The model also shows a venting of pent-up frustration, termed "directed wrath."

WELFARE STATE CAPITALISM

Black people cannot afford the social injustices of capitalism. They cannot afford a system which creates privileged classes within an already superexploited and underprivileged community. They cannot afford a system which organizes community resources and then distributes the resulting wealth in a hierarchical fashion, with those who need least getting most.[22]

Private-Sector Corporate Profits

When the owning class invests its money in corporations, it expects something in return. What it gets in return are profits (see Figure 5.2). These derive from paying workers less than the market value of what they have produced. In other words, this is a return to capital, not to labor.

These corporate profits have accounted for at least 10 percent of all national income throughout most of this century. In the period under study, they rose from $119.7 billion to $124.4 billion in constant 1984 dollars, after subtracting the owners' taxes, profits from transactions with government and welfare recipients, and adjustments for inventory valuation and capital depreciation. There was significant fluctuation over the period, but profits in 1984 reached their highest level in 20 years and appear to be climbing to new heights.

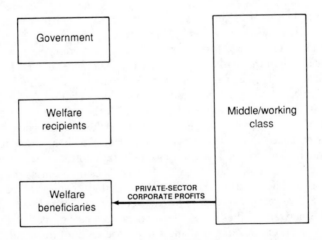

Figure 5.2. Welfare State Capitalism: Private-Sector Corporate Profits

Focusing on black Americans, such private profit taking has allowed the white owning class to acquire billions of dollars of income each year as profits from its sales of the goods and services produced by those in the black middle and working class. In 1965, the white owning class extracted more than $6 billion (1984 dollars) from the market value of what the black middle and working class produced. By 1984, that transfer had climbed to nearly $9.5 billion.[23]

Personal Taxes

By 1984, Americans were paying nearly $700 billion in taxes every year (see Figure 5.3). And as Table 5.1 indicates, when tax burdens imposed by federal, state, and local governments are combined, it is quite clear that the United States does not have a progressive tax system. Americans who make most of the money still have most of the money after government is paid. In 1980, for example, economist Joseph Pechman found the poorest one-tenth of American families making 1.3 percent of all adjusted family income before taxes and 1.3 percent of it afterward. At the other end of the income spectrum, the wealthiest one-tenth made 33.1 percent of all adjusted family income before taxes and had 33.9 percent of it after all taxes had been paid.[24]

In 1965, the black middle and working class paid some $1,870 (1984 dollars) in taxes for every man, woman, and child in average three-person families. That figure grew to a peak of $3,297 in 1979 and was still $2,924 by 1983—despite a major federal income tax cut over the previous three years. As a group, the black middle and working class was paying nearly $50 billion in taxes each year by 1983, and black and white workers combined were paying some $559 billion.[25]

Now add to all of this the fact that the United States had no wealth tax as such. In other words, besides local real estate taxes, individuals are taxed only on the yearly income derived from their stocks, trust funds, bank accounts, and so on,

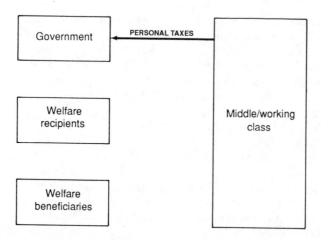

Figure 5.3. Welfare State Capitalism: Personal Taxes

TABLE 5.1 CUMULATIVE DISTRIBUTION OF ADJUSTED FAMILY INCOME, 1980

Population Decile	Proportion of Adjusted Family Income Retained	
	Before Taxes (%)	After Taxes (%)
Bottom 90%	66.9	66.1
Bottom 80%	51.6	51.2
Bottom 50%	21.0	21.0
Bottom 10%	1.3	1.3

Source: Joseph Pechman, Who Paid the Taxes, 1966–1985? (Washington, D.C.: Brookings Institute, 1985), p. 52. Reprinted by permission of the publisher.

instead of being taxed annually on the overall value of such wealth. Inheritance and estate taxes are applied once the individual dies, but even those are fraught with loopholes. Prior to death, for instance, a wealthy person may (1) gradually liquidate the estate by giving it away in untaxed annual gifts to each heir, (2) sell property to the inheritor(s) for a nominal fee, or (3) create trust funds that will be taxed only when the inheritors collect their yearly allotment. Finally, the entire estate is subject to a $600,000 federal estate tax deduction and is subject to inheritance taxation only when first put into trusts. (Unspent trust money can be passed along to the next heirs without incurring any inheritance taxation.)[26] Estate and gift taxes, as a result, have been providing only about 1 percent of all governmental revenues despite the millions upon millions of dollars' worth of wealth that exists and is passed on every year.[27]

In the end, then, huge family fortunes can be amassed and handed down from generation to generation without much government interference. Meanwhile, the average American working for a wage or salary winds up paying the lion's share of the ever-increasing (nonprogressive) government tax burden.[28]

Corporate Subsidies

Direct Subsidies. Each year the *Survey of Current Business* compiles the amount of government subsidies paid to nongovernment enterprises, primarily in the agricultural, construction, and transportation industries. This figure includes both direct cash payments and the calculated value of "benefits in kind" (see Figure 5.4). Converted to 1984 dollars, the owning class's share of those subsidies amounted to $11.8 billion in 1965, grew to a peak of $17.5 billion in 1983, and dropped to $16.1 billion a year later. This meant that in 1965, the black middle and working class transferred over $600 million to the white owners by means of these governmental subsidies. By 1983, that figure had grown to more than $1.3 billion, and it was only slightly less the following year.[29]

Contract Profits. The owning class is also reaping after-tax profits from business transactions with government, although these profits declined somewhat between 1965 and 1984. At the beginning of that period, as the Vietnam War raged, the after-tax profits from sales to government were estimated to be $7.4 billion in 1984 dollars. That figure dropped below $4 billion in the early 1980s but was $4.3 billion

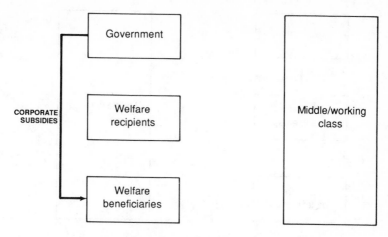

Figure 5.4. Welfare State Capitalism: Corporate Subsidies

in 1984. Meanwhile, this was costing the black middle and working class nearly $400 million in 1965 and still more than $300 million by 1984.[30]

These are conservative estimates when considering that many of government's biggest purchases—such as most of its defense equipment—are made without competitive bidding from industries in which profit rates are often considerably higher than the average corporate profit rates used here.[31]

Interest Profits. Government indebtedness continues to mount, and thus government continues to pay more and more interest to its lenders. This has meant an increase in real-dollar after-tax profits for the owning class. From a 1965 figure of $4.5 billion, for example, it is estimated that that class has recently begun to acquire over $6 billion a year—an increase of 40 percent in 20 years. As a result, the white owning class has come to extract nearly another half billion dollars annually from the paychecks of the black middle and working class.[32]

Public Assistance

Public assistance refers to the host of government programs designed to ease the load of being indigent in the United States of America, such as AFDC, Medicaid, food stamps, rent subsidies, and Supplemental Aid for the Aged, Blind, and Disabled (see Figure 5.5). They provide low-income Americans with money and vouchers with which to purchase necessities like food, shelter, clothing, and medical assistance. Beginning primarily with Franklin Roosevelt's New Deal and accelerating dramatically during and after Lyndon Johnson's Great Society era, such relief payments have grown to sizable proportions: in 1984, some 74 need-based programs provided millions of indigents with over $134 billion worth of "relief."[33] The Congressional Research Service refers to these programs as the "welfare system." But the story does not end here, for the recipients do not eat,

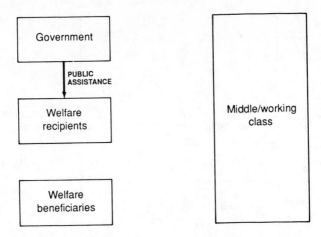

Figure 5.5. Welfare State Capitalism: Public Assistance

wear, and live under these checks and coupons. They spend them, and in the process, they provide additional profit for the owning class.

Conduit Capitalism

Charles V. Hamilton was one of the first to note the "conduit" function played by nearly all relief recipients.[34] As indicated earlier, this occurs when various proportions of their governmentally funded purchases flow on to the owning class—wealthy landlords, the stockholders of pharmaceutical companies, nursing home operators—as profits from these transactions (see Figure 5.6). Although it is difficult to determine how much money each of these vendors is making by serving

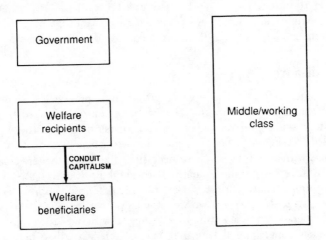

Figure 5.6. Welfare State Capitalism: Conduit Capitalism

the poor, it is possible to estimate what the owning-class vendors as a group have made. For example, applying the average after-tax corporate profit rates to the billions spent on need-based public assistance programs, real-dollar vendor profits flowing to the owning class nearly tripled between 1965 and 1984. The figure had risen to some $1.4 billion by the latter date, and more than $100 million came out of the pockets of the black middle and working class.[35]

How does this actually occur? Consider the following examples of this phenomenon.

Case 1. In June 1985, the city of New York was housing 2,900 homeless families in welfare hotels. Each family lived in a single room, fewer than half of which had refrigerators and almost none of which had stoves or allowed cooking facilities. The city paid landlords a monthly average of $1,900 per room for these accommodations.[36]

Case 2. Builders, contractors, and operators in the notorious nursing home industry make millions of dollars from government while elderly patients reportedly go underfed and underattended and are occasionally even being found in shock from cold or dehydration or starving and fighting each other for food.[37]

Case 3. Industries producing health care items—companies like American Home Products, G. D. Searle, Merck, SmithKline, Sterling Drug, Eli Lilly, Johnson & Johnson, Miles Laboratories, Pfizer, Squibb, and Upjohn—reap some of the highest profits in the corporate world.[38] Through Medicaid, the American taxpayer has certainly paid a significant share of their hefty profits.

America's political-economic system does seem to reinforce existing class relationships. This becomes even more obvious in light of the figures.

In 1965, the American political economy transferred more than $7.5 billion (1984 dollars) from the paychecks of the black middle and working class to the investment portfolios of the white owning class. That figure climbs to $143 billion when considering the black and white middle and working classes combined. To look at it another way, it amounted to some 14 percent of both black and total middle- and working-class income.

Although fluctuating with the owning class's private-sector profits in the years that followed, the total transfer had risen to more than $150 billion by 1984, exceeding $11.5 billion from the black middle and working class. This was still a full 10 percent of increased black middle- and working-class income. Thus the average American, black or white, is now working more than one month out of every year in order to supply money to the small group of whites who own the bulk of the nation's corporate stock—a "tribute" of sorts for the privilege of living and working in the country owned by the white elites.[39]

Government was directly involved in about one-fifth of this transfer. It was also indirectly involved in the amount transferred through private-sector profits, given its nonprogressive tax system, economic regulations or lack thereof, many of its maintenance services, and so on.

The Trickle-down Fallacy

Both liberal and conservative politicians from time to time espouse varying versions of "supply-side economics," an economic theory based on the premise that if the wealthy are allowed to get wealthier, a certain amount will "trickle down" to everyone else, making the entire society better off in the long-run. Reality, however, poses some serious questions for that theory.

The rich have indeed gotten richer. The poorest owning-class family, for example, made $54,961 (1984 dollars) in 1965 and $73,230 by 1984. At the same time, the average American family, black or white, was clearly better off in 1984 than it was in 1965. However, the real-dollar income of the average middle- and working-class family has actually declined by more than $1,000 since the late 1970s. And for black middle- and working-class families, real-dollar income has fallen more than $3,000 over that same period. Finally, families in the lower class saw their average real-dollar income increase significantly between 1965 and 1973 as the Great Society welfare programs took effect. That income, nonetheless, dropped an average of over $1,500 per family between 1973 and 1984, with black families paralleling the entire group.

A paradox is beginning to emerge. The after-tax income gap between the middle and working class and the owning class has continued to widen, while their respective shares of all family income have remained relatively steady. The top 5 percent of American families have consistently made some 16 percent of that income, while the middle three-quarters of the families have been making roughly 79 percent of it.[40] Just as mystifying are the trends apparent in Figure 5.7.

The growth in the after-tax income gap is most apparent here. First, however, there was some modest leveling in the late 1960s during the Great Society period, at least for black middle- and working-class families. (Note the rise of line 2 between 1965 and 1968.) And this did seem to correspond to a decline in tribute payments (see line 3). Yet thereafter, as owning-class tribute reaches a plateau of sorts (at least until 1982), the income gap increases significantly after the mid-1970s. (Note the downward slopes of lines 1 and 2, beginning in the mid-1970s.) How can the income gap between the classes be widening while tribute and income shares have remained relatively steady?

Focusing on the relationship between the middle and working class and the owning class, there are at least four viable explanations. The first two are essentially mathematical, and though they are the most obvious, they do not explain one of the crucial phenomena. The other two have greater potential for explaining that phenomenon, but they are more tentative.

By simple mathematics, if the owning class receives more than three times its proportionate income share over time (5 percent of the population receiving 16 percent of all income) and the middle and working class receives only slightly more than its proportionate share over the same period (75 percent of the population making 79 percent of all income), the income gap is bound to grow as the pie expands. Consider it in these terms. The average member of the owning class is receiving more than three times as much of each additional dollar of national income as the average member of the middle and working class. Thus the more

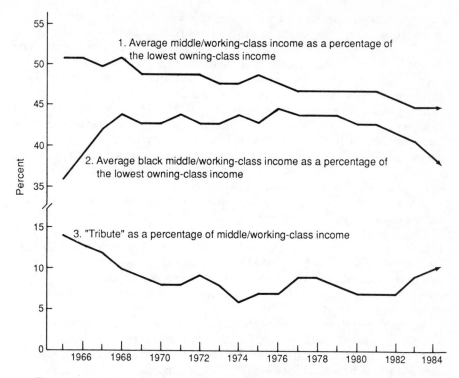

Figure 5.7. Income Gaps and Tribute Paid, 1965–1984 (Sources: Current Population Reports, Survey of Current Business, *Statistical Abstracts of the United States*, and Congressional Research Service Report No. 85-194 [1984])

additional dollars there are, the more the income gap will widen between these two groups.

But looked at from another vantage point, as the owning class has received billions of dollars in tribute, the total family income pie has expanded in 16 of the 20 years under study, while each class has maintained its percentage share of that expanded pie. That would seem to support the trickle-down theory. The owning class continues to get its disproportionate share and thus grows relatively richer. Nevertheless, the non-owning classes, by pulling down a steady share of an expanding pie, find a growth in real-dollar income as well. Or do they?

It is at this point that the first explanation falls short. Although it helps explain the real-dollar increase in owning-class income, the real-dollar income of the middle and working class has actually been declining. As measured by median family income, it has fallen by $3,301 real dollars for blacks and $1,026 for the entire class between 1978 and 1984. Consequently, something else must be going on.

A second mathematical approach also appears to hold out some explanatory hope. The welfare state capitalism model revolves around the ownership of corporate capital. Therefore, as the owning class has come to own a smaller share of the nation's corporate stock (for the variety of reasons discussed in Chapter 4), its share of profits and subsidies has declined, reducing its tribute as calculated by the model. Nevertheless, the fact that members of the owning class have shifted their savings into other forms of wealth does not mean that they are no longer acquiring income from such investments. As a matter of fact, one can only assume that they would not have switched investments if they did not feel that that would be a financially lucrative move. In the end, then, the owning class appears to be garnering some of its increased income from "noncapitalist" investments outside the model used in this study, such as real estate ventures. Yet even though that may help explain some peculiarities in the tribute trends, it does not explain the real-dollar decline in middle- and working-class income.

Although it is more difficult to measure, given the limitations of available income data, two additional approaches offer hope for resolving the paradox.

First of all, amid the shift from an industrial-dominated economy to a service-dominated one, evidence is mounting that a division is developing within the middle and working class. Skilled technicians and professionals continue to do well in the technological era, while much of the rest of the work force is slipping into the secondary labor market, as low-paying service jobs replace unionized factory positions.[41]

George Sternlieb and James Hughes note the general phenomenon when looking at constant-dollar income distributions between 1973 and 1982. During that period, there was growth in the proportion of the population making $35,000, clear shrinkage of the $15,000–$35,000 group, and growth in the percentage making less than $15,000.[42]

The growth at the top of the middle and working class reflects the increase in managerial and professional positions integral to an expanding postindustrial service economy. But why the loss of income in the rest of the middle- and working-class category? Consider the fact that between 1973 and 1982, for example, the United States lost 1.3 million manufacturing jobs, which paid an average of $17,000 per year, while adding an even larger number of service positions that paid an average of only $12,000 per year. More Americans came to be employed by McDonald's than by General Motors. Not surprisingly, the unionization rate for the overall work force slipped below 20 percent—lower yet if government workers are excluded. Nationwide, real-dollar average hourly wages have been declining for production and nonsupervisory workers in general, with roughly one-half of all new jobs created between 1976 and 1985 paying a family head poverty-level wages. This was also due in part to the fact that the minimum wage had been frozen at $3.35 per hour since 1981. An additional indicator of declining standards of living in the service economy is the fact that the number of persons without health insurance rose 32 percent between 1976 and 1985.[43]

As further evidence of this intraclass division, the income share of the second lowest quintile of American families has fallen by a full 1 percent since the mid-1970s, while the middle quintile has fallen 0.5 percent. Conversely, the second highest quintile has increased its share by 0.4 percent, and the highest quintile by a full 2 percent—with the likelihood that only part of that gain is accounted for by the owning class. On the face of it, those figures may appear minuscule; however, they take on added significance in light of the tremendous consistency of the distribution over the course of the prior decade.[44]

Consequently, although the entire group's income share remains the same, the majority of the middle and working class appears to be losing ground because of the ongoing change in the labor market. The median income of the middle and working class is actually declining, while its average income and income share remain steady. How can that happen? This appears to occur because their group average and total group share are pulled up by the disproportionately large earnings of those at the top of the category.

Yet these figures actually understate the declining position of the bulk of the middle and working class for at least four reasons:

1. The large baby boom generation has begun to reach its peak earning years.
2. The number of multiple-income families has been growing markedly.[45]
3. Baby boomers have married later and had smaller families than their predecessors, allowing for more discretionary per capita income, even when hourly wages were declining.[46]
4. Cheap Third World labor is likely to continue bidding down American wages in the postindustrial United States. For example, South Korea, Brazil, Mexico, Hong Kong, Taiwan, and Singapore each has an average wage of less than $3.00 per hour.[47]

Thus the present does not appear as bad as it has become, and the future looks even less promising for many in the next generation of middle- and working-class families. But even for the present, this situation only appears to be intensified by the next tentative explanation.

Real-dollar government spending has increased significantly over this period. Therefore, given a nonprogressive tax structure, the increased tax burden may well have consumed most of, if not more than, what the bulk of the middle and working class gained as a result of an expanded economic pie. The average owning-class family, by contrast, would have received enough from their disproportionate share of the increased income so that they could pay their proportion of the tax bill and still emerge with a sizable increase in after-tax income.

Using public assistance spending as a highly visible example, the decline in real-dollar average family income may well reflect redistribution downward within the lower 95 percent of American families. As a measure, spending on public assistance programs has increased by more than 700 percent in real dollars since 1965. Thus, given a progressive income structure and a nonprogressive tax structure, the large majority of the middle and working class may well have spent a sizable share of its larger piece of pie to help the poorest 20 percent of American families retain their posttransfer 5 percent of overall income.[48] The average owning-class family, by contrast, would have received enough increased gross income to come out ahead even after the poor had been paid.

In conclusion, there is little evidence to support the supply-side economic theory; in fact, the opposite seems to be true. As tribute declined in the late 1960s and early 1970s, all classes made real-dollar income gains, while the black middle and working class significantly narrowed the income gap between themselves and the white owners of capital. As tribute began to rebound, all but owning-class income dropped markedly, and income gaps increased.

There is reason to believe that tribute will continue to rise. As described in Chapter 2, the advent of the postindustrial economy has further strengthened the bargaining position of the owners of capital. With expanding opportunities to invest virtually anyplace on the face of the earth, venture capitalists are likely to be increasingly successful at extracting concessions from government. Consequently, wealth and income gaps will continue to widen. The rich will get richer and more powerful, while most of the remainder of society becomes relatively and absolutely poorer and more subordinate.

Directed Wrath

> Tax money is collected from the upper-lower and lower-middle classes (black and white)—whom I call the "middies"—and funneled through the conduit system to private hands in another segment of the economy. And all the while the ignorant, unsuspecting "middies" think their money is going to help "shiftless, lazy welfare cheats." Both the middies and the conduits are being pillaged.[49]

Watching its standard of living decline since the mid-1970s, the middle and working class has become frustrated. It is instructive, however, to note who ends up as a primary target of its wrath (see Figure 5.8).

The words *welfare recipient* seem to conjure up one of two images in the minds of many middle Americans, particularly whites. The first is the black female heading up a household with numerous small or adolescent children, having lived somewhat comfortably on the dole for years and probably receiving more aid than

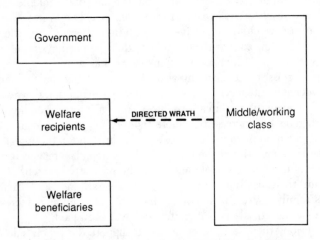

Figure 5.8. Welfare State Capitalism: Directed Wrath

she is legally entitled to receive. The second, even more resented, is the shiftless black male hanging out on the street corner when he could actually be working.

Yet there is a considerable difference between public assistance myth and public assistance reality. Take the test presented here.

Test

The typical American relief-receiving family:

1. resides in a   (a) metropolitan area,   (b) nonmetropolitan area.
2. is   (a) white,   (b) black,   (c) American Indian,   (d) other.
3. has the following number of dependent children: (a) 1,   (b) 2,   (c) 3,
   (d) 4 or 5,   (e) 6 or more.
4. has been on the dole for   (a) less than a year,   (b) 1–3 years,
   (c) 4–5 years,   (d) 6–10 years,   (e) 11–15 years,   (f) over 15 years.
5. has a father who is   (a) deceased,   (b) incapacitated,
   (c) unemployed,   (d) absent from the home.
6. has only children   (a) under 6 years old,   (b) 6–11 years old,
   (c) 12–17 years old,   (d) 18–20 years old.

If your answers were anything close to "an urban black female-headed household with six or more small or adolescent children, having been on the public dole for more than six years," and if you also happen to believe that many of these recipients are ineligible or could be working but have chosen not to, you harbor many of the misconceptions that seem to permeate much of the middle and working class.[50]

The typical relief-receiving family is white, with one child under 6 years of age, and has been on relief less than a year. More than 60 percent have been on less than three years, while only about 15 percent are truly chronic, staying with the system for 8 years or more.[51]

Focusing on AFDC, the bellwether of the relief package, more than 70 percent of the recipients are children, and the size of relief-receiving families has actually been declining. As for the heads of these households, a small minority are deemed to be "able-bodied," and most of these are mothers who are the sole resident parents of small children. The number of able-bodied adult males receiving such relief has been estimated at 1 to 2 percent of the caseload[52]—not a particularly high figure in a period when 5 to 10 percent of those actively seeking work could not find it. And it has been estimated that some 90 to 95 percent of all recipients are legally eligible, with nearly half of the ineligibles receiving benefits due to administrative errors.[53] In the most recent comprehensive study, the Department of Health, Education and Welfare actually found less than 3 percent of AFDC cases "suspected of fraud," 1.6 percent with "possible questions of fraud," and 0.8 percent with "sufficient facts to support" such charges. Less than 0.2 percent were ultimately prosecuted.[54] Overall, then, the amount of middle- and working-class money going to "welfare abusers" is minuscule compared to the amount of their paychecks that are transferred to the owning class in the form of tribute each year.

Second, many people persist in believing that most able-bodied recipients could find work if they were not so lazy. There has been little systematic measurement of such unemployed recipients' desire to work; however, examples like the following are all too common.

> The subway system, about half of which is above ground, needed its track cleared of snow. It put out the word that it would pay people $5 an hour to do the job.
>
> The next morning they began to show up; hundreds at first, then thousands. No easy trick, mind you. Many of the streets weren't plowed yet. Public transportation wasn't running. People had to get up at 4 A.M. or 5 A.M and fight their way through thigh-high snow—sometimes miles—to get this job. Yet thousands did.
>
> The predictable thing happened. The city didn't want thousands. It wanted, at most, a few hundred. So, fist fights broke out over places in line and the people had to claw their way onto the buses. The buses then had to force their way through an angry mob that pounded on them and threatened to overturn them. Left behind, one enraged group of job applicants looted a nearby liquor store. . . .
>
> One of the men who made the bus, explaining the riot, said: ". . . Those folks could see the job, they could smell it. They wanted it bad."[55]

Another myth is that these recipients live quite comfortably "on welfare." A look at two of the more generous states simply does not bear that out. In Illinois, for example, a family of four was eligible to receive a monthly maximum of $385 in AFDC payments, $219 in food stamps, and $18 in subsidized credit. That still left them 30 percent below the federal poverty line.[56] Or consider Sharon Hunt of New York City, who was attempting to raise two daughters on her monthly welfare grant of $340:

> After $110 is deducted to pay the rent for her public-housing apartment on the Lower East Side, Miss Hunt's total welfare grant leaves about $2.55 in cash a day for each member of the family. Her food-stamp allotment is $115 a month, or about $1.28 a day for each family member, amounting to about 43 cents for each of three meals.
>
> . . . Miss Hunt says she still has difficulty adjusting to the anxiety that hits her when one of her sons visits and in one day drinks the juice that was meant to last for five, or when the baby screams in the night and there is no money for emergencies.
>
> "It shouldn't hurt to be born in America," Miss Hunt observed. "It does, though."[57]

A very real dilemma often develops. Using California as an example, the minimum wage provides a monthly income of roughly $580 per month. Minimum-wage jobs, however, often do not come with benefits such as health insurance. Therefore, a single parent can work, or not work and receive more income via welfare, plus health insurance through the Medicaid program. Now, is this an indictment of the welfare system or an indictment of the paltry wage and benefit packages in the secondary labor market wherein an increasing proportion of American workers are left to work?[58]

Nevertheless, polls conducted during a particularly telling period reflect an increased animosity toward "welfare" when times are tough for more than just the welfare recipients—animosity felt by average Americans, black and white.[59] Amid the real-dollar leveling of the mid-1960s, such attitudes were relatively favorable. For example, a majority of Americans felt that spending on "welfare and relief programs" was either not enough or about right.[60] Yet once those programs proliferated and the real-dollar incomes of middle- and working-class citizens began to decline, this tone changed considerably. In the late 1970s, for instance, 58 percent of Americans disapproved of most government-sponsored "welfare" programs, and two out of three respondents mistakenly believed that public assistance costs even made up a major part of their locality's expenditures.[61]

How, then, does one move to counteract this illusion of lazy, conniving, promiscuous welfare chiselers? The majority of Californians, for example, cited a desire to reduce "welfare expenditures" as their primary reason for supporting Proposition 13.[62] Nationwide, more than 40 percent of Americans favored cutting relief programs "a lot," and an "overwhelming number" of those favoring service cuts cited "welfare and social services" as clearly their most preferred target.[63] As part of the rationale, more than one-third of Americans incorrectly believed the majority of recipients were receiving more than they were legally entitled to [64] and thus when asked which welfare reforms were most needed, the majority of Americans called for "better screening methods." The second most common response was to get those who can work off the welfare rolls.[65]

At the government level, the amount of real-dollar expenditures on public assistance quit growing in the 1980s, and the posttransfer income of the bottom one-fifth of American families declined 4.4 percent in real dollars.[66]

Thus, in absolute terms, the rich were getting richer and the poor were getting poorer in the 1980s, and that reality is both reinforced and enhanced by the functioning of the welfare state capitalism model, summarized in Figure 5.9.

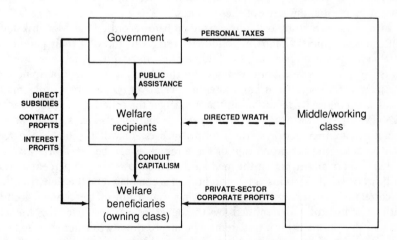

Figure 5.9. Welfare State Capitalism Model

What keeps people in the middle and working class and the lower class going in the face of the political-economic realities just described? At least part of it can be explained by a faith in a long-standing bit of mythology.

AMERICAN MYTHOLOGY

Horatio Alger (1834–1899) was a successful author who inspired generations of American youth with tales such as *Ragged Dick, Tattered Tom,* and *Luck and Pluck,* wherein penniless heroes gained wealth and fame through a combination of goodness and courage. Thus the "Horatio Alger myth" comes to read something like this: It is possible to go from rags to riches in the United States if one displays the right combination of abilities, hard work, thrift, and wise investment. As a consequence of that belief, the existence of considerable economic inequality must be taken as a given, the necessary result of healthy competition between free, variably talented individuals. A century later, the myth seems alive and well, for rich and poor, black and white.[67] But consider the realities.

To begin with, the ranks of the owning class are not impenetrable. However, how one usually enters these ranks today might well cause poor Horatio Alger to turn uncomfortably in his grave.

> A young reporter asked a leading capitalist how he made his fortune: "It was really quite simple," the capitalist answered. "I bought an apple for five cents, spent the evening polishing it, and sold it the next day for 10 cents. With this I bought two apples, spent the evening polishing them, and sold them for 20 cents. And so it went until I had amassed $1.60. It was then that my wife's father died and left us a million dollars."[68]

Lester Thurow, studying families with incomes of more than $100,000 and wealth holdings averaging $1.5 million, found 57 percent of these families to have inherited substantial amounts of these estates.[69]

In an in-depth study of Connecticut probate records, Paul Menchik found much the same thing. Comparing children's estates to those of their parents, he estimated that some 30 percent of a child's estate will be directly left over from the parents' estate. However, if one assumes that the child invests the inheritance, the figure jumps to 50 percent at bond rates and well over 50 percent if stock market indexes are employed. He also notes that the larger the inheritance, the more of it is likely to survive; for example, if one person's lifetime resources are 10 percent higher than another person's, the first person's estate will be some 25 percent higher because a higher proportion of those resources can be saved and invested. The end result of all this is that the median child dies possessing 85 percent as much wealth (in real dollars) as his or her parents had accumulated by the time they died. The correlation coefficient is .635, meaning that a full 40 percent of a child's wealth is statistically determined by the level of parental wealth. Menchik concludes that if one is born to parents who are 10 times wealthier than someone else's, one is likely to die at least eight times wealthier than the other person.[70]

It is also true, however, that more than 40 percent of the "great" and "less great" fortunes have been compiled without the benefit of substantial inheritance, but Thurow has found that this economic success is rarely the result of a lifetime of scrimping and saving. Rather, it comes as virtually "instant wealth." The person gambles or invests and happens to win, which is obvious when one looks at how quickly most of these fortunes were accumulated, often in a matter of a few years and seldom in two or more leaps. Therefore, this success comes to be seen much more as a matter of luck and seldom as the result of lifelong hard work and frugality.

Thurow concludes that only about 10 percent of economic success is explicable by how hard one works or how frugal one has been. The rest is determined by a society's population trends, unemployment level, tastes, and so on, leaving some 70 to 80 percent of economic success unexplained by the standard variables such as education, experience, and personality traits. Hard work may be necessary, but it is certainly not sufficient, and there is little indication that it is even necessary. A person may well work hard and even save, but that is not likely to place that person on the path to a great fortune. Rather, the latter tends to be a "random walk": One happened to be fortunate enough to have chosen Xerox or IBM in the 1950s rather than the broad array of other possible investments—and, of course, one was among the small minority that had much of anything to invest in the first place.[71]

In sum, it is possible to become wealthy other than by inheritance, but that leap requires luck more than anything else. Alger's goodness and courage seem to play very little part in the process. Consequently, short of inheriting a healthy sum of money from a long-lost relative or hitting a number in the lottery, the odds are that the hardworking, penny-pinching janitor from the ghetto simply has no realistic hope of acquiring a fortune in his lifetime. His children and grandchildren will not see one either. As a matter of fact, they will almost certainly find themselves punching a time clock as well.

Focusing on males, for example, the hard reality is that nearly two out of three sons will end up working at a job of the same general status as their fathers. And when the white-collar category is limited to professionals and managers, almost three in four sons will remain outside of this group, just as their fathers did.[72]

So, if hard work and frugality do not really help much in scaling the class wall, must the overwhelming majority of Americans be content to "bet on the horses" as their only realistic hope of gaining a share of the means of production? Even though Thurow has indicated that all the abilities in the world are nowhere near the surest ticket to a ride on the wealth train, it seems reasonable to believe that if nurtured, such abilities might help increase income as a step toward attaining wealth. Indeed, there is empirical evidence that schooling helps determine one's job, which in turn determines income.[73] Yet beneath an economic hierarchy based largely on inheritance and luck stands an educational system (discussed in Chapter 9) that actually serves to impede members of the lower and middle and working classes from taking even a first tiny step toward economic success: making enough so that there is money left at the end of the month to enter the game of chance through one's investments.

Income is indeed related to educational attainment, regardless of a person's age. A college graduate makes an average of 54 percent more than a high school graduate, nearly three times more than a grade school graduate, and so on.[74] But who gets the higher levels of education? Looking at Table 5.2, it becomes clear that the more income parents have, the more likely their children will be afforded the opportunity to further their education. And there are some indications that the ante has been going up. The New York Times, for example, unearthed the following:

> The rising demand of American youth for the limited vacancies in medical and law schools appears to be creating an increase in questionable and even illegal efforts to gain admission.
>
> Court records and interviews with knowledgeable authorities suggest that payments totaling millions of dollars are being made to these schools by parents and friends of prospective students to assure their acceptance. Covert bids of as much as $250,000 have been made for one place in the freshman class of a California medical school.[75]

Educational attainment seems to be intergenerationally linked, at least in part, by the socioeconomic position of the student's parents.[76] But looking beneath the opportunity to study a greater number of years, it is just as revealing to note that the quality of the person's elementary and secondary educational experiences may well be affected by the socioeconomic status of that person's parents.

Because nearly one-half of all school funding comes from local property taxes, there are substantial discrepancies in the amount of money available to spend on the public schools. In the state of Ohio, for instance, one district spent less than $900 per pupil, while another was able to spend more than $4,400 and still enjoy a much lower tax rate.[77]

It seems safe to say that in today's real world, a person who is not born in the owning class will almost certainly never end up there, regardless of abilities, hard work, thrift, and knack for making wise investments. When there is nothing left at the end of the month to invest in either the stock market or further education for one's children, the family simply lacks the ante even to get into the game. In extremely rare cases, a Samuel Newhouse, Henry Kaiser, or a W. Clement Stone will indeed rise from rags to riches largely by virtue of his own efforts—and such examples help keep the Horatio Alger myth alive. However, virtually every other American will work very hard to make profits for someone else and will remain

TABLE 5.2 COLLEGE EDUCATION BY FAMILY INCOME, 1982

Family Income Level	Children Attending College (%)
Less than $10,000	15
$10,000–14,999	23
$15,000–24,999	27
$25,000–34,999	37
More than $35,000	54

Source: U.S. Department of Commerce, Bureau of the Census, "Characteristics of American Children and Youth," Current Population Reports (Washington, D.C.: GPO, 1982).

essentially locked into the class position into which he or she was born. Indeed, there is a light at the end of the tunnel, but for the overwhelming majority of Americans it simply amounts to a false hope, a cruel hoax, as they continue to bite the bullet of their own economic exploitation.[78]

SUMMARY

To what extent does the U.S. political-economic system function to transfer income between classes? The welfare state capitalism model, focused on income transfers between 1965 and 1984, found a system that exploits the middle and working class, struggles to maintain the lower class at subsistence, further enhances the dominant position of the capital-owning class, and leads to an at least temporary diversion of middle and working class wrath toward the lower class while maintaining groundless hopes of interclass mobility.

NOTES

1. Charles V. Hamilton, "Conduit Colonialism and Public Policy," Black World (October 1972), pp. 40–45.
2. See Jude Wanninski, The Way the World Works (New York: Basic Books, 1978); George Gilder, Wealth and Poverty (New York: Basic Books, 1981); Irving Kristol, Two Cheers for Capitalism (New York: Basic Books, 1978); Milton Friedman, Capitalism and Freedom (Chicago: University of Chicago Press, 1962); Arthur Laffer and James Seymour, The Economics of the Tax Revolt (Orlando, Fla.: Harcourt Brace Jovanovich, 1979).
3. Louis Harris poll, 1983.
4. The Census Bureau defines families as households in which two or more people live and are related by marriage, birth, or adoption.
5. James O'Connor, The Fiscal Crisis of the State (New York: St. Martin's Press, 1973), pp. 6–7. Also see Ralph Miliband, The State in Capitalist Society (New York: Basic Books, 1969); Larry Hirschorn, "The Political Economy of Social Services Rationalization," in R. Quinney (ed.), Capitalist Society (New York: Dorsey, 1979).
6. Paul Samuelson and William Nordhaus, Economics (New York: McGraw-Hill, 1985), p. 565.
7. For a more detailed discussion of the power inherent in capital ownership, see Marcus Pohlmann, Political Power in the Postindustrial City (Millwood, N.Y.: Associated Faculties Press, 1986), chaps. 3–4.
8. Internal Revenue Service, Statistics of Income (Washington, D.C.: GPO, 1985); Richard Edwards (ed.), The Capitalist System (Englewood Cliffs, N.J.: Prentice-Hall, 1978), p. 306; New York Times, May 8, 1986. Many others consider the owning class to be much smaller than this; see C. Wright Mills, The Power Elite (New York: Oxford University Press, 1956), p. 122; Michael Best and William Connolly, The Politicized Economy (Lexington, Mass.: Heath, 1982), p. 76.
9. For further discussion of the black class structure in the United States, see St. Clair Drake and Horace Cayton, Black Metropolis (Orlando, Fla.: Harcourt Brace Jovanovich, 1945); Thomas Dye, The Politics of Equality (Indianapolis: Bobbs-Merrill, 1971); William J. Wilson, The Declining Significance of Race (Chicago: University of Chicago Press, 1980).

10. For example, see Karl Marx, *Value, Price, and Profit* (New York: International Publishers, 1935).
11. *Time* (August 29, 1977), p. 17.
12. *New York Times*, March 13, 1981; May 10, 1988; November 15, 1988; Edward Greenberg, *Capitalism and the American Political Ideal* (New York: Sharpe, 1985), pp. 160–166.
13. Adapted from Herbert Gans, *More Equality* (New York: Pantheon, 1972). Also see Frances Fox Piven and Richard Cloward, *Regulating the Poor* (New York: Vintage, 1971); Charles V. Hamilton, "The Patron-Recipient Relationship and Minority Politics in New York City," *Political Science Quarterly* (Summer 1979); Robert Allen, *Black Awakening in Capitalist America: An Analytical History* (Garden City, N.Y.: Anchor/ Doubleday, 1969), esp. chaps. 1, 4, 5, 7.
14. For a more detailed discussion of the "slump and boom" phenomenon, see Samuelson and Nordhaus, *Economics*, chap. 10; Howard Sherman, *Radical Political Economy* (New York: Basic Books, 1972), chap. 7.
15. For a more complete explanation of this "conduit" function, see Hamilton, "Conduit Colonialism and Public Policy."
16. *Time* (August 29, 1977), pp. 16–17.
17. For a fuller discussion of what the indigent have in common, see Michael Harrington, *The New American Poverty* (New York: Viking Penguin, 1984); Pohlmann, *Political Power*; *Christian Science Monitor*, February 15, 1985, pp. 18–19; *New York Times*, December 21, 1986.
18. Quoted in *Time* (December 1, 1986), p. 27. For a fuller discussion of the unique circumstances that have befallen the black underclass, see William J. Wilson, *The Truly Disadvantaged* (Chicago: University of Chicago Press, 1987); Douglas Glasgow, *The Black Underclass* (San Francisco: Jossey-Bass, 1980); Douglas Glasgow, "The Black Underclass in Perspective," in National Urban League, *The State of Black America, 1987* (New York: National Urban League, 1987), pp. 129–144; Chicago Tribune Staff, *The American Millstone: An Examination of the Nation's Permanent Underclass* (Chicago: Contemporary Books, 1986); Sylvester Monroe and Peter Goldman, *Brothers* (New York: Newsweek/William Morrow, 1988).
19. Chicago Tribune Staff, *American Millstone*, p. 83. Note that the term *poor* has been avoided in describing the lower class. This has been done because the term is normally associated with the arguably underestimated "poverty" figures published by the federal government. (For example, see Wilson, *Truly Disadvantaged*, pp. 170–171.)
20. U.S. Department of Labor, Bureau of Labor Statistics, as cited in *Information Please Almanac* (New York: Viking, 1979), p. 60. Also see Sherman, *Radical Political Economy*, pp. 50–51.
    Note that a sizable minority of the "lower class" also work for a wage. (See *New York Times*, November 19, 1987.) Thus, in a sense, these people also end up in the middle- and working-class category. They too are paid less than the market value of what they produce, contributing to owner profits. And they too pay taxes, some of which find their way to the bank accounts of the owning class. Nonetheless, this total transfer is relatively small, for even counting public assistance, this group earns only 5 percent of all national income. And owning virtually no property, members of the lower class pay very little in property taxes.
21. *New York Times*, July 10, 1977. For further discussion of this "vulnerability," see Andrew Levison, *The Working Class Majority* (Baltimore: Penguin, 1974); Arthur Shostak, *Blue Collar* (New York: Random House, 1969).
22. Allen, *Black Awakening*, p. 274.
23. Adjusted after-tax corporate profit figures from the *Survey of Current Business* were converted to constant 1984 dollars using the consumer price index. The constant-dollar contract profit, interest profit, and conduit profit amounts were then subtracted to avoid

double-counting. Estimates of the percentage of corporate stock held by the top 5 percent of American adults were used to calculate the share of these profits garnered by the owning class.

These figures exclude profits made by partnerships and proprietorships, which tend to be small firms with relatively few employees that account for only approximately 10 percent of all sales. Inasmuch as a number of their white owners would fall into the owning-class category, ignoring profits from these firms makes the private-sector profit figure slightly more conservative.

Population statistics were used to calculate black Americans as a percentage of the total middle and working class from whom owning-class profits have been extracted. Because blacks have regularly made less income than their white counterparts, their proportionate contribution to the corporate profit figure was deflated by multiplying it by a ratio of average black middle- and working-class (MC/WC) income divided by average middle- and working-class income as a whole:

$$ BD = TD \times \frac{BF}{TF} \times \frac{BI}{AI} $$

where BD = total black MC/WC dollars involved at this juncture
    TD = total dollars involved at this juncture
    BF = black MC/WC families (60 percent of all black families)
    TF = total MC/WC families (75 percent of all U.S. families)
    BI = average black MC/WC family income
    AI = average MC/WC family income

The annual income transfers as a result of private profit taking are shown in the following table (in billions of 1984 dollars):

	Black MC/WC Families	All MC/WC Families		Black MC/WC Families	All MC/WC Families
1965	6.29	119.7	1975	5.54	76.8
1966	6.44	113.0	1976	6.29	84.6
1967	6.41	103.2	1977	7.29	101.6
1968	6.11	96.0	1978	8.14	110.6
1969	5.30	81.3	1979	7.75	104.4
1970	4.94	72.1	1980	5.98	80.1
1971	5.17	74.6	1981	6.73	83.2
1972	6.55	84.0	1982	5.46	74.2
1973	6.27	91.5	1983	7.66	101.6
1974	4.32	61.6	1984	9.41	124.4

24. Joseph Pechman, *Who Paid the Taxes, 1966–1985?* (Washington, D.C.: Brookings Institution, 1985), p. 52.
25. Figures from *Statistical Abstracts of the United States* for all taxes paid each year, were multiplied by middle- and working-class percentage of national income for all taxpayers, with black middle- and working-class taxes deflated as in note 23. The results figures were converted to 1984 dollars using the consumer price index.
   The results were as follows (in 1984 dollars per capita):

	Black Taxpayers	All Taxpayers		Black Taxpayers	All Taxpayers
1965	1,870	2,597	1975	2,770	3,112
1966	2,164	2,810	1976	2,934	3,155
1967	2,418	2,879	1977	3,169	3,445
1968	2,525	2,936	1978	3,246	3,528
1969	2,839	3,263	1979	3,297	3,507
1970	2,845	3,197	1980	3,042	3,343
1971	2,710	3,011	1981	3,133	3,443
1972	2,917	2,278	1982	3,015	3,277
1973	2,973	3,341	1983	2,924	3,178
1974	2,990	3,286			

These figures are conservative estimates, however, not only for the reason cited in the text but also because the recent reduction in the federal income tax burden has most likely made the overall tax structure regressive. If that is true, the middle and working class is no doubt paying even more of the nationwide tax burden today. It should also be noted that federal social security payments are not being included as taxes in this study, even though that is a payment that is not optional.

26. For some concrete cases in point, see Joseph Ruskay, "Tax Reform: The Loopholes Still with Us," *The Nation* (March 22, 1971), pp. 368–371.

27. Trend information was derived from *Statistical Abstracts of the United States* and *Survey of Current Business*.

28. For a somewhat dated but relatively comprehensive discussion of this subject, see Keith Butters et al., *Effect of Taxation on Investments by Individuals* (Cambridge, Mass.: Riverside Press, 1953).

29. See note 23 for calculation procedures and comments. The annual figures were as follows (in billions of 1984 dollars):

	Black Middle and Working Class	Entire Middle and Working Class		Black Middle and Working Class	Entire Middle and Working Class
1965	0.62	11.8	1975	0.46	6.4
1966	0.74	13.0	1976	0.48	6.4
1967	0.65	10.5	1977	0.59	8.2
1968	0.66	10.4	1978	0.71	9.7
1969	0.70	10.7	1979	0.69	9.3
1970	0.76	11.1	1980	0.71	9.5
1971	0.75	10.8	1981	0.75	10.2
1972	1.05	15.1	1982	0.93	12.7
1973	0.86	12.6	1983	1.32	17.5
1974	0.47	6.7	1984	1.22	16.1

30. *Survey of Current Business* figures on federal, state, and local government purchases of services and durable and nondurable goods and structures, less all money going directly to employee compensation, conservatively assuming that no profit was accrued by the owning class in such transactions, converted to constant 1984 dollars.

Profits-to-sales ratio was calculated by dividing the after-tax corporate profit figures by *Survey of Current Business* figures on "corporate receipts" from sales and services less allowances, rebates, and returns (excluding capital gains and losses and investment income not associated with taxpaying businesses). This results in a conservative estimate, as a sizable majority of these purchases have been made without competitive bidding; thus profit rates are no doubt higher than usual in this arena (*New York Times*, March 8, 1985; April 9, 1985; May 30, 1988).

Corporate profits were then calculated as a proportion of government purchases each year, and the shares captured by the owning class and paid by the black middle and working class were calculated as in note 23. The resulting annual figures were as follows (in billions of 1984 dollars):

	Black Middle and Working Class	Entire Middle and Working Class		Black Middle and Working Class	Entire Middle and Working Class
1965	0.39	7.4	1975	0.28	3.9
1966	0.42	7.3	1976	0.28	3.8
1967	0.47	7.6	1977	0.33	4.6
1968	0.45	7.0	1978	0.35	4.7
1969	0.36	5.5	1979	0.30	4.0
1970	0.30	4.4	1980	0.22	3.0
1971	0.32	4.6	1981	0.26	3.5
1972	0.38	5.5	1982	0.25	3.4
1973	0.32	4.6	1983	0.29	3.8
1974	0.19	2.7	1984	0.33	4.3

31. *New York Times*, May 8, 1986; *Common Cause* (March-April 1988), pp. 18–22.
32. After-tax profit estimates were calculated by first establishing a functional investor profit rate on loaned money. Given that banks do most of the lending to government and that roughly 90 percent of bank revenues come from interest payments, banks' net (after-tax) income was divided by their current revenues, all using Federal Reserve Board figures. These calculated "profit rates" were then applied to total interest paid on government debt each year. The resulting after-tax profits from lending to government were then reduced to the share gained by the owning class and paid by the black middle and working class as calculated in note 23. The resulting annual figures were as follows (in billions of 1984 dollars):

	Black Middle and Working Class	Entire Middle and Working Class		Black Middle and Working Class	Entire Middle and Working Class
1965	0.24	4.5	1975	0.33	4.6
1966	0.25	4.4	1976	0.31	4.1
1967	0.29	4.6	1977	0.32	4.5
1968	0.29	4.5	1978	0.33	4.5
1969	0.32	4.9	1979	0.32	4.3
1970	0.37	5.4	1980	0.30	4.0
1971	0.44	6.3	1981	0.29	3.9
1972	0.46	6.6	1982	0.33	4.5
1973	0.36	5.3	1983	0.40	5.3
1974	0.31	4.4	1984	0.48	6.3

33. See Vee Burke, "Cash and Non-cash Benefits for Persons with Limited Income," Congressional Research Service Report No. 85-194 (Washington, D.C.: GPO, 1984).
34. Hamilton, "Conduit Colonialism and Public Policy."
35. Public assistance figures for 1968, 1972, 1973, and 1975–1984 from Burke, "Cash and Non-cash Benefits"; estimates for other years based on Burke and on *Statistical Abstracts of the United States* totals for AFDC, Supplementary Aid for the Aged, Blind and Disabled, Medicaid, food stamps, and "general assistance."

Focus is on cash paid to welfare recipients and items and services purchased for them, such as school lunches and medical care. Whereas approximately one-half was cash and one-third medical payments in 1968, by 1983 only one-quarter was cash, one-third was still medical payments, 15 percent was food, and 10 percent was housing payments. It is presumed that the cash is spent and not saved or invested.

These public assistance totals are then multiplied by the average corporate profit rate for each year as in note 30, and the shares going to the owning class and paid for by the black middle and working class are calculated as in note 23. The resulting annual figures were as follows (in billions of 1984 dollars):

	Black Middle and Working Class	Entire Middle and Working Class		Black Middle and Working Class	Entire Middle and Working Class
1965	0.03	0.5	1975	0.09	1.3
1966	0.05	0.8	1976	0.10	1.4
1967	0.06	1.0	1977	0.12	1.7
1968	0.07	1.1	1978	0.13	1.8
1969	0.07	1.0	1979	0.11	1.5
1970	0.08	1.2	1980	0.08	1.1
1971	0.08	1.2	1981	0.10	1.3
1972	0.10	1.5	1982	0.09	1.2
1973	0.09	1.3	1983	0.10	1.3
1974	0.06	0.9	1984	0.11	1.4

It is also assumed that the administrative portion of these government expenditures is offset by the higher-than-average profits gained in many of these transactions. In addition, there are some indications that the administrative costs of these programs are actually relatively low; see *Social Security Bulletin Annual Statistical Supplement, 1972*, p. 57, where it is estimated that the administrative costs for the Supplementary Aid to the Aged, Blind and Disabled program were only 1.8 percent of its budget in 1972.

There is some overlap between the "conduit profits" and the "contract profits" discussed earlier. Nonetheless, the earlier figures are conservative enough to more than compensate for that.

36. *New York Times*, June 15, 1985. For a similar example, see National Urban League, *State of Black America, 1987*, p. 12.

37. *The Progressive* (September 1975), p. 11.

38. *Forbes* (January 1, 1972; May 5, 1972).

39. The annual total tribute paid was as follows in billions of 1984 dollars:

	Black Middle and Working Class	Entire Middle and Working Class	Share of Income (%)		Black Middle and Working Class	Entire Middle and Working Class	Share of Income (%)
1965	7.6	143.9	14	1975	6.7	93.0	7
1966	7.9	138.5	13	1976	7.5	100.3	7
1967	7.9	126.9	12	1977	8.7	120.6	9
1968	7.6	119.0	10	1978	9.7	131.3	9
1969	6.7	103.4	9	1979	8.7	123.5	8
1970	6.5	94.2	8	1980	7.3	97.7	7
1971	6.8	97.5	8	1981	7.5	102.1	7
1972	8.5	122.7	9	1982	7.1	96.0	7
1973	7.9	115.3	8	1983	9.8	129.5	9
1974	5.4	76.3	6	1984	11.6	152.5	10

As indicated in note 20, these numbers are slightly inflated by the fact that some welfare recipients also work for a wage and thus supply a portion of this tribute. In addition, an increased share of private-sector profits have been made from the labor of workers in foreign countries, this also inflates the contribution made by the American middle and working class. Nonetheless, these numbers are conservative estimates for the variety of reasons discussed in the notes and text. Thus they provide a resonable estimate of the total transferred to the owning class from the paychecks of the middle and working class.

40. See *Current Population Reports*, P-60 Series; Internal Revenue Service, *Statistics of Income Bulletin*.

41. For example, see Pohlman, *Political Power*, chaps. 1, 3, 6.

42. George Sternleib and James Hughes, *Income and Jobs: USA* (New Brunswick, N.J.: Center for Urban Policy Research, 1984), chap. 5; *New York Times*, July 31, 1987. And see *Los Angeles Times*, April 2, 1988, for statistical evidence of this trend in black America specifically.

43. See Sternleib and Hughes, *Income and Jobs*; National Urban League, *State of Black America, 1987*, pp. 11, 72; Congressional Research Service, *Measures of Racial Earnings since 1970* (Washington, D.C.: GPO, 1988); Frank Levy, "The Vanishing Middle Class and Related Issues," PS (Summer 1987), pp. 650–655; *New York Times*, February 1, 1987; August 17, 1987; November 19, 1987; *Memphis Commercial Appeal*, December 10, 1986; January 18, 1987.

44. For further evidence from within the black community, see Wilson, *Declining Significance of Race*, esp. p. 173.

45. Sternleib and Hughes, *Income and Jobs*, chap. 5; *New York Times*, January 26, 1988; Congressional Research Service, *Measures of Racial Earnings*; Levy, "Vanishing Middle Class."

46. Levy, "Vanishing Middle Class."

47. *New York Times*, June 26, 1987.

48. Pechman, *Who Paid the Taxes?* For a clear view of the consistency of the income share held by the lower class, see Table 2-1 in Chapter 2.

   Much of the public assistance increase occurred early in the period under study. There are indications that the real-dollar value of AFDC and food stamp payments have actually declined since 1970 (*New York Times*, July 30, 1987), although the Medicaid portion of public assistance appears to have increased enough to make up for this decline.

49. Hamilton, "Conduit Colonialism and Public Policy," pp. 42–43.

50. The correct answers are 1-a, 2-a, 3-a, 4-a, 5-d, and 6-a; *Statistical Abstracts of the United States, 1986*, p. 382.

51. Ibid. Also see *New York Times*, February 23, 1987; Manning Marable, *How Capitalism Underdeveloped Black America* (Boston: South End Press, 1983), pp. 43–44; Harrington, *New American Poverty*, p. 28.

52. *U.S. News and World Report* (April 3, 1972), p. 57.

53. *New York Times*, May 22, 1977.

54. U.S. Congress, Joint Economic Committee, 93d Cong., 1st sess., "Issues in Welfare Administration," *Studies in Public Welfare*, Paper No. 51, pt. 2, March 12, 1973 (Washington, D.C.: GPO, 1973).

55. Donald Kaul, "Over the Coffee," *Des Moines Register*, January 18, 1977. Also see Leonard Goodwin, *Do the Poor Want to Work?* (Washington, D.C.: Brookings Institution, 1972); Harrington, *New American Poverty*, p. 28.

56. *Time* (December 1, 1986).

57. *New York Times*, March 23, 1982.

58. For example, see Harrington, *New American Poverty*, chap. 3.

59. For some good examples of how such animosity crosses racial lines, see ibid., p. 30; Philip Au Claire, "Public Attitudes towards Social Welfare Expenditures," *Social Work* (March-April 1984), p. 143.

60. Gallup poll, November 1964.

61. *New York Times*, August 3, 1977; June 28, 1978. Also see Greenberg, *Capitalism*, pp. 159–160.
62. *New York Times*, June 9, 1978.
63. *New York Times*, August 3, 1977; June 28, 1978. Also a Gallup poll in February 1979 found 54 percent of Americans in favor of cutting "welfare" programs in order to balance the federal budget, 29 percent for cutting "defense," and no other option attracting the approval of even 10 percent.
64. Gallup poll, December 1978.
65. Gallup poll, June 1977.
66. High-income cutoff point for the bottom 20 percent of American families was $13,058 in 1980 but had declined to $12,489 by 1984 (in 1984 dollars; *Current Population Reports*, P-60 series).

   No adjustments have been made for benefit-in-kind transfer income. First, it is not disposable income, and thus it ought not be counted in the same way. Second, such calculations are methodologically suspect. For example, if we calculate the disproportionate benefit the poor receive from Medicaid, why not also calculate the disproportionate benefits the wealthiest gain from national defense, State Department trade efforts, domestic infrastructure, and so on? Third, even if such benefits are included —see Edgar Browning, "The Trend toward Equality in the Distribution of Net Income," *Southern Economic Journal* (July 1976)—they are still funded largely by the middle and working class.

   Public animosity toward "welfare" began to moderate in the 1980s—apparently because, among other things, program growth stopped and the plight of the indigent became increasingly visible and closer to home. For example, see Au Claire, "Public Attitudes"; *New York Times*, June 15, 1987; Louis Harris poll and Washington Post/ABC News poll quoted in *New York Times*, November 19, 1987.
67. For example, see Goodwin, *Do the Poor Want to Work?*; Harrington, *New American Poverty*, p. 148; Charles V. Hamilton, *American Government* (Glenview, Ill.: Scott, Foresman, 1982), pp. 561–562.
68. *New York Times*, February 19, 1984.
69. Lester Thurow, *Generating Inequality*, (New York: Basic Books, 1975), ch. 6.
70. Paul Menchik, *Conference on Research in Income and Wealth* (New York: National Bureau of Economic Research, 1979).
71. Thurow, *Generating Inequality*, esp. chaps. 5, 6.
72. For example, see U.S. Department of Commerce, Bureau of the Census, *Current Population Surveys; Occupational Changes in a Generation Survey* (1973).
73. Richard Coleman and Lee Rainwater, *Social Standing in America, 1978* (New York: Basic Books, 1978).
74. U.S. Department of Commerce, Bureau of the Census, *Statistical Abstracts of the United States, 1986*, p. 446.
75. *New York Times*, April 23, 1978.
76. National Center for Education Statistics, *Digest of Education Statistics* (1979), p. 93.
77. Figures available from the secretary of state, state of Ohio. For more detailed discussion of the effects of class on educational attainment, see Christopher Jencks, *Inequality: A Reassessment of the Effect of Family and Schools in America* (New York: Basic Books, 1972); Richard De Lone, *Small Futures: Children, Inequality, and the Limits of Liberal Reform* (Orlando, Fla.: Harcourt Brace Jovanovich, 1979).
78. For a detailed discussion of the structural impediments to socioeconomic mobility for the black underclass in particular, see Wilson, *Truly Disadvantaged*; Glasgow, *Black Underclass*.

PART THREE

Blacks in American Politics

CHAPTER SIX

The Judicial Arena

> Inasmuch as the primary object of a government, beyond the mere repression of physical violence, is the making of the rules which determine property relations of members of society, the dominant classes whose rights are thus to be determined must perforce obtain from the government such rules as are consonant with the larger interests necessary to the continuance of the economic processes, or they must themselves control the organs of government.
>
> Charles Beard[1]

The United States prides itself on being a nation ruled by laws and not by individuals. The country's written constitution is central in guaranteeing individual rights and the political process that will enforce them. In addition, such written "rules of the game" are beyond the immediate reach of the governing elites at any point in time. But what if the rules of the game, not to mention their interpreters and enforcers, are seriously biased from the outset?

This chapter will suggest that much of the American political system designed at the constitutional convention in Philadelphia was crafted and has functioned to protect the unequal distribution of property. Democracy was limited in part to protect certain rights and liberties for all citizens; however, a number of these limitations have also served to protect historic inequalities, which for black Americans are tremendous.

THE FOUNDING FATHERS

In analyzing the Constitution, scholars have tended to praise the democratic spirit and foresight of the Founding Fathers and to laud the brilliantly adaptable document and governmental system they devised. Indeed, many of the Founding Fathers may well have been brilliant and visionary men dedicated to at least an 18th-century vision of rights and democracy. And the document they designed has endured—longer than any written constitution in the history of the world. It has also helped preserve an array of individual liberties. But that is not the whole story—nor was it supposed to be.

> We hold these truths to be self-evident: That all men are created equal; that they are endowed by their Creator with certain unalienable rights; that among these are life, liberty, and the pursuit of happiness; that, to secure these rights, governments are instituted among men, deriving their just powers from the consent of the governed.[2]

105

That, of course, was Thomas Jefferson. But his was not the only influential voice of the period. Many were much more concerned with protecting the existing distribution of property.

Gouverneur Morris of Massachusetts, for example, wrote that "men don't unite for liberty or life, . . . they unite for the protection of property."[3] John Adams added, "The moment the idea is admitted into society that property is not as sacred as the laws of God, and that there is not force of law and public justice to protect [it], anarchy and tyranny commence."[4] Consider also the words of two of the best known of the Founding Fathers, Alexander Hamilton and James Madison.

> The difference of property is already great amongst us. Commerce and industry will increase the disparity. . . . Your government must meet this state of things, or combinations will . . . undermine your system.
>
> The people, sir, are a great beast. . . . The same state of the passions which fits the multitude, who have not a sufficient stock of reason and knowledge to guide them, . . . very naturally leads them to a contempt and diregard of all authority.[5]

> An increase of population will of necessity increase the proportion of those who will labour under all the hardships of life, and secretly sigh for a more equal distribution of its blessings. These may in time outnumber those who are placed above the feelings of indigence. According to the equal laws of suffrage, the power will slide into the hands of the former.
>
> . . . Whenever the majority shall be without landed or other equivalent property and without the means or hope of acquiring it, what is to secure the rights of property against the danger from an equality and universality of suffrage, vesting complete power over property in hands without a share in it . . .
>
> Landholders ought to have a share in the Government. . . . They ought to be so constituted as to protect the minority of the opulent against the majority.[6]

Such sentiment reflected the views of political philosopher John Locke, whose *Second Treatise on Civil Government* was very influential in shaping the outlooks of America's founders. Locke, for example, was so obsessed with the protection of property that his writings included provisions for rebelling against an unresponsive government but never against the sanctity of private property. If the latter were challenged, all rights were to be suspended until the threat to property had been effectively overcome.[7]

But to understand more fully the fears of Locke, and especially those of Madison and other Founding Fathers, it is important to put all of this into historical perspective.

Most of the Founding Fathers were men of significant personal wealth.[8] Although a strong national government made sense for the purposes of regulating their interstate commerce and protecting their property from both foreign and domestic invaders, they were highly suspicious of what the lesser propertied majority might do if given a proportionate share of the political power. Such fears were fed by social movements beginning to surface in Massachusetts, Rhode Island, New Hampshire, and Pennsylvania. Small farmers, in particular, were beginning physically to resist foreclosures and forcibly to free debtors from prison, while pressing for voting rights and a shift to paper currency in order to help them overcome their extensive debts.[9]

Shays's Rebellion was one of the most frightening of these developments. In the winter of 1787, Daniel Shays led an armed group in a series of raids across the Massachusetts countryside, spreading to the very outskirts of Boston. Not only did they free prisoners, but they also attacked courts, lawyers, and legislators. Mired in debt and weary from years of seemingly futile peaceful protest, they were now violently demanding lower taxes, a repudiation of past debts, and other concessions. By the time they were finally subdued by the state militia, 11 people lay dead and dozens wounded.[10]

> All communities divide themselves into the few and the many. The first are the rich and well-born, the other the mass of the people. The voice of the people has been said to be the voice of God; and however generally this maxim has been quoted and believed, it is not true in fact. The people are turbulent and changing; they seldom judge or determine right. Give therefore to the first class a distinct permanent share in the government. . . . Can a democratic assembly who annually revolve in the mass of the people be supposed steadily to pursue the public good? Nothing but a permanent body can check the imprudence of democracy.[11]

As they gathered in Philadelphia, then, the Founding Fathers had a good bit more on their minds then "life, liberty, and the pursuit of happiness" for all. A number of them also set out to protect their property interests—including their enslaved human property.

THE CONSTITUTION OF THE UNITED STATES

> The Constitution is a law for rulers and people, equally in war and peace, and covers with the shield of its protection all classes of men at all times and under all circumstances.[12]

> The Constitution was a compromise between slaveholding interests of the South and moneyed interests of the North for the purpose of uniting the thirteen states into one great market. For commerce, the northern delegates wanted laws regulating interstate commerce, and urged that such laws require only a majority of Congress to pass. The South agreed to this, in return for allowing the trade of slaves to continue.[13]

Did the elitists succeed in incorporating their views into the United States Constitution? To answer that question, we must first consider how their conservative political philosophy was included in the governmental system outlined in Articles 1 through 6 and then focus on the nature of the civil rights guaranteed in various other constitutional passages.

Chief Justice Charles Evans Hughes said, "We are under a constitution, but the constitution is what the judges say it is."[14] The United States Supreme Court assumes the role of final constitutional interpreter by virtue of Article 3, which states, "The judicial power shall extend to all cases, in law and equity, arising under this constitution." And since the Court's decision in *Marbury v. Madison* (1803), it has also reviewed the constitutionality of laws passed by legislatures. So we must consider the conservative biases built into the Constitution not only by the Founding Fathers but also by the Supreme Court justices who have interpreted their words.

The Governmental System

First we shall examine the conservative devices built into the governing process (many of which will be discussed in greater detail in Chapters 7 and 8). Then we will note additional care taken to secure the sanctity of private property, particularly as it extends to contracts between individuals.

Governmental Process. The governmental process set out in Articles 1 through 6 established numerous roadblocks to majority rule—for example, checks and balances within the Congress, among the three branches, and between the national and state governments. As a case in point, legislation had to pass both houses in identical form, was subject to a presidential veto, and would be reliant on executive or state level implementation. It was much easier to block laws than to pass them. Also, since there was no provision for national referenda, all legislation had to pass through that maze of governmental decision makers.

As James Madison put it:

> [If] you take in a greater varieties of parties and interests; you make it less probable that a majority of the whole will have a common motive to invade the rights of other citizens. . . . A rage for paper money, for an abolition of debts, for an equal division of property, or for any other improper or wicked project, will be less apt to pervade the whole body of the Union than a particular member of it.[15]

And who would pick the governmental decision makers? The ones with the longest term of office, United States senators, were actually chosen by state legislatures until a constitutional amendment more than 125 years later. The chief executive was to be elected by an electoral college rather than directly by the people. And although the House of Representatives (like state legislatures) would be chosen directly by the people, it was half a century before "the people" came to include most nonpropertied white men, a century and a half for most white women, and two centuries for most black Americans.

Property-related Clauses. To be doubly safe, a number of explicit property-related clauses were added, and although they never specifically mentioned slavery or race, the implications for most black Americans were quite clear. For example, Article 1, Section 9, essentially granted legal sanction to the importation of slaves for the next 20 years. Article 4, Section 2, read, "No person held to service or labour in one state . . . escaping into another, shall . . . be discharged from such service or labour, but shall be delivered up on claim of the party to whom such service or labour may be due." And there was the infamous "three-fifths compromise" in Article 1, Section 2, reducing enslaved human beings to the legal status of three-fifths of a noncitizen, merely to be counted for the purposes of determining a state's share of federal taxation and its congressional representation. Both provisions—the mandatory returning of runaway slaves and the three-fifths compromise—were in effect for nearly a century, ultimately requiring a civil war to undo.

As for property in general, the Fifth Amendment guaranteed that "no person shall . . . be deprived of . . . property, without due process of law; nor shall private property be taken for public use, without just compensation." An army and a navy were established to defend the nation's territory—most of which was owned by a relatively small group of elites. A militia was created to suppress insurrections. The Congress was empowered to regulate commerce. And state governments were explicitly barred from coining their own money, allowing the repayment of debts in paper currency, or otherwise "impairing the obligation of contracts."

This hyperconcern over property, debts, and contracts really ended up amounting to the following: The Constitution of the United States would protect one's right to make unlimited profits, far beyond the necessities of life, while at the other end of the spectrum, it would be illegal to refuse repayment of a debt, even if one was starving to death. Jefferson's "right to life" would not imply a right to eat.

Finally, the entire document was never placed before the American people for ratification. Instead, it was ratified by state legislatures, and those legislatures, like their counterpart in Washington, were composed almost exclusively of white males who possessed a significant amount of property, just like the people who were allowed to elect them. What is more, ratification was marked by rumors of bribery, misinformation, and economic coercion, including advertiser boycotts of antifederalist newspapers and the calling in of debts of Constitution opponents.[16]

When it came to interpretation of this document by the judicial elites the legislative elites had appointed, it was more of the same. In *Trustees of Dartmouth College v. Woodward* (1819), the Supreme Court judged that corporations were "persons" in the eyes of the law and thus eligible for constitutional protection. In *Pollock v. Farmers' Loan and Trust Co.* (1895), the Court invalidated the graduated federal income tax, leading a New York bank president to praise the court as the "guardian of the dollar, defender of private property, enemy of spoilation, [and] sheer anchor of the Republic."[17] The Court would also protect a national bank and other even more blatant monopolies, imprisonment of anticapitalist dissenters, deportation of immigrant radicals, violent strikebreaking, Ku Klux Klan actions, and Jim Crow laws. And until 1937, it found that the Constitution protected child labor, sweatshops, and 16-hour workdays, as the 5th and 14th amendments were interpreted as forbidding the state and federal governments from depriving corporate owners of their property without "due process of law."

For black Americans, all of this simply promised to reinforce the legacies of slavery. The political system had been consciously designed to impede fundamental change, while the protection of existing property relations would further slow black efforts to overcome an inequality imposed on them by their many years of enslavement.

Constitutional Rights

But what about the civil rights guaranteed to all residents of the country? To begin with, realize that there was no Bill of Rights until four years after the constitutional convention, when ratification appeared to be in some doubt, and that the first 10 amendments involved negative and not positive rights: protecting people from governmental intrusion but not guaranteeing governmental protection.

These constitutional rights are clearly negative. Government is not to make laws that prohibit religious practice or free speech and assembly. Yet the Constitution does not guarantee a job at a livable wage, health care when one is desperately ill, or quality educational opportunities. Freedom of the press does not guarantee one an avenue for expression unless one owns a press. Government may not search one's house without a warrant, but there is no guarantee of a house to live in. These are but a few of many possible examples.

Also realize that the absence of positive guarantees inhibits full utilization of rights protected against governmental interference. For example, one may choose not to register and vote, if one's employer likes to employ only "good Negroes." Being dependent on governmentally determined eligibility for public housing and a welfare check may well chill one's willingness to be identified as an active protester against governmental policy.[18] A caseworker can make a warrantless search of a welfare recipient's home. A poor woman may well lose her constitutionally protected right to an abortion if she has no means to pay for it. And despite democratic "one person, one vote" rhetoric, the wealthy are the only ones in a position to influence elections and elected officials by virtue of large personal campaign contributions.

One of the most glaring examples of this inhibition of rights can be seen in the institutional barriers to bringing a lawsuit into the United States judicial arena. For example, in the context of the wealth and income inequalities described in Chapters 4 and 5, consider the fact that bringing a single employment discrimination suit can cost $100,000, exclusive of attorneys' fees.[19] The U.S. Supreme Court eased this burden somewhat in the 1960s by allowing successful plaintiffs to recover such costs from defendants (*Newman v. Piggie Park Enterprises*, 1968). Thereafter, however, at least two decisions seem to reduce the likelihood that the fee recovery principle will encourage indigent people to bring lawsuits (*Marek v. Chesny*, 1985; *Evans v. Jeff D.*, 1986).

Race and Civil Rights

For most black Americans, it took a civil war to gain recognition that even negative rights were applicable to them. But those rights have been applied and extended inconsistently. Both the emphasis on negative rights and their erratic enforcement have caused considerable uncertainty at any point in time—the kind of uncertainty that is supposed to be minimized in a constitutional system.

Prior to the Civil War, black rights were suppressed time and again. In *Prigg v. Pennsylvania* (1842), for example, the U.S. Supreme Court upheld the Fugitive Slave Act requiring slaveowners' human property to be returned. In *Jones v. Van Zandt* (1847), the Court even went so far as to describe slavery as "a sacred compromise" in the Constitution. Then, in *Dred Scott v. Sanford* (1857), the justices made quite clear where they placed the large majority of black Americans in the constitutional order of things. Nearly a century after the Revolutionary War, the Court declared that 4 million black slaves were chattel and not citizens. They had no constitutional rights at all, but their owners' possession of them was protected by the "due process" clause of the Fifth Amendment. In other words, such property could not be taken from slave owners without giving each of them full due process of law.

Following the Civil War, three key constitutional amendments altered the ground rules. The 13th Amendment, ratified in 1865, outlawed slavery. The 14th, ratified three years later, required each state to recognize the citizenship of "all persons born or naturalized in the United States," as well as extend them due process and equal protection under state laws. The 15th Amendment (1870) prohibited the federal and state governments from denying any (male) citizen the right to vote "on account of race, color, or previous condition of servitude." How the Supreme Court interpreted these amendments, however, is another story altogether.

Once Reconstruction ended and the federal troops were gone, former slaves had little other than the letter of the law to protect them. Faced with intense racial discrimination in the job market, as well as outright physical intimidation, most ended up in economic peonage hardly distinguishable from their previous legalized enslavement. Their right to vote was denied through a series of election laws that appeared racially neutral on their face—including highly arbitrary tests of a voter's literacy (literacy tests) and special taxes that had to be paid at the polls in order to be allowed to vote (poll taxes)—a disenfranchisement upheld by the U.S. Supreme Court in decisions such as *Williams v. Mississippi* (1898). In addition, a host of segregationist Jim Crow laws emerged to circumvent 14th Amendment guarantees. For example, a Louisiana law required that blacks ride on separate railroad cars, and the Supreme Court upheld such laws in its infamous *Plessy v. Ferguson* (1896) decision. Such segregation of the races was not seen as denying blacks "equal protection of the laws."[20]

Segregated, without the vote, reduced to near economic enslavement, and living in continual fear of white violence, little seemed to have changed for the large majority of black Americans. Nevertheless, in the face of all of this, there was increasing organized resistance. The NAACP, for example, was born out of the Niagra Movement and began to press for black rights on a number of fronts. Communities were organized. Information was disseminated. Protest marches were launched. Elected officials were lobbied. Probably most noteworthy of all, federal lawsuits were filed on behalf of those so blatantly being denied basic human rights. The successes and failures in this last arena are the primary concern of this chapter.

Education. In this area, successes were achieved in legally requiring equal educational opportunities from elementary to graduate schools. The Supreme Court, however, now seems to have drawn the line on the extension of these rights, despite the continued existence of a largely segregated public school system and the serious discrepancies in educational quality discussed in Chapter 3.

From the late 1930s to the late 1960s, some major strides were made in the legal battle to acquire truly equal educational opportunities for black children. In *Gaines v. Canada* (1938), for example, the Supreme Court ruled that true equality required that the state of Missouri provide equal law schools for its black students, rather than simply paying their way to attend in another state. Twelve years later, in *Sweatt v. Painter* (1950), the Court ruled that Texas's separate black law schools were not equal, in part because of their "isolation from the individuals and institutions with which the law interacts." And in *McLaurin v. Oklahoma* (1950), the Court judged that segregation within an integrated school impaired a black student's "ability to study, to engage in discussions and exchange views with other students, and, in general, learn his profession."

The landmark case, of course, was *Brown v. Board of Education* (1954). Legally segregated public schools were no longer to be tolerable under the "equal protection" clause of the United States Constitution. "Separate" governmental treatment would cease to be viewed as ever being "equal." However, when pressed for some immediate action to enforce that decision, the Supreme Court backed off a bit; in *Brown v. Board of Education* (1955), it simply required implementation "with all deliberate speed." Nevertheless, the Court did not stand idly by. It barred blatant evasions in *Cooper v. Aaron* (1958), *Watson v. Memphis* (1963), and *Griffen v. Prince Edward County* (1964), and it ultimately did call for speedier compliance in decisions such as *Green v. County School Board* (1968), *Alexander v. Holmes County* (1969), and *United States v. Montgomery County Board of Education* (1969). Then, in *Swann v. Charlotte* (1971), a unanimous Court even upheld measures such as court-ordered busing in situations where local school authorities had failed to redress long histories of segregation; and in *Runyon v. McCrary* (1976), it ruled that an all-white private school could not discriminate on the basis of race either.

But as the composition of the Court changed, so did the thrust of its decisions. As Richard Nixon's more conservative appointees replaced members of the more liberal Warren Court, it was not long before the brakes began to be applied. The newly constituted Supreme Court, under Chief Justice Warren Burger, would not prove to be nearly as aggressive in attacking educational inequities like segregation. As a matter of fact, it would rein in some of the previous efforts.

In *Keyes v. School District No. 1* (1973), the Court ruled that an "intent to segregate" must now be demonstrated before desegregation was required. Thus the considerable school segregation that had resulted from the nation's blatantly segregated residential patterns was no longer subject to court-ordered remedies. In *San Antonio v. Rodriguez* (1973), the justices upheld the funding of public schools by property tax formulas, despite the huge differences in school district resources that resulted. In *Milliken v. Bradley* (1974), they also strictly limited busing across school district lines, further fueling white flight to the suburbs for the purposes of avoiding school integration. And in *University of California v. Bakke* (1978), they allowed race-conscious affirmative action efforts in college admissions, but only if race was just one of several factors considered and no inflexible quotas were used. Most recently, in *Grove City College v. Bell* (1984), the Burger Court ruled that the federal government may not cut aid to an entire school simply because one part of the school is found to be discriminating—in this case against women, but the implications were clear for blacks as well.[21]

The same sorts of ebbs and flows in Court protection are apparent in other areas. Let us look at six more: elections, jobs, housing, public facilities, criminal punishment, and the right to speak in protest.

Elections. In the realm of suffrage, it took a full century to begin to enforce the 15th Amendment in recalcitrant states. The most basic right in a democratic system, the right to vote, was withheld from nearly half of America's black citizens for some 100 years after a civil war and a constitutional amendment had supposedly laid the question to rest. The delay resulted in large part from the Supreme Court's dogged reluctance to put the most fundamental right in a democracy above the conservative principle of federalism.

The United States Constitution leaves it up to the states to establish who is eligible to vote. According to Article 1, Section 4, "The times, places, and manner of holding elections for senators and representatives, shall be prescribed in each state by the legislatures thereof; but the Congress may at any time by law make or alter such regulations." Why the Congress for so long avoided its responsibility in this area will be explored in chapters 7 and 8. For now, note that the Supreme Court of the United States essentially sat on its collective hands throughout the second half of the 19th century, refusing to intervene in such "state matters," particularly significant given the absence of forceful congressional efforts to right this blatant wrong.

The first half of the 20th century was somewhat better, although in many ways it simply demonstrates the inconsistency with which the federal courts attacked the evasive manuevers of these states. In *Guinn v. United States* (1915), the Court finally put an end to the notorious "grandfather clauses," which had denied registration preferences to all whose grandparents had not been registered to vote—virtually all southern blacks. Given the dominance of the Democratic party in the South, however, southern representatives were essentially chosen in the Democratic party's primary elections. Thus when the Court declared in *Newberry v. United States* (1921) that primary elections were "in no real sense" part of federal elections, registered blacks could simply be excluded from these southern primaries and in essence be stripped of any real control over who would ultimately be elected in the region. *Nixon v. Herndon* (1927) barred state governments from writing such restrictions into state law, but *Grovey v. Townsend* (1935) allowed such exclusion if done by the parties themselves.

The Court changed composition and orientation in the late 1930s. This time, the change was in a more liberal direction. In *United States v. Classic* (1941), the Court reversed *Newberry* and found primaries to be an essential step in the federal election process. In *Smith v. Allwright* (1944) they reversed *Grovey* and ruled that because states were so directly involved in regulating such primaries, these were not purely private activities. And when states tried to repeal all related statutes in order to make the primaries truly private affairs, such efforts were rejected by the Court in *Rice v. Elmore* (1947) and *Terry v. Adams* (1953). Primary elections had come to be seen as integral parts of the electoral process and thus subject to the provisions of the 15th Amendment.

Nevertheless, by the early 1960s, a number of other laws and practices still left the overwhelming majority of southern blacks either unregistered or underrepresented. To reverse these would require strong Court-supported action on the part of the federal government.

States like Louisiana, for example, drew their election districts in ways that would minimize the impact of registered black votes—and one of the most blatant of these plans was struck down by the Court in *Gomillion v. Lightfoot* (1960). Yet the real action was just beginning.

In *Harper v. Virginia Board of Elections* (1966), the U.S. Supreme Court finally struck down the poll tax in federal elections as a violation of "equal protection of the laws." A combination of the 1964 Civil Rights Act and the 1965 Voting Rights Act (both to be discussed in detail in Chapter 8) allowed considerable federal intervention in the "times, places, and manner of holding elections," previously a nearly exclusive state purview. For example, federal examiners were allowed to register voters under certain circumstances, and a number of states had to "preclear" new voting regulations with federal officials. The U.S. Supreme Court, for its part, upheld the role of federal examiners in *South Carolina v. Katzenbach* (1966) and preclearance in *Allen v. State Board of Elections* (1969).

Enter the Burger Court, however, once again hesitant to intervene in "state matters" in the absence of clear "purposeful intent to discriminate." The issue was apportionment schemes that had the result of reducing black representation. For example, in *Whitcomb v. Chavis* (1971), *Beer v. United States* (1976), and *Mobile v. Bolden* (1980), the Court upheld the practice of multimember district at-large elections, despite their dilution of geographically concentrated black votes. And in *City of Richmond v. United States* (1975), it allowed urban annexations of white suburbs, which also clearly served the purpose of diluting the black vote.

Nevertheless, in *Williamsburg v. Carey* (1977), the Court refused to block race-conscious New York gerrymandering designed specifically to enhance black representation. In *Rome v. Georgia* (1980), it did finally block an annexation plan—though only because the subsequent apportionment did not "fairly reflect the strength of the black community after annexation," not because of the discriminatory effect of the annexation itself. And in *Thornburgh v. Gingles* (1986), the Court upheld the revised Voting Rights Act's "discriminatory results" standard (rather than requiring "purposeful intent to discriminate") in finally overturning a set of large multimember election districts as racially discriminatory.

Despite the ultimate bans on racially discriminatory grandfather clauses, white primaries, literacy tests, poll taxes, and some racial gerrymandering, there are still a variety of impediments to black suffrage. Economic and physical intimidation employed by individual whites against individual blacks, for instance, are forms of discrimination for which judicial remedy has proved much more difficult than when government is the offender.[22]

Jobs. The 1964 Civil Rights Act banned racial discrimination in the workplace, and in *Griggs v. Duke Power Company* (1971), the Supreme Court rejected employment standards unrelated to job performance when the result was to exclude black workers. But regardless of discriminatory impact, the Court demanded discriminatory intent before it would overturn performance-related tests (*Wash-*

ington v. Davis, 1976) or existing seniority systems (*Teamsters v. United States*, (1977).

The federal government did establish affirmative action requirements, follow-ing John Kennedy's first mention of the concept in his 1961 Executive Order 10925. Yet in terms of enforcement, the Supreme Court has drawn an important distinction. Affirmative action plans, even for the Burger Court, were acceptable as remedial efforts in job-training programs (*United Steelworkers v. Weber*, 1979), federal government set-asides for black contractors (*Fullilove v. Klutznick*, 1980), hiring when attempting to overcome past discrimination by that agent (*Sheet Metal Workers v. EEOC*, 1986; *Firefighters v. Cleveland*, 1986), and promotion when seeking to rectify such past discrimination (*United States v. Paradise*, 1987; *Johnson v. Transportation Agency*, 1987), but they were not constitutionally permissible in guiding layoffs, particularly where a legitimate seniority system was in place (*Memphis Firefighters v. Stotts*, 1984) or in the absence of a very clear and compelling state interest (*Wygant v. Jackson Board of Education*, 1986). Thus the last hired could continue to be the first fired, which significantly tempers training, hiring, and promotion assistance in an economy that regularly experiences both boom and slump periods. In addition, many existing state and local government set-asides for black contractors would no longer be allowed (*Richmond v. Croson*, 1989).

Housing. In 1917, Louisville, Kentucky, was forbidden from engaging in blatantly segregationist zoning (*Buchanan v. Warley*). In addition, state and local govern-ments were barred from enforcing discriminatory "restrictive covenants" written into the deeds of houses (*Shelley v. Kramer*, 1948). Then *Reitman v. Mulkey* (1967) struck down California's attempt to place private real estate transactions outside of governmental review. *Jones v. Mayer* (1968) resurrected an 1866 civil rights act to guarantee blacks equal opportunity to "purchase, lease, sell, hold, and convey real and personal property." And *Hunger v. Erickson* (1969) would not allow the city of Akron to require popular referenda before any fair-housing ordinances could go into effect.

But having the right to acquire a home anywhere in town and having the means to do so are two quite separate things. Even when the government helps out with housing assistance, equal rights still get denied. For example, many blacks have been forced by economic necessity to rely on public housing; thus the location of public housing has also become a focus of attention in the battle to secure equal housing opportunities. Into the fray bounded the Burger Court, with its "purposeful intent to discriminate" standard. In *Arlington Heights v. Metropolitan Housing District* (1977), for example, the Court ruled that the segregating effects of the city's zoning laws, as they affected predominantly black public housing, were not enough to violate the equal-protection clause. There must be clear evidence of discrimi-natory intent.

Public Facilities. The 1875 Civil Rights Act barred racial discrimination in public accommodations; yet the U.S. Supreme Court struck down those provisions in 1883 (*Civil Rights Cases*), arguing that the segregationist practices of private hotels, theaters, railroads, and the like did not involve "state action" as required to justify such a law under the 14th Amendment. Jim Crow became the order of the day in many such businesses until the 1960s. In *Burton v. Wilmington Parking Authority* (1961), the Supreme Court ruled that a private restaurant with a lease in a state-owned building could not discriminate without violating the equal-protection clause. The Civil Rights Act of 1964 finally prohibited all such discrimination and was upheld by the Court in *Heart of Atlanta Motel v. United States* (1974) and *Katzenbach v. McClung* (1974).

Nevertheless, the battle was not over. In particular, a number of these facilities were converted to private clubs in order to restrict patronage. And although the Court disallowed such a dodge in *Daniel v. Paul* (1969), it ruled that no state action was involved when a Moose Lodge refused to serve blacks, even though it was operating under a state liquor license (*Moose Lodge No. 107 v. Irvis*, (1972). Beyond that, *Tonkins v. Greensboro* (1959) allowed public swimming pools to be sold to segregating private operators, and *Palmer v. Thompson* (1971) allowed Jackson, Mississippi, to close all of its city pools rather than integrate them.

Criminal Punishment. It was not until 1935, in *Norris v. Alabama*, that the U.S. Supreme Court finally outlawed the systematic exclusion of blacks from juries, and not until 1986, in *Vasquez v. Hillery*, did it extend this to grand juries. Thus the Sixth Amendment guarantee of an "impartial jury," on the books for two centuries, was at last deemed applicable to black Americans. Yet in *Swain v. Alabama* (1965), the Court refused to bar a prosecutor's use of preemptory challenges to exclude blacks from juries unless there was a clear racial pattern in such exclusions. And although *Batson v. Kentucky* (1986) did not accept such preemptory challenges simply on the grounds that blacks are less likely to convict other blacks, realize that prosecutors do not have to give any reason for such exclusions. Thus *Swain* is still governing for all practical purposes, and blacks often continue to be convicted by all-white juries even in racially mixed communities.

Probably the most blatant example of continuing racism in this area concerns the ultimate punishment: the death penalty. In *Furman v. Georgia* (1972), the Supreme Court halted further executions until the procedure for assigning the death penalty was reformed. In part, the Court felt that existing practice had allowed its application in an "arbitrary and capricious" way toward black defendants. Four years later, in *Gregg v. Georgia*, the Court seemed satisfied that additional safeguards such as separate sentencing hearings had alleviated the problem. Executions resumed, and by the spring of 1987, some 70 people had been executed, 42 of them black. Of the nearly 1,900 people on death row awaiting execution in the mid-1980s, 42 percent were black.

Enter University of Iowa researcher David Baldus, statistics in hand, to complicate the picture even further. Controlling for 230 separate factors in 2,484 Georgia cases, Baldus concluded that killers of whites were 4.3 times more likely to receive a death sentence than killers of blacks.[23] Though it did not challenge the accuracy of those findings, the U.S. Supreme Court refused to allow such general statistical evidence to invalidate the procedure by which Georgia assigned the death penalty in this particular case (*McCleskey v. Kemp*, 1987). In dissent, Justice William Brennan lambasted his fellow justices by stating, "Since *Furman v.*

Georgia, the court has been concerned with the risk of the imposition of an arbitrary sentence, rather than the proven fact of one." And he went on to warn, "We remain imprisoned by the past as long as we deny its influence in the present."

The Right to Speak in Protest. The First Amendment decrees that "Congress shall make no law . . . abridging the freedom of speech . . . or the right of the people peaceably to assemble, and to petition the Government for a redress of grievances." In addition, as of *Gitlow v. New York* (1925), such restrictions were extended to state legislatures by means of the 14th Amendment. Nevertheless, in practice, "no law" has come to mean "some laws." For example, *Schenck v. United States* (1919) allowed the suppression of protest if it created a "clear and present danger." *Gitlow* also made an exception if the speech was likely to create a "bad tendency" in its audience. *Cox v. New Hampshire* (1941) allowed governments to require a permit for all "parades and processions." And *Chaplinsky v. New Hampshire* (1942) found "the lewd and obscene, the profane, the libelous, and the insulting or 'fighting words' (words that would provoke others to fight)" similarly unprotected by the First Amendment.

For the black community, such concerns became particularly relevant in the 1950s and 1960s, as civil rights protests proliferated. Once again, the Court's signals were mixed. Irving Feiner, for example, gave an impromptu address on a street corner in a predominantly black area of Syracuse. Among other things, Feiner declared, "The Negroes don't have equal rights; they should rise up in arms and fight for their rights." In *Feiner v. New York* (1951), the United States Supreme Court upheld his conviction for "disorderly conduct," arguing that the First Amendment does not protect "incitement to riot." More than a decade later, however, the more liberal Warren Court found that large numbers of black protesters, even when confronting a larger number of angry whites, were protected by the First Amendment (*Edwards v. South Carolina,* 1963; *Cox v. Louisiana,* 1965). But even though the Court allowed such highly inflammatory protests on public streets and even in a public library (*Brown v. Louisiana,* 1965), it would not allow them at a jail (*Adderly v. Florida,* 1966).

If the Constitution is what the Supreme Court says it is, what rights does it guarantee for black Americans? Lewis Steele has referred to the United States Supreme Court as "nine men in black who think white."[24] That may be a little too simplistic, as the Court's posture on race-related issues has varied considerably, depending on the political orientation of the Court. Another way to look at that, however, is that the United States really does not have a constitutional system in which basic human rights are etched clearly in stone for all time. Instead, it has a constitutional democracy, in which majority opinion can affect both who sits on the federal bench and how those justices decide cases—particularly in light of the fact that judges must make decisions that have a realistic chance of being implemented effectively by more democratically vulnerable agents.

A classic case in point is the recently revived controversy over whether private institutions may discriminate on the basis of race. The Constitution clearly states that governments may not; but many of the victories (especially in the areas of jobs, housing, education, and public facilities) required nongovernmental agents to cease discriminating as well. The real legal foundation for a number of these decisions was a pair of relatively obscure post–Civil War laws (now codified as 42 USCS 1981 and 1982). In decisions such as *Jones v. Mayer* (1968) and *Runyon v. McCrary* (1976), these laws were resurrected by the Warren Court and extended by the Burger Court in order to bar discrimination by private agents. However, when confronted with a private-sector employee's discrimination suit in 1988, newly confirmed Justice Anthony Kennedy cast the swing vote as the even more conservative Rehnquist Court decided it was time to reconsider this entire principle (*Patterson v. McLean Credit Union*, 1984). Such Court activity only reconfirms the contingent nature of all such judicial "victories."

IMPLEMENTATION

There is one more piece in the judicial puzzle. Despite what the Founding Fathers said in the Constitution and unevenness in interpretation, even outright legal victories mean nothing until they are implemented.

First, the organization of the U.S. judicial process is a clear example of federalism at work. There are federal courts and there are state courts, both with their own unique jurisdictions. The federal system is comprised of U.S. district courts (which hold the initial trials), U.S. courts of appeals, and finally, the U.S. Supreme Court. Their jurisdiction is limited to national matters, as spelled out in Article 3 of the U.S. Constitution, and they must ultimately rely on the federal marshals of the U.S. Justice Department to carry out their decisions. Parallel to that, the 50 state systems are organized in a similar manner. Although the names of the specific courts vary from state to state, each state has local trial courts, most have intermediate courts of appeals, and all have a state supreme court. Jurisdiction covers state laws, which include most familiar crimes, and enforcement falls on the shoulders of state and local police departments.

The Judicial Process

Courts of Appeals. The ultimate arbiter in this entire process, of course, is the Supreme Court of the United States. It is that court's responsibility to determine whether challenged state or federal government actions have offended the dictates of the United States Constitution, the "supreme" law of the land. But given that the United States does have a formal written constitution that has been amended a mere 17 times in 200 years, how can Supreme Court interpretation of it vary as much as it has? Why are there no permanent victories?

The answer to such questions lies in both the nature of the document and the nature of the justices who must interpret it. To begin with, terms like "due process of law" are ambiguous; thus interpretation is required as different circumstances arise. Second, justices vary in the way they define their roles. At one extreme are those justices who decide primarily on the basis of what they feel the Founding Fathers meant, while at the other extreme are those who give equal weight to "social need" at any given point in time. Activist justices like Thurgood Marshall and William Brennan continually vote to declare the death penalty unconstitutional, even though the Founding Fathers' generation did not consider even dismemberment in the course of execution to be "cruel and unusual punishment" for some offenses. Clearly, who sits on any interpreting court becomes extremely important.

And just who does sit on the U.S. Supreme Court—or any of the federal courts, for that matter? That is determined by a relatively simple process. The president of the United States chooses a nominee to replace a retiring or deceased justice. That nominee is reviewed for professional competence and integrity by the American Bar Association. Then, if the president is satisfied with the ABA's evaluation, the nominee is placed before the United States Senate for confirmation and—over the course of the 20th century—is almost always confirmed.

So who ends up with these appointments? As Lewis Steele and others have indicated, they are generally white Anglo-Saxon men who come from relatively wealthy backgrounds.[25] Their demographic profile closely resembles that of the elites who own most of the nation's wealth. Black Americans are noticeably underrepresented. Only one black justice has ever sat on the U.S. Supreme Court, and only about 7 percent of lower federal court justices are black, most of them appointed by President Jimmy Carter.

There are at least four obvious reasons for these results. First of all, justices are drawn from the ranks of the legal profession, and only 3 percent of United States lawyers are black. Second, the justices are appointed and confirmed by elected representatives whose collective profile is quite similar to their own (the reasons for the representatives' homogeneity will be discussed in Chapter 7). Third, the prestigious law schools that tend to supply nominees have long been bastions of wealthy white elites (a subject explored further in Chapter 9). Fourth, the American Bar Association is a very conservative organization, prompting black lawyers to form their own bar association to try to counter that influence.[26] Once again, institutionalized racism is in plain view.[27]

In a speech in June 1986 during his brief campaign for the presidency, Pat Robertson declared that Supreme Court rulings "are *not* the law of the land."[28] Seemingly illogical at the time, Robertson's statement was essentially correct—though not necessarily for the reasons he had in mind. To understand the validity of his remark is to understand another very important lesson about the judicial arena in the United States.

Appeals court decisions do not automatically translate into enforced behavior for a number of reasons. Most important, such courts do not have their own administrative arms or police forces. They are reliant on the executive branches of government to carry out their decisions, and executive bureaucracies often have their own political agendas. The justices in these courts also lack the staff, budget, and time to keep an eye on how their decisions are being enforced. Thus, by default, laws actually come to mean what law enforcement agents say the courts said they meant. And if their interpretation is unsatisfactory, back to the beginning the challengers must go, to the trial courts.

Trial Courts. Only a tiny fraction of lower court decisions ever work their way up the appeals hierarchy. Consequently, trial courts' interpretations and judgments normally stand as the law of the land. Although the national government is supposed to look after the basic rights of all American citizens, no matter where they live, the reality is that local judges end up deciding just what the national government had in mind. And it is at this level that the judicial process is least insulated from political pressure. Litigants have recognizable faces and networks of associates. Decisions often have direct and immediate effects on the local community. State trial judges are often elected to their positions, serving limited terms, and even the life-tenured federal judges informally have to be approved by elected U.S. senators from their state. On top of that, very few trial judges are black. There was not one black trial judge in the South from the end of Reconstruction to 1965. Even as of the mid-1980s, there were fewer than 350 black trial judges in the entire nation.

The implications for enforcement of Supreme Court victories are obvious. Because blacks have not fared as well in lower courts,[29] victories at higher levels have been impeded. In Virginia, for example, state and local governments were allowed to delay school integration by abolishing compulsory school attendence policies and closing integrated schools—including all the public schools in one county.[30] In addition, all-white schools have been integrated by busing in black students, but all-black schools remain all-black, as whites are seldom bused to black schools for the purpose of desegregation.[31]

Law Enforcement Agents. The zeal with which law enforcement agents enforce court-interpreted federal law also varies, depending on the political inclinations of the particular agents and the elected officials who appointed them. Examples of such uncertainty-producing inconsistency can be found at the highest levels of the federal law enforcement bureaucracy. Contrast, for instance, the approaches of Attorneys General Nicholas Katzenbach and Ed Meese or Equal Employment Opportunity Commission (EEOC) Chair Eleanor Holmes Norton and Civil Rights Commission (CRC) Chair Clarence Pendleton. Ronald Reagan's assistant attorney general, William Bradford Reynolds, was even quoted as saying, "We are not going to compel children who don't choose to have an integrated education to have one.[32] And no sooner had the U.S. Supreme Court upheld the Voting Rights Act's "results" standard in its *Thornburgh* decision, Reynolds was stating that the Justice Department did not intend to employ that standard when preclearing new state election laws.[33] Meanwhile, Jeffrey Zuckerman, nominated by Reagan to be the general counsel to the EEOC, argued at his confirmation hearing that blacks and women could best end discrimination in the workplace by simply working more cheaply than whites.[34] Such politicized administration at this level, where media scrutiny is most intense, would seem to be only the tip of a very large iceberg.

Specifically, consider what local practice has meant for enforcement of the rights of those accused of a crime. Given these realities, it is no wonder that the black poor constitute nearly half of the American prison population.

The Criminal Justice System

Both individual and institutionalized racism are readily apparent in the criminal justice system. From arrest to bail decisions to sentencing, black Americans can never be certain where and when such racism will appear. Although this discussion in no way seeks to make excuses for the behavior of criminals, it does raise serious questions about the equity of treatment in a system that intentionally allows a considerable degree of discretion at each stage.

A 1960s presidential crime commission found that 9 in 10 Americans do things that could land them in prison.[35] Nevertheless, it is not a cross section of the American population that ends up being arrested and convicted of such criminal behavior. Instead, America's prisons are overflowing with low-income individuals, nearly half of whom are black.

Police. At the street level, complaints of excessive and discriminatory uses of police force did not end in the 1960s.[36] Beneath such behavior on the part of white police officers lurk stereotyping, fears, and anger. In December 1986, for example, an all-white New Orleans suburb was experiencing an increasing number of burglaries. In response, its sheriff ordered that any black seen in the area be stopped and questioned.[37] The nationwide doubling of black police officers between 1972 and 1986 should help increase the equity of treatment by police, but even if police treatment becomes more equitable, even larger problems lurk elsewhere in the system.

Bail. Once arrested and charged, there is the question of bail. Presumed innocent until proved guilty, the criminal suspect is not to be punished by imprisonment prior to conviction and sentencing. Therefore, the suspect normally should be released, with bail set high enough to ensure that he or she will appear at the subsequent proceedings but not so high as to be considered "excessive," which would violate the Constitution. In reality, of course, the poor are often unable to post bail and thus end up in jail for months awaiting trial.[38] Meanwhile, they are not as able to assist in their own defense, for example, by lining up witnesses; and if convicted, they will ultimately be less likely to get probation because they have not been working regularly.

Legal Representation. More than 90 percent of all criminal cases will end outside of court with a "plea bargain" whereby the charge is reduced in return for a guilty plea. Whether a case is settled in or out of court, the quality of legal representation is extremely important. Fully 90 percent of people in prison cannot afford to hire a lawyer and thus have one appointed by the court. What are such lawyers paid? The national average in 1985 was $196 per case.[39] It should be no surprise, then, when stories like the following begin to surface:

> James Messer, a poor man, was charged with murder. The first lawyer appointed to defend him begged off, citing community outrage at the crime. So did the second. A third lawyer adopted a low-key strategy: He made no opening statement, called no witnesses, did not object to evidence and engaged in only cursory cross examination. At the sentencing hearing following conviction, he did not ask the jury to spare Mr. Messer's life, did not offer mitigating details inviting mercy and hinted that execution was appropriate. Mr. Messer soon found himself on Georgia's Death Row.
>
> Kevin Griffin's lawyer, a South Carolina public defender, had a hundred other clients. He was forced to begin Mr. Griffin's rape trial on short notice, with little

chance to investigate and after working on another case until 11:30 the previous night. There was no time to prepare Mr. Griffin or anyone to testify. Mr. Griffin convicted after a one-day trial, received 40 years.

Peter Schwander was charged with robbery in Louisiana. His trial lawyer made no independent investigation of the facts, nor did he speak with Mr. Schwander before trial. After conviction, Mr. Schwander's appellate lawyer worked without critical parts of the trial record. Mr. Schwander was sentenced to 30 years in prison.[40]

Juries. The juries that bring these sentences are hardly representative either. Normally chosen randomly from the list of enrolled voters, they exclude the disproportionate number of lower-income people who have not registered. Then, from the group that is chosen, hourly workers may be excused on the basis of "hardship." Thus the juries end up disproportionately populated by middle-class white business persons and professionals.[41]

Not surprisingly, then, a stockbroker gets a small fine for making $20 million in an illegal stock manipulation, whereas the same day a black man gets one year in prison for stealing a $100 television from the back of a truck.[42] There are indications that the poor are notably less likely to get suspended sentences or probation.[43] Even controlling for prior criminal records, blacks appear to get longer sentences than whites for the same crimes.[44] The race of the victim is significant as well. In the early 1980s, the average sentence for a black raping another black was four years, a white raping another white was five, a white raping a black was six, and a black raping a white was 16.[45]

Incarceration. Despite an explicit constitutional prohibition of "cruel and unusual punishment," the United States harbors the harsh realities of prisons and mental hospitals for the criminally "insane." The conditions inside many U.S. prisons have been widely publicized. Extortion, robbery, assault, and homosexual rape are commonplace in overcrowded and underfunded prisons, in which much of the policing is often left to the convicts themselves. Less publicized is the role mental hospitals have come to play in all of this. "Troublemakers," many of them black, have at times been subjected to mind-altering drugs, shock treatments, aversion therapies, and even lobotomies.[46]

Overall, then, even the limited negative rights guaranteed by the United States Constitution are inconsistently interpreted and enforced, creating very real uncertainty in the minds of black Americans. This, the least political of the several government arenas, seems destined by design to ebb and flow in its judgments, to the point of reinforcing the most fundamental inequalities in the status quo by its lack of consistent action to the contrary.

Radicals and the Law

Despite the inherent limits of the rights expressed in the U.S. Constitution, as well as the uncertainty created by some obvious ebbs and flows in their interpretation and implementation, the judicial arena has proved relatively receptive to a number of black demands for equal opportunities within the present economic structure. But when radical voices that challenge the historical maldistribution of property are raised, the interpreters and implementers of the Constitution seem to revert to the original purpose of protecting property above and beyond all else. American history is replete with radical individuals and groups who were under the erroneous impression that such challenges were protected under the Bill of Rights. For the majority of black Americans, seemingly locked in the economic subordination that is slavery's legacy, this is not good news.

Radicals in General. At the constitutional level, the signals are mixed. Consider advocates of communism as an alternative to capitalism. In De Jonge v. Oregon (1937), the U.S. Supreme Court decided that states must respect the First Amendment rights of communists to assemble, although in Dennis v. United States (1951) it reversed itself amid the anticommunist hysteria of the McCarthy period. Six years later, in Yates v. United States (1957), the Court reversed itself again. Now there was to be constitutional protection for communists' advocacy of an abstract doctrine that called for the overthrow of the existing political-economic system but not for direct advocacy of such an overthrow. And as late as 1961, in Scales v. United States, the Court upheld the conviction of a man for his active membership in a Communist party branch that the Court apparently felt had stepped over the boundary. Ironically, in Brandenburg v. Ohio (1969), the Court began requiring that advocacy be likely to incite lawlessness before it could be banned, and thus the Ku Klux Klan was not to be prosecuted under a more restrictive Ohio statute, while in Haig v. Agee (1981), the Court allowed the executive branch to renew and revoke passports selectively on political grounds. Thus socialist scholars like Regis De Bray and Ernest Mandel could be prevented from accepting lecturing invitations at American universities and ex-patriot Margaret Randell could be deported for her left-wing political advocacy.[47]

Historically, such constitutional waiverings have left the door open for considerable government harassment of radical groups. The federal government has used vague laws against "conspiring" to harm the United States, as when it jailed Eugene Debs and other socialist leaders during World War I. States used "criminal syndicalist" laws to repress the emergence of radical labor unions like the International Workers of the World (IWW), one of the few early union efforts that was both racially integrated and dedicated to socialism. Localities have often used "disorderly conduct" ordinances to arrest radical demonstrators. Tolerated were even more blatant and systematic repressions like the Red Raids of 1919 and the McCarthy hearings of the early 1950s, the latter leading to the practice of "blacklisting" radicals so that they could not work. Yet in 1978, when then United States ambassador to the United Nations Andrew Young spoke of "political prisoners" in the United States, he was resoundingly chastised by many elected officials and much of the mass media. Nevertheless, it is difficult to ignore the "political trials" of groups like the Chicago 8, the Panther 21, and the Wilmington 10 or those of individual dissidents like Dr. Benjamin Spock or Phillip and Daniel Berrigan.

Black Radicals. The judicial process has been particularly harsh on blacks who were deemed to be delivering "dangerous" messages. Most were dealt with at levels well below the United States Supreme Court. They simply seemed to fall out of the protective reach of the United States Constitution.

Jamaican-born black nationalist Marcus Garvey, for example, was able to attract thousands of largely low-income blacks to his Universal Negro Improvement Association, an organization that, among other things, urged blacks to form and patronize separate, communally owned black businesses. His success prompted federal authorities like William Burns and J. Edgar Hoover anxiously to discuss the need to deport such a "notorious Negro agitator." Meanwhile, Garvey also began to build up a series of black businesses, often by soliciting investors through the mail. Soon he and three other officers of one such firm were indicted for mail fraud. Although the sole witness could not even remember what the advertisement had said, Garvey alone was convicted and given the maximum sentence, which included five years in prison. Two years later, under political pressure, President Coolidge commuted his sentence but also ordered his deportation.

Actor Paul Robeson, an outspoken socialist, never even participated in a political protest march, let alone became involved in disruption or violence. Nevertheless, in 1949 he stated, "It is unthinkable that American Negroes will go to war on behalf of those who have oppressed us for generations against a country [the Soviet Union] which in one generation has raised our people to the full dignity of mankind."[48] Thereafter, he was effectively blacklisted, and his income fell from $100,000 in 1947 to $6,000 in 1952. Although never convicted of any crime, he would have to leave the United States in order to make a living.[49]

Radical minister Ben Chavis was arrested on numerous occasions in the course of political protests, only to be acquitted each time his cases ultimately got to trial. He was finally successfully jailed as one of the Wilmington 10. They were convicted of arson, although all three witnesses against them later recanted their testimony.

Black activist Martin Sostre, an outspoken critic of heroin use in the ghetto, was arrested in New York and convicted of selling $15 worth of heroin to an informer. He was then sent to prison in 1967, even after the only witness against him, the informer, recanted his testimony. Sostre was finally granted amnesty in December 1975—after the political scene had quieted considerably.[50]

Socialist Frank Shuford, whom the prosecutor would label a "revolutionary troublemaker," was arrested for shooting two store clerks in Santa Ana, California. Although at home with family and friends at the time, he was convicted by an all-white jury and sentenced to 30 years in prison even though there was no material evidence and neither clerk could identify him.[51]

In early 1970, scholar Angela Davis, an avowed communist, began to assist in the defense of the Soledad Brothers, three black prisoners accused of killing a prison guard. She also continued to speak out against both racism and capitalism. Soon she was fired from her teaching position at UCLA and shortly thereafter was sought for "conspiracy" in connection with a bungled prisoner escape plot. Even though she had no previous arrest record, she became only the third woman ever to be placed on the FBI's "Ten Most Wanted" list, which described her as "armed and dangerous," a classification that placed her life in jeopardy. Arrested in October 1970, she was held for days in solitary confinement while outside, the president of the United States publicly called her a "terrorist." Ultimately extradited to California for trial, the evidence was so thin that she was subsequently acquitted by an all-white jury.

Black Panther leader Huey Newton was convicted of felony assault with a knife in 1964 and manslaughter in 1968. Thus he was in jail during a key period from October 1967 through August 1970. Ultimately he got new trials, and all charges were dismissed. Nevertheless, in 1978 he was convicted of being in illegal possession of a gun, and while out awaiting final judicial action, he was rearrested in 1985 for embezzling government funds from a children's education and nutrition program and again for being a felon in possession of a gun. Subsequently, he was imprisoned and began serving 15 months to 3 years for the 1978 conviction.

In April 1969, some 21 members of the Black Panther party were indicted for conspiracy to kill a police officer and for placing dynamite in a large department store and on subways. They spent two years in jail awaiting trial and then another 15 months in court before a jury unanimously acquitted them after only 2½ hours of deliberation.

Black Panther Johnny Spain was even less fortunate. He spent 21 years in prison as a result of two separate murder convictions—one for a 1966 killing and the other related to an aborted prison escape. In March 1988, his convictions were finally reversed, and he was released at the age of 38.

So when Andrew Young spoke out in 1978, there were indeed numerous black persons in prison at least in part as a result of their radical political activities, including 24 Black Panthers, 25 members of the Black Liberation Army, and 12 members of the Republic of New Africa organization.[52] The 1981 annual report of Amnesty International, for example, accused the FBI of fabricating evidence in order to convict members of the Black Panthers.[53]

Nevertheless, those are cases that at least got to a court of law, however unequal the justice applied. A number of outspoken black activists, many of them not even radicals, were less fortunate yet. They were dealt with directly by such agents as mobs, local police, or the FBI.

For decades following Reconstruction, black "troublemakers" were lynched, while state and local law enforcement agents stood idly by or occasionally even assisted. Meanwhile, the federal government deferred to "states' rights" and refused to intervene, as they had in the days of slavery. Such respect for federalism cost many blacks their lives, despite 14th Amendment guarantees of due process and equal protection under the laws, not to mention Eighth Amendment prohibitions against cruel and unusual punishment.

A more recent example of this phenomenon occurred during the period of civil rights activism between 1957 and 1968. For the nearly 100 civil rights activists murdered during that period, there were few arrests and no murder convictions.

The case of George Jackson is instructive. Serving an indeterminate sentence for a $70 robbery committed in his youth, after 10 years in prison he gradually became radicalized. He proceeded to write books and organize fellow inmates until he was shot to death in an alleged escape attempt in August 1971. An FBI agent later testified about a plot to kill Jackson by contriving what would look like an escape attempt.[54]

Local police often were not nearly as circuitous in their approach. For example, unarmed black students were gunned down during protests in Orangeburg, South Carolina, and Jackson, Mississippi, and more than 40 Black Panthers were shot and killed by police between 1968 and 1971. One of the most blatant incidents occurred in Chicago in December 1969. In a predawn raid, police claimed they met with armed resistance. In fact, Black Panther leaders Fred Hampton and Mark Clark were found shot to death in their beds, and later congressional investigations would implicate the FBI in the plot to assassinate them.[55]

FBI harassment of black activists is now well documented. Its "Counterintelligence Program" (COINTELPRO) was designed, in Director J. Edgar Hoover's own words, "to expose, disrupt, misdirect, discredit, or otherwise neutralize" radical black groups.[56] Between 1956 and 1971, it carried out 295 actions against black groups and individuals. These included extraordinary efforts to undermine Rev. Martin Luther King, Jr., a political activist working for racial integration and black people's right to register and vote. Hoover publicly called King "the most notorious liar in the country," and internal FBI memos talked about the need "to destroy Doctor Martin Luther King." Just prior to his receiving the Nobel Peace Prize, for example, the FBI sent King and his wife separate packages. Coretta Scott King received cassette tape recordings of alleged sexual trysts involving her husband, while Martin received a letter that implicitly invited suicide:

> King, there is only one thing left for you to do. You know what it is. You have just 34 days in which to do it. The exact number has been selected for a specific reason. It has definite practical significance. You are done.[57]

Undaunted by such efforts, King continued his civil rights activities until assassinated in 1968. As chairperson of the U.S. House committee that investigated that assassination, Congressman Louis Stokes concluded that he was murdered because "he had begun to wake up poor people in this country, not only poor black people but also poor white people."[58]

OPTIONS FOR BLACK AMERICA

What are the overall potentials and limitations of the judicial arena in the search for racial justice in America? On the positive side, this arena is more insulated from majority rule and is thus a logical place for minorities seeking to force the majority to behave. Rights can be sought without the same need to compromise found in more political arenas, and it takes fewer people, connections, and political resources to enter the game. However, it does require a very important political resource—money—and it is costly in terms of both legal fees and lost wages. It is also a very slow process, with victories often coming years after the initial discriminatory behavior. In addition, such victories can be stalled or reversed in implementation or by subsequent court decisions. Also, it does not require the kind of mass mobilization and organization that can generate the political pressure necessary to sustain the victories. Furthermore, it is in many ways actually depoliticizing, for it is largely an elite-level activity that promotes passive spectatorship rather than activism at the grass-roots level. Finally, it is not nearly as neutral a process as it looks on paper, especially the more the demands challenge the distribution of wealth in the society.[59]

What, then, can be done in terms of reforming the judicial arena to allow it more effectively to protect the most basic rights of black Americans?

Positive rights must be written into the Constitution—rights to housing, health care, a job at a livable wage, and an adequate guaranteed annual income for people unable to work. The nation's political structures must be altered to be more responsive and responsible. Only then will it be realistic to expect passage and effective implementation of the legislation "necessary and proper" to carry the positive rights into being. In particular, it is time to suggest reductions in a number of the checks and balances built into the political system (specifics will be discussed shortly and in the next two chapters) given the major reason why the Founding Fathers put them there in the first place.

As for interpretation and adjudication, there is clearly a need for more black judges. Despite a few exceptions, there is mounting evidence that a judge's behavior on the bench will reflect his or her social and economic background.[60] As black judge Bruce Wright put it:

> Black judges who have themselves escaped the gravitational pull of the ghetto, but who still bear the marks of their narrow escape, know the rough tensions of a two-culture existence. There is, therefore, a special insight of compassion which only a black judge can bring to the law.[61]

As the system's "gatekeepers," it is critical that judges possess the necessary perspective, sensitivity, and openness to new legal issues and approaches.

A new method of selecting judges should be considered in order to remove legal interpretation as far as possible from political influence. Judges at all levels could be appointed instead of elected. Such appointments could be done by random selection from a large list of candidates approved by their peers. The list could be weighted to ensure that blacks, women, and other previously excluded groups would have far more equal demographic representation on the bench. Such a process would help minimize the introduction of politics and racism into the judicial arena, while helping to maximize the "rule of law."

Finally, at the implementation stage, more black officers are needed at all ranks in federal, state, and local law enforcement agencies. In addition, these agencies could be placed in the judicial rather than the executive branch so as to limit politics in implementation as well. And as a constructive check, neighborhoods should be given a significant role in choosing, overseeing, and disciplining the police who regularly patrol them.

NOTES

1. Charles Beard, quoted in Howard Zinn, A *People's History of the United States* (New York: Harper & Row, 1980), p. 89.
2. Declaration of Independence.
3. Quoted in Max Farrand (ed.), *The Records of the Federal Convention of 1787*, vol. 1 (New Haven, Conn.: Yale University Press, 1937), p. 536.
4. John Adams, *Works*, vol. 6 (New York: AMS Press, 1971), p. 9.
5. Quoted in Farrand, *Records of the Federal Convention*, pp. 424, 432; and in Mary Jo Kline (ed.), *Alexander Hamilton* (New York: Harper & Row, 1973), p. 45.
6. Quoted in Farrand, *Records of the Federal Convention*, pp. 422, 423, 421; and in M. Meyers (ed.), *The Mind of the Founder* (Indianapolis: Bobbs-Merrill, 1973), pp. 504–505.
7. John Locke, "Second Treatise on Civil Government," in Maurice Cranston (ed.), *Locke on Politics, Religion, and Education* (New York: Collier, 1965).
8. Charles Beard, *An Economic Interpretation of the Constitution*, (New York: Macmillan, 1962).
9. Samuel Morrison, *The Oxford History of the American People* (New York: Oxford University Press, 1965), p. 274.
10. David Szatmary, *Shays's Rebellion: The Making of an Agrarian Insurrection* (Amherst: University of Massachusetts Press, 1980).
11. Quoted in Zinn, *People's History*, p. 95.
12. *Ex parte Milligan* (1866).
13. Zinn, *People's History*, p. 97.
14. Quoted in Dexter Perkins, *Charles Evans Hughes* (Boston: Little, Brown, 1956), p. 16.
15. Clinton Rossiter (ed.), *The Federalist Papers* (New York: New American Library, 1961), pp. 83–84.
16. Jackson Turner Main, *The Social Structure of Revolutionary America* (Princeton, N.J.: Princeton University Press, 1965).
17. Quoted in Ira Katznelson and Mark Kesselman, *The Politics of Power* (Orlando, Fla.: Harcourt Brace Jovanovich, 1987), p. 190.
18. See Frances Fox Piven and Richard Cloward, *Regulating the Poor* (New York: Vintage, 1971), pp. 299–300.
19. Julius Chambers, "The Law and Black Americans: Retreat from Civil Rights," in National Urban League, *The State of Black America, 1987* (New York: National Urban League, 1987), pp. 26–27.
20. See W. E. B. Du Bois, *Black Reconstruction* (New York: Russell, 1935).
21. See Meyer Weinberg, *A Chance to Learn: A History of Race and Education in the United States* (New York: Cambridge University Press, 1977), chaps. 1–3, 7.
22. For example, see Charles V. Hamilton, *The Bench and the Ballot: Southern Federal Judges and Black Votes* (New York: Oxford University Press, 1973), chap. 8.
23. David Baldus et al., "Comparative Review of Death Sentences: An Empirical Study of the Georgia Experience," *Journal of Criminal Law and Crimonology* (June 1983).
24. Lewis M. Steele, "Nine Men in Black Who Think White," *New York Times*, October 13, 1968.
25. Ibid. Also see Herman Schwartz, *Packing the Courts: The Conservative Campaign to Rewrite the Constitution* (New York: Scribner, 1988).
26. Joel Grossman, *Lawyers and Judges: The ABA and the Politics of Judicial Selection* (New York: Wiley, 1965); Joseph C. Howard, "Why We Organize," *Journal of Public Law*, vol. 20 (1971), pp. 381–382.
27. For example, see Helen Edwards, *Black Faces in High Places* (Orlando, Fla.: Harcourt Brace Jovanovich, 1971).
28. *New York Times*, June 28, 1988.

29. Kenneth Vines, "Federal District Judges and Race Relations Cases in the South," *Journal of Politics* (May 1964), pp. 337–357.

30. Bob Smith, *They Closed Our Schools*, (Chapel Hill: University of North Carolina Press, 1965).

31. Willis Hawley, *Strategy for Effective Desegregation: A Synthesis of Findings* (Nashville, Tenn.: Center for Education and Human Development Policy, 1987); Charles V. Willie, "The Future of School Desegregation," in National Urban League, *State of Black America, 1987.*

32. *New York Times*, November 20, 1981.

33. *Washington Post*, August 30, 1986, p. A1.

34. See Chambers, "Law and Black Americans," for this and other examples of enforcement laxity and policy reversals during the Reagan presidency.

35. Katznelson and Kesselman, *Politics of Power*, p. 207.

36. *Newsweek*, July 4, 1977; *New York Times*, March 2, 1975; April 15, 1979; Joan Walsh, "Police Brutality Divides Milwaukee," *In These Times* (September 9, 1981), p. 6; Theodore Becker and Vernon Murray, *Government Lawlessness in America* (New York: Oxford University Press, 1971); Manning Marable, *How Capitalism Underdeveloped Black America* (Boston: South End Press, 1983).

37. *New York Times*, December 23, 1986.

38. Stuart Nagel, "Disparities in Criminal Procedure," *UCLA Law Review* (August 1967), pp. 1272–1305; Herbert Jacob, *Urban Justice* (Englewood Cliffs, N.J.: Prentice-Hall, 1973), p. 103.

39. *New York Times*, February 28, 1986.

40. Ibid.

41. Herbert Jacob, *Justice in America* (Boston: Little, Brown, 1972), p. 104.

42. Leonard Downie, Jr., *Justice Denied* (New York: Praeger, 1971).

43. Nagel, "Disparities in Criminal Procedure."

44. *Denver Post*, May 1, 1977.

45. Calvin Larson, *Crime, Justice, and Society* (Dix Hills, N.Y.: General Hall, 1984), p. 225.

46. Michael Parenti, *Democracy for the Few* (New York: St. Martin's Press, 1983), pp. 175–181.

47. *New York Times*, June 4, 1982; November 16, 1986.

48. Quoted in Edward Greenberg, *The American Political System* (Boston: Little, Brown, 1983), p. 75.

49. Ibid., pp. 73–75. See Martin Duberman, *Paul Robeson* (New York: Knopf, 1989).

50. *New York Times*, December 25, 1975; Zinn, *People's History*, p. 508.

51. Parenti, *Democracy for the Few*, pp. 158–159.

52. Ibid., p. 164.

53. *New York Times*, September 11, 1981.

54. Eric Mann, *Comrade George* (New York: Harper & Row, 1974); Zinn, *People's History*, pp. 509–510; *Guardian*, April 21, 1976.

55. *Chicago Tribune*, April 20, 1976; June 12, 1976; Zinn, *People's History*, pp. 455, 542–543.

56. *Village Voice*, September 9, 1981, p. 25.

57. Zinn, *People's History*, p. 453. Letter quoted from David Wise, "The Campaign to Destroy Martin Luther King," *New York Review of Books*, November 11, 1976, pp. 40–41.

58. Emily Rovetch (ed.), *Like It Is* (New York: Dutton, 1981), p. 42.

59. See Derrick Bell, *And We Are Still Not Saved: The Elusive Quest for Racial Reform* (New York: Basic Books, 1987); Harold Cruse, *Plural but Equal: Blacks and Minorities in America's Plural Society* (New York: Morrow, 1987).

60. Randall Black, *Private Pressure on Public Law: The Legal Career of Justice Thurgood*

Marshall (New York: Kennikat, 1973); Michael D. Smith, "Social Background and Role Perception of Black Judges," paper presented at the annual meeting of the American Political Science Association, New Orleans, September 4–8, 1973; Gilbert Ware (ed.), *From The Black Bar: Voices for Equal Justice* (New York: Putnam, 1976); Bruce Fein, *Significant Decisions of the Supreme Court, 1978–1979 Term* (Washington, D.C.: American Enterprise Institute, 1980), pp. 22–23; George W. Crockett, Jr., "The Role of the Black Judge," *Journal of Public Law* 20 (1971), pp. 398–399.

61. Quoted in Lucius Barker and Jesse McCorry, *Black Americans and the Political System* (Cambridge, Mass.: Winthrop, 1976), p. 158.

CHAPTER SEVEN

The Electoral Arena

> The vote has become a fetish with many Negroes, but there is little evidence
> that social problems anywhere in the world are solved by fetishism.
> Ralph Bunche, 1944[1]

For nearly a century after the abrupt end of Reconstruction, the majority of black Americans were effectively denied their constitutionally guaranteed right to vote. With the assistance of civil rights and voting rights acts in the 1960s and 1970s, however, blacks finally were able to register and vote much more freely. The results were dramatic. For example, whereas there were fewer than 500 black elected officials in the entire country in 1965, that number had grown to more than 6,000 in 20 years. Nevertheless, the impact on public policy and subsequently on the life conditions of many of these newly enfranchised citizens has not been comparably dramatic. To begin making some sense of that, serious questions must be raised about America's democratic system. This chapter will examine the nature and functions of the electoral process; the next will consider the response of legislative and executive officials.

ELECTIONS AND DEMOCRACY IN AMERICA

Just what are the prerequisites of self-government? If there was only one person around, the question would be purely academic. The sole citizen would relate to his or her environment by making all the decisions that governed that person's own actions within it. But once that individual joins a "community," a procedure is needed for determining the community's interests in matters of social concern. Now, if these communal decisions remain in the hands of "the people" rather than in the hands of one person or an exclusive few, this arrangement can be loosely labeled a democracy. And a common way for a democracy to reach decisions is by majority rule. In a small town, a town meeting might be called every Friday night, where the residents could come together for the purpose of making these decisions by majority preference. But if the population is large and the issues many and complex, some division of labor becomes necessary. Thus a representative democracy is born, whereby politicians are elected to make the decisions, and they must be chosen and reviewed in a manner that will enable them to know and represent the interests of the people (or at least a majority of the people) in matters of public policy.

Political theorist Joseph Schumpeter addressed the prerequisites of a representative democracy, concluding that the essential element is citizen opportunity to vote for either the politicians in office or a set of competing politicians wishing to get into office. Thus the role of the voter becomes somewhat analogous to that of the consumer in the market economy, choosing freely from among a limited number of competing candidates.[2]

Elections thus allow the general public to set the broad outlines of governmental policy by virtue of whom they elect or reject. To facilitate that, political parties arise to help clarify electoral choices, as well as to allow the subsequent government to organize itself in a more efficient manner. In the United States, however, both the election process and political party process are inherently biased against fundamental redistributive change.

From the founding of the country, the electoral process was not designed to empower the masses; suffrage was limited to propertied white males, and the United States Senate was to be elected by state legislators. Those restrictions have since been modified, but a number of others continue to institutionalize race and class inequities. For example, registration and campaign finance procedures are prejudiced against working- and lower-class people, and a two-party system guarantees that the major parties will be virtually incapable of educating and leading the public in any direction that would fundamentally challenge the socioeconomic status quo.

For black Americans, these realities are becoming increasingly obvious. Wherever blacks have been enfranchised, they have nearly always followed prescribed electoral strategy. They have often been geographically concentrated in areas of strategic importance to the two major parties. Controlling for socioeconomic status, they appear to turn out at a higher rate than the population as a whole. And they have voted as a relatively cohesive bloc for the dominant party in nearly every election since the Emancipation Proclamation. Unfortunately, for reasons such as those alluded to already, the electoral system is severely limited in its capacity to allow serious challenge to the worst of the legacies of slavery.

That is not to say that success in the long battle to gain suffrage has been a hollow victory. Electoral mobilization has led to control over some institutional levers of political power, enabling a number of blacks to improve their life situations. It has also provided an organizational structure for sustaining the vigilance and pressure needed to perpetuate those gains. In addition, the right to vote—regardless of political-economic system—is a necessary condition for advancing the causes of equality and self-determination. In the American context, however, the electoral process alone would not appear to be a sufficient mechanism for achieving those results. Acquiring and exercising the right to vote may well be more than "fetishism," but it presently leaves black Americans a far cry from self-determination in a racially just America.

THE BLACK ELECTORAL EXPERIENCE

Once dubbed "the greatest Democratic ward in the country" by President Franklin Delano Roosevelt, [Chicago's] 24th ward . . . has always been good about delivering the vote. It was the first West Side ward to elect a black alderman, a black committeeman and a black state representative. For Mayor

Harold Washington, the ward delivered a resounding 99.5 percent of its vote. . . . Walter Mondale won 98 percent.

Yet for a community that has had such an impact at the polls, it shows few signs of benefiting in return.[3]

In the 1960s, nearly 3½ centuries after blacks first arrived on the American continent, large legal impediments to their self-governance remained. Nevertheless, the majority of southern blacks were finally able to register and vote for the first time since Reconstruction, and the number of black elected officials increased dramatically. Still, pockets of resistance remain to this day, and electoral gains have been tempered by, among other things, the limits of the electoral process itself.

The Battle for Suffrage

Enslaved blacks had no political rights whatsoever. The *Dred Scott* decision made that point quite emphatically. In addition, Staughton Lynd and others emphasize that even so-called free blacks faced considerable racial discrimination, including discrimination in their efforts to cast a ballot.[4] The struggle for an unimpeded right to vote would be a long and arduous one, and many people would give their lives to the endeavor, both figuratively and literally.

The first major victories were marked by the Emancipation Proclamation and the Civil War amendments to the United States Constitution. Slavery was terminated, and the Constitution was amended to state that "the right of citizens of the United States to vote shall not be denied or abridged by the United States or any State on account of race, color, or previous condition of servitude." In addition, "No State shall make or enforce any law which shall abridge the privileges or immunities of citizens of the United States; nor shall any State deprive any person of life, liberty, or property without due process of law; nor deny to any person within its jurisdiction the equal protection of the laws."

For the overwhelming majority of black Americans, most of whom would reside in the South for at least another half century, these legal pronouncements had meaning as long as northern troops were around to enforce them. When the Republican party abandoned Reconstruction in order to gain the presidency in 1876, all of that changed rapidly. In terms of suffrage, legal impediments like poll taxes, literacy tests, and all-white primaries, as well as both physical and economic intimidation, quickly disenfranchised nearly all southern blacks.

Even after many migrated North, discrimination remained the rule of the day. In urban political machines, for example, blacks were recruited but often confined to parallel party organizations. These organizational appendages would turn out the black vote for white Democratic candidates and in return would receive limited amounts of patronage and sometimes a few black seats in party and governmental decision-making bodies. The relationship of the black community to the Chicago political machine is one well-analyzed example, while the New York City machine and its parallel Union of Colored Democrats is an even more extreme case in point.[5] At the state level, by contrast, practices such as racial gerrymandering were commonplace, with election district lines drawn to distribute the black vote in such a way as to dilute its impact. For example, the black community would be divided so that no voting district would have a black majority.

Chapter 6 documented how over time the federal courts struck down a number of the discriminatory practices just mentioned. Between 1957 and 1970, the Congress added vigor to the enforcement of such constitutional rights by passage of a series of civil rights and voting rights acts. In particular, new voting laws and regulations in suspect election districts had to be precleared by the federal courts, registration records had to be kept much more systematically, and penalties were increased for the violation of voting rights. Federal judges could appoint referees to review the qualifications of rejected applicants, the Commission on Civil Rights was created to investigate abuses, and the attorney general of the United States was authorized to bring lawsuits where necessary. A second reconstruction was under way.

Political Participation

Millions of previously disenfranchised black Southerners stepped forward to claim the right so long denied them. In the eleven southern states from Virginia to Texas, the surge was quite apparent. Whereas 1.5 million blacks voted in 1960, that figure jumped to 2.2 million by 1964, 3.1 million by 1968, 3.6 million by 1972, and 4 million by 1976. Mississippi saw its black turnout rate increase from 6 percent to 59 percent over this period, meaning that nearly 3 out of 5 eligible black voters were at last registered and voting. Alabama's increased from 14 percent to 55 percent. Arkansas witnessed an increase from 38 percent to 81 percent.

With the legal barriers all but eliminated, blacks' political participation soon approached, and in a number of ways exceeded, that of their white counterparts. Although their overall voting rate has continued to lag some 5 percentage points behind that of whites, when blacks and whites of the same socioeconomic status are compared, blacks register and vote at higher rates. In addition, even without controlling for socioeconomic position, blacks tend to be more active in other forms of participation, such as campaigning and lobbying.[6]

Nevertheless, this relative gain vis-à-vis whites must be viewed against participation trends across national black and white constituencies. Although blacks have been participating at a slightly higher rate than their white socioeconomic counterparts, the participation rates of both groups are quite low by international standards, and participation has been declining steadily since 1960.

To begin with, both black and white Americans vote at lower rates than voters in virtually every other democracy in the world. Turnout rates in other Western democracies, for example, almost always exceed 75 percent, and in a number of countries they regularly exceed 90 percent. In this country, less than one-half of all registered blacks voted in the most recent presidential elections; scarcely more than one-third normally vote in either congressional primaries or congressional general elections, and the numbers normally fall somewhere in between for elections at the state and local levels.[7] Black voting, like white voting, has been declining rather steadily since the mid-1960s, despite the sizable addition of previously disenfranchised southern blacks. For example, where black turnout was nearly 60 percent in the presidential elections of 1964 and 1968, it has hovered around 50 percent ever since and was lower yet in 1988.

Why are a large number of black Americans choosing not to exercise their franchise? Despite the limited data available on the black electorate,[8] political analysts have suggested a number of tentative explanations. Some of them are true for whites as well, while others are unique to the black experience.

To begin with, physical intimidation did not cease with the passage of the civil rights and voting rights acts, and the kind of economic dependence discussed in Chapter 4 has continued to leave the black community particularly vulnerable to economic intimidation, such as threats of being fired or losing credit.[9] In addition, the Atlanta-based Voter Education Project has found a number of registration offices to be located in intentionally remote places and only open during unusual hours.

Yet well before that, a major politicizing agent was disappearing at precisely the wrong time. The urban political machine was being dismantled just as large numbers of blacks began to migrate into the nation's large cities. In particular, a reform movement was stripping the machines of the kinds of patronage that had proved so useful in the process of politically mobilizing earlier immigrant groups. This had at least three significant consequences.

First, many in the black community came instead to be galvanized around charismatic individuals like Marcus Garvey, Martin Luther King, Jr., and Malcolm X. The problem there was that when the charismatic leaders were gone, it was much more difficult to transfer their power to others and thereby hold the organizations together.

Second, there was more of a tendency to mobilize around large and highly charged issues like police brutality and desegregation. Yet, as the machine had quickly discovered, it is usually much easier to politicize large numbers of people and sustain their political energies over the long term by using divisible and more tangible patronage benefits like jobs, food, and personal help. Not only that, but determining the correct policy for addressing communitywide issues can polarize the group, while divisible benefits can be widely dispersed, providing a little something for everybody and thus keeping the organization together.

Finally, local machine patronage was being displaced in part by national programs with national eligibility standards and a large national bureaucracy to administer them. No longer would recipients have to "deliver the vote" in order to qualify for governmental assistance. And even more depoliticizing would be the fact that the bureaucrats on whom many now relied were far removed from electoral control. There was simply less reason for low-income ghetto residents to register and vote. In addition, there was certainly less incentive to undertake the very tedious work of finding and funding candidates, registering voters, and getting out the votes on election day.[10]

Beyond the decline of the politicizing party machine is the comparably depoliticizing litigation orientation discussed in Chapter 6. Instead of requiring grass-roots political activism, heavy early reliance on the judicial arena promoted passive spectatorship among many potential activists in the black community.

The most commonly heard explanation for black nonparticipation, however, is that black Americans fall disproportionately into lower socioeconomic groups—groups that have traditionally participated less often. That obviously explains some of the variation between black and white voting rates. But participation levels in the black community do not vary much on the basis of socioeconomic position.[11]

More useful to note is the tremendous variation in black turnout from one election to the next; witness the outpourings of support for black candidates like Mayor Harold Washington in Chicago (1983) and Democratic presidential candidate Jesse Jackson (1984 and 1988). Walton and others have found that blacks have a high level of group consciousness, and their turnout appears to be very responsive to specific race-relevant combinations of candidates and campaigns, as well as organizational efforts.[12]

The Voters' Choice

Once registered and voting, how did black Americans cast their ballots? Despite popular misconceptions to the contrary, blacks have not voted as a monolith. Nonetheless, they have voted more cohesively for a longer period of time than virtually any other racial or ethnic group in American history. Before tracing that electoral behavior, however, first consider some of the dominant voting strategies advocated over time.

Alternative Voting Strategies. As the 1984 presidential election approached, prominent black leaders such as Andrew Young, Richard Hatcher, and Mickey Leland formed groups like the 1984 Election Strategy Group and the Black Leadership Family.[13] There was considerable debate over whether the time was ripe for Jesse Jackson to seek the presidency and, even if he did, whether black leaders should support him or Democratic front-runner Walter Mondale. The debate reflected two important currents that had run through black electoral strategy for more than half a century. The following discussion will briefly touch on both of those (major party and black candidate strategies) as well as others.

Major-Party Strategy. This approach accepts the premise that in a two-party system like the one in the United States, one of the two major parties will always hold the power. Thus the wisest approach is to try to maximize influence over those parties. That can be done in one of two ways.

Black elected officials such as Walter Fauntroy, Andrew Young, and others have long advocated working within the dominant political party most predisposed to black interests at any particular point in time. That has come to be the Democratic party over the course of the past half century.

Meanwhile, newspaper editor and author Chuck Stone called for "political oscillation" between the two major parties, essentially delivering the black vote to the highest bidder. As Vernon Jordan put it, "The black vote must be earned with ironclad commitments to the programs and policies black people need."[14] With such a thought in mind, CORE's Floyd McKissick talked about creating an "apparatus, not a party . . . [to] develop an independent platform which it will attempt to sell to the Democrats and Republicans."[15]

Third-Party Strategy. Another general approach advocates stepping away from the two relatively unresponsive major parties and supporting one of four basic types of minor parties: (1) multiracial protest parties that form to rally people around a particular cause, like the Liberty party in its opposition to slavery; (2) multiracial ideological parties that in each election run candidates dedicated to their world view, such as the Communist party of the United States; (3) black independent parties, like the Lowndes County Freedom Organization in Alabama; or (4) black parallel parties operating as black branches of one of the major parties, such as the Mississippi Freedom branch of the Democratic party.[16]

Black Candidate Strategy. One of the best articulations of this position was presented by the Organization of Afro-American Unity in 1964. Stressing the need for racial solidarity, it argued that a primary goal must be to

> organize the Afro-American community block by block to make the community aware of its power and potential; we will start immediately a voter-registration drive to make every unregistered voter in the Afro-American community an independent voter; we propose to support and/or organize political clubs, to run independent candidates for office and to support any Afro-American already in office who answers to and is responsive to the Afro-American community.[17]

Nonelectoral Strategy. Finally, there are those like black studies professor Robert Allen who argue against participating in the electoral process at all. Allen states, "Dabbling in elections on the pretext of 'organizing and educating' is an unnecessary waste of scarce resources. This activity may inflate egos, but it does little to build a mass-based organization."[18] Instead, forms of organized resistance and "direct action" are advocated. These will be discussed in Chapter 10.

Major-Party Support. Ever since Emancipation and the Civil War amendments, the black vote has gone largely to one of the two major parties of the day. For approximately the first 70 years it was the Republicans and for the past 50 years the Democrats in elections for national office.

Although polling data was not generated until quite recently, there are indicators of this early partisan loyalty. In the House of Representatives, for example, all black representatives were Republicans prior to 1932 and have been Democrats since then. Polling, begun in the latter period, has consistently shown that the majority of blacks identify with the Democratic party and side with that party on most prominent political issues.

The Republican Era (1865–1912). It is not difficult to understand why early allegiance went to the party of Lincoln, the Republicans, and not the southern-based and blatantly racist Democrats. Not only had the Republicans led the "good fight" during the Civil War, but they subsequently produced the Civil War amendments, Radical Reconstruction of the South, and the 1866 Civil Rights Act. Yet the honeymoon began to waiver with Rutherford B. Hayes's sellout of Reconstruction in 1876. Soon the southern Republican party actually began to divide along racial lines, culminating in the Lily White Republicans and the Black and Tan Republicans. This split at the state and local levels helped the southern Democrats push through the notorious black codes and Jim Crow laws that would quickly reduce most of the nation's blacks to a degrading and physically perilous "second-class citizenship."

Era of Transition (1912–1936). The Great Migration landed many blacks in large cities accessible by rail. There they were recruited by the local Democratic machines, and their votes could be bartered for small amounts of patronage. At the national level, this new relationship was nearly cemented by President Woodrow Wilson. He had courted black voters, at least in very general language, despite his party's powerful southern wing. Nevertheless, after being elected with the help of a number of defecting black votes, he rather quickly proceeded to eliminate the few federal patronage jobs blacks had attained, and he even took steps to segregate the federal bureaucracy. The Republicans, for their part, were so cavalier about their black support that 1928 presidential candidate Herbert Hoover even endorsed the Lily White faction in the South—helping him do better in that region than any other Republican had up until that time.[19] Despite continued reticence on the part of the Democrats, black loyalty to the national Republican party began to waiver in the 1928 and 1932 presidential elections.

The Democratic Era (1936–present). Although the national Democratic party did not seat a black as even an alternate convention delegate until 1924, was running a presidential candidate (Franklin Delano Roosevelt) who had served in the Wilson administration and openly avoided direct appeals to black voters, and had been deafeningly silent on relevant issues such as fair employment opportunities, the right to vote, and lynching (with southern Democrats actively opposing antilynching legislation), its implementation of a social welfare state seems to have been warmly received in the economically depressed black community. Thus the presidential election of 1936 marks a major watershed of sorts. Even though the electoral transition would not really be complete until 1944[20] and the shift in party identification would take until 1964,[21] the switch from Republican to Democratic voting in national-level elections was nearly revolutionary in 1936.

Under the increasing pressure of a growing civil rights movement, the Democrats made moves that would cement their gain. Besides continuing to press forward with their social welfare agenda, the 1940 Democratic platform contained a very moderate plank endorsing enforcement of the 14th Amendment and nondiscrimination in government service. President Roosevelt created the Fair Employment Practices Commission in 1941. The 1944 party platform contained clear support for enforcement of the 15th Amendment. The 1948 convention adopted a civil rights plank even though that created a serious regional split within the party. President Harry Truman desegregated the military and presented civil rights legislation to the Congress. And then came the civil rights and voting rights acts, Lyndon Johnson's War on Poverty, a host of other Great Society programs, support for busing and affirmative action, a quasi-quota system for guaranteeing black representation at the party's presidential conventions, and the 1989 election of Ron Brown as the first black to head a major political party in U.S. history.

Consequently, blacks now generally cast over 85 percent of their votes for Democratic presidential candidates, and in the process they have come to comprise a full one-quarter of those candidates' electoral constituencies.

In the meantime, the Republicans were sending mixed signals. Sensing an opening in the previously solid Democratic South, the Republicans sought to capitalize on the serious split within the Democratic party over the issue of black rights. For example, President Eisenhower was quite slow in protecting the civil rights movement in the South, and Richard Nixon adopted an overt "southern strategy," with his law-and-order and antibusing positions as well as his unsuccessful nominations of two allegedly racist justices to the U.S. Supreme Court. Nevertheless, the Republicans also created Heritage Groups within the party to reach out to various racial and ethnic constituencies, and this soon led to the development of Republican Black Nationality Clubs. In addition, there was a call for "positive action" to secure more black representation at the 1976 Republican national convention. Yet, moving into the Reagan period, the party's position was essentially that blacks would be better off without special treatment or much of the social welfare state, benefiting along with everyone else from the national economic growth Republicans claimed to be providing.

Having traced those general, national-level trends, however, it should be noted that some definite qualification is in order. After the great national-level switch of 1936, for instance, plenty of black Republican votes were still cast at the state and local levels, against the established Democratic machines in the North and against racist Democratic candidates in the South. At this subnational level, blacks have been very issue oriented, often voting against the individual candidates who seemed to pose the greatest threat to perceived black interests.[22] In addition, the black community has had its share of internal splits; for example, Marcus Garvey appealed to disenchanted lower-income blacks who had not been well received by many of their more established black counterparts upon the migrants' turn-of-the-century arrival in northern cities. Meanwhile, even at the level of presidential elections, there have been some significant divisions in the black vote. In the Democratic era, for example, blacks cast 40 percent of their votes for Republican Dwight Eisenhower in 1956 and 30 percent for Republican candidate Richard Nixon in 1960.

Minor-Party Support. A number of blacks have also moved away from the two major-party organizations altogether. Black experience with third parties, for example, predates the Civil War and spans all four of the minor-party types mentioned earlier. And although electoral victories have been few, this involvement has no doubt provided a number of the less tangible benefits: mobilization, consciousness raising, education, and hope among them.

Multiracial Protest Parties. Three of the best-known examples are the Liberty, Populist, and Progressive parties. Free blacks were an important component of the antislavery Liberty party during the 1840s and 1850s. Blacks were also significant contributors to the Populist party's efforts in the 1890s, although they came to be treated rather shabbily in that allegedly progressive organization as race became a major issue dividing its crucial southern constituency. They were also courted to a limited extent by the reformist Progressive party a couple of decades later, although specific black grievances were essentially avoided.

Multiracial Ideological Parties. From rather early on, the American Communist party made overt appeals to the black community. That was also true, to a lesser degree, of a variety of socialist parties. Historians differ as to reasons, but blacks have never been attracted to such parties in sizable numbers. At the very least, the parties' primary focus on class conflict did not seem to leave enough room for consideration of racism as an independent phenomenon.[23]

Black Political Parties. On a number of occasions, blacks have chosen to step outside predominantly white major and minor parties to form creative political organizations of their own. Independent parties have provided aggregation and articulation of distinctly black perspectives, and parallel black parties have allowed black members of the two major parties to challenge their dominant white factions, especially at the state and local levels. Examples of the former in the 19th century are the Colored Independent party (Pennsylvania) and the Negro Protective party (Ohio). More recent examples have included the Lowndes County Freedom Organization (Alabama), the United Citizens party of South Carolina, and the national Freedom Now party. Recent examples of parallel parties are the Mississippi Freedom Democratic party and the National Democratic party of Alabama.[24]

One final phenomenon requires close scrutiny: the drift of many black voters, particularly young blacks, away from strong partisan attachment altogether.

Black Independents. Available data indicates that the number of black "independents" increased markedly in the 1970s, much as it did in the nation as a whole. Even more specifically, the number of blacks identifying themselves as strong partisans dropped from a peak of nearly 60 percent in 1968 to roughly 40 percent or less thereafter.[25] Hanes Walton estimates that one-third of the black electorate is no longer closely affiliated with either of the two major parties but instead floats back and forth between their candidates, depending on the particular issues and personalities involved.[26] Of greatest significance is the fact that this phenomenon is most apparent among blacks under 30 years of age. In 1986, for example, more than half of all blacks over 30 years of age expressed a "strong" commitment to the Democratic party, while that was true for just one-third of those under 30. In addition, strong partisanship was declining considerably faster in the black community than in the nation as a whole.[27] Thus the black vote may well be increasingly less predictable as time goes on.

Electoral Gains

No white candidate is likely to feel and express, as a black could, the ache and anger of black communities ravaged by joblessness and the snatching away of even those rickety ladders that offered some promise of a way up and out of hopelessness for poor blacks.[28]

Black Elected Officials. Thousands of black Americans presently hold elective office, but achieving that has been a very long battle, with untold black representation lost in the interim. To begin with, poll taxes, literacy tests, racial gerrymandering, outright intimidation, and other tactics deprived blacks of input during some pivotal years. In 1880, for example, blacks held majorities in some 311 counties but were almost completely disenfranchised. By 1970, when basic voting rights were finally being protected, blacks held majorities in only 102 counties.[29] The state of Mississippi, where blacks have comprised more than 40 percent of the population since slavery, did not elect a black member of Congress from the end of Reconstruction until 1986. Statewide malapportionment, prior to the 1962 *Baker v. Carr* decision, deprived black voters of proportional representation for crucial decades in which they had heavy concentrations in large northern cities. In addition, disposable income has almost always been in short supply, forcing many black candidates to run underfunded campaigns.

Nonetheless, most of these obstacles are finally beginning to be overcome. As a result, black elected officials have proliferated. That increase has been most dramatic in the South. Whereas only 72 blacks held elective office there in 1965, for example, that figure had jumped to 2,128 by 1976. Meanwhile, at the state and local levels across the country, no black has yet to be elected to a governorship; nonetheless, a number have served as mayors of large cities, including Atlanta, Baltimore, Birmingham, Chicago, Detroit, Gary, Los Angeles, Newark, New Orleans, Philadelphia, and Washington, D.C. Nationally, there have been more than 15 black members in the House of Representatives since 1972. And even though no black has held the office of president or vice president, blacks have been the nominees of third parties for over a century. Congresswoman Shirley Chisholm was a bona fide candidate for the Democratic nomination in 1972, winning more than 150 delegates to the Democratic national convention. Jesse Jackson broke through a number of the major party barriers. In 1984, he garnered 16 percent of the Democratic primary vote (more than 3 million votes) and gained nearly 400 convention delegates. In 1988, he did far better yet, winning more than 29 percent of the primary vote (nearly 7 million votes) and gaining over 1,000 convention delegates.

The actual gains resulting from these electoral victories are a bit more difficult to calculate. There now exist a Congressional Black Caucus and a Caucus of Black State Legislators, both of which are in a position to press for black causes (see Chapter 8). And although there is little empirical evidence to suggest that major governmental priorities are much different when blacks hold public office, having institutional power over revenue raising, budgets, staffs, and statutes has still made some difference. In terms of tangible rewards at the local level, for example, there have been more black appointments, more governmental contracts extended to black-owned businesses, and fewer reported incidences of police brutality. Intangible gains include more role models, hope, pride, politicization, articulation of black demands, and opportunities to break down white stereotypes.[30] At the very least, having Wilson Goode in the Philadelphia mayor's office once held by Frank Rizzo and seeing Richard Arrington as mayor of the city that previously employed Sheriff Bull Connor have almost certainly increased government sensitivity to black perspectives.

But there have been some serious limitations as well. It is true that there are more than 6,000 black elected officials, but that is still scarcely more than 1 percent of all the elected officials in the country. And even in the seven states most directly covered by the 1965 Voting Rights Act, blacks make up 26 percent of their populations but hold only 6 percent of the elected positions—and less than 2 percent of the elected county spots.[31]

One of the most visible prizes has been winning the office of mayor, but some of the specific limitations faced by black mayors are instructive. The large majority are weak mayors in council-manager forms of government, and approximately one-half represent towns of less than 2,000 people—towns like Cotton Plant, Arkansas; Waterproof, Louisiana; and Mount Bayou, Louisiana.[32] The roughly two dozen black mayors of cities larger than 100,000 people face other limitations. The reform movement has stripped them of most of the patronage their predecessors employed to hold together a governing coalition. Their cities are generally so desperately poor that Paul Friesema has called black control of them a "hollow prize."[33] And a primary reason why most of these black mayors have been able to win is that there are now black majorities or near majorities in most of these cities—primarily because many of the more affluent whites have fled to the suburbs. The fact that they have taken their tax base with them may be even more problematic than the further racial polarization that their flight represents.[34]

White Elected Officials. Contrary to a popular misconception, blacks do not automatically vote for black over white candidates when the choice is available. In the 1967 mayoral race in Philadelphia and the 1984 and 1985 Democratic primaries in New York City, the majority of black voters opted for white candidates over black alternatives. Nor is the black community destined to be indefinitely pleased with the performance of a black representative. The black mayor of West Memphis, Arkansas, for example, lost much of his black base and was replaced by a white man. In the overwhelming majority of electoral situations, black Americans find themselves facing only white choices. It is in this circumstance that the electoral process seems to have proved especially deficient.

Although a minority group, black voters have generally followed the standard prescription for electoral success. They tend to live in strategic areas and to deliver their vote as a bloc. It is generally assumed that the Democratic party requires clear victories in large northern cities and most of the southern states. For the past half century, blacks in these strategic locations have cast their ballots for Democratic candidates, forming the party's most cohesive and identifiable voting bloc. Yet this loyalty has not translated into comparable political rewards. What is more, white Democrats' concern for black problems seems to be declining at a time when national Democratic party reliance on the black vote has never been higher: Blacks now cast some 25 percent of Democratic presidential candidate votes, while white America has given a majority of its votes for the Democratic presidential candidate only once since World War II, in the Democratic landslide election of 1964.

The 1976 presidential election and its aftermath are a classic case in point. Jimmy Carter received 50.1 percent of the popular vote and only 297 electoral votes. He won 47 percent of the white vote and 95 percent of the black vote. In addition, black votes for Carter exceeded his margin of victory in 13 states, with a total of 216 electoral votes. Yet, as his first term expired, only one in three blacks approved of the president's job performance, and not even one in four was satisfied with what he had tried to do for the black community.[35] Part of the reason can be found in limits inherent in the American electoral process (discussed next) and in the American legislative process (discussed in Chapter 8).

A CONSERVATIVE ELECTORAL PROCESS

The American electoral process, as presently structured, is simply incapable of empowering most Americans. Instead, it has evolved into an effective mechanism for helping to conserve the unequal distribution of wealth and power in the society—impeding rather than facilitating fundamental change. We shall touch on several examples of this conservative nature.

The Electoral Process

To begin with, as indicated at the outset of this chapter, there is little opportunity for direct popular rule. Rather, the American electorate is left to pursue national demands through elected representatives. But there are still plenty of impediments to even indirect popular input. The registration and campaign finance procedures discriminate against those in the lower socioeconomic classes. Electoral choices are severely limited. It is difficult for government to respond to the issue preferences expressed at election time, clear as they may be. And a host of major decisions fall beyond the reach of elected officials anyway.

Initiatives. The one exception to the lack of direct democracy is the initiative process at the state and local levels. Citizens can draft their own legislation, and if enough compatriots sign their petition, the issue can be brought to the electorate for a direct vote. In a number of states, the proposal becomes statutory law if approved by a majority of the voters, just as if it had been passed by the state legislature. Nevertheless, the petitioning process normally requires an intimidating amount of time and energy. This option was not available at state and local levels until the turn of the 20th century, and there is no comparable provision at the national level.

Registration Laws. In nearly every state, a citizen must be registered to vote by a specified date, generally a few weeks prior to election day. The exact procedure varies from state to state, but a person must normally register at a government office that is a distance from his or her home and is only open from roughly 8 A.M. until 5 P.M. Monday through Friday—the precise hours when most hourly workers are required to be at their jobs. In addition, some states demand reregistration if the person has not voted in the last four years, and virtually all states require reregistration if one moves to a new election district. The result is that nearly one-third of the electorate (more than 50 million voters) remains unregistered at any point in time, and as many as two out of three claim that they would have voted if they had been registered.[36] The United States is the only Western democracy that requires this much of a registration hurdle, and it clearly discriminates against lower-income people for whom registration center locations and operating hours pose greater burdens.[37]

Campaign Finance. As campaign costs have proliferated in the era of television advertising, large campaign contributors have come to play an ever more critical role. It now costs more than $1 million to run a typical large-city mayoral or statewide campaign and thousands of dollars to run for many lower offices—sums beyond the means of most potential candidates and very difficult to raise in small contributions. Thus wealthy individuals and organizations must often be wooed. As Sheila Collins put it:

> What was not fully appreciated was that by the time blacks entered electoral politics as a significant national voting bloc, the rules of power had changed. It was not the ability to deliver votes to a candidate that counted, but the ability to deliver money.[38]

The Congress, in fact, saw this developing and passed the 1974 Campaign Finance Act in the wake of the Watergate scandal. Among other things, it set limits on the amount of money an individual could give to a particular campaign. Two years later, however, the Supreme Court seriously weakened the act by declaring key parts of it to be violations of First Amendment freedom of expression (*Buckley v. Valeo*). Specifically, the Court disallowed limits on the amount of money one could contribute to one's own campaign and the amount an individual or group could spend independently on a candidate's behalf.

Another glaring loophole was the allowance for Political Action Committees (PACs). Although a single donor can give a maximum of only $1,000 to any particular PAC and each PAC cannot contribute more than $5,000 to any individual candidate, there are no limits on the number of PACs that can form or the number of them to which any person can contribute. As a result, 3,400 PACs gave more than $83 million to congressional candidates in 1982—largely to incumbents, especially conservative Republican incumbents. A mere four years later, the total contribution had grown to $130 million.[39] And although presidential campaigns now are financed primarily out of the federal treasury—with each major-party candidate allowed $40.4 million in 1984—PACs still spent an additional $12 million on behalf of candidates that year (and the Republican party spent $65 million).[40]

By the time all was said and done, major-party candidates spent over $2 billion in 1984, more in 1988, and that does not even include the millions of additional dollars spent on their behalf. Where does all this money come from?

To begin with, people in the upper socioeconomic classes simply have more money to give and know more people who have money. Thus it should come as no surprise that virtually all campaign funds are generated by the owning class.[41] With blacks essentially excluded from those socioeconomic circles, the reality of campaign funding effectively shuts out black America.

Weak Political Parties. After studying the functions of political parties, Walter Burnham concluded that "critical elections" are a dynamic mechanism that helps political systems adapt to fundamental changes in their environment. In the course of these, parties respond by organizing themselves around the new, most polarizing issue in the society. This shift enables them to represent the spectrum of interests generated by the change. For example, the Civil War divided the nation, and the party system responded with the northern Republicans opposing the southern Democrats on ensuing issues such as reconstruction policies. Burnham argues, however, that the American party system failed to respond adequately to the issues and interests that stemmed from the industrial revolution. Instead of capitalist and socialist parties emerging to reflect paramount opposing interests within an industrial economy—as was the case in virtually every multiparty democracy on earth—both major American parties accepted capitalism as a given.[42]

> We don't have a two-party system in this country. We have Demopublicans. It's one party of the corporate class, with two wings—the Democrats and the Republicans. They both say the other can't do the job for the working people, and they're both right.[43]

But even had the parties polarized around the issue of how capital was to be owned and operated, it is doubtful whether the structure of America's parties would have allowed a conversion of these positions into meaningful electoral choices. After a lifetime of studying America's political parties, E. E. Schattschneider concluded that "decentralization of power is by all odds the most important single characteristic of the American major party."[44] How does decentralization affect meaningful electoral input?

Lack of Unity. Under a parliamentary system, a national party's platform has real meaning, for candidates elected under that party's banner will be held to voting the party line. Their allegiance is guaranteed by the fact that they will have been nominated to run by the party's national committee, and thus their loyalties are secured by both the party's screening process and their own desires to run for office again someday. Consequently, the party (or the working coalition of parties) that wins a majority of the legislative seats not only gets to choose the country's chief executive (or prime minister) but can also be counted on to carry out the policies promised in the party platform.

In the United States, by contrast, chief executives and legislatures are elected separately, and there is no guarantee that the executive and both branches of the legislature will be controlled by the same political party. In fact, in only one-third of the governments since 1956 have the president and both houses of Congress been of the same party. Approximately 60 percent of state governments likewise currently fall under mixed-party control.

Beyond that, each of the two major parties is composed of a national organization, 50 state branches, and thousands of local ones—many of which have little in common other than name. This is true because the national committee is weak, without any significant sanctions for disciplining either state and local organizations or the candidates who often independently seek their nominations. Even the party's presidential candidate has been chosen in a series of statewide primaries and caucuses, with the national party normally convening simply to ratify that choice. Thus the national party platform is not binding in any way on candidates elected under the party label.

Unsurprisingly, party unity in the halls of the nation's legislatures is limited, for the elected representatives rarely owe anything to a party organization. Using 90 percent loyalty as a standard for determining party voting cohesiveness on any particular bill, Julius Turner found that from 1921 to 1948, only 17 percent of the roll calls in the U.S. House of Representatives met that criterion, and the figure declined further thereafter.[45]

In the absence of party discipline, the positions taken by the candidates of the two major parties overlap considerably. And in the Congress, some Republicans vote more liberally than some members of the generally more liberal Democratic party, and some Democrats vote more conservatively than members of the generally more conservative Republican party. Thus party label is not a reliable indicator of a politician's policy learnings and is therefore not reliable as a voting cue.

Political parties appear to be losing their ability to influence voter choices. Nationwide, for example, the proportion of self-identifying independents rose from less than 10 percent of registered voters in the 1920s to more than one in three voters by the 1970s and 1980s. Also, a sizable number of people have begun to split their ticket, meaning that they vote for members of different parties on the same ballot.[46]

Democratic Implications. Party weakness reduces the ability of elected officials to overcome some of the impeding checks and balances established by the Founding Fathers. Without party discipline, it becomes extremely difficult for hundreds of independently elected respresentatives to pass and implement comprehensive legislation through the policymaking maze (described at length in Chapter 8). That is no doubt why a number of the more conservative Founding Fathers so adamantly opposed the formation of political parties.[47]

The absence of meaningful party platforms and the party discipline necessary to enforce them contributes to a lack of accountability. Candidates can and do say one thing in the campaign and do another once in office.[48] This would be significantly less likely if candidates were more effectively bound to a national party platform.

Political parties stand to serve four primary functions: (1) to educate voters about policy matters, (2) to lead voters toward the policies the party has formulated, (3) to organize elections, and (4) to organize government after the elections. As it turns out, America's weak parties perform only half of these very well. The major parties generally do a respectable job of conducting elections and providing a structure whereby subsequent legislatures can choose their leaders and committees. They are far less successful in the other two areas. Campaigns are increasingly being left to hired campaign consultants, the most sophisticated of whom take continuous tracking polls to determine what the voter wants to hear at any point in time. The candidate then tailors his or her image accordingly. Then polls are used to determine whether the candidate's messages are satisfying those public wishes, however uninformed. Little leadership or education is likely to come from that process.

The vapidity of contemporary media-oriented campaigns will be discussed further in Chapter 9, as will the growth of mass media as an independent political force in its own right. One other agent has grown in political strength as parties have slipped even further into insignificance. That agent is the interest group.

Interest groups tend to fill the void left by declining political parties. The United States, with the weakest political parties among the various democracies, has the broadest array of active interest groups. That development poses a serious problem. It leaves individual representatives more vulnerable to lobbying pressure than in a stronger party system. Therefore, almost every vote must be carefully cast so as to avoid offending a resource-rich special-interest group.

Even if the United States had a strong-party parliamentary system, another potent arrangement would continue to make it difficult for the electoral process to provide viable alternatives that challenge the underlying socioeconomic structure. That arrangement is the two-party system.

The Two-Party System. As Sheila Collins puts it, "One of the most carefully guarded preserves of United States class rule [is] the two-party system."[49]

Figure 7-1 is designed to help clarify the inherently conservative logic of a two-party system. This is true in particular because the two major parties are free to take their more ideologically extreme supporters for granted and do battle over the moderates in the middle. Those at the ideological extremes really have no place else to go if they wish to vote for a viable candidate, and for a major party to move too far in order to appease them is to risk abandoning the center to the other party. Thus party platforms and policies are moderated to appeal to the middle and rarely

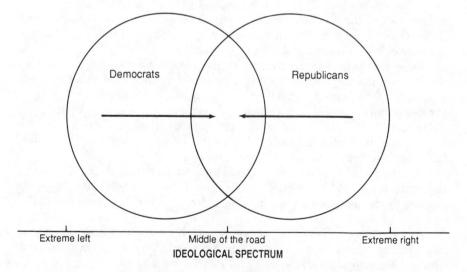

Figure 7.1. The Conservative Two-Party System

provide alternatives sharply different from the status quo.[50] The Democratic party, for example, requires a minimum of 15 percent showing in its primaries in order to gain any convention delegates. In the process, it can avoid the potential embarrassment of smaller groups even raising controversial issues at the televised national convention.

From the voters' perspective, this leaves many of them voting against the more offensive of two moderates rather than having the chance to vote for a viable candidate who is strongly advocating positions in line with the voters' own predilections. The 1980 presidential election between Ronald Reagan and Jimmy Carter was a classic case in point. The campaign came to revolve around which social programs to cut and which defense programs to increase. Neither candidate suggested fundamental alterations in either the existing welfare or warfare states. Polls found more than half the voters unable to distinguish any "important differences" between the candidates, less than one-third perceiving any such differences between the parties, and more than one-third of the Reagan voters claiming to have voted against Carter rather than for Reagan.[51]

So why has a multiparty system not developed? The answer cannot be found in the absence of powerful cleavages in the society. No other Western nation has anywhere near as many interest groups or a history of such violence surrounding interest clashes in areas such as labor and race relations. More significant are the following seven factors.

Single-Member Districts. Under this arrangement, a single representative is chosen from each election district. Finishing first is all that counts; thus voting for anyone other than one of the two most viable candidates is essentially wasting one's vote (the electoral college system for electing the president is a classic example of this winner-take-all arrangement). And the two most viable candidates are almost invariably those put forward by the two major parties.

In a multimember district where public officials are selected by proportional representation, there is much more incentive for third-party voting. Although there are numerous forms of proportional voting, a general example should still be instructive. If the district is to choose three members of Congress, for example, the top three vote getters would then go to the House of Representatives, with a third-place finish just as good as a first. The voter is less likely to be wasting a vote by casting it for a third-party candidate, as that person will not need nearly as many votes to acquire a seat. If such a system had been in place in northern Mississippi, for instance, and if the white votes were split at all, black voters could have concentrated their votes on a single black candidate and would most likely have had a black representative well before 1986.

In fact, there have been a few experiments with proportional representation at the local level in the United States. In the case of New York City, however, it was dropped shortly after two Communists were elected to the city council in 1947.

Plurality Elections. Not only is just one person chosen from each district in most cases, but that person normally need only have a plurality of the votes. In other words, the person who gets the most votes wins, even if he or she does not get an electoral majority. Once again, this encourages people to concentrate their attention on the top two candidates, as a second- or third-place finish is meaningless. Were a majority to be required, as it sometimes is in nonpartisan general elections at the local level, finishing other than first can still land one in a run-off election between the top finishers. In such a case, there would be more incentive for the voter to consider third-party candidates.

Getting on the Ballot. Besides the disincentives to vote for third-party candidates when they appear on the ballot, it is often quite difficult for them even to get on the ballot in the first place. Most states require some sort of petitioning process, although some actually waive this requirement if a party received a certain percentage of the vote in the previous election—obviously favoring the two major parties. Otherwise, the petitioning process can be difficult. For statewide office, California recently required 125,000 signatures, Pennsylvania demanded 36,000 collected within a three-week period, Arizona required more than 7,000 in 10 days, New York insisted on 20,000 spread over more than half of the congressional districts, and so on. In addition, the signee often must not have signed any other petition or voted in another party's primary, and some states throw out an entire petition if it has even one illegal name on it.

The results? In 1968, George Wallace made one of the best third-party showings for president in the history of the United States. Yet he had been able to get his name on the ballots of only a little over half the states. By the 1980 presidential election, however, independent John Anderson and Libertarian Ed Clark mounted successful court challenges against many of the most restrictive of these state election laws, and each was finally able to have his name on all 50 state ballots. Nevertheless, the *New York Times* estimated that it still took 1.2 million signatures and $750,000 to accomplish that feat.[52]

Public Financing Formulas. As mentioned earlier, the 1974 Campaign Finance Act provided for public financing of presidential campaigns. In 1988, each of the two major party candidates received $46.1 million of taxpayers' money with which to fund his campaign. A third-party candidate can qualify for public monies only after gaining at least 5 percent of the national vote. In 1980, for example, John Anderson polled 7 percent and became the only third-party candidate ever to qualify, receiving roughly $4 million after the election.

Equal Time on the Airwaves. The 1934 Communications Act specifies that stations that provide free airtime to one candidate must provide "equal time" to opponents. In practice, however, that has seldom applied to third-party challengers. Most significantly, that provision can be legally waived for interviews, documentaries, coverage in newscasts, and even candidate debates. In 1980, for example, John Anderson was excluded from the Carter-Reagan debates on national television. And, beyond the formats just mentioned, television and radio stations simply are not likely to be extending free airtime to any candidate. Thus financially strapped third parties must purchase advertising time if they wish to receive any significant media exposure at all.

Police Harassment. As the Watergate hearings revealed, federal law enforcement agents had been using legally dubious procedures to monitor the activities of certain "suspicious" third parties, mostly socialists. Phones were tapped, offices were broken into, mail was read, and so on.[53] Of course, this was nothing new in American history. Socialist parties have mounted about the only serious nationwide threat to two-party hegemony. In 1918, Socialists held 1,200 offices in 340 cities, including 79 mayors in 24 states, 32 state legislators, and one member of Congress. Shortly thereafter, the police raids began. Meetings were disrupted, and leaders were deported or jailed, often on trumped-up charges.[54]

Miscellaneous Obstructions. There are other impediments to serious third-party challenges. The United States Postal Service has quit providing reduced-rate postage to third parties. In their long-standing positions of domination, representatives of the two parties have continually been able to gerrymander voting districts to help secure their own seats. The ratings-conscious mass media have definite inclinations to reduce all campaigns to a two-person "horse race" of sorts; third-party candidates are simply ignored for the most part.

For all these reasons, American third parties have been inconsequential—especially by international comparison. At the national level, third-party representatives in Congress have been extremely rare, and only once did a minor party presidential candidate receive more than one vote in four, when defecting Republican and former president Theodore Roosevelt polled 27.4 percent of the popular vote.

Governmental Limitations. Governmental leeway is being seriously circumvented by the economic realities of the postindustrial economy. Increasingly desperate for capital investment, government must contour public policy ever more closely to the needs of those who own highly mobile corporate capital. Therefore, the two major parties can be expected to become even more conservative in their overall policy orientations.

Yet in an economic system like the one in the United States, the large majority of decisions that affect people's lives are made in the private sector anyway, and there is no reason to expect either of the two dominant parties to challenge that. As Robert Allen put it:

> Political power in America is dependent upon those who control valued resources and critical institutions, not vice versa. And those who have this power cannot be voted out of their positions by the public at large, because the base of their power lies outside the formal political sphere. Their base of power lies in the corporations and the large public institutions which are interdependent, but largely removed from the sway of public pressure.[55]

Electoral Aftermath

Whether they are black or white, the ability to cast a vote every four years to help determine which millionaire will represent them does not bring poor people flocking to the polls. Since their votes are ineffective, their real political power is not increased by voting, and consequently their motivation to continue voting is lowered still further.[56]

Is C. T. Vivian, quoted here, correct about the nature of the electoral choices available? To what degree has the American electorate demonstrated disinclination to participate in this very conservative electoral process? And how does this arrangement function to preserve the political-economic status quo?

Elite Candidates. The large majority of America's public officials and candidates for those positions tend to be wealthy middle-aged white Anglo-Saxon Protestant males.[57] Richard Hamilton, among others, has found that because they live, work, and play separately:

> The white Protestant upper-middle class (and also the equivalent upper class) form an "isolated mass." They are separated and cut off from the rest of the society and as a result have their own separate consciousness and understandings about what is going on elsewhere in the society.[58]

This raises questions as to whether these men can effectively represent many of the interests of non-elites. For example, why suppose that they can be sensitive to the psychological devastation a breadwinner feels when even temporarily unemployed? Why expect them to feel concern for the plight of junkies or prison inmates when such people are so far removed from their daily lives? Why be surprised when they put abstract principles such as "maintaining the international balance of power" ahead of concern for tenants' rights to heat and hot water 24 hours a day, cockroach extermination, and the like?

Turnout Decline. Table 7.1 shows that the turnout rate for Americans in general closely parallels the turnout in the black community. Most Americans do not vote, even in national elections. Beyond that, more than two-thirds do not belong to any organization that takes stands on political issues, and only a very small minority contributes in any way to the campaign process.[59] It is also a fact that even fewer

TABLE 7.1 ELECTORAL TURNOUT IN NATIONAL ELECTION YEARS, 1960–1988 (percentage of eligible voters)

Presidential Years		Off-Year Elections	
1960	63	1962	46
1964	62	1966	45
1968	61	1970	44
1972	56	1974	36
1976	54	1978	37
1980	52	1982	41
1984	52	1986	39
1988	50		

Source: U.S. Department of Commerce, Bureau of the Census. Statistical Abstracts of the United States (Washington, D.C.: GPO).

TABLE 7.2 INTERNATIONAL ELECTORAL TURNOUT, 1978 (percentage of eligible voters)

Malta	94.4	Norway	82.8
Australia	92.6	New Zealand	82.7
Austria	91.9	Israel	78.2
Sweden	91.4	Ireland	75.7
Italy	90.8	Canada	74.9
Iceland	90.3	Great Britain	72.8
West Germany	89.9	Japan	72.6
Belgium	88.3	India	60.5
Denmark	88.2	United States (presidential)	54.4
Netherlands	87.5	Switzerland	51.7
France	83.5	United States (midterm)	37.0

Source: The Economist (December 1978).

tend to turn out for state and local balloting. In addition, whereas presidential voting turnout exceeded 60 percent of the eligible voters in all but the period immediately following the extension of women's suffrage (doubling the electorate) and the period of disruption during World War II, such participation has been decreasing rather markedly since the early 1960s and now hovers around 50 percent.

It can be seen from Table 7.2 that this level of participation is quite low in relation to representative democracies around the world. As alluded to before, the United States has one of the lowest levels of electoral involvement on earth.

Just who are the tens of millions of nonvoters, and why are they not participating? Increasingly less is learned by looking for indications in their demographic characteristics. Voting studies have demonstrated that the nonparticipant is more likely to be under 25 years of age, to be from the South, and to have a low level of education and income;[60] but as the number of nonvoters increases to the point of becoming a majority, the nonvoting population begins to look demographically similar to the population as a whole.[61] Of more help are direct surveys. Arthur Hadley found a relatively common response among nonvoters. They would consider voting if there were "better candidates; someone who tells the truth; someone you can trust."[62] Such mistrust and alienation have soared since the 1960s, accompanied by a precipitous decline in people's regard for the two major political parties.[63] (These problems are discussed at length in Chapter 10.) That dissatisfaction is also reflected in political "tune-out."

As an indication of their tuning out politics, most Americans do not know which party controls the Congress and cannot name their representative in the House of Representatives, let alone recall that person's party affiliation. As a matter of fact, a majority do not even know that they have two senators, let alone know their names and parties. Thus it should not be surprising that less than 20 percent can identify how their senator or representative voted on any piece of legislation.[64]

Two researchers conclude:

Most candidates in most elections are unknown quantities for the average voter. Typically, voters will be aware of the candidate's party affiliation and whether or not he is an incumbent, but not much more. Furthermore, [even] these elements of information may come to the attention of the voter only if they are indicated on the ballot.[65]

As a consequence, competition for national office has diminished, and the reelection of incumbents is virtually assured.

Less Competition. In 1956, for instance, only 41 percent of the members of the House of Representatives had won their seats by gaining 60 percent or more of the vote in their districts. By 1986, more than three out of every four representatives had won by such a margin. Or, to look at it another way, consider the number of races that were generally classified as "competitive—meaning that the winner won by no more than 55 percent of the vote. In 1936, about one-third of the races fit that classification. By 1984 and 1986, the figure had declined to less than one in eight House contests.[66]

Secure Incumbents. Not only are the races becoming less competitive, but it is often the same people who are running away with these contests election year after election year. For example, 25 incumbent presidents have sought reelection, and nearly three-quarters of them have been successful. No sitting president has been denied his party's renomination since the direct primary was added in 1912. On Capitol Hill, members of the U.S. House of Representatives have been successful in 90 to 98 percent of their reelection bids, exceeding 98 percent in 1986 and 1988. In the Senate, more than 80 percent have been just as successful. And on the state and local level, it appears to be more of the same. In New York City, for example, 95 percent of state senate, 92 percent of state assembly, and 93 percent of city council incumbents were successful when challenged in their bids for reelection.[67]

Incumbents are able to secure their positions in part by the process of gerrymandering. As the dominant officeholders, they are normally in a position to have significant input in the decisions as to where to draw the district lines, and they tend to draw them in ways that enhance their own possibilities of reelection.[68] Such secure seats explain in large measure why nearly 90 percent of all PAC money goes to incumbents.[69]

Systemic Preservation. In the end, instead of being ruled by the many, America finds itself ruled by the few. Elections do not serve to guarantee that the elected politicians will know and represent the interests of all the people. Instead, a minority of poorly informed voters turns out to choose between wealthy white men who run with the help of large campaign contributors and relatively meaningless party labels. These men then take capitalism as a given and are predisposed toward policies that help preserve present economic arrangements.

Yet it becomes more than a matter of insensitivity to popular needs. The electoral process itself, at least for those who participate in it, also helps to deflect pressure to change the socioeconomic structure described in Chapters 3–5. Frustrations are channeled through nonthreatening exercises in democratic futility. Limited political energies are exhausted. Finally, as Murray Edelman puts it, elections are "rituals of symbolic reassurance which serve to quiet resentments and doubts about particular political acts" and to "reaffirm belief in the fundamental rationality and democratic character of the system."[70]

OPTIONS FOR BLACK AMERICA

The Voting Rights Act reflects . . . America's "instrumentalist bias," its preoccupation with the formal, outward trappings of democratic government, . . . and its neglect of the substantive underpinnings of real democracy.[71]

If the American electoral process is to be converted into a mechanism whereby black citizens can have meaningful input into the political decisions that affect their lives, there is a definite need to accomplish and then move beyond what Lester Salamon has referred to as "instrumentalist" solutions. As with the judicial process, structural changes must also be pursued if and when the moment of political power presents itself. Overall, then, a variety of impediments must be cleared from the path of authentic one-person, one-vote democratic input. In addition, substantive choices must be provided by removing other barriers.

Toward Equal Input

Increasing Voter Turnout. To begin with, a variety of alternatives have been suggested for increasing participation, some of which have proved successful where they have been tried. These range from making the registration and voting procedures more flexible to automatic registration and compulsory voting.

Approximately 3 in 10 eligible voters are currently not registered, and political scientists Raymond Wolfinger and Steven Rosenstone have estimated that at least one-third of those unregistered individuals could be added to the rolls by simply making all states' registration laws as liberal as those in the most permissive state.[72] Examples of such permissiveness include presenting a registration application to every high school senior, registration by mail, and election-day registration at the polls.

Alan Cranston and others in the U.S. Senate have introduced a bill that would require states to allow registration by mail, election-day registration, and registration at government offices directly serving the public. The more extreme position is to call for automatically registering people when they attain the age of eligibility, as is done in all the other Western democracies.

But even if one can register at a variety of places—at the Board of Elections, a county fair, or at home during a registration drive—on virtually any day of the year, one must vote at a specific place, on a specific day, during a limited number of hours. There is the option of an absentee ballot, but that normally requires thinking of the election in advance, picking up the ballot at a single location, and having the completed ballot notarized before mailing it. Proposals for change range from making voting hours more flexible (say, 6 A.M. to 7 P.M. over a five-day period) to not drawing jurists from the list of registered voters (a practice that seems to intimidate some potential registrants) to the creation of either tax incentives to encourage voting or fines to discourage nonparticipation. Even the most extreme of these suggestions have been administered successfully in a number of democracies.

National Initiatives. Once enfranchised, the general public obviously cannot be expected to study and vote on every issue that faces all three basic levels of government. The nation has simply become too large and complex for the town-meeting principle to apply much anymore. Nevertheless, there are still individual issues that could well be decided by the electorate as a whole. Initiatives have been used at the state and local levels for decades, without the dire consequences that some theorists fear must accompany mass decision making.[73] As a matter of fact, it is hard to argue that even the most controversial of successful public initiatives, such as Proposition 13 in California, is any more bizarre than some of the legislation that elected representatives have concocted over the years, such as the internment of Japanese Americans during World War II.

Since the mid-1970s, a number of national initiative proposals have been considered on Capitol Hill. In 1977, for example, Senator James Abourezk proposed to allow a national initiative if the corresponding petitions were signed by at least 3 percent of the number of voters that had voted in the previous presidential election—2 to 3 million signees by recent standards. The signatures would have to be obtained in at least 10 different states, and three issue areas would be excluded from consideration by this method: constitutional amendments, declarations of war, and calling out federal troops.

A decade later, Senator Mark Hatfield introduced virtually the same legislation, arguing that a national initiative option would

> be an exercise of the sovereign power of the American people to govern themselves . . . (provide) a concrete means for citizens' participation in the policymaking function of our Government . . . lessen the sense of alienation from their Government felt by millions of Americans . . . enhance the accountability of Government . . . [and] produce an open, educational debate on issues which otherwise might have been inadequately addressed.[74]

Community Control. A variety of proposals emerged in the 1960s suggesting that more political decisions directly affecting neighborhoods needed to be made at the neighborhood level. For example, residents in the affected neighborhoods could be authorized to hire and fire certain police officers and teachers and to award certain public contracts.[75]

Deprivatizing Decisions. Corporate owners and managers have always made major decisions that had implications not only for large numbers of their own workers but for their surrounding communities as well. Decisions to move a production operation or have more of the work done elsewhere and shipped back for final assembly ("contracting out") are two of the best known of such judgments. To date, almost all of these have been seen to fall outside the purview of democratic control, and that needs to change—either through more public control of corporate decisions or more community input by way of local workers owning the corporations in the first place.

In the interest of public control, Oregon's Employment Stability Act, proposed in 1981, would have required departing businesses with more than 50 employees to (1) provide one year's notice even before any significant layoffs could occur, (2) compensate an abandoned community by paying 85 percent of any "adjustment costs," (3) pay for the relocation of all workers, (4) pay employee benefits for a full year after closing, and (5) give the Oregon Bureau of Labor and Industry the first option to buy the abandoned business. Similar legislation has been proposed in nearly two dozen states, and congressmen Perry Bullard, William Ford, Donald Riegle, and Peter Kostmayer and senators Howard Metzenbaum and Harrison Williams introduced national variants. Meanwhile, in 1988, the federal government did succeed in passing a bill that requires businesses employing more than 100 people to give 60 days' notice to their employees before closing.[76]

Beyond public input into the decisions of large companies whose stock is held by the small owning class, there is also the alternative of broadening ownership to include far more residents of the local community. In 1983, for example, 10,000 steelworkers in Weirton, West Virginia, spent nearly $200 million to buy the failing steel plant where they worked. That move succeeded, but near Pittsburgh, local government has been pressured to exercise eminent domain so that steel-workers could buy up an abandoned plant from a resistant company.[77] Far more sweeping is a proposal recently considered in Sweden. It would tax individual income and corporate profit in order to establish a fund that labor unions could use to buy up the nation's corporate stock—a gradual approach to socialism.

Election Rules. Section 5 of the 1965 Voting Rights Act needs to be extended, not phased out. Every new election law in the country should be precleared to guarantee that it will not result in racial discrimination. At the very least, this could help put an end to racial gerrymandering. Courts have recently been requiring a showing of "discriminatory intent" when the lines were drawn before they will strike such lines as illegal. Preclearance, by contrast, would shift the burden of proof to those drawing the lines. They would have to prove that discrimination would not result.[78]

Another area for reform is the parties' nomination procedures. Short of centralizing the entire process, certain changes would improve representation in the present procedure. The Democratic party needs to abandon its "15 percent rule," which requires a candidate to get at least 15 percent of a state's primary votes in order to be awarded any convention delegates. Elimination of that rule would give fairer representation to citizens voting for a less dominant candidate. In addition, both parties should be encouraged to extend, not narrow, their affirmative action efforts. Not only should there be race and sex quotas for delegations to the national nominating conventions, but there should be class quotas as well. More people from the middle, working, and lower classes need to participate directly in whatever decisions occur, and the national parties should develop a formula that would allow them to use party funds to subsidize the convention expenses of those who need such assistance.

Campaign Financing. Private money needs to be as far removed from the electoral process as possible. People with large personal fortunes should not have added influence over elections or elected officials by means of campaign contributions. To accomplish this, the nation needs to work toward full public financing of all political campaigns. A more equitable version of the existing presidential model could be adopted at all levels. In addition, the cost could be reduced by requiring radio and television stations to provide a set amount of free airtime to all candidates, with no purchases of additional time allowed. That practice already exists to a degree in countries as diverse as Great Britain and Japan. If current representatives remain resistant to providing such funds to their challengers, a constitutional amendment may be in order, requiring public financing as a necessary extension of the right to vote.

A constitutional amendment also apparently will be necessary to reverse the U.S. Supreme Court's ruling of 1976. Once public financing is in place, candidates must not be free to spend their own fortunes in their campaigns, even if they would rather do that than accept public financing. In addition, there should be no private spending on a candidate's behalf. If the Court feels that the First Amendment presently precludes such a rule, democracy would seem to require that the First Amendment be altered to allow for this change.

Toward Real Choices

Multiparty System. Once voter input becomes more equalized, a viable multiparty system seems essential if real choices are to be available. To achieve that will require serious alterations in the various rules that presently reinforce the inherently conservative two-party arrangement. For example, multimember districts are needed in which representatives are chosen by proportional representation. Lenient national standards should govern the petitioning process, so that small parties can more easily find their way onto general election ballots. The Federal Election Commission must be reconstituted to include minor-party representatives, and this newly constituted body must find a formula for public financing of campaigns that funds all established parties in the same way that the two major parties are presently funded. In addition, the equal-time provision must be rewritten to guarantee that all parties certified by the FEC receive their fair share of free time on the airwaves.

Stronger Political Parties. Besides opening the door to a larger number of political parties, those parties must be strong enough to lead, educate, and govern once they come through that door. If they are to be expected to propose meaningful platforms and execute those policies if elected, existing rules and practices must be altered. Most important, the nation needs to move toward a parliamentary system. Party nominees should be chosen by party members in caucus settings, not by the more ephemeral primary process. In addition, this caucus system must be centralized enough so that each party speaks with one voice across the various states and disloyal elected officials can be summarily denied nomination the next time around. Public financing and television airtime should be channeled through the party organizations, not given directly to candidates. Finally, top administrators should be chosen from the ranks of the elected legislatures. Both this last proposal and the strengthening of party control over representatives elected under party banners would go a long way toward overcoming the almost unbelievable American "legislative maze" discussed next.

NOTES

1. Ralphe Bunche in Dewey Grantham (ed.), *The Political Status of the Negro in the Age of FDR* (Chicago: University of Chicago Press, 1973), p. 88.
2. Joseph Schumpeter, *Capitalism, Socialism, and Democracy* (New York: Harper & Row, 1950), pp. 273–283.
3. Chicago Tribune Staff, *The American Millstone: An Examination of the Nation's Permanent Underclass* (Chicago: Contemporary Books, 1986), pp. 34–35.
4. Staughton Lynd, "Slavery and the Founding Fathers," in Melvin Drimmer (ed.), *Black History: A Reappraisal* (Garden City, N.Y.: Anchor/Doubleday, 1969). Also see Hanes Walton, Jr., *Black Political Parties* (New York: Free Press, 1972), pp. 20–23.
5. Harold Gosnell, *Machine Politics: Chicago Model* (Chicago: University of Chicago Press, 1934, 1968); James Q. Wilson, *Negro Politics* (New York: Free Press, 1965).
6. See Sidney Verba and Norman Nie, *Participation in America* (New York: Harper & Row, 1972), pp. 153–154. Also see Johnnie Daniel, "Changes in Negro Political Mobilization and Its Relationship to Community Socioeconomic Structure," *Journal of Social and Behavioral Sciences* (Fall 1969); Johnnie Daniel, "Negro Political Behavior and Community Political and Socioeconomic Structural Factors," *Social Forces* (March 1968); Frederick Wirt, *Politics of Southern Equality* (Hawthorne, N.Y.: Aldine, 1970).
7. Hanes Walton, Jr., *Invisible Politics: Black Political Behavior* (Albany, N.Y.: State University of New York Press, 1985), pp. 108–109.
8. It is important to note that the data on the causes of black political behavior is severely limited. As Hanes Walton, Jr., so aptly points out, nearly all that is known has been drawn from national samples of fewer than 400 blacks, even though a sample of 1,500 is normally required in order to reduce the sampling error to 3 percent. The black population was not systematically sampled as a separate entity but simply as one of the many facets of the American electorate. That significant limitation must be kept in mind when reviewing explanations in the text. See Walton, *Invisible Politics*, pp. 78–82.
9. See Lester Salamon and Stephen Van Evera, "Fear, Apathy, and Discrimination," *American Political Science Review* (December 1973), pp. 1288–1306; Douglas St. Angelo and Paul Puryear, "Fear, Apathy, and Other Dimensions of Black Voting," in Michael Preston et al., *The New Black Politics* (White Plains, N.Y.: Longman, 1982); Charles V. Hamilton, *The Bench and the Ballot: Southern Federal Judges and Black Votes* (New York: Oxford University Press, 1973), chap. 8.
10. For example, see Theodore Lowi's Preface to the Second Edition of Gosnell, *Machine Politics*.
11. Walton, *Invisible Politics*, chap. 5; Verba and Nie, *Participation in America*, p. 157.
12. Ibid.; St. Angelo and Puryear, "Fear, Apathy, and Other Dimensions."
13. *Washington Post*, March 6, 1983, p. A2; also see *New York Times*, November 16, 1987.
14. Chuck Stone, *Black Political Power in America* (Indianapolis: Bobbs-Merrill, 1964); quoted in *New York Times*, July 23, 1979.
15. Quoted in Robert Allen, *Black Awakening in Capitalist America: An Analytical History* (Garden City, N.Y.: Anchor/Doubleday, 1969), p. 143.
16. A rationale for the latter two strategies can be found in Stokely Carmichael and Charles V. Hamilton, *Black Power* (New York: Random House, 1967), chaps. 4–5.
17. Quoted in George Breitman (ed.), *The Last Year of Malcolm X* (New York: Merit, 1967), p. 109.
18. Allen, *Black Awakening*, p. 273.

19. See Paul Lewinsohn, *Race, Class, and Party* (New York: Grosset & Dunlap, 1965), pp. 173–174.

20. Following the switch that occurred from 1936 to 1944, blacks could normally be counted on to cast at least 80 to 90 percent of their votes for the Democratic presidential candidate, a nearly complete reversal of what could be found prior to 1936.

21. Democratic party registration and identification jumped abruptly from roughly 50 percent prior to 1964 to more than three-quarters of all black partisans thereafter. A sizable number of black independents did appear in the 1970s and 1980s, however, and they will be discussed later in this chapter.

22. See Walton, *Invisible Politics*, pp. 140–146.

23. See Wilson Record, *Race and Radicalism* (Ithaca, N.Y.: Cornell University Press, 1964); Wilson Record, *The Negro and the Communist Party* (New York: Atheneum, 1971); Henry Williams, *Black Response to the American Left, 1917–1920* (Princeton, N.J.: Princeton University Press, 1973); Harold Cruse, "Revolutionary Nationalism and the Afro-American," *Studies on the Left* (1962).

24. See Walton, *Black Political Parties*.

25. Everett Carll Ladd, *Transformations of the American Party System* (New York: Norton, 1978); Warren Miller et al., *American National Election Studies Data Sourcebook, 1952–1978* (Ann Arbor, Mich.: ICPSR, 1979).

26. Walton, *Invisible Politics*, pp. 120–124. Other important analyses of the contemporary black electorate include Rod Bush (ed.), *The New Black Vote* (San Francisco: Synthesis Publications, 1984); James Jennings and Melvin King, *From Access to Power: Black Politics in Boston* (Cambridge, Mass.: Schenkman, 1986).

27. Gallup/Joint Center for Policy Studies poll, Summer 1986, reported in the *Memphis Commercial Appeal*, August 5, 1987, p. A9. Also see *New York Times*, October 27, 1988.

28. M. Carl Holman, president of the National Urban Coalition, quoted in *New York Times*, April 20, 1983.

29. Walton, *Invisible Politics*, p. 83.

30. See Leonard Cole, *Blacks in Power* (Princeton, N.J.: Princeton University Press, 1976); William Keech, *The Impact of Negro Voting* (Chicago: Rand McNally, 1968); Sharon Watson, "Do Mayors Matter?" paper presented at the annual meeting of the American Political Science Association, Washington, D.C., August 1980; Edmund Keller, "The Impact of Black Mayors on Urban Policy," *Annals of the American Academy of Political and Social Science* (September 1978).

31. ABC-TV, *Nightline*, January 15, 1986.

32. For example, see Sheila Collins, *The Rainbow Challenge: The Jackson Campaign and the Future of American Politics*, (New York: Monthly Review Press, 1986), p. 90.

33. Paul Friesema, "Black Control of Central Cities: The Hollow Prize," *Journal of the American Institute of Planners* (March 1969).

34. For example, there are black majorities in Atlanta, Baltimore, Birmingham, Camden, Detroit, Gary, Newark, New Orleans, Oakland, Richmond, and Washington, D.C. There are near majorities in cities like Chicago, Cleveland, Hartford, Memphis, Philadelphia, and St. Louis.

35. See Marcus Pohlmann, *Political Power in the Postindustrial City* (Millwood, N.Y.: Associated Faculties Press, 1986), pp. 128–129; *New York Times*, January 18, 1980; March 28, 1978. For a more general discussion of this subject, see George Sinkler, *The Racial Attitudes of American Presidents* (Garden City, N.Y.: Doubleday, 1972).

36. New York Times/CBS poll, 1976. Also see Raymond Wolfinger and Steven Rosenstone, "The Effect of Registration Laws on Voter Turnout," *American Political Science Review* (March 1978).

37. For example, see Benjamin Ginsberg, *The Consequences of Consent* (Reading, Mass.: Addison-Wesley, 1982), pp. 80–87.

38. Collins, *Rainbow Challenge*, p. 89.
39. Maxwell Glen, "Republicans and Democrats Battling to Raise Big Bucks for Vote Drives," *National Journal* (September 1, 1984), p. 1618; Thomas Edsall, *The New Politics of Inequality* (New York: Norton, 1984); *Public Citizen* (May-June 1988), p. 14.
40. Elizabeth Drew, *Politics and Money* (New York: Macmillan, 1983), p. 107.
41. See David Adamany, "Money, Politics, and Democracy: A Review Essay," *American Political Science Review* (March 1977), p. 291; Edsall, *New Politics of Inequality*.
42. Walter Burnham, *Critical Elections and the Mainsprings of American Politics* (New York: Norton, 1970).
43. William Winpinsinger, president of the International Association of Machinists, *Guardian* (Fall 1981).
44. E. E. Schattschneider, *Party Government* (New York: Holt, Rinehart and Winston, 1942), p. 129.
45. Julius Turner, *Party and Constituency: Pressures on Congress* (Baltimore: Johns Hopkins Press, 1970), pp. 16–17.
46. Walter Burnham, "American Politics in the 1970s: Beyond Party?" in W. N. Chambers and Walter Burnham (eds.), *The American Party System* (New York: Oxford University Press, 1975). Also see Arthur King (ed.), *The New American Political System* (Washington, D.C.: American Enterprise Institute, 1979), pp. 390–392; Burnham, *Critical Elections;* Walter De Vries and Lance Tarrance, *The Ticket-splitter* (Grand Rapids, Mich.: Eerdmans, 1972); David Re Pass, "Issue Salience and Voter Choice," *American Political Science Review* (June 1971).
47. See Richard Hofstadter, *The Idea of a Party System* (Berkeley: University of California Press, 1969); Henry Jones Ford, *The Rise and Growth of American Politics* (New York: Macmillan, 1898).
48. See Charles O. Jones, "The Role of the Campaign in Congressional Politics," in M. Kent Jennings and Harmon Ziegler (eds.), *The Electoral Process* (Englewood Cliffs, N.J.: Prentice-Hall, 1966); Warren Miller and Donald Stokes, "Constituency Influence in Congress," *American Political Science Review* (March 1963), pp. 45–56.
49. Collins, *Rainbow Challenge*, p. 228.
50. For further discussion of the moderating influence of the American political party system, see Clinton Rossiter, *Parties and Politics in America* (Ithaca, N.Y.: Cornell University Press, 1960); Austin Ranney, *Curing the Mischief of Faction* (Berkeley: University of California Press, 1975); Burnham, *Critical Elections*, p. 90.
51. *New York Times*, November 16, 1980; *Gallup Opinion Index* (December 1980), p. 30; Everett Carll Ladd, "The Brittle Mandate," *Political Science Quarterly* (Spring 1981).
52. *New York Times*, April 1, 1980.
53. For example, see Howard Zinn, *A People's History of the United States* (New York: Harper & Row, 1980), pp. 542–543; Edward Greenberg, *The American Political System* (Boston: Little, Brown, 1983), pp. 290–293.
54. James Weinstein, *The Decline of American Socialism* (New York: Monthly Review Press, 1967).
55. Allen, *Black Awakening*, p. 187.
56. C. T. Vivian, *Black Power and the American Myth* (Philadelphia: Fortress, 1970), p. 98.
57. Donald Matthews, *The Social Background of Political Decision-makers* (New York: Random House, 1955); Donald Matthews, *U.S. Senators and Their World* (Chapel Hill: University of North Carolina Press, 1960); David Stanley et al., *Men Who Govern* (Washington, D.C.: Brookings Institution, 1969); Gabriel Kolko, *The Roots of American Foreign Policy* (Boston: Beacon Press, 1969); Thomas Dye, *Who's Running America?* (Englewood Cliffs, N.J.: Prentice-Hall, 1983).
58. Richard Hamilton, *Class and Politics in the United States* (New York: Wiley, 1972), p. 507. Also see Lewis Lipsitz, "On Political Belief: The Grievances of the Poor," in Phillip Green and Sanford Levinson (eds.), *Power and Community* (New York: Pantheon,

1970); Kenneth Dolbeare and Murray Edelman, *American Politics* (Lexington, Mass.: Heath, 1981), pp. 260–268.

59. Lester Milbraith and M. L. Goel, *Political Participation* (Chicago: Rand McNally, 1977).
60. Ibid., chap. 4; William Flanigan and Nancy Zingale, *Political Behavior of the American Electorate* (Boston: Allyn & Bacon, 1978), chap. 1.
61. Arthur Hadley, *The Empty Polling Booth* (Englewood Cliffs, N.J.: Prentice-Hall, 1978).
62. Ibid., p. 116.
63. Gallup poll, July 13, 1980; Samuel Eldersveld, *Political Parties in American Society* (New York: Basic Books, 1982), p. 417–418. For a general discussion of nonvoters and their level of alienation, see Walter Burnham, "The Changing Shape of the American Political Universe," *American Political Science Review* (March 1965); Penn Kimball, *The Disconnected* (New York: Columbia University Press, 1972); Studs Terkel, *Division Street: America* (New York: Pantheon, 1967); Murray Levin, *The Alienated Voter* (New York: Holt, Rinehart and Winston, 1960); Lipsitz, "On Political Belief."
64. Robert Erickson and Norman Luttbeg, *American Public Opinion* (New York: Wiley, 1973), p. 25; Subcommittee on Intergovernmental Relations, *Confidence and Concern* (Washington, D.C.: GPO, 1973), p. 215; Judson James, *American Political Parties* (New York: Harper & Row, 1974), p. 173; Fred I. Greenstein, *The American Party System and the American People* (Englewood Cliffs, N.J.: Prentice-Hall, 1970), p. 14.
65. Flanigan and Zingale, *Political Behavior*, p. 130.
66. *New York Times*, June 15, 1987.
67. Marcus Pohlmann, "The Electoral Impact of Partisanship and Incumbency Reconsidered," *Urban Affairs Quarterly* (June 1978), p. 500.
68. Robert Sickels, "Dragons, Baconstrips, and Dumbbells: Who's Afraid of Reapportionment?" *Yale Law Journal* (July 1966); Edward Tufte, "The Relationship between Seats and Votes in Two-Party Systems," *American Political Science Review* (June 1973).
69. *New York Times*, June 15, 1987.
70. Murray Edelman, *The Symbolic Uses of Politics* (Urbana: University of Illinois Press, 1964), p. 17.
71. Lester Salamon, "Protest, Politics, and Modernization in the American South," doctoral dissertation, Harvard University, 1971, pp. 627–628.
72. Wolfinger and Rosenstone, "Effect of Registration Laws."
73. For a classic example, see William Kornhauser, *The Politics of Mass Society* (New York: Free Press, 1959).
74. *Congressional Record*, vol. 125, no. 11 (February 5, 1979).
75. For example, see Carmichael and Hamilton, *Black Power*, pp. 166–172.
76. See Bennett Harrison and Barry Bluestone, "The Incidence and Regulation of Plant Closings," in Larry Sawers and William Tabb (eds.), *Sunbelt/Snowbelt* (New York: Oxford University Press, 1984), pp. 368–402; William Tabb, "A Pro-people Urban Policy," in William Tabb and Larry Sawers (eds.), *Marxism and the Metropolis* (New York: Oxford University Press, 1984), p. 371; *Public Citizen* (May-June 1988), pp. 15–17.
77. *New York Times*, January 16, 1984; *The Business of America* (San Francisco: California Newsreels, 1984).
78. John O'Loughlin, "Racial Gerrymandering," in Michael Preston et al. (eds.), *The New Black Politics* (White Plains, N.Y.: Longman, 1982).

CHAPTER EIGHT

The Legislative Arena

The Congress, the presidency, and the bureaucracy are intricately intertwined in the process of writing, passing, and executing the federal laws of the land. Thus they combine to form the legislative arena. Like its judicial and electoral counterparts, this arena is conservative by design. Beyond the unrepresentative demographics of its members, its rules and procedures make fundamental change extremely difficult to accomplish.

Legislation must be initiated by either the president or the Congress. It must then often command majorities at more than 40 separate congressional junctures. It can be stalled at any one of those junctures and can even be checked by the threat of a filibuster in the Senate. And once the legislation survives this procedure, the president can veto it, and it will take two-thirds majorities on both house floors to override. And even if that succeeds, the executive bureaucracy may fail to enforce the law after it is enacted. Clearly, legislated change, especially if at all controversial, is much easier to stop than to pass. The system is inclined toward small incremental changes rather than major comprehensive ones.

As a consequence, the legislative apparatus has been very difficult to move in the struggle to secure basic civil rights for black Americans. Although blacks have achieved passage of some major pieces of legislation, those gains have come sporadically, at a very high cost, and have proved difficult to sustain.

In the 20th century, for example, despite a half century of formal lobbying, decades of allegiance to the reigning Democratic party, and more than a decade of mounting organized protest, the Congress and the president continually failed to respond to black interests in a meaningful way. Finally, between 1957 and 1970, three civil rights acts, two voting rights acts, and a constitutional amendment to ban the poll tax became law.

The cost of gaining that legislation was high. Violent racial unrest stirred in more than 150 cities, leaving more than 100 people dead and thousands injured. Massive demonstrations and nonviolent civil disobedience also occurred across the nation. Although by no means a supporter of violence, even Martin Luther King, Jr., argued that at times you have to create a crisis in order to force a dialogue. In a political system so closely wedded to the status quo, that should not be surprising.

The battle does not end with the passage of legislation, however, as the laws then have to be implemented if change is actually to occur. Given the system of federalism, for example, much of that implementation is left to local white bureaucrats, many of whom come from the very areas that denied the rights in the first place.

But even more important is the fact that the federal government can take back what it gives out. This became quite obvious during the Reagan years, for instance, when social programs were cut back and enforcement of some major civil rights laws was relaxed. Without independent control over certain levers of power, blacks end up dependent both on white-created legislation and white administration of those laws.

In this latter regard, however, there have been a few hopeful signs. The growth of the Congressional Black Caucus has been a significant development, as has the increasing black presence at the top and bottom levels of the executive bureaucracy. Nevertheless, the legislative arena remains very resistant to change.

THE CONSERVATIVE DANCE OF LEGISLATION

There's a breakdown in the . . . machinery. There are 100 gauntlets and 1,000 vetoes. . . . You simply can't sustain any kind of policy through that process.[1]

The "dance of legislation"[2] now often begins in the White House. After being advised by various members of the executive bureaucracy, the president sends a legislative proposal to the Congress. That proposal must wend its way through a veritable maze on Capitol Hill in order to gain passage. If passed, it returns to the president's desk to be signed—assuming that its final form is still acceptable. Then it must be implemented, at which point the executive bureaucracy returns to center stage.

The following discussion will consider each of these primary actors separately: the president, the Congress, and the bureaucracy. What results is a portrait of a massive and lumbering legislative machine, biased against fundamental change except in times of severe crisis.

The Presidency

The president has come to be the single most important actor in the legislative process. But before beginning, note that the president has really become the presidency. In the late 1920s, Herbert Hoover performed his executive functions with the help of one secretary and two assistants. Today, presidents are assisted by the Executive Office of the President, which employs more than 5,000 specialized staff persons. The risk inherent in relying on such a corps and the much larger federal bureaucracy for information and advice is that the president could well become a captive of these advisers.

Presidential Power. In many ways, the growth and bureaucratization of the presidency reflect its expanded responsibilities and power. A good bit of this expansion can be attributed to both the march of events and technological developments.

Crises such as the Civil War and the Great Depression presented opportunities for unprecedented extensions of "emergency" presidential powers. During the Civil

War, Abraham Lincoln assembled troops, drew money from the United States Treasury, and suspended a number of constitutional rights—all while the Congress was not even in session. To reduce panic during the Great Depression, Franklin Delano Roosevelt declared a "bank holiday"—closing the banks for 100 days simply by executive decree. In addition, since the United States has become increasingly involved in world politics, the president's role has grown even greater. As the single spokesperson for the nation as a whole, the president comes to be delegated considerable power in international affairs, especially if the public can be convinced that the country faces a serious foreign threat.[3] Presidents now have nearly 500 pieces of legislation that extend them "emergency powers" under various circumstances, not to mention the precedents set by Lincoln, Roosevelt, and others. And all of that is true despite efforts to limit such accumulated powers with legislation such as the 1973 War Powers Act and the 1976 National Emergency Act.

The growth and development of the mass media has also added potent tools to the arsenal of presidential power. Presidents can now speak directly to the nation, and they seem capable of commandeering media access virtually whenever they wish. Theodore Roosevelt pioneered strategic use of the press, and Franklin Roosevelt made comparably good use of the radio airwaves. John Kennedy and Ronald Reagan became masters of the most invasive medium of all, television. There is simply no way 535 members of the U.S. Congress, for instance, can speak singularly enough to compete with most presidents in the mass media.

Besides the opportunities afforded by perceived emergencies and media access, two constitutionally defined entities, the veto and the executive budget, have also evolved into potent weapons.

Since the days of Andrew Jackson, presidents have been vetoing legislation purely on policy grounds. Presidents originally felt this should be done only if they deemed the Constitution to have been violated by the legislation; nowadays, presidents feel free to veto simply because they do not like the policy. Even the threat of such a veto can normally force the Congress either to a compromise or to abandon the legislation altogether. The Congress needs to marshal two-thirds majorities in both houses if the veto is to be overridden, and that has seldom proved to be possible. Less than 4 percent of the approximately 2,500 presidential vetoes have ever been overridden by the Congress, and that figure does not include presidential "pocket vetoes" or the many situations in which the mere threat of a veto was enough to scuttle the legislation.

Probably the most important fact is that much successful legislation has come to be originated in the White House.[4] Armed with the authority cited in Article 2, Section 3, of the Constitution ("[The president] shall from time to time give to the Congress information of the state of the Union, and recommend to their consideration such measures as he shall judge necessary and expedient"), the president is often setting the Congress's agenda, swaying both what will be discussed and the range of alternatives that will be considered. Of particular significance is the practice of introducing a full executive budget, a prerogative first formalized by President Harry S Truman.

Note the significance of the presidency in the process that results. Information is generated from a 3 million–person bureaucracy and compiled by the Office of

Management and Budget—which happens to have some 600 staff members of its own. The president then sends the proposed legislation to the Congress, draws on the Congressional Liaison Office to help lobby it through, and sends top administrators to testify at committee hearings. In addition, accommodative legislators realize that come reelection time, the president can introduce additional legislation targeted to their constituents—a military base here, a water or highway project there. Once these rarely controversial rewards skip through the legislative process, those members of Congress are then invited to the White House for a photo session when the bill is signed, producing impressive pictures that will be beamed back home to appear in the local media.

Finally, the president not only has the first word but one of the last as well. In particular, through appointments and personal leadership, the president can affect the enthusiasm with which the federal bureaucracy will implement any congressionally passed legislation.

Presidential Bias. Just how close to the people is this increasingly powerful president? One can get a sense of that by looking both at the demographics of the individuals who have held that office and how one gets access to them.

To begin with, all but one of the American presidents has been a white Protestant man, and the exception was a white Catholic man. In addition to the narrowness of perspective likely to stem from such backgrounds, virtually all of them have been millionaires either when they arrived or once they left. While, beyond that, most of the people they come to appoint to high office reflect the same elite characteristics.[5]

How does one get to speak to a president to make one's views known? Unless called on for advice, one of the only certain avenues is to buy one's way in. The Watergate hearings revealed that one could speak to Richard Nixon for a $50,000 campaign contribution,[6] and during the Iran-*contra* hearings it came to light that a $300,000 private contribution to the Nicaraguan *contras* warranted a conversation with President Ronald Reagan.[7]

Nevertheless, even if one of these increasingly powerful presidents had the inclination to redistribute wealth and power from elites to non-elites, he or she would encounter plenty of obstacles.

The Congress

Once legislation has emerged from the White House and been introduced on Capitol Hill, the dance becomes incredibly convoluted. Senator David Pryor (D-Ark.) characterized it as a "slow-motion system of inefficiency and procedural imprisonment." According to Senator Paul Trible (R-Va.), "the whole policy-making process stands at the brink of incoherence." Retiring Senator Thomas Eagleton (D-Mo.), exhausted and disillusioned, referred to it as an "unmanageable circus." Senator David Evans (R-Wash.) concluded, "There's a feeling of lack of accomplishment, or maybe more accurately a sense that the whole system is breaking down."[8] And Representative Richard Bolling (D-Mo.) wrote:

> In the many years I have been a member of Congress, [it] has revealed itself to me
> as ineffective in its role as a coordinate branch of the Federal Government,

negative in its approach to national tasks, generally unresponsive to any but parochial economic interests. Its procedures, time-consuming and unwieldy, mask anonymous centers of irresponsible powers. Its legislation is often a travesty of what the national welfare requires.[9]

The Legislative Maze. The most basic steps in this process were designed by the Founding Fathers, and the rest have emerged over time as the Congress has grown in size and responsibilities. Consider a typical piece of contested budgetary legislation as it successfully wends its way through this tangled maze.

1. Bill is introduced in the House.
2. Speaker refers the bill to committe.
3. Committee chair refers the bill to subcommittee.
4. Subcommittee approves its version of the bill.
5. Full committee approves its version of the bill.
6. Speaker places the bill on the House calendar.
7. Rules committee sets rules for the bill's debate.
8. Full House approves the rules.
9. Full House passes its version of the bill.
10. Senate leader refers the House bill to committee.
11. Committee chair refers the bill to subcommittee.
12. Subcommittee approves its version of the bill.
13. Full committee approves its version of the bill.
14. Leadership places the bill on the Senate calendar.
15. Full Senate passes its version of the bill.
16. House rejects changes, calls for a conference.
17. Senate agrees to join in a conference committee.
18. Conference committee passes a compromise version.
19. Full Senate accepts the compromise bill.
20. Full House accepts the compromise bill.
21. President signs the bill into law.[10]

Now the spending has been authorized. Repeat the entire process when it comes time for the spending to be appropriated (that is, when the checks are actually to be written). Since the Budget Act of 1974, the Congress is striving to initiate its own budget rather than being so dependent on the president's agenda. In this newest budgetary process, the maze must be traversed in order to set targets and then negotiated again when time comes for official authorization in the fall. Also, a bill may be referred to more than one committee each time around if its subject matter spills over into other committees' jurisdictions.

This is a highly conservative process. An opponent of a bill need only muster majority support at one of the many discretionary junctures and the bill may well die. In addition, if all else fails, the opposition can launch a filibuster in the Senate, or the president may be persuaded to veto the legislation, increasing the steps necessary for passage.

Because the Senate allows unlimited debate, a member can simply hold the floor for days and thus prevent any other debate or votes from taking place. Rule

22 was added to allow the full Senate to halt such a filibuster. As the rule presently reads, 16 colleagues must be willing to incur the wrath of the filibustering member by signing a cloture petition. Once that is done, a vote can be taken, and 60 votes ends the debate. Fewer than 20 percent of cloture votes have been successful, and many cloture efforts fail for lack of 16 signatures in the first place. And since the mid-1970s, even the traditional filibuster has become somewhat obsolete.

There are now new and improved methods of filibustering that are impervious to the cloture rule. One involves the presentation of an endless stream of amendments, calling for a roll-call vote on each. Another is even more inventive. In the spring of 1987, for example, a group of Senate Republicans sought to forestall a vote on a military appropriations bill. John Warner (R-Va.) refused to vote on the routine motion of approving the previous day's journal. As the full Senate must vote to excuse a fellow senator from voting, a roll call was ordered on Warner's refusal. Dan Quayle (R-Ind.) then refused to vote on that motion, and a roll call was taken on Quayle's refusal. On and on it went.[11]

A presidential veto is always a possibility as well. Overrides of presidential vetoes have been relatively rare.

Thus if a proponent of a bill suspects defeat at any of the multiple legislative steps or can reasonably anticipate a filibuster or a presidential veto, the legislation is in serious trouble. Either the bill will never be introduced, a huge majority will have to be mustered to overcome the opposition, or a compromise will have to be struck with the bill's opponents. Even a single opponent can create havoc for virtually any proposed piece of legislation. Little wonder that it seems to take a severe national crisis before anything approaching fundamental comprehensive change can be steered through this incredible maze.[12]

Institutional Bias. In addition to the heavy inclination toward stasis created by the formal procedures of the Congress, a number of informal realities shape the legislative dance. Bureaucratization and the increasing role of interest groups are readily apparent, as are various coping mechanisms. But even free of all the pressure, there is little reason to believe the typical congressperson is going to be inclined toward fundamental change.

The bureaucratization of the Congress is difficult to overlook. There are now more than 300 specialized committees and subcommittees on Capitol Hill, and their actions or inactions determine the fate of virtually all legislation. For example, nearly two-thirds of strong committee recommendations survive on the floors of both houses of Congress. Not only do the individual congresspersons serving on these various committees play enhanced roles, but staff people are also proliferating in both numbers and importance. As recently as 1947, there were approximately 500 committee staff persons and another 2,000 working directly for individual representatives. A mere four decades later, those numbers had increased more than fivefold, to more than 3,000 committee staffers and 10,000 direct employees. Given the volume of legislation to be addressed and the resultant pace at which most representatives are forced to operate, there is little time for study or reflection.[13] Instead, detail and even much agenda setting are left to these unelected staffers. As Representative Michael Harrington put it before retiring,

"The country has no goal, no sense of direction, no vision. Congress is a bureaucracy. We have government by managers and engineers."[14]

In addition, as the process has become decentralized, the role of the special-interest groups has been enhanced. As best as can be estimated, roughly 7,000 groups have representatives in Washington. More than half are corporations, another third are professional or trade associations, 4 percent are so-called public-interest groups, and less than 2 percent represent civil rights or minority groups.[15] Possessing a far greater wealth of information than the average representative, these groups regularly appear at committee hearings to fill the record with facts and figures that support their particular position. They also arm friendly representatives with information as those congresspersons press the position outside committee chambers. Beyond that, interest-group activity on the Hill is virtually unregulated, and modern electronic technology allows them to communicate to a representative's constituents almost instantaneously to try either to reward or to punish the elected official for each action or inaction.

Faced with a 1,325-page procedural manual, interest-group pressure, and an absence of strong party organizations to insulate them (see Chapter 7), it begins to become obvious why the Congress has developed a number of coping mechanisms that allow its members to protect their seats without challenging the existing maldistribution of wealth and power. For example, the majority of bills are introduced largely as political gestures, designed to appease constituents with the appearance of active support for their causes. Most never reemerge from committee, and thus "the Congress" as a body can be blamed for their deaths. Serious legislation also gets bogged down; consequently, much of it ends up getting lumped together into huge "continuing resolutions"—massive budgetary laws that simply continue existing levels of spending when changes have not been able to find their way through the maze. These allow the status quo to be maintained by including something that virtually every representative wants continued. Thus "pork barrel" legislation lives on, as each district continues to get its pet highway or water project, military base, or whatever. Little wonder that the Reagan administration's Grace Commission on government waste found huge inefficiencies—for example, it found that 2,700 of the nation's 3,000 military bases could be shut down without doing any damage whatsoever to national security.

As a result, the Congress has tended to become a rather cozy and stagnant club in which members gratiously trade favors in order to stay in office.[16] Rather than risk engendering controversy, it is far easier to keep a low profile, leave the existing priorities of the Congress essentially as they are, and tend to constituent service. Such service is enhanced by going along with one's colleagues in order to gain their support—support in getting seats on committees and subcommittees particularly relevant to one's home district, not to mention ultimate passage of legislation that will benefit members of the district. Then, as seniority accumulates, a representative can become a chairperson, a position that will allow more protection of these constituent tidbits by virtue of the chair's agenda-setting discretion.

Even if every member of Congress had a safe seat and none of the obstructions or lobbyist pressures existed, there are still good reasons to believe that these representatives would not be inclined to alter the present distribution of wealth and power in the United States. These are largely middle-aged, upper-class, professional, white males—unusually homogeneous by international standards. Their congressional compensation puts them in the top 1 percent of the population, with a combined income and benefit package of between $150,000 and $350,000 per year.[17] They are asked to address problems in the factory environment having never worked in one and to write medical-care legislation without having ever had to stand in line at a public hospital.[18] A number have had financial interests in the very corporations with which they were dealing.[19] Representative Ron Dellums (D-Cal.) concluded that they tend to be "mediocre prima donnas who don't understand the level of human misery in this country."[20]

Nonetheless, members of Congress must stand for reelection periodically. The bureaucrats who populate the next tier in the process are almost completely insulated from popular pressure, have certain institutional agendas of their own, and are regularly influenced by lobbyists.

The Bureaucracy

It is no secret that the Founding Fathers set out to create a federal government that would be dominated by the legislative branch. The experience with England's King George III had not left most of them yearning for another dominant executive. There is clear evidence today that the executive branch has grown much larger than its legislative counterpart. The current United States Government Manual, for instance, contains approximately 40 pages devoted to the Congress and some 600 pages describing the executive branch. It has not always been that way.

When George Washington took the oath of office in 1789, he was to administer a federal bureaucracy of approximately 780 people. By the time Andrew Jackson assumed the office of president nearly a half century later, there were still fewer than 2,000 federal bureaucrats. Over the course of the next 100 years, the federal bureaucracy would grow significantly. By 1930, for example, Herbert Hoover was overseeing an executive branch that numbered 600,000. As the federal government has assumed more responsibilities, particularly with the emergence of Franklin Roosevelt's New Deal, the figure has grown to nearly 3 million. That means the federal bureaucracy has increased almost fivefold in the last half century alone.

Besides the proliferation of federal responsibilities, however, there is another important explanation for this bureaucratic expansion. It appears to be far easier to create a new agency than to eliminate an existing one. For example, Common Cause studied this phenomenon between 1961 and 1976. Over that period, 236 agencies were created and only 21 were dissolved.[21] Once programs develop constituencies, it is very difficult to steer cuts past the members of Congress who represent the programs' constituents. Recall that the process of Congress is quite sensitive to the reelection needs of its members.

Bureaucratic Power. Not only have bureaucracies developed a resilience to the congressional ax, but these unelected public officials have also accumulated a sizable amount of independent political power. Harry Truman once confessed, "I thought I was president, but when it comes to these bureaucracies, I can't make them do a damn thing."[22]

Application Discretion. When the Congress passes a law, it will almost always contain at least some ambiguous language. This allows flexibility as the law is applied by the bureaucracy. Among other things, this practice saves the Congress from having continually to rewrite its legislation to fit each new situation that arises. So while the Congress passes some 600 laws per year, the federal bureaucracy issues 10 times that many regulations. The *Federal Register,* which records all such administrative laws, often ends up containing more than 60,000 pages of fine print.

Besides filling in the gaps between the lines of congressionally passed laws, the bureaucracy also has ample opportunity to shape those laws in the course of enforcement. Each day bureaucrats must make decisions such as who meets federal guidelines and thus qualifies for federal monies or who is out of compliance with a federal regulation and thus faces penalties. This power is enhanced by the fact that most such decisions are seldom visible by either the Congress or the public. To keep ever more decisions out of the public eye, the executive branch has increased penalties for leaking information and has often been harsh in its punishment of whistle-blowers—insiders who choose to go public with embarrassing revelations about internal bureaucratic matters.[23] The low visibility of these decisions adds extra insulation, at times even from top-level administators appointed to oversee these activities.

Agenda Setting. Besides application discretion, bureaucrats are also crucial sources of information and advice. They generally possess some of the most extensive expertise in their fields of specialization, and they also tend to be the ones asked to compile relevant data describing what is occurring in those areas. More and more of them even have their own public relations staffs. Consequently, they have ample opportunity to set the legislative agenda in the course of evaluating what has worked in the past and proposing what needs to be done in the future. As a case in point, when the air force asks for a new bomber, few people are in a position to second-guess the bureaucrats' assessment of the situation—especially since the size and complexity of government have left elected officials further and further removed from what is actually going on in the various fields. At the very least, short of major complaints or scandals, such bureaucrats are in a strong position to have their current budget and practices reapproved.

Job Security. A combination of civil-service status and unionization further insulates the bureaucracy. The overwhelming majority have attained their positions through civil-service procedures. They listed their qualifications, took a test, were ranked, and were later appointed by the Civil Service Commission primarily on the basis of that ranking. Not only are elected officials left out of their hiring, but the bureaucrats can thereafter only be fired for serious cause, such as dereliction of duty. When they choose subtly to drag their feet rather than enthusiastically enforcing a law they oppose, elected officials can do little about it. The tiny percentage of top-level administrators, appointed rather than hired through the civil service, can be pressured and fired, but those appointed administrators are not in the position to do much more than persuade and cajole the bureaucrats beneath them. Career civil servants, a number of whom are also unionized, normally cannot be effectively commanded to do much of anything. They ultimately proceed as they choose.

Institutional Bias. A variety of bureaucratic realities militate against having this extensive power turned against the status quo. Close relationships tend to form between bureaucrats and the groups of people they serve or regulate. Meanwhile, regulation itself is often obstructed by a fragmentation of authority.

Clientelism. For a variety of reasons, bureaucrats develop close affinities with their clients. To begin with, clients are valuable allies in each agency's never-ending quest to retain current levels of funding, if not increase them. As the Federal Communications Commission (FCC) fought the development of cable television, for example, the commercial networks became even closer political allies. Such affinity is also enhanced by the fact that individuals often move back and forth between the bureaucracy and their clientele group, a practice called the revolving-door syndrome. As a case in point, Edward Herman found 21 of 33 FCC commissioners returning to the communications industry once they left the commission; most of the others retired.[24] More than one-half of all regulatory appointees previously served in the industry they are to regulate.[25]

A significant result of these trends has been the development of what have been termed "iron triangles." These are tight, mutually accommodative relationships among the client, the agency, and the related congressional committee. A classic example is the close working relationship of the oil industry, the Department of the Interior, and congressional committees that oversee commerce, the environment, energy, and natural resources. Because committee power increases with seniority, there is much time for the ranking members of these congressional committees to grow close to the clients and bureaucrats in the triangle.

Regulatory Limitations. Government agencies appear adept at retaining services for clients. They have more difficulty when it comes to punishing people in the course of law enforcement. Besides protecting clientele groups, such regulatory bodies are often understaffed; for example, the Bureau of Motor Carrier Safety has only nine people to monitor things like the transportation of hazardous wastes across the country. In addition, authority is often fragmented across a whole host of departments, agencies, and subagencies. In the area of civil rights enforcement, for example, that duty is spread across the likes of the Civil Rights Division of the Justice Department, the Department of Education, the Department of Health and Human Services, the Civil Service Commission, the Office of Federal Contract Compliance in the Department of Labor, the Equal Employment Opportunity Commission, the Civil Rights Commission, the Federal Housing Authority, and the Department of Housing and Urban Development. In such a tangle of overlapping, fragmented authority, it is often difficult to determine precisely who has failed when a law goes underenforced.

BLACKS IN THE LEGISLATIVE ARENA

> Although the Congressional Black Caucus has taken strong, progressive positions over the years, . . . it has been a voice crying in the wilderness. The legislation black congresspersons would need to pass in order to demonstrate that there was real hope for the majority of black Americans . . . suggests changes the United States political system is incapable of making. As a result, the Congressional Black Caucus and other black leadership forums have increasingly functioned to enhance the individual careers of the black middle class—those who can profit from the incremental benefits the system is capable of granting, rather than the distributive justice it will not concede.[26]

Over the course of United States history, the interests of black Americans have been particularly affected by decisions or nondecisions in the federal legislative arena—which has just been shown to be practically impervious to fundamental change. Although the federal government has delivered some helpful major pieces of legislation at times, that has normally occurred only when accompanied by both considerable social turmoil and the leadership of a strong and congenial president.

The Presidency

Given the increasing nationalization of American politics over time, as well as the resistance to racial justice often confronting black Americans at the state and local levels, it is not surprising that black political attention soon turned to Washington. It often turned in particular to the one official elected nationwide and least likely to be beholden to any single state or local constituency: the president of the United States.

We shall focus in this section on only part of the presidential response: the appointments, orders, and general postures of key presidents. In our discussion of the Congress, we shall take up major pieces of legislation often initiated by presidents and steered through under their leadership.

Presidential appointments and other actions reflect real ebbs and flows in presidential commitment to black interests. A few presidents reluctantly and cautiously bucked racist attitudes prevalent in the nation by delivering things like patronage for a small number of blacks, highly visible token appointments, high-level meetings with carefully selected black leaders, and a sizable amount of rhetoric. At other times, the reception was not warm, unless a crisis was at hand.

The Slavery Period. Prior to the end of the Civil War, these presidential actions tended to be almost completely antithetical to the interests of black Americans. George Washington, for instance, sought restitution for several thousand slaves taken by British troops toward the end of the Revolutionary War. John Adams pressed Great Britain and Mexico for formal agreements that would guarantee the return of runaway slaves. During the Civil War, President Abraham Lincoln only selectively emancipated the slaves, allowing the institution to continue in slave states that were fighting under the Union banner. Meanwhile, most presidents from Washington through Lincoln pressed for active enforcement of domestic fugitive slave laws but minimally enforced the 1808 ban against further importation of slaves.

The Civil War Era. Nonetheless, Lincoln did wage the Civil War, at least in part because of the escalating turmoil over the issue of slavery. He negotiated a treaty with Great Britain to suppress the African slave trade, and he eventually announced the emancipation of all slaves held in the United States. Yet his successor, Andrew Johnson, was nearly impeached fighting the imposition of Reconstruction on the South, and Rutherford B. Hayes ultimately abandoned the policy altogether in order to win the presidential election of 1876.

The 1876 electoral vote was so close between Hayes and Democrat Samuel Tilden that it literally hung on disputed results in South Carolina, Louisiana, and Florida. When, among other things, the Republican candidate agreed to press for official termination of Reconstruction by withdrawing federal troops from the South, that seemed to break the impasse. The House of Representatives resolved the dispute in Hayes's favor, Hayes became president of the United States, and soon the troops were gone.

The Jim Crow Period. What followed was a period that ranged from presidential indifference to outright hostility. Republican presidents generally could be counted on to continue delivering small amounts of patronage, but that was about the best of it. Amid legal resegregation, black disenfranchisement, and increasing numbers of lynchings, presidents were doing little to protect black Americans. Nevertheless, as blacks attempted to escape some of the worst of this by migrating to the North, some token gestures were forthcoming. Woodrow Wilson appeared to be offering some of the first direct presidential overtures in a very long time. What he proceeded to deliver was quite another thing, however. Although he appointed Robert H. Terrell as a municipal judge in Washington, D.C., he also eliminated virtually all black patronage and promoted segregation both in Washington and in the federal bureaucracy. President William Howard Taft had appointed William H. Lewis assistant attorney general, but such tokenism marked the extent of presidential concern.

Gains amid Turmoil. As the Great Depression drove national unemployment rates to some 25 percent and food riots occurred in the streets, something had to be done. In response, President Franklin Roosevelt initiated the New Deal. Beyond pressing for the establishment of a social welfare state, however, he offered little that directly addressed the discrimination and violence plaguing blacks in both the North and the South at the time.

Virtually nothing was forthcoming until blacks began to rebel violently in cities such as New York and Detroit. A. Phillip Randolph threatened to lead a massive march on Washington just as United States involvement in World War II was beginning. Roosevelt finally responded by appointing a number of blacks to advisory positions in various federal departments, comprising what came to be called his Negro Cabinet. He also issued Executive Order 8802 prohibiting racial discrimination in defense-related industries and in government. Then, as an enforcement vehicle, he created the Fair Employment Practices Commission to investigate discrimination in industries servicing the federal government. However, the commission had no authority to punish the companies when such discrimination was encountered, and it was reluctant to cancel government contracts with discriminating companies in the middle of a war effort. Therefore, besides embarrassing a few such firms into compliance, job discrimination continued pretty much unabated.

As the Congress of Racial Equality (CORE) began to escalate civil rights activities with marches, "freedom rides," and the like, Harry S Truman became the first president openly to advocate full equal rights for black Americans. He created a civil rights committee to provide advice and a more effective committee to battle discrimination in businesses under government contract. In 1948, he issued Executive Order 9981, which finally desegregated the military, and he introduced various pieces of civil rights legislation in the Congress. He also continued the practice of appointing blacks to significant positions, including the federal bench. Nevertheless, it was not until after he had chosen not to seek reelection that he called for a national civil rights policy backed by the "full force and power of the Federal Government."[27]

Dwight Eisenhower favored military segregation as late as 1948, although once elected he continued federal pressure to eliminate discrimination among government contractors. Meanwhile, he never formally announced his support of the 1954 *Brown v. Board of Education* decision, was slow to send federal troops to Little Rock to enforce court-ordered school desegregation, and was silent when Martin Luther King, Jr., was sentenced to four months at hard labor in Georgia's Reidsville State Prison.

John F. Kennedy made a very timely phone call to the jailed Dr. King at a crucial point late in the 1960 presidential campaign, but he was far slower to respond once he took the oath of office. He avoided the entire subject of race in his inaugural address, did not include racial issues as a topic for any of his initial task forces, was slow to press for Civil Rights Commission hearings, and appointed racist judges to the federal bench in the South. It took two years before he finally pressed for desegregation of public housing, and even then, only about one unit in five was affected. He settled for a watered-down effort at desegregating military residential units, and he did not cut federal aid to states that continued to discriminate in public employment.

Nonetheless, the civil rights movement was gathering force across the South, and the atmosphere was becoming even more highly charged. Reverend Theodore Hesburgh served on the Civil Rights Commission during this period, and he concluded that the civil rights issue imposed itself on the Kennedy administration, rather than the other way around. "The time schedule was not guided from the White House, but it was guided by the march of events and the White House had to react to it."[28]

Besides appointing a number of black administrators, judges, and advisers—appointments now obligatory for Democratic presidents—Kennedy finally was forced more directly to join the battle against discrimination in voter registration.

At first, he simply endorsed the private Voter Education Project but did not commit the Justice Department to active assistance. Yet as images from Birmingham and elsewhere seared the public consciousness in the spring of 1963 and as plans for a huge March on Washington went forward, Kennedy moved. He agreed to send temporary voting referees wherever less than 15 percent of a local black population was registered and the attorney general of the United States filed a formal complaint. He also appointed the Equal Employment Opportunity Committee and the Committee on Equal Opportunity in Housing, and he issued Executive Order 10925, which included the first federal mention of affirmative action.

As Lyndon Johnson took office, racial unrest was reaching its peak. Massive demonstrations swept the South, and more than 100 urban ghettos went up in flames. In that volatile setting, Johnson moved quickly. Besides major appointments—Robert Weaver as the first black head of a cabinet department (Housing and Urban Development), Andrew Brimmer to the Federal Reserve Board, Thurgood Marshall as solicitor general and later first black justice on the U.S. Supreme Court—the Johnson presidency would be marked by the greatest legislative gains in black American history. Nevertheless, even though a combination of events and presidential leadership had succeeded in overcoming the conservative legislative maze, implementation would be another story. The institution of federalism would impede strong enforcement of many of these long-awaited gains. Like Eisenhower and Kennedy before him, President Johnson would be hesitant to introduce federal observers, examiners, and troops. On paper, a second reconstruction was under way, but this one would be implemented much more cautiously than the first.

Despite some initial hesitancy, however, the Johnson administration did finally begin to enforce the laws. Soon, much legal discrimination had been successfully eliminated. Major legal impediments to voting, employment, and housing opportunities had been swept aside. But as the unrest began to dissipate, the pendulum began to swing back the other way.

A Return to Reticence. In 1968, while numerous public opinion polls indicated that white America felt that government had gone too far in its assistance of blacks, Richard M. Nixon won the presidency on a platform that had clear racial undertones. If elected, he would work to end school busing and would bring "law and order" back to the country—the latter being a thinly veiled promise, in part, to crush inner-city rebellions. Although ghetto unrest had been put down rather effectively by the time he was inaugurated, once in office Nixon proceeded to implement a number of regressive policies. His administration would be relatively lax in its enforcement of the civil rights legislation on the books,[29] and it would quite openly work to reduce enforcement of court-ordered school busing. Probably its most significant legacies, however, were the appointments of four relatively conservative justices to the Supreme Court and the development of amorphous block grants to replace many of the much more narrowly targeted and redistributive project grants that had emerged as part of Lyndon Johnson's Great Society efforts.

Eight years of Ronald Reagan would mean even more of the same. Between

1981 and 1989, not only would the Justice Department all but cease to enforce busing orders and affirmative action laws, but the solicitor general would argue against the constitutionality of such policies when they came before the Supreme Court. Beyond that, hostile federal judges were appointed, and the Equal Employment Opportunity and Civil Rights commissions were stacked with persons who opposed many existing civil rights laws and practices. Social welfare efforts would be reduced, and aside from the appointment of Samuel Pierce as secretary of the Department of Housing and Urban Development (HUD) and of Collin Powell to finish the term as national security adviser, about all that the Reagan administration offered to blacks was a promised share in the economic growth Reagan claimed was resulting from his laissez-faire economic policies—a share that never materialized for most blacks.

Ronald Reagan's successor, George Bush, like Richard Nixon's successor, Gerald Ford, entered office with a more conciliatory posture than his predecessor. One of Bush's first acts was to appoint Louis Sullivan as secretary of the Department of Health and Human Serivces. However, where the domestic policies of the Ford administration diverged only minimally from the conservative Nixon approach, there was little reason to believe that Bush would deviate much from Reagan's domestic agenda either, despite his promise of a "kinder and gentler America."

Jimmy Carter provided a brief interlude between Nixon–Ford and Reagan–Bush, but even he failed to deliver what many blacks had expected. The appointments were indeed forthcoming. Patricia Harris was appointed to a cabinet-level post as secretary of HUD. Clifford Alexander was made secretary of the army. Andrew Young was tapped to be United States ambassador to the United Nations. Wade McCree was chosen as solicitor general. Michigan newspaperman Louis Martin was brought in as a special adviser—as he had been under both Kennedy and Johnson. A record number of blacks were appointed to the federal bench. And a civil rights office was even created in the powerful Office of Management and Budget. Nevertheless, a policy of fiscal restraint thwarted hopes of any major federal efforts to reinvigorate the Great Society, and relations with the White House became so strained that the president was not even invited to the 1979 legislative weekend of the Congressional Black Caucus.

The Congress

Legislation. Mired in its own incredibly convoluted procedures, the Congress has generally been even less responsive to black interests than the presidency. In the absence of both forceful demands propelled by serious social turmoil and strong presidential leadership, it has done little to attack the individual and institutionalized racism that has so long plagued black America.

The Slavery Period. Not only was slavery tolerated in the nation and its territories, but it was legal even in the nation's capital until the outbreak of the Civil War. The Fugitive Slave Act, passed in 1793, mandated the return of runaway slaves, and it was fortified by provisions included in the Compromise of 1850. This was hardly the extent of legalized discrimination. Even free blacks were barred from the militia, navy, marines, and postal service. They were also all but barred from obtaining a passport, and they were denied preemption rights to public lands.

The Civil War Era. In the aftermath of the Civil War, the Congress (devoid of much southern opposition) moved boldly to strike down the legal vestiges of slavery. This "reconstructive" effort included the Wade-Davis bill, the Reconstruction Act of 1867, creation of the Freedmen's Bureaus, three proposed amendments to the U.S. Constitution, and the Civil Rights Act of 1875.

The Wade-Davis bill marked the Congress's effort to be harsher on ex-Confederates than President Lincoln was being. In particular, it sought to preclude a much larger number from voting, and it demanded more guaranteed loyalty from newly reconstructed southern states. However, when the president refused to sign the bill, the Congress was not capable of overriding his will.

Following Lincoln's death, however, the Congress became more responsive to black interests, and its majority Republic party courted newly enfranchised black voters who faced racist violence, intimidation, and emerging black codes in the postwar South. Of particular significance, the Congress proceeded to adopt the Reconstruction Act over President Andrew Johnson's veto. The act divided the old Confederacy into five military districts and imposed martial law. For readmission into the Union, each state had to implement universal (male) suffrage to those swearing allegiance to the Union, write new state constitutions acceptable to the Congress, and ratify the 14th Amendment to the Constitution.

The Freedmen's Bureau was established to deliver a number of badly needed services to dislocated southern blacks, as well as some southern whites. It provided food, health care, education, and resettlement assistance. It also intervened on behalf of black workers to establish workable contracts with their new employers, and it provided its own courts when local courts were deemed to be unreliable.

The Civil War amendments to the Constitution were another significant gain. Each was passed by the Congress and then ratified by the states between 1865 and 1870. The 13th Amendment banned slavery and involuntary servitude in the United States and its territories, unless the involuntary servitude was part of a legitimate punishment for a crime. The 14th prohibited states from abridging federal "privileges and immunities"; denying life, liberty, or property without "due process of law"; and denying "equal protection of the laws." The 15th declared that the right to vote was "not to be denied or abridged by the United States or by any State on account of race, color, or previous condition of servitude."

At the very end of this period, the Congress passed the Civil Rights Act of 1875. It outlawed the exclusion of blacks from public accommodations, including privately owned hotels, theaters, boats, and railroads. The law would be struck down by the Supreme Court eight years later, and it would be nearly another century before those rights would be restored.

The Jim Crow Period. In the lull from the Hayes compromise in 1876 until the turmoil of the Great Depression period of the 1930s, the Congress proved incapable of doing much to protect southern blacks from increasing oppression. Legalized segregation and disenfranchisement were tolerated, as was outright violence. In fact, the Congress actually contributed to some of this. For example, in 1878 it prohibited the use of federal troops in elections and 16 years later cut all appropriations for election marshals. This, of course, left blacks voters to fend for themselves. Final amnesty was granted to the remainder of the previously "disloyal" southern Confederates in 1898. Probably most alarming of all was the fact that an antilynching bill never did emerge from the legislative maze. Nonetheless, the period was not devoid of progress: The 1883 Pendleton Act created a merit system for hiring federal bureaucrats. That legislation inadvertently helped blacks by limiting opportunity for discriminatory federal hiring.

Gain amid Turmoil. As social unrest rocked the nation throughout much of the period between 1930 and 1968, some direct aid and protection finally began to emerge from Washington in response to black demands. Domestic crises once again would provide the catalyst necessary to overcome the inherent stasis of the legislative process.

As early as 1930, under intense pressure from the NAACP in particular, the U.S. Senate blocked the nomination of John J. Parker to serve on the Supreme Court. Parker was alleged to have once stated that "participation of the Negro in politics is a source of evil and danger to both races."[30] As discussed earlier, the Congress is much better equipped to stop proposals than it is to pass them. But the level of crisis was about to allow even the latter.

New Deal legislation in the 1930s was designed to address many of the violent and nonviolent biracial demands arising out of the Great Depression. Emergency relief was provided. Social welfare programs such as Aid to Families with Dependent Children (AFDC) were created. Unemployment compensation was established, as was a minimum wage and a 40-hour workweek. Collective bargaining was protected, legalizing unionization. A variety of federal jobs were created to put unemployed people back to work. Child labor was prohibited. And the Social Security system was brought into being.

Following World War II, violent and nonviolent protest would gather momentum. This time, however, the rebels were predominantly black Americans demanding the enforcement of rights they had gained nearly a century earlier. Once again, the Congress found ways to respond.

The Civil Rights Act of 1957 was the first major piece of civil rights legislation to find its way through Congress since 1875. It established the Civil Rights Commission to investigate violations of the 14th and 15th amendments. It authorized the attorney general of the United States to protect federal voting rights, including criminal prosecution of judges. And nondiscriminatory criteria were established for the selection of federal jurors.

The Civil Rights Act of 1960 mandated that stricter voting records be kept, and if a "pattern or practice of discrimination" could be demonstrated, federal judges were authorized to adjudicate voter registration disputes, or the attorney general could appoint federal referees to resolve them. It also made it a federal crime to use interstate commerce to threaten or carry out a bombing and added much stiffer penalties for people convicted of violent acts such as this.

The Civil Rights Act of 1964 was the most sweeping piece of legislation to date, and it passed by virtue of the fact that the Senate was able to invoke cloture over a filibuster for the first time since 1917. The act mandated the desegregation of public schools and accommodations and set forth provisions for equal employment. Federal aid was to be withheld from discriminatory state and local governments. It extended and broadened the role of the Civil Rights Commission and created the Equal Employment Opportunities Commission (EEOC). A Community Relations Services division was created in the Commerce Department to mediate race-related social disputes. In the area of suffrage, it required even stricter record keeping, authorized the Commerce Department to compile registration and voting statistics in areas suggested by the Civil Rights Commission, prohibited disenfranchisement due to minor errors, tightened limitations on literacy tests, and provided a process whereby either the prospective registrant or the attorney general could appeal voter application denials to an independent three-person federal panel.

The Congress also addressed the issue of poll taxes. Even though a congressional ban could not get past filibusters in the Senate, a constitutional amendment did survive all the way to ratification in February 1964. Thus the 24th Amendment was added to the Constitution barring "any poll tax or other tax" from precluding a person from voting in a primary or general election for federal office.

The capstone to the suffrage fight was the Voting Rights Act of 1965. It directed the attorney general to bring suit challenging the constitutionality of poll taxes in state elections and provided authority to bring suit against other practices based purely on statistical evidence. When a federal suit was pending, federal courts were authorized to ban the discriminatory practice in question temporarily. In addition, all literacy tests and other suspect practices were suspended in states where less than half of their eligible voters turned out in the 1964 presidential election. Those states were Alabama, Alaska, Georgia, Louisiana, Mississippi, South Carolina, Virginia, and North Carolina. Finally, designated election districts were required to submit all new voting qualifications to federal judges for preclearance.

Meanwhile, President Johnson was steering his Great Society programs through a Congress that had two-thirds Democratic majorities in both houses—enough to overcome a "conservative coalition" of Republicans and southern Democrats. This round of social legislation included food stamps, Medicaid, Head Start, Legal Aid, community mental health centers, Model Cities projects, and other programs.

Three final legislative actions warrant mention. The 1968 Civil Rights Act prohibited racial discrimination in the rental or sale of housing, unless a private owner chose to make the transaction without the use of a real estate broker. The Supreme Court nominations of two alleged racists, Clement Haynsworth and G. Harrold Carswell, were rejected by the Senate.[31] And the Voting Rights Act of 1970 banned any new literacy tests.

A Return to Reticence. With those legislative gains in place and racial turmoil finally abating, a political backlash loomed on the horizon.[32] From Richard M. Nixon's inauguration in 1969 through the end of George Bush's term, conservative

Republicans held the White House all but four years, with Republicans even controlling the Senate for six. In the interim, little in the way of redistributive policies would emerge from the legislative arena under conservative Democrat Jimmy Carter either. Thus the legislative maze was back intact, and no new major civil rights legislation would be forthcoming. As a matter of fact, the real battles would be over efforts to reduce black gains from the previous era.

As examples of this assault on previous gains, consider the following. There were serious efforts to pass antibusing legislation and to reduce the federal courts' jurisdiction over school desegregation and affirmative action. A fair-housing bill was defeated in 1981. And the renewal of the 1965 Voting Rights Act faced some stiff opposition. The resulting reality even led Ronald Reagan's conservative EEOC chairman Clarence Thomas to lament that "there are greater penalties for breaking into a mailbox than there are for violating someone's basic civil rights."[33]

Nevertheless, the period was not all bleak. The Voting Rights Act was ultimately renewed, additional enforcement provisions were amended to the Fair Housing Act, and in 1988 the Civil Rights Restoration Act nullified the primary negative effect of the Grove City College v. Bell (1984) decision by allowing an entire institution to be denied federal funds even if only one of its branches has been found to be discriminating.

Blacks in Congress

August Hawkins (D-Calif.) observed:

> Twenty years ago, black members couldn't even eat in the House dining room. It was an unwritten rule. They were made to feel unwelcome. Now I'm chairman of the committee that has jurisdiction over that dining room.[34]

By contrast, Manning Marable noted:

> There is something essentially absurd about a Negro politician in racist/capitalist America.[35]

Black interest groups face certain rather formidable disadvantages in their efforts of lobby bills through the federal legislative maze. In particular, their primary constituency is relatively small—less than 12 percent of the national population. In addition, it is relatively poor, making it difficult to fund large lobbying offices in Washington or to endow cooperative politicians with sizable campaign contributions. Political scientists Harold Wolman and Norman Thomas concluded that "few blacks are actively consulted by the White House, the agencies, or the key congressional leaders."[36] Unfortunately, that appears to be as true today as it was when they wrote in 1970. Thus, short of crisis situations, attaining fundamental change through the legislative process will be very difficult indeed. Nonetheless, there are still important things to be gained by having at least small amounts of clout in the corridors of the Congress, even if those gains do not add up to fundamental change. In particular, blacks can gain their share of patronage from the congressional pork barrel, while the inherent conservatism of the Congress can be used by crafty insiders to help stave off assaults on gains won during periods of unrest.

Black Representatives. Lobbying white elected officials is one way to proceed. However, well placed black congresspersons can provide other important inroads. Parren Mitchell (D-Md.) describes one approach:

> During a recent lame duck session [of Congress], when few people expected much to happen, I introduced an amendment to the Surface Transportation Act of 1982, which represents a $71 billion expenditure over four years. My amendment provided a 10 percent set-aside for minority businesses—that represents $7 billion over four years. Now, that's using the system. I would also point out that, in 1975, under the Public Works Act, I introduced an amendment to create a 10 percent set-aside. From that, we received $400 million of a $4 billion expenditure. In reality it amounted to over $625 million that flowed into minority businesses.[37]

From 1869 until 1901, only 20 blacks served in the House of Representatives and 2 in the Senate, all representing "reconstructed" southern states. First to be elected were Jefferson Long (R-Ga.) and Joseph Rainey (R-S.C.). Thereafter, the majority of representatives came from the Carolinas, and both senators (Hiram Revels and Blanche Bruce) came from Mississippi. Nevertheless, the number of black legislators diminished rapidly following the Hayes compromise of 1876, and the last one scarcely made it to the 20th century.

Black congresspersons would reappear on Capitol Hill in 1929, however, and their numbers would grow steadily from the 1940s until the 1980s. Chicago sent the only blacks to Congress in the period from 1929 to 1944; one of them, Oscar De Priest, was the last black Republican to serve in the House, holding office from 1929 until 1934. He was then succeeded by Democrat Arthur Mitchell, who gave way to William Dawson in 1942. Dawson was joined by Harlem's Adam Clayton Powell two years later, and the black contingent gradually grew to nine members by 1969. That number reached a peak of 24 as of the 1988 elections.

Virtually all of these black congresspersons, in Reconstruction and thereafter, have represented heavily black districts. Edward Brooke (R-Mass.), the only black senator in this century, is the most obvious exception. Whites still appear uncomfortable voting for blacks, a fact not only reflected in the absence of black senators but also in the complete absence of black governors. Until those white attitudes change, the number of black representatives is not likely to grow much larger. Blacks hold majorities in only 13 congressional districts and exceed 30 percent in less than 50 others. Nonetheless, despite their relatively small numbers, many of these black representatives have held positions that provide opportunities to affect change.

Adam Clayton Powell was chairman of the House's Health, Education, and Welfare Committee. Other chairs have been Robert Nix head of the Post Office and Civil Service Committee; Ron Dellums, Committee on the District of Columbia; Parren Mitchell, Small Business; Augustus Hawkins, Education and Labor; and William Gray, Budget. As for key subcommittees, Charles Diggs headed the Foreign Affairs Subcommittee on Africa, and John Conyers the Judiciary

Subcommittee on Criminal Justice.[38] Besides insider opportunities to gain black patronage and block unfriendly bills, such positions provide opportunities to research and publicize issues. As Ron Dellums put it, "It does give me the opportunity to set the agenda, explore issues, [and] bring witnesses that have never been presented."[39] In addition, they provide opportunities to travel and speak, not to mention the Committee on the District of Columbia's jurisdiction over a predominantly black constituency.

> The Congressional Black Caucus remains committed to the position that government must be an active force for the enhancement of social justice and human dignity. We have had to become leaders and fight aggressively to protect constitutional freedoms and social justice for not just minorities but for all Americans.[40]

The Congressional Black Caucus. In an effort to maximize what little black presence existed on Capitol Hill, Charles Diggs made an overt attempt to unite with Adam Clayton Powell and William Dawson in the mid-1950s. By 1969, their numbers had grown to nine, and Powell would become the first chairperson of a now more formal organization called the Democratic Select Committee. They renamed themselves the Congressional Black Caucus in 1971, and within a decade their ranks would more than double.

Beyond organizing legislative efforts in the Congress, the primary functions of the caucus include collecting data, formulating budgetary proposals, initiating investigations (for example, investigating the 1971 police killings of Chicago Black Panthers Mark Clark and Fred Hampton), and pressuring the president. Unfortunately for the caucus, its formation has coincided with a marked decline in social unrest and a string of less than cooperative presidencies. Consequently, the group has often found itself on the defensive. Even its source of funds was challenged by a 1981 change of rules that prohibited caucuses from using public space and funds if they received outside monies. In response, the caucus formed three separate branches that essentially operate away from Capitol Hill: a foundation to raise money, a legislative service organization to do research, and a political action committee for channeling campaign funds to critical campaigns.

The caucus so functions in order to accomplish at least two stated purposes. It seeks both to provide a black perspective in the Congress and to press for equal opportunities.

First, it intends to lend a black perspective to legislative deliberations. To maintain the uniqueness of that input, in 1975 it rejected the membership of Fortney Stark, Jr., a white California Democrat who represented a district that happened to be 30 percent minority. After a month of careful consideration, they concluded that for symbolic reasons as well as a substantive unity of perspective, they would remain an exclusively black organization.

Second, the caucus is committed to equal opportunity in America. Given that its members tend to represent the major black ghettos across the country, its general policy goals were not difficult to define. As then CBC chairman Charles Rangel put it, "We have no permanent friends, no permanent enemies, just permanent interests of black and minority constituents."[41] But charting approaches to serve those interests has not always been easy. In 1972, for example, the caucus split over the presidential candidacy of its own member Shirley Chisholm, and it also could not reach consensus about whether to send representatives to the National Black Power Convention being held in Gary, Indiana, that year. Nevertheless, the caucus has shown a remarkable amount of unity overall, especially in its resolve to battle attacks on major legislative gains won in previous periods.[42]

> To say that we will pursue vigorous enforcement of civil rights laws does not mean that we accept—uncritically and unthinkingly—present approaches and assumptions.[43]

The Bureaucracy

As stated earlier, laws ultimately mean whatever the people assigned to enforce them define them to mean. Those same administrators filter the information generated by their agencies as they set the nation's legislative agenda. They can facilitate the policy orientations of the elected representatives. They can also obstruct and undermine.

In the Reagan administration, for example, the solicitor general was normally in court arguing against federal civil rights extensions. The Civil Rights Division of the Justice Department was on record as being opposed to affirmative action laws, and the entire administration simply did not actively enforce them. Neither Justice nor the Education Department pressed school desegregation; Assistant Attorney General William Bradford Reynolds declared, "We are not going to compel children who don't choose to have an integrated education to have one."[44] In addition, the Internal Revenue Service was not inclined to challenge the tax-exempt status of private schools that discriminated by race.

Top-level presidential appointees are not alone in shaping the implementation of federal legislation. Lower-level federal administrators as well as state and local law enforcement officials—both groups normally drawn from the local area—are ultimately left the responsibility of enforcing many of these laws. Local officials, for example, ended up monitoring many of the desegregation efforts mandated by the 1964 Civil Rights Act. The attorney general and his Washington staff simply could not observe every hotel registration, school admission, and hiring decision. That, of course, created certain problems when the implementing officials were the same type of people whose failure to protect blacks had led to this legislation in the first place. Of some consolation to black America, however, is the fact that a sizable portion of lower-level federal bureaucrats are now black. For example, whereas there were only 620 blacks in the entire federal bureaucracy in 1883, that figure has grown to more than 400,000—a percentage exceeding the proportion of blacks in the population as a whole.[45]

Overall, then, at the planning and implementation stages, a combination of presidential influence, bureaucratic realities, and federalism can have a significant impact on the shape federal legislation will ultimately take. Escaping the legislative maze is only part of the task.

Case Study: The 1964 Civil Rights Act

The 1964 Civil Rights Act came into being in the midst of the most extensive and intense black unrest in the history of the United States. Its route to passage provides a good example of how all the pieces fit together. It also indicates just how tortuous this procedure can be, even in the most optimal of times.

President John F. Kennedy submitted the bill to the Congress in June 1963 as what he called the "fires of frustration and discord" were sweeping the nation.[46] He then made speeches in support of the legislation, lobbied key congresspersons, and sent his cabinet members up to the Hill to testify on its behalf.

Emanuel Cellar (D-N.Y.), chair of the House Judiciary Committee, received the bill from the speaker and referred it to his Subcommittee No. 5. Public hearings then proceeded for months. Ultimately, an even stronger bill emerged out of subcommittee and was passed by the full Judiciary Committee.

Sailing in the Senate was not as smooth. Mississippi Democrat James O. Eastland, chair of the Senate Judiciary Committee, did all he could to scuttle the bill. Only one witness was heard over an 11-day period, and then the bill was tabled. It was quite clear to proponents that it would be extremely difficult to dislodge the civil rights bill from Eastland's committee.

Meanwhile, back in the House, problems were building as well. Howard Smith (D-Va.), who chaired the House Rules Committee, was refusing even to call the committee together. With no rule, the bill could not go to the House floor, where passage actually looked likely. At that critical juncture, however, John Kennedy was assassinated and Lyndon Johnson assumed the office of president. Johnson, former majority leader in the Senate and a very skillful legislator, moved quickly to dislodge the bill from the House Rules Committee. He organized enough support to force the rules consideration to the House floor if necessary. Smith finally conceded the inevitable, and the House soon had its rules—rules that did not favor quick and simple passage, however.

More than eight months from its introduction, the civil rights bill had finally reached the House floor. There, under relatively loose rules, 122 amendments were offered, and nine full days of debate ensued. Nonetheless, the marginally amended bill was finally passed by a vote of 290–130.

There had been no movement in the Senate Judiciary Committee. Consequently, majority leader Mike Mansfield took a calculated gamble. He would circumvent Senator Eastland, despite the political risks of alienating the chair of such a powerful committee. In an extremely rare move, he took the House bill directly to the Senate floor by way of a parliamentary manuever that was approved by a vote of 54–37. Those 54 senators were taking a considerable political risk, for any one of them might someday need timely and friendly consideration in the Senate Judiciary Committee. Nevertheless, the process moved forward, despite the risks.

The next obstruction was a Senate filibuster. Southern senators, led by the likes of Richard Russell (D-Ga.), began to exercise their procedural right to unlimited debate. Needing 67 votes to invoke cloture at that time, undecided votes had to be corralled. Proponents reached compromises with the waiverers that narrowed the bill's scope and significantly weakened its enforcement components. Nonetheless, cloture was finally imposed by a 71–29 vote, another relatively rare occurrence. The 71 senators seemed to be willing to risk ill will and subsequent retaliations.

Despite 99 separate attempts at amendment, the bill came to a final vote on the Senate floor, where it passed 73–27. Because the bill differed from the original House version, however, more delay loomed.

Prodded by the all-out lobbying effort of one of the most politically astute presidents in the history of the nation, there was enough support in the House to avoid a conference committee and take the matter directly to the House floor. This time the once-defeated chair of the Rules Committee proved more cooperative, and there was a full House vote within one month. The civil rights bill, as amended by the Senate, passed the House by a vote of 289–126 slightly over a year after it had first been introduced.

The bill was then signed into law by President Johnson, and the friendly Warren Court rather quickly upheld the constitutionality of key passages. Nevertheless, the battle was far from won. Short of sending legions of federal observers and law enforcement officials, implementation of the 1964 Civil Rights Act would be left to state and local judges and administrators. Enactment would be slow, arduous, and, as recent developments indicate, never final.[47]

OPTIONS FOR BLACK AMERICA

The Congressional Black Caucus, in order to be effective within the electoral context, would have to understand and directly attack the structural conditions of black subordination. Otherwise, structural constraints will continue to undermine seeming advances won through electoral politics and incremental strategies.[48]

A variety of these "structural constraints" need to be addressed not only by the CBC but by all groups and individuals who acquire power and hope to facilitate the institutionalization of a more open and just system. Among other ways, change can be facilitated by significantly reducing the number of checks and balances that presently comprise the legislative maze, by institutionalizing more direct popular control at the bureaucratic level, and by both increasing the number of black officials in the legislative arena and using those positions to educate and mobilize mass constituencies.

Reducing Checks and Balances

A Parliamentary System. One of the most sweeping changes would involve amending the U.S. Constitution so as to convert from a presidential to a parliamentary arrangement similar to those used in virtually every other representative democracy in the world. Instead of electing the president and the Congress separately, the electorate would simply choose the entire Congress at once. When a majority of the elected legislators agreed to work together, that majority would pick the president and cabinet from their own ranks, forming a government. That government would be far more united in its initiation, passage, and implementa-tion of a legislative program, and when it could no longer hold together for this purpose, new elections would be called. When the public expressed its general will at election time, the legislative process would be much more capable of responding.

Fewer Specific Checks. Among the specific checks that need to go are unlimited debate in the Senate—the procedure that has given rise to the filibuster. Also needed are standing rules in both houses of Congress that would automatically limit debate and amendments unless majorities vote to alter them for a given bill. In addition, both houses must design rules that make it easier for majorities to extract bills from committee. And even though it poses less of a problem under a parliamentary arrangement, the presidential veto should still be eliminated.

Less Federalism. Besides streamlining the federal legislative process, state and local checks need to be reduced as well. Public policy must be more centralized. More federal laws must be formed and implemented by federal bureaucrats who have not been chosen from the areas they serve. This could be accomplished by first classifying all federal jobs as either involving policy-related discretion or not involving such discretion. For example, most nonclerical employees implementing the welfare system or employed by the FBI would be in the first category, while most postal employees would be in the latter one. Then, those in the first category would be recruited under the Civil Service System from across the nation, and thereafter as many as possible would be randomly assigned outside the region from which they applied. They would also be rotated periodically from one region to another (similar to much of the foreign service). In addition, the Justice Department needs to be expanded and given a freer rein to observe and intervene locally in the implementation of federal law.

Institutionalizing Popular Control

A number of agencies are needed to empower the general public in its relationships with both the governmental bureaucracy and the private sector. Omsbudsmen, as are prevalent in Europe, could serve as liaisons between service recipients and the agencies assigned to deliver those services.[49] To provide citizens with assistance in the private sector as well, a Consumer Protection Agency could aid them in challenging questionable practices of private corporations, much as the Environ-mental Protection Agency protects the environment. Lastly, a much stronger Legal Aid program would enable all citizens, regardless of income, to use the courts to redress grievances arising in either the public or private arena.

Affirmative Action

It continues to be important to appoint more blacks to executive, staff, and bureaucratic positions throughout the legislative arena. Besides lending black perspectives to governmental agenda setting and policymaking, as well as providing hope, role models, and other more symbolic advantages, the presence of blacks in these positions may cause other blacks to be less hesitant about approaching various governmental entities in active pursuit of their interests.[50] In addition, such affirmative action efforts will give blacks opportunities to amass the kind of experience and contacts necessary to penetrate the higher levels of executive decision making in the federal government.[51]

Educating and Mobilizing

These types of streamlining and institutionalization facilitate change. Even after the system becomes more open, however, public demand for specific policy changes must continue. Several black members of Congress have suggested ways of enhancing that probability by using the full scope of existing governmental positions.

In an interview with Jeffrey Elliot, Representative Major Owens (D-N.Y.) indicated that one of his primary goals was "to push prerogatives of a congressperson to the limit." As he put it, "Congress gives me a platform. . . . And I intend to use that platform to offer leadership."[52]

In more specific terms, Congressman Gus Savage (D-Ill.) concluded:

> Being a legislator is only one side of the coin. But there's another side—namely, the ability to serve as an informal mass educator, a mobilizer, and an agitator when necessary. As I see it, my job is to galvanize people, to energize people. . . . For example, I think I was better able to contribute to the Nuclear Freeze campaign outside Congress than I was as a member. I led 200,000 people in a Nuclear Freeze demonstration in Lisbon, Portugal.[53]

Individual leaders can do only so much. Of far more importance is institutionalizing this consciousness-raising process, and it is to that end that the discussion now turns.

NOTES

1. David Stockman, former director of the Office of Management and Budget, *New York Times*, April 12, 1984.
2. Coined by Eric Redman in *The Dance of Legislation* (New York: Simon & Schuster, 1973).
3. For example, see Kenneth Dolbeare and Murray Edelman, *American Politics* (Lexington, Mass.: Heath, 1981), pp. 352–353.
4. For a fuller description of this evolution, see Lawrence Chamberlain, *The President, Congress, and Legislation* (New York: Columbia University Press, 1946), pp. 450–464.
5. *New York Times*, February 4, 1977.
6. Howard Zinn, *A People's History of the United States* (New York: Harper & Row, 1980), p. 535.
7. Testimony before the Select Committees on the Iran-Contra Investigation, 100th Cong., 1st sess., May 21, 1987 (Washington, D.C.: Government Printing Office,

1987). See Chapter 7 for a more detailed discussion of the influence of money in contemporary electoral campaigns.

8. Quoted in Jim Fain, "The Nation Is the Loser," *Memphis Commercial Appeal*, May 23, 1988.

9. Richard Bolling, *House out of Order* (New York: Dutton, 1965), p. 17.

10. For an excellent visual depiction of this process, see Marjorie Hunter and Tom Bloom, "The Longest-running Game in Town," *New York Times*, June 24, 1985.

11. *New York Times*, May 21, 1987.

12. See Charles Lindbloom, "The Science of Muddling Through," *Public Administration Review* (Spring 1959); Aaron Wildavsky, *The Politics of the Budgetary Process* (Boston: Little, Brown, 1974).

13. See Congressional Quarterly, *Weekly Reports* (September 3, 1977), p. 1855.

14. Quoted in Marguerite Michaels, "Why Congressmen Want Out," *Parade* (November 5, 1978).

15. Kay Lehman Schlozman and John Tierney, *Organized Interests and American Democracy* (New York: Harper & Row, 1985), Table 5-4.

16. Roger Davidson and Walter Oleszak, *Congress against Itself* (Bloomington: Indiana University Press, 1977).

17. *New York Times*, May 30, 1978.

18. Richard Hamilton, *Class and Politics in the United States* (New York: Wiley, 1972); Leroy Reiselbach, *Congressional Politics* (New York: McGraw-Hill, 1973).

19. Congressional Quarterly, *Weekly Reports* (September 1, 1979), p. 1823.

20. Quoted by Alex Poinsett, *Ebony* (June 1973), p. 64.

21. Common Cause, *Sunset* (Washington, D.C.: Common Cause, 1976).

22. Quoted in Thomas Cronin, *The State of the Presidency* (Boston: Little, Brown, 1975), p. 19.

23. John Hayes, *Lonely Fighter* (Secaucus, N.J.: Lyle Stuart, 1979); Helen Dudar, "The Price of Blowing the Whistle," *New York Times Magazine* (October 30, 1977); *New York Times*, April 14, 1982; *Washington Post*, October 3, 1982.

24. Edward S. Herman, *Corporate Control, Corporate Power* (New York: Cambridge University Press, 1981), p. 179.

25. *New York Times*, October 3, 1976.

26. Sheila Collins, *The Rainbow Challenge: The Jackson Campaign and the Future of American Politics* (New York: Monthly Review Press, 1986), p. 92.

27. Quoted in John Hope Franklin, *From Slavery to Freedom: A History of Negro Americans* (New York: Knopf, 1980), p. 451.

28. Interview by Joseph O'Connor, March 27, 1966, John F. Kennedy Library.

29. Gary Orfield, *Congressional Power* (Orlando, Fla.: Harcourt Brace Jovanovich, 1975), p. 73.

30. Quoted in Franklin, *From Slavery to Freedom*, p. 385. Also see Kenneth Goings, "The NAACP Comes of Age: The Defeat of Judge John J. Parker," in Winfred Moore et al. (eds.), *Developing Dixie: Modernization in a Traditional Society* (Westport, Conn.: Greenwood Press, 1988).

31. Joel Grossman and Stephen Wasby, "The Senate and Supreme Court Nominations: Some Reflections," *Duke Law Journal* (August 1972).

32. In addition to the assassination of national civil rights leader Martin Luther King, Jr., and the police repression discussed in Chapter 6, explanations for the demise of the turmoil can be found in Peter Goldman, *Report from Black America* (New York: Simon & Schuster, 1970), pp. 113–132.

33. Interview in Jeffrey Elliot (ed.), *Black Voices in American Politics* (Orlando, Fla.: Harcourt Brace Jovanovich, 1986), p. 150.

34. Quoted in *New York Times*, March 11, 1983.

35. Manning Marable, *How Capitalism Underdeveloped Black America* (Boston: South End Press, 1983), p. 170.
36. Harold Wolman and Norman Thomas, "Black Interests, Black Groups and Black Influence in the Federal Political Process," *Journal of Politics* (November 1970), p. 875.
37. Interview in Elliot, *Black Voices*, p. 37.
38. For further examples of black committee and subcommittee chairs, see Hanes Walton, Jr., *Invisible Politics: Black Political Behavior* (Albany: State University of New York Press, 1985), pp. 198–200.
39. *New York Times*, March 11, 1983.
40. Interview in Elliot, *Black Voices*, p. 46.
41. *New York Times*, March 18, 1974.
42. For further discussion see Marguerite Ross Barnett, "The Congressional Black Caucus," in Michael Preston et al. (eds.), *The New Black Politics* (White Plains, N.Y.: Longman, 1982).
43. Clarence Thomas, EEOC chairman in the Reagan administration, in Elliot, *Black Voices*, p. 153.
44. Quoted by Louis Stokes in ibid., p. 48.
45. United States Civil Service Commission, *Minority Group Employment in the Federal Government* (Washington, D.C.: GPO).
46. *Vital Speeches*, July 1, 1963, pp. 546–547.
47. For a more complete discussion of this legislative journey, see Milton Morris, *The Politics of Black America* (New York: Harper & Row, 1975), pp. 267–276. For an even more detailed analysis of a comparable example, the 1965 Voting Rights Act, see Stephen Lawson, *In Pursuit of Power* (New York: Columbia University Press, 1985). For an example of an important bill that did not emerge from the legislative maze this unscathed, see Mary Eisner Eccles, "Backers Defend Revised Humphrey-Hawkins Bill," *Congressional Quarterly Weekly Reports* (November 26, 1977), pp. 2475–2476.
48. Barnett,. "Congressional Black Caucus," p. 52.
49. For example, see Stanley Anderson, *Ombudsmen for American Government* (Englewood Cliffs, N.J.: Prentice-Hall, 1968).
50. Morris, *Politics of Black America*, p. 295.
51. For example, see Dean E. Mann, "The Selection of Federal Political Executives," *American Political Science Review* (March 1964).
52. Interview in Elliott, *Black Voices*, p. 68.
53. Ibid., p. 9.

CHAPTER NINE

The Information Arena

Recent public opinion polls provide ample evidence of growing political alienation and mistrust across the American citizenry. These feelings are not, however, accompanied by large-scale challenges to either the race and class structures described earlier or the political system that reinforces them. To the contrary, public opinion polls have actually found, for example, that a clear majority of Americans favored federal aid to help Chrysler Corporation out of its economic difficulties,[1] a reduction in social welfare programs designed to help individual indigents out of their economic predicaments,[2] and a regressive rather than progressive tax arrangement to pay the government tab.[3] Although the American public appears generally frustrated by basic political-economic outcomes, it nevertheless tends to support structures and policies that reinforce the status quo.

To understand such a mind-set requires looking beyond Easton's input, output, and conversion processes and focusing on the feedback mechanisms and political environment (see Chapter 2). Thus our analysis now turns from the conservative natures of the judicial, legislative, and electoral processes to two important conservative influences on the knowledge and opinions that underlie popular demands or the lack thereof: schools and the mass media.

EDUCATION

A primary role of the educational system in virtually every nation is to engender faith in the country's basic institutions. The United States is certainly no exception. In both subtle and not so subtle ways, the American educational system functions to generate support for the political-economic system. We shall consider examples ranging from the overt pledge of unquestioning allegiance to the national flag to the more covert "hidden curriculum" built into behavioral expectations such as "Obeys promptly and willingly" on elementary school report cards. We shall conclude with specific examples of how such institutionalized bias has affected the black community.

Overt Indoctrination

> In the political sphere, the child is taught he is free, a democrat with a free will and a free mind, lives in a free country, makes his own decisions. At the same time he is a prisoner of the assumptions and dogmas of his time, which he does not question because he has never been told they exist.[4]

Patriotic Rituals. The pledge of allegiance at the beginning of each school day and the playing of the national anthem before each interscholastic athletic event are the most obvious examples of the educational system's efforts to indoctrinate its students. As a matter of fact, comparing political indoctrination in the United States and the Soviet Union, American scholars George Bereday and B. B. Stretch found more elementary school time devoted to such overt political indoctrination in the United States.[5]

The Curriculum. Only slightly more subtle are the ways in which such reinforcing mechanisms are built into the school curriculum. Beginning in the elementary school, students are taught that the Congress and elections are the essence of the American political process, while structural biases are ignored.[6] For example, by arbitrarily separating the study of government and economics, the interrelationship between money and politics can be more easily overlooked. The focus tends to be on the fairness of the procedures and not structural biases—for example, "Is everyone eligible to vote?" as opposed to "Does the maldistribution of wealth give the wealthy clear advantages in terms of electoral input?" From such myopia comes the conclusion that the nation is a model representative democracy, open to a virtually unlimited array of individuals and interest groups.

People who have assumed positions of power over the course of American history are glorified. Christopher Columbus is exalted as a courageous and skillful seaman; his brutal treatment of the Arawak Indians, however, is never mentioned.[7] The genocide inflicted on Native Americans, the inhumanity of slavery, the second-class citizenship women and blacks endured for more than a century after the American Revolution—all of these are mentioned but played down. Instead, curricula overflow with heroics during the Revolutionary War against Britain, the brilliance of the Constitution, and the honesty of Abraham Lincoln.

How has this come to be? For one thing, many of the teachers do not know any better themselves; their own educational experiences, even through graduate school, are often just as devoid of critical analysis.[8] As Jonathan Kozol puts it:

> It is a clever North American deception to allow professor, scholar, editor alike to say what they please when we know well what they please is what we like. When wishes, ideas and dreams themselves can be confined like this, words can be free. The bulls, once surgically restrained, receive all barnyard privileges.[9]

Like any other institution that provides a product, schools require money to operate. Where does that money come from? For the public schools, some of it is drawn from government tax revenues. However, especially at the university level, more and more of this money comes from wealthy people in the private sector—often with ideological strings attached.

The owning class has long had a vested interest in the information, training, behavioral moderation, and other services schools provide. For instance, it benefits from the development of a pliant and productive work force and from a citizenry that will not seek to upset the political-economic apple cart. Schools generate information and new technologies that can improve corporate efficiency and international competitiveness. They provide reliable child care while parents work, child care that might otherwise have to be provided by employers. For those and many other reasons, it has made sense for the owning class to contribute its way into the cores of the schools.

Corporations donate books and audiovisual materials that both outline their perspective on the free enterprise system and provide a corporate view of contemporary policy issues such as health and environmental policies that pose threats to their profits. They sponsor contests that reward schools and students for demonstrating traits they desire. At the college level, they fund research institutes, faculty positions, and even entire departments in areas of interest to them,[10] and they sponsor faculty-business seminars and "executives on campus"—both of which allow the virtues of free enterprise to be extolled.[11]

Separate "think tanks," created by corporations, grind out information often used in the classrooms, much of it free of charge. Top scholars are lured by attractive salaries to work within the research agendas established by the particular organization. Examples of think tanks whose research reinforces the existing political-economic system include the American Enterprise Institute, the Brookings Institution, the Heritage Foundation, the Institute for Contemporary Studies, the International Institute for Economic Research, and the Institute for Educational Affairs.

Besides purchasing opportunities to influence faculty and students, direct monetary contributions to a school can also affect internal school decisions as to resource allocation, curriculum, and even the hiring and firing of faculty members and administrators. In the spring of 1978, for example, activist Jane Fonda spoke at Central Michigan University. In protest, Dow Chemical Company subsequently cut its substantial funding to that university. Such decisions are bound to have a chilling effect on the types of speakers many schools will dare bring to campus. Beyond that, governing boards of trustees are generally dominated by members of the owning class, often by those who have given the largest amount of money to the particular school. These boards have final say over a school's resource allocation, curriculum changes, and hiring and firing decisions.[12]

Therefore, even when teachers have been exposed to more critical perspectives, they are often treading on very thin ice if they try to introduce such perspectives into the elementary, secondary, and often even collegiate classroom.[13] Teachers, librarians, school administrators, and even school board members can be intimidated by powerful wealthy patrons and by reactionary groups and individuals as well. Often acting for what they see as patriotic or moral reasons, these reactionaries inadvertently do much of the censoring for the owning class. For example, they monitor library holdings, textbook selections, the hiring of teachers, invitations to speakers, selection of field trips, and the like, to watch for "dangerous" deviations from the status quo. Should they disagree with the educators' decisions, those responsible can at times be brought to their knees by subsequent smear tactics.[14]

Treatment of Alternative Views

> [An] important mission of the school is . . . teaching [children] to think that
> whatever country they live in is the best country in the world; that its ways of
> thought and life are better than anyone else's.[15]

Students are often taught to limit criticism of the nation's institutions and
practices unless they can demonstrate a superior alternative. Yet, at the same time,
there are overt biases against conflicting ideas and alternative arrangements. These
can be seen both in how these get treated when taken up and in explicit rules about
the conditions under which they can be examined at all.

Consider the following passage from a standard world geography textbook
published in the 1970s; the assertion has been untrue since about 1960:

> There is good reason to believe that the average Chinese is not getting enough
> food to keep healthy, and in many cases even to keep alive.[16]

Such overt slants are only the most obvious examples. There are often explicit
restrictions on the circumstances under which such ideas can be studied in the first
place. The state of Ohio, for instance, requires schools to teach "capitalism" before
students can be exposed to "socialism." The state of Florida requires a course titled
"Americanism and Communism," and the statute explicitly states:

> No teacher or textual material assigned to this course shall present Communism
> as preferable to the system of constitutional government and the free enterprise,
> competitive economy indigenous to the United States.[17]

To be doubly certain that the populace will not be unduly exposed to such
contrary thinking outside the classroom, the federal government has placed
restrictions on printed materials that can be imported, foreign speakers that can be
heard, and even countries that can be visited. For example, American citizens are
not free to visit socialist Cuba at their own discretion, and they are not allowed to
import Cuban books or magazines. In addition, visas have been denied to foreign
radicals invited to speak in American schools, churches, and even the United
Nations.

Covert Indoctrination

> It is [the teacher's] duty and responsibility to control the raw energies and desires
> of his charges and replace them with calmer, more moderate ideals. What would
> many happy citizens and trustworthy officials have become but unruly, stormy
> innovators and dreamers of useless dreams, if not for the efforts of their
> schools . . . Thus it is the school's task to subdue and control man with force and
> make him a useful member of society.[18]

Not only does the educational system overtly function to build system support
and suppress serious contemplation of radical alternatives, but it also quietly

socializes students into behavioral patterns that will make them both pliant citizens and pliant workers. From early on, they are taught to obey, memorize, and carry out tasks designed by others rather than to think for themselves, innovate, and challenge existing arrangements.

This should not be surprising in light of the genesis of mandatory public education. The early stirrings of industrialization created upheaval across the economic, social, and political landscapes. Urbanization and wage labor would replace the intimacy and relative independence of small-farm existence, requiring the cultivation of a different set of skills and behavioral patterns. Government was called on to help facilitate this transition. The "teeming masses" would need to be trained and stabilized at the same time. Thus public education was born and expanded.

In 1881, for example, the business-oriented Citizens' Association of Chicago issued a report criticizing existing public schools for failing to provide "practical training, that training of hand and eye which would enable those leaving our schools to be useful and productive members of society almost immediately after leaving school."[19] Frustrated industrialists even began to create their own schools. At that point, however, public education finally adapted itself—at least in part to conform more closely to corporate needs. Innovations like polytechnical high schools were created, and work-related training began receiving considerably more attention across the entire educational scene.[20] Today this orientation has become so ingrained that it is hardly ever given a second thought.

Consider the following letter, written by a Michigan public school principal:[21]

Dear Mr. and Mrs. Smith:
    It gives me a great deal of pleasure to inform you that Mary has completed the . . . school year with perfect attendance. This is an outstanding achievement, especially in this day and age when industry and schools are finding much abuse in this area.
    Regular attendance, whether it be at school or on the job, doesn't just happen. It takes much self-discipline, and is a great habit to form. . . .

Sincerely,
Richard Jones
Principal

The Hidden Curriculum. Open virtually any elementary school report card, and on one side there are spaces for placing grades achieved in the various academic subjects. On the other side is a behavioral checklist, and the items in that list are very telling. Besides recording the number of absences and number of times the student was tardy, many of the following behavioral traits are typically included and evaluated: accepts and respects authority, obeys promptly and willingly, follows directions, finishes work on time, respects the property of others, practices self-control, and is generally well mannered. By high school, Samuel Bowles and Herbert Gintis found subordinate and well-disciplined students rewarded, while the following traits were actually penalized: creativity, aggressiveness, independence, outspokenness, skepticism, helpfulness, emotion, and individuality.[22] And then there is competition.

Set into mean-spirited competition against other children, he learns that every man is the natural enemy of every other man. Life, as the strategists say, is a zero-sum game: what one wins, another must lose, for every winner there must be a loser. . . . He may be allowed to work on "committees" with other children, but always for some trivial purpose. When important work is being done—important to the school—then to help anyone else or get help is called "cheating."[23]

Grades are given, and class rank is noted. Standardized tests are administered, and rankings again take center stage. Honors students are given special privileges in the school building. As a capstone to the entire experience, top students receive special note at the graduation ceremonies. Although students are not encouraged to be free-thinking individuals, they are expected to be self-centered and competitive—ideal traits for their future roles as cogs in the large corporate machine. They can then be motivated by individual material incentives and are less likely to band together for their mutual protection and empowerment.

In addition, as John Holt puts it:

The schools, as they separate and label children, a few winners and a great many losers, must convince them, first, that there must always be a few winners and many losers, that no other human arrangement is possible, and secondly that whether winner or loser they deserve what comes to them. Only thus can we be sure that the winners will defend the system and the losers accept it without rancor. . . . The successful students are trained to think that being superior they have a right to more of life's goodies, a right to order other people around. The losers are trained to like what they get.[24]

Not only is the educational system training an appropriately skilled and manageable work force, but it is in fact preparing future workers by replicating many aspects of their future workplace. Students get used to a 40-hour workweek, work as drudgery done for external as opposed to intrinsic rewards, and acceptance of hierarchical authority and competition. On top of that, through mechanisms like tracking, students are introduced to structural inequality—limitations that predetermine the results of the larger competition before the race ever begins.

The resulting reality is all too predictable, as recounted by a third grade teacher:

The first rule of education for me was discipline. Discipline is the keynote to learning. Discipline has been the great factor in my life. I disciplined myself to do everything—getting up in the morning, walking, dancing, exercise. If you won't have discipline, you won't have a nation. We can't have permissiveness. When someone comes in and says, "Oh, your room is so quiet," I know I've been successful.[25]

. . . by a welder at a Ford plant:

How would you like to go up to someone and say, "I would like to go to the bathroom?" If the foreman doesn't like you he'll make you hold it, just ignore you. Should I leave this job to go to the bathroom I risk being fired. The line moves all the time.[26]

. . . and by authors Bowles and Gintis:

> Let your school system go hand in hand with the employment of your people; you may be quite certain that the adaption of these systems at once will aid each other.[27]

The Equalizer Myth. As Samuel Bowles puts it, "The ideological defense of capitalism rests strongly on the assertion that the equalizing effects of education can counter the disequalizing forces inherent in the free market system."[28] Some of those disequalizing effects were outlined in Chapters 3–5. But, in fact, the educational system quietly tends to reinforce the inequalities.

Both unemployment and income correlate rather well with years of education, meaning that the more education one has, the less likely one is to be unemployed and the more income one is likely to make. Thus, on the face of it, publicly provided educational opportunities would seem to offer a springboard to economic prosperity. As a popular public-service advertisement continues to remind students, "To get a good job, you need a good education."

Unfortunately, the employment status and income of a child's parents correlate with the number of school years completed, meaning that the children of better-off parents generally finish more school years. In addition, parental economic position often affects the quality of the school attended. Lower-income neighborhoods have less of a property tax base from which to fund their public schools, those schools are less attractive places to teach, and so on. And none of that begins to address the fact that elite private schools offer educational opportunities and prestige beyond the financial reach of most parents, not to mention the additional job contacts these schools and more affluent parents can provide after graduation.[29]

Overall, then, education can affect one's economic position in life, but the economic class into which one is born has a significant impact on one's education. Thus one's ultimate class position is more a function of the class into which one was born. Once again, then, the race is fixed from the outset. All of which led Christopher Jencks and his Harvard colleagues to conclude that the only realistic way to redistribute wealth and thus alter the American class structure is to have government use its taxing and spending powers to redistribute directly. As they saw it, the educational system provides only an illusion of equal opportunity; to expect it to lead the way toward more societal equality is little more than wishful thinking.[30]

Of course, such illusions and wishful thinking can prove to be quite useful. Everett Reimer, in his book *School Is Dead*, puts it this way:

> Schools have held out unprecedented hope of social justice. To the elite they have been an unparalleled instrument, appearing to give what they do not, while convincing all that they get what they deserve.[31]

The Black Educational Experience

The state of New Jersey provided schooling for black residents as early as 1777, and religious and humanitarian groups set up private schools for free blacks in several other states. But black slaves were systematically denied most types of education. In many places, it was actually illegal to teach a slave to read. As a result, W. E. B. Du Bois estimated that only about 5 percent of former slaves were literate as of 1865.[32] Much of that was to change following the Civil War.

Freedmen's Bureaus were instrumental in helping pave the way for the creation of elementary, secondary, and college-level schools for former slaves, including assistance in the establishment of such well-known institutions as Howard, Fisk, and Atlanta universities and the Hampton Institute. By 1870, some 247,333 black students were attending 4,329 schools, and the cost to the Freedmen's Bureaus exceeded $5 million.[33]

The Freedmen's Bureaus were not the only organizations helping to expand black educational opportunities. Various black and white religious denominations, as well as private foundations like the Peabody Educational Fund, also became involved. Thus black schools continued to expand, and a few colleges like Oberlin and Berea were racially integrated despite strong social pressure to the contrary.

The school doors were opened even further with the series of Supreme Court decisions culminating in *Brown v. Board of Education* (1954). Thereafter, a combination of the growing civil rights and black power movements, not to mention riots in the streets, paved the way for even more racially equal educational opportunities. Busing and affirmative action plans were implemented, and curricula began to include more black perspectives; black history was taught in increasing numbers of high schools, and black studies programs emerged on a number of college campuses. In addition, whereas there was only one predominantly black college in 1854, there were more than 100 such schools by the early 1970s.

Once established, however, the black educational experience included all of the previously mentioned conservative influences and then some. There has been more than an ample amount of overt and covert indoctrination, as well as clear evidence that educational opportunites are far from equal.

As an example of overt indoctrination, it is now becoming increasingly acceptable to study the political thought of Martin Luther King, Jr., a staunch Christian and an avowed pacifist. However, pity the poor elementary or secondary school teacher who tries to give equal time to the writings of black militants and socialists such as Malcolm X, Langston Hughes, Angela Davis, or Manning Marable, even in many predominantly black school settings.

After being fired for reading a poem by Langston Hughes to a class of black students in a Boston public school, Jonathan Kozol recalls what he was told:

> No literature . . . which is not in the course of study can ever be read by a Boston teacher without permission from someone higher up. When I asked her about this in more detail, she said further that no poem anyway by any Negro author can be considered permissible if it involves suffering.[34]

In his book *Death at an Early Age*, Kozol also retells the story of a teacher speaking to third- and fourth-grade black students in a ghetto school where "the books are junk, the paint peels, the cellar stinks, the teachers call you nigger, and the windows fall on your head." With fervent sincerity, the teacher tells them:

> You children should thank God and feel blessed with good luck for all you've got. There are so many little children in the world who have been given so much less. Thank God you don't live in Russia or Africa.[35]

Covert indoctrination is, of course, much more subtle. Black education has been replete with examples. Besides behavioral modification, for years schools encouraged blacks to have what Lucius Barker and Jesse McCorry term a "subject orientation"—remaining passive and detached politically.[36] In addition, black pride, identity, and self-esteem were repressed by ignoring virtually all black history and culture. Even after the civil rights and black power movements forced some of that to change, problems remain. Particularly disturbing is evidence that a large number of black students are being prematurely tracked into nonacademic vocational programs, further reinforcing the legacy of slavery.[37]

Most blatant of all are the inequities in school funding and quality, shown here as they have related specifically to blacks. As indicated in Chapter 5, public school spending varies considerably in relation to the property values in the given school districts. In the state of Ohio, for example, the wealthiest districts spent nearly five times as much on each student as the poorest ones. With blacks found disproportionately in poorer neighborhoods, the implications of such class bias in school funding are clear. The situation may be getting even worse as middle-class whites flock to private schools and exhibit less willingness to increase funding for public education. In the South, for instance, predominantly white schools outspent their predominantly black counterparts by a 3 to 2 ratio during the Jim Crow days at the turn of the century; the differential soon grew to 3 to 1 and is often even greater than that today.[38] Rather than serving as an equalizing influence, such an educational arrangement actually seems to decrease both equality of opportunity and equality of results.

MASS MEDIA

Consciously or not, the mass media exert considerable influence in American politics. In the course of both public affairs and entertainment presentations, the media do much to generate support for the existing American political-economic system.

Sources of Influence

The mass media are the nation's television, radio, newspaper, and magazine organizations. How have they come to be so politically influential? In presenting the news, for example, they have considerable discretion over what to cover, the placement and slant of the story, and the headlines and pictures that will accompany it. They are integral in the determination of the nation's public policy agenda. Problems and alternatives are generally not discussed seriously until emphasized by the media.

The importance of that agenda-setting role is amplified by the size of the audiences. Television is the most dramatic example. More than 98 percent of all American homes currently have at least one television set, and it is turned on an average of 6 to 7 hours each day. (The average 16-year-old has spent more time in front of the television than at school.) TV Guide is the top-selling magazine in the country, and during peak winter viewing hours, fully half of the American population can be found in front of television screens.

This power is enhanced by the monopolization of media ownership. Such monopolies allow a relatively small number of individual elites to exercise much discretion. Let us consider the concentration of ownership in the two dominant media, television and newspapers.

From the inception of television in the 1940s until well into the 1970s, CBS, NBC, and eventually ABC had almost a complete monopoly. Between the national networks and their affiliates, they essentially owned the airwaves. More recently, however, the number of independent stations has boomed, thanks in large part to viewer subscription cable television. Nevertheless, the three major networks and their affiliates still attract some three-quarters of the television audience most of the time, and a good many of the independents end up running and rerunning shows produced by the three major networks.

In the press, monopolization is also considerable and has been steadily increasing. Press chains (single companies that own a variety of newspapers) controlled nearly one-half of all papers in 1970, and that figure grew to some three-quarters by the end of the decade, at which point 12 chains controlled more than one-third of all the nation's newspapers. Then came the merger mania of the 1980s. In one three-month period, for instance, the Tribune chain purchased the *Newport News* for $130 million (104,000 circulation), Media News Group purchased the *Dallas Times Herald* for $110 million (244,629 circulation), Ingersoll purchased the *New Haven Register* and *New Haven Journal-Courier* for $170 million (218,519 circulation), Times Mirror purchased the *Baltimore Sun* for $400 million (356,927 circulation), and Gannett purchased the *Louisville Courier Journal* and the *Louisville Times* for $300 million (295,965 circulation). Over a four-year span, Gannett purchased the two Louisville papers just mentioned as well as the *Jackson Clarion-Ledger*, the *Jackson Daily News*, the *Des Moines Register*, and the *Detroit News*—spending $705 million and adding 1.3 million readers. On top of that, chains have even begun to buy up other chains; in one instance, Samuel Newhouse purchased Booth Newspapers for $305 million.[39]

The largest of the chains are Gannett, Knight-Ridder, Newhouse, Times Mirror, Tribune, and Dow Jones, who combined currently own nearly 200 daily newspapers and sell approximately one-third of all the individual papers purchased each day. This process has left only about 500 newspapers in the entire country that are not part of a press chain, and those tend to be in small markets and to draw all but their local stories from a handful of wire services dominated by United Press International (UPI) and the Associated Press (AP). Beyond that, less than 4 percent of American cities still have competing newspapers under separate ownership.

Not only is ownership concentrated within each medium, but ownership concentration across media is growing as well. At last count, Gannett, for example, owned 91 dailies, 38 nondailies, 6 television stations, and 14 radio stations. An individual newspaper, the *Washington Post* (part of the Times-Mirror chain), owned a television station, a radio station, a newsmagazine, and a news wire service. The Federal Communications Commission places some limits on this conglomeration;

for example, only one outlet in a given medium per owner is permitted in a given market, and an individual company is not allowed to own more than 12 television stations or control more than 25 percent of the television viewing market. Nevertheless, such rulings scarcely make a dent in the overall monopolization of the nation's media, and because the rulings generally are not applied retroactively, they affect only new acquisitions.

The end result is that three television networks, two wire services, and a half dozen newspaper chains have a powerful hold on what is known in the United States. Who actually owns these media giants? As few as 10 business and financial corporations hold the controlling shares of stock in CBS, NBC, ABC, 34 subsidiary television stations, 201 cable television systems, 62 radio stations, 59 magazines (including *Time* and *Newsweek*), and 58 newspapers (including the *New York Times, Los Angeles Times, Washington Post,* and *Wall Street Journal*).[40] WNET, the flagship channel in the Public Broadcasting Service (PBS), is heavily reliant on the Ford Foundation. Chapter 4 made it clear who controls these banks, financial corporations, and foundations, and do not forget that the owning and non-owning directors of these organizations sit on each other's boards, even within the media business.[41]

In Pursuit of Profit

What drives the decisions of this highly monopolized industry so integral to the political-economic system? As virtually the entire mass media industry is privately owned and operated for a profit, it normally must first serve the investment interests of its primary stockholders. As it turns out, this pursuit of profit has often resulted in news and entertainment presentations that have a sort of political lobotomizing effect on the audience.

Serving Investors. Focusing on television, Fred Friendly draws the following conclusion from his experiences as president of CBS News:

> By default we have permitted the investor's equity to control what is basically a public-service industry.[42]

As evidence, he ranks the top priorities guiding television's choice of what shows would appear:

1. Nielsen ratings
2. Effect of those ratings on advertisers
3. Effect of those ratings on expected earnings and thus stock market position
4. The company's corporate image in the press, among the community leaders, and at the FCC
5. Public service and good taste[43]

As an example of just how effective the three major commercial networks are at following these criteria, consider their economic success. Advertisers pay them hundreds of thousands of dollars for each minute of prime-time advertising, adding up to over $1 billion a year for each network. Profit rates are higher than in most business operations in the country. For example, the networks often make more than 30 percent profit on gross revenues and 200 to 300 percent on invested capital. So lucrative is such access to the airwaves that local television stations sell for millions of dollars, and even individual radio stations are regularly approaching $1 million in value.

Highly profitable, although on a somewhat smaller scale, newspapers also rely heavily on attracting advertisers. All newspapers combined draw nearly twice as much advertising revenue as the three major television networks. Such dependence is reflected in the allocation of newspaper space. Whereas roughly one-quarter of all television airtime is consumed by advertisers, 40 percent of space in the press is devoted to news while the other 60 percent is filled with advertisements. "Newspaper" actually seems to be a misnomer.[44]

The mass media, then, are comprised of private corporations whose primary reason for being is to return maximum profits for their stockholders. The figures indicate that they take their job seriously and are quite good at it. But besides leading them to sell advertisers a sizable share of the nation's mass communications,[45] this profit orientation also appears to have had a noticeable impact on the content of the news and entertainment that appears the rest of the time. This reality has definite political consequences.

Programming Impact. Media critic John Leonard concludes that "the history of the United States [is being brought to us] not by the Senate and the House, but by Occidental Bank and Weed Eater."[46] He is implying that what the public knows and considers important may well be heavily affected by what large advertisers will and will not sponsor. What shapes those advertising decisions? The primary concern of corporations who spend thousands upon thousands of dollars for these opportunities to circulate information about their products almost always has to be reaching the largest buying audience possible. To attract advertisers, mass media companies must be able to attract and hold large audiences with the content of what they present.

> The most serious threat to television and its claim to First Amendment freedoms is not the Federal Communications Commission or the Supreme Court, or an Imperial Presidency, but the runaway television ratings process. The current obsession with surveying the "habits" and "pulse" of television sets, rather than the response of and impact on human beings, has resulted in an industry preoccupied with short-term indicators and profits.[47]

What Friendly found true for television, Gannett's Al Neuharth found true for newspapers.[48] There is a real tendency in the mass media to follow audience inclinations rather than to lead. But it is not enough simply to attract the audience by serving them something that will catch their attention and conform to their existing values and attitudes. It is also essential to hold them. Thus once they have been attracted, it is much safer to anesthetize than to provoke or offend.

Television news gives highest priority to sensational stories that can be captured on film, such as auto accidents and multiple homicides. Thus the airwaves come to be dominated by what media critic Ben Bagdikian calls "fires, sex, and freaks."[49] In between such stories, local stations serve up a hefty portion of "happy talk" banter between the various on-camera personalities.[50] On the national level, ABC plucked Roone Arledge from the *Wide World of Sports* to head up its news division in order to "liven up" the network's news programming. Absent, even at most newspapers, is probing in-depth investigative reporting, especially on subjects like workplace safety, poverty, and product liability.

Even election coverage, essential to the functioning of a healthy democracy, tends often to be narrow, superficial, and sensational. Unable to attract and hold large audiences with extensive discussion of issues, the focus shifts to clichés and candidate images. Is he "strong on defense"? Is she "fiscally responsible"? What passes for investigative reporting is often voyeurism into candidates' personal lives for the sensationalism that entails. Come election day, the results are reported as if it were a horse race. In a crowded primary, for example, a winner must be declared and crowned, even if that person received only 15 or 20 percent of the vote.

Actually, radio and television stations are required by the Federal Communications Commission to devote at least 5 percent of their broadcasting time to "public affairs." If it were not for that rule, there might be even less news-related programming on the airwaves. Documentaries, for example, tend to be expensive to produce and tend not to draw large audiences. Even controversial documentaries like *The Selling of the Pentagon* and *The Corporation* do poorly in the Neilsen ratings. And as the three major networks have gradually lost some of their monopoly status to cable television, increased competition seems to have led to even less inclination to absorb the financial losses entailed in documentaries. Instead, the viewer is given "newsmagazines" and early-morning quasi-news programming like *The Today Show*.

Media critic John O'Connor described public affairs programming as follows:

> It is something the FCC likes to find in the program log of stations at license renewal time as an indication, however meaningless, that the customary quest for profits was tempered by an occasional gesture toward the real world beyond old movies and sitcoms."[51]

Entertainment, of course, tends to be even more mind-numbing. Most cable stations, like network TV, present a steady parade of game shows, soap operas, mindless situation comedies, and police dramas. As Norman Lear put it, "With painful predictability, the networks putter with the same tired formats, adding more sex here and more violence there—more mindlessness. . . ."[52]

Profit-seeking media corporations and their advertisers also have a vested interest in defending a profit-based economic system. Thus the world view underlying most public affairs and entertainment programming is not difficult to identify.

The Dominant Values

Conferring Values. Like the educational process, the mass media are an important part of American socialization. Faith in welfare-state capitalism must be reinforced, as must the illusion that the political system guarantees democratic control. This is accomplished by omission and commission in both public affairs and entertainment programming.

By omission, challenging perspectives often fall out of public affairs presentations. For example, newspapers run regular syndicated editorials by a number of spokespersons for the extreme conservative position, such as William F. Buckley, Jr., George Will, and James Kirkpatrick. However, absent are regular columns by socialists such as I. F. Stone, Michael Harrington, or Noam Chomsky. In the electoral arena, third-party candidates and their potentially threatening views are ignored almost completely. Even in their heyday, documentaries tended to concentrate on subjects like divorce, youth crime, and incest rather than topics whose analysis could threaten the political-economic status quo, such as labor unions, the military-industrial complex, or the positive side of life in socialist countries.[53]

News coverage often bears the stamp of the same underlying values. Political scientist Michael Parenti notes, for instance, that labor issues get twisted to make the workers look irresponsible and greedy.[54] He also notes that the mass media both downplayed and underestimated the size of two of the largest demonstrations in the nation's history—a half million people marching on Washington to protest Reagan policies in September 1981 and a full million marching in New York City to oppose nuclear weapons in June 1982.[55] The flip side of this form of slant is local media's inclination to inflate positives and play down problems in their immediate communities in order to boost the community's image in the eyes of potential investors. As a local business themselves, these media outlets have much at stake in the overall economic climate of their host community.

Similar things can be found on the entertainment side. As Erik Barnouw put it, "Television entertainment is propaganda for the status quo."[56] For example, no television series has had a black militant or a courageous socialist as a hero. Quite the contrary, black militants and socialists, when they do appear, are normally portrayed as dangerous caricatures. Meanwhile, police shows condition the audience to accept police repression of such dissenters.[57]

Contributing Factors. At least four forces contribute directly to this ideological posture. Media personnel and their standard operating procedures, advertisers, and government all contribute to the fostering of what Ralph Miliband terms "a climate of conformity."[58]

To begin with, decision makers in the media business are demographically homogeneous. Once again, they tend to be relatively well-to-do white men. In addition, all of the employees are ultimately answerable to members of the owning class who hold the controlling shares of stock in their particular company. Both realities contribute to the media's conservative content.[59] On top of that are a set of operational parameters that further encourage conformity—for example, time and money restraints that prompt news journalists to feed off one another's stories.[60] Besides these internal factors, the mass media face external influences as well. As Leonard Matthews, president of the American Association of Advertising Agencies, put it,

> To expect private companies to go on supporting a medium that is attacking them is like taking up a collection for money among the Christians to buy more lions.[61]

Although they are ultimately guided by the desire to maximize audience exposure and thus profits, advertisers will occasionally use their advertising money for overtly political purposes when they feel circumstances require it. At the national level, the thrust of *Lou Grant* came to be seen as too ideologically liberal, incurring the wrath of various right-wing organizations. Kimberly-Clark then pulled its advertising money, and the show was soon dropped.[62] General Electric withdrew its sponsorship from an interview Barbara Walters conducted with Jane Fonda. Coming at the time of her popular film *The China Syndrome*, GE feared that it would contain "material that could cause undue public concern about nuclear power."[63] At the local level, Brooklyn's Williamsburgh Savings Bank pulled its advertising from a local newspaper that had run a story on the practice of bank redlining (designating certain neighborhoods as too risky for investment). The tobacco industry's mere threat of withdrawing such money seems capable of censoring media coverage of that industry in Winston-Salem, North Carolina.[64]

Advertisers also draw on their stock of wealth in other ways to make certain that their own perspectives are presented on important political issues of the day. For example, they buy media time and space so that they can present their political points of view directly. Such "advocacy advertising" proliferated in the late 1970s and soon involved well over $1 million a year.[65] Texaco and Mobil, for instance, have both run numerous ads extolling "corporate perspectives" on various issues. In addition, their regular commercial advertising is replete with conservative values as well, such as conditioning people to accept the virtues of profit-driven capitalism.[66] The same values permeate many public-service ads, most of which are delegated to the Advertising Council, a body comprised largely of corporate owners and executives.[67] These same corporations sponsor journalism prizes for outstanding work—within acceptable parameters—and fund trips to lavish conferences at which journalists can discuss issues of interest to the corporations.

Finally, government plays a role as well. The United States Information Agency, for example, has put out pamphlets like *The Problems with Communism*. Even more blatant is the fact that the "fairness doctrine," established in the Federal Communications Act, required all broadcasting stations to provide "balanced" coverage of controversial issues but explicitly stated that this did not include the "Communist perspective."[68]

The Black Experience

> Black people find themselves in a country with the legal and constitutional guarantee of freedom of the press but lacking the actual power to exercise that right because there is not freedom in the press. As a result, all Americans, but

especially black people, suffer through distortion and deletion. Journalism has used its power of appraisal to mentally disenfranchise us.[69]

The legacies of slavery have been reinforced in numerous ways by the mainstream mass communications system in the United States. Not only have blacks suffered from the general reinforcement of the political-economic status quo, but the dominant media have tended either to ignore black Americans or to caricature them brutally and destructively. In response, blacks have opted to found their own mass communications networks—black newspapers, black-oriented radio stations, and the political component of a number of black churches.

Blacks and the White Media. In terms of race, one need only look at the dearth of black stockholders, executives, and employees in the major national media to begin to understand why blacks have long been portrayed as caricatures and why black issues emerge so slowly in the public consciousness. But the problem runs far deeper than the general impact on society as a whole, for black consciousness itself has been particularly affected by these practices.

Underrepresentation. As Hanes Walton, Jr., put it, "The perennial problem confronting black political opinion is that it cannot stop one sphere of society from creating its picture of reality but it must constantly reshape the distortions it creates to fit its own perceptions."[70] One of the primary reasons for this phenomenon would seem to be the disproportionately small number of blacks in the decision-making ranks of the mass media.

Blacks are underrepresented at all levels of the media business. They own roughly 50 of the over 8,000 radio stations in the country and only 3 of the more than 700 television stations. Two of 134 top network executives are black. *Tony Brown's Journal,* aired over the Public Broadcasting System, is about the only example of a black-produced program that is nationally televised and deals with black America in a serious way. Six of 1,769 daily newspapers have blacks in executive management positions. In the entire national press corps, there are only two syndicated black columnists (Carl Rowan and William Raspberry) and approximately 30 black editorial writers, while only 4 percent of all print journalists are black and a majority of daily newspapers have no minority journalists at all.[71] What is more, the modest gains blacks have been making seem to have leveled off in recent years.[72]

On the entertainment side, with the exception of programs like *The Bill Cosby Show,* the reality is even bleaker. There are virtually no blacks in decision-making positions here either. Even the much acclaimed television series *Roots,* for example, had no black producers, no black assistant producers, no black writers, and no black directors.[73]

This dearth of blacks in discretionary positions has a number of implications. It no doubt leads to some inequity of treatment within the media ranks. On *Roots,* for example, two white actors earned more money for their performances than did all of the black cast combined.[74] More significant is the impact of what ends up being presented in the press and over the airwaves.

One of the ways [in which] institutionalized racism is manifest is that the news media do not consider the condition of the black community to be newsworthy. The income gap between whites and blacks has widened. Segregation is greater in the North now than it was 25 years ago. Police brutality is still one of the major sources of irritation in the black community. Black teenage unemployment never fell below 35 percent during the entire decade of the 1970s. And more. Yet, little media attention was focused on these forms of racism. [75]

Invisibility. As Jesse Jackson suggests, there is little coverage of chronic problems black Americans face. Court-ordered school busing is a classic case in point. Governmentally required busing of black students to inferior segregated schools received virtually no media coverage prior to the 1950s, whereas court-ordered busing of blacks to white schools filled the newspapers and the airwaves. [76] The nation's two syndicated black columnists can both cite numerous examples of this phenomenon. In the midst of the 1967 Watts unrest, for example, William Raspberry recalls searching the back issues of the *Los Angeles Times* without finding a single prior story on the area. [77] Carl Rowan goes as far as to conclude that "the country's rulers are using the media to obscure truths about racism, poverty, injustice, and economic and political repression." [78]

Black Images

Television programming still reflects stereotypes and prejudices that perpetuate feelings of inferiority in blacks and superiority in whites. Until minorities gain access in policy-making positions in programming, in both radio and television shows alike, . . . [television shows such as] CBS's "Baby, I'm Back" and others like [it] will continue to poison the minds of viewers. [79]

While blacks have tended to be ignored in public affairs programming, they have often been blatantly caricatured on the entertainment side. One need not watch many episodes of *Good Times, Sanford and Son,* or *The Jeffersons* to hark back to the bad old days of Amos and Andy, Aunt Jemima, and Rochester. *The Bill Cosby Show,* like *Roots* before it, is one of the very few examples in which black characters are not presented as lightweight buffoons, mammies, superstuds, and criminals, fueling the stereotypes of white America. [80]

As Jesse Jackson put it, "Television's major violation of us is a consistent combination of distortion and deletion which projects us as less intelligent, more violent, less hard-working, and less universal than we are." He goes on to conclude that "television's projection of us almost makes welfare, poverty, unemployment, and blacks synonymous." [81]

Such stereotyping does not stop with television. Harvard's Jeanne Chall, for instance, found blacks badly underrepresented and stereotyped in children's books as well. [82]

Impact

It cannot be denied that by adding a few black faces on television, the medium which probably has the greatest impact on the black population, the white cultural rulers have taken a major step toward co-opting, distorting, and essentially nullifying [black America].[83]

Feeding white stereotypes and indifference to black problems are only the most obvious results of such distortions. Just as devastating is the apparent impact on blacks' self-perceptions and political world views.

Blacks watch approximately 16 percent more television than whites, and they listen to more radio than they watch television—some 25 hours per week.[84] They are exposed to the full gamut of mass media messages. This probably explains why blacks exhibit the same inclination as whites to distrust political and economic leaders, who are often critically analyzed in the media. Blacks also have relatively low levels of political satisfaction. At the same time, both blacks and whites strongly support the rarely attacked political-economic system itself. Also, quite similar to whites, nearly three-quarters of all blacks identify themselves as moderate or conservative, while only 17 percent conceive of themselves even as liberal, and very few as radical.[85] Meanwhile, in contrast to whites, black Americans as a group tend to have lower feelings of political efficacy and greater deference to authority.[86]

The end result is a black population that tends to mistrust the officials who operate the system they feel they have little control over, yet they remain loyal to that system and deferent to its leaders' authority. The degree to which any of this can be linked to the content of the media is uncertain, but at the very least, the media are reinforcing such perceptions by their failure to expose and attack the underlying structures themselves. Jesse Jackson reached this conclusion:

> To the degree . . . journalism accurately and fairly informs and educates the public, to that some degree will it retain its moral authority and believability. Right now, as far as black people are concerned, it has been weighed and found wanting.[87]

It is in part out of such dissatisfaction with the white media that the black media have arisen, proliferated, and become important in the black community. In addition, the deficiencies of the white media contributed to the sizable role of the black church as a forum for political communication.

The Black Media

> The forces that operated on the Negro population for three centuries and more were of such nature as to create a distinctly separate Negro world within the American community.[88]

Although often constrained by relatively small budgets, attributable in large part to a difficulty in attracting white advertisers, black newspapers and radio stations can at least function without some of the shortcomings exhibited by their white counterparts. Black people are normally in the key decision-making positions, lending more of a black perspective to public affairs coverage and what entertainment is provided. Black-related issues are covered far more regularly, and black images are not as apt to be tarnished by the ignorance or prejudices of whites.

Consequently, these media allow black Americans a less obstructed forum for political communication among themselves and for analyzing events from a black perspective, even if the larger American population remains reliant on the dominant sources.

> Negro newspapers of the twentieth century took up the cudgel in behalf of the underprivileged. They became the medium through which the yearnings of the race were expressed, the platform from which the Negro leaders could speak, the coordinator of mass action which Negroes felt compelled to take, and a major instrument by which many Negroes were educated with respect to public affairs.[89]

Black media emerged in the 19th century, with the first black newspaper appearing in 1827. One of the earliest and best known was the *North Star*, produced by Frederick Douglass primarily for the purpose of articulating antislavery points of view. Since those early days, some 2,700 different black papers have appeared, reaching a peak of proliferation in the 1950s. They grew in circulation with the advent of the Great Migration northward. As blacks became concentrated in central cities, several papers had circulations exceeding 100,000 by 1920 and twice that 20 years later.[90]

In recent years, approximately 200 black-owned newspapers have existed at any one point in time. Most have been weeklies. New York City is typical, featuring weeklies plus the *Daily Challenge* (a daily) and the *New York Page* (a monthly). In political outlook, again using New York City examples, they range from more racially separatist and politically radical papers like the *Big Red* and the *City Sun* to more integrationist and politically moderate papers like the *New York Voice* and the *Amsterdam News*. In between are a variety of newspapers ever more influential in increasingly black urban centers, such as Longworth Quinn's *Michigan Chronicle* (Detroit), John Sergstracke's long-standing *Chicago Defender*, Carlton Goodlett's *San Francisco Sun Reporter*, and Charles Tisdale's *Jackson Advocate* (Jackson, Mississippi).

Over the airwaves, there are two relatively small but increasingly important black-oriented radio networks, the National Black Network and the Mutual Black Network. In addition, Bob Law's *Night Talk* is a syndicated radio show. On television, *Soul Train* and *Black Journal* are nationally syndicated as well, and cable television offers the Black Entertainment Network.

As far as common content, black radio stations focus far more on the work of black entertainers and types of music and humor traditionally popular in the black community. On the public affairs side, Alan Morrison concluded that these stations have "continued to voice the aspirations, articulate the demands and protests, and mirror the progress and problems of . . . Negro Americans."[91] Most of these sources have been restrained in their criticism of black elected officials and leaders. Instead, they have normally opted to discuss and critically analyze political issues of the day, without much of the general media's emphasis on "fires, sex, and freaks," and they spend a fair amount of time countering myths and attacks propounded in the white media.[92] In addition, they provide a forum for black leaders that for a long time tended to be limited to the black church.

THE BLACK CHURCH

The foundations of modern black politics are found within the black church.[93]

The black church has often served as an important network for political communication over the course of black history in the United States. The visibility and the extent of the church's political role is a phenomenon relatively unique to the experience of black Americans.

Independent black churches first began to appear in significant numbers during the period of the American Revolution, and they really flourished after the Civil War. The African Methodist Episcopal Church, for example, grew from 20,000 members in 1856 to more than 200,000 members by 1876. Black Baptists grew from 150,000 in 1850 to 500,000 by 1870.[94] Thereafter, their memberships soared again. Reaching a membership peak around 1910, their numbers have fallen some since.[95]

Somewhat by default, the churches became central black institutions in the realm of politics. As John Hope Franklin explained it, "The lack of opportunities for Negroes to participate fully in the affairs of other institutions caused many to concentrate their energies and attention on the church."[96] Among other things, they recruited and provided a training ground for black political leaders and offered a forum for political communication and organization—especially during the darkest days of Jim Crow exclusion.[97] Ministers actually held positions at state constitutional conventions, on school boards, and in other public organizations during Reconstruction, and ministers like Martin Luther King, Jr., and Ralph Abernathy were at the forefront of the civil rights movement that would finally sweep away the Jim Crow laws. Thereafter, although ministers would play less of a direct role, they and their churches would continue to play important supporting roles in black politics.[98]

Not confined by the economic necessity to turn a profit, as are most mass media, the black church has been in a relatively unique position to facilitate a truly freewheeling discussion of political and economic alternatives. Nevertheless, black churches have been accused by some critics of having significant inherent limitations.

The church, for example, has been accused of often directing attention primarily to spiritual well-being and life after death and at times even implying that blacks are somehow personally responsible for much of their own plight.[99] This, among other factors, is said to have led a number of these churches to be painfully apolitical at crucial times in black history. For example, Manning Marable and others have noted an almost deafening silence during lynchings, post-Reconstruction disenfranchisement, unabated economic exploitation, and attacks on black radicals.[100] Gary Marx even went so far as to speak of the churches' "opiate" effect in the political arena, implying that they often stifle political energies rather than promoting aggressive political activism.[101] And a sizable number of black ministers have at times even taken up the conservative banner, as in fighting to retain segregation.[102]

To be fair, it is important not to lump all black churches and religious leaders together. There has been considerable variation in both the level of political activism and political-economic ideology. From reactionary Christian fundamentalism to the liberalism exhibited by many members of the Southern Christian Leadership Council to the progressive radicalism of many of the Black Muslims to advocates of liberation theology, black churches and leaders have supported a tremendous range of political orientations. [103]

OPTIONS FOR BLACK AMERICA

Consider the efforts of Emma Bowen. Her Black Citizens for Fair Media had as many as 200 organizational members, including churches and professional associations. At its strongest, it met regularly with network-owned television stations in New York City to discuss black grievances, including more training and hiring of black broadcasters and more documentaries on black problems. [104] Beyond the attainment of political-economic power, what else needs to be done to alter the conservative socialization process? Focus will be placed on the two secular components of the information arena, education and the mass media.

Education

> What all this boils down to is, are we trying to raise sheep—timid, docile, easily driven or led—or free men? If what we want is sheep, our schools are perfect as they are. If what we want is free men, we'd better start making some big changes. [105]

School Governing Boards. One of these changes needs to be in the composition of the school boards and trustees who make the ultimate decisions concerning curricula, speakers, field trips, hirings and firings, and the like. To reduce the influence of the wealthy, these positions could be filled randomly, leaving each person whose name is drawn the option to decline. But this would nevertheless involve filling these slots with people who have been indoctrinated by the existing educational system; thus the specific changes to be demanded of them must be discussed.

School Curricula. School curricula will require fundamental alterations, and teachers and administrators must be protected from political pressures during this implementation, as through the random selection of their highest superiors. Curriculum reform could begin with unification of the study of politics and economics; their interrelationships must be analyzed as a regular part of the curriculum. Alternative ideologies and political-economic systems must be studied at the same time that the dominant ones are taught. And people and events in American history must be evaluated critically rather than perfunctorily glorified. Overall, the schools must perform their socialization role by teaching even the youngest students to think and choose rather than simply to believe.

Behavioral Instruction. The emphasis in behavioral lessons must shift dramatically as well. The schools have to move away from training robotlike individuals who are motivated primarily by individual incentives and competition. Instead of class rankings on the basis of rote knowledge and social conformity, emphasis should be on traits like creativity, innovation, independent thought, critical analysis, outspokenness, cooperation, and other-orientation. When those behavioral characteristics begin to dominate the elementary school checklists, progress will have been made.

School Funding. Schools need to be funded in a much more equitable fashion. No public school should have to operate on less than 90 percent of what the wealthiest public or private school has to spend. One way to raise the additional money necessary so as continually to elevate a number of the public schools to that level would be to set up a progressive school-funding arrangement on a national basis. Employers and employees could each be required to contribute a percentage of their incomes, in proportion to what they are making. These federal revenues would then be set aside for equalizing school funding only. This would not only help guarantee more equal educational opportunities, but it would tax most heavily many of the people who have gained the most from the educational system.

Mass Media

> For the press, . . . the freedom is not simply a right and a privilege, it is a duty. You, more than any other institution, are trustees of the nation, because no one else gives their opinion so openly and so regularly.[106]

In terms of content, more freedom-restricting governmental censorship is not the answer. Instead, a variety of structural changes seem more appropriate to the goal of fundamentally altering current media practices.

Black Perspectives. Black presence needs to be increased in existing media and regulatory bodies. Virtually as true now as when the postriot Kerner Commission concluded it in 1968, "Along with the country as a whole, the press has too long basked in a white world, looking out of it, if at all, with white men's eyes and a white perspective. That is no longer good enough."[107]

To begin with, the Federal Communications Commission needs black commissioners, and it in turn needs to impose strict affirmative action hiring guidelines on radio and television stations. In addition, blacks must be placed in managerial positions throughout the Public Broadcasting System. Public funds must be made available for starting up black media companies. This could involve setting aside portions of PBS monies for black public broadcasting stations and providing low-cost financing for black entrepreneurs seeking to start stations in the commercial sector.

Less Elite Control. The conservative mass media should be subject to stiffer antitrust laws. No investor, for example, should be allowed to hold stock directly or indirectly in more than one media company, to control more than 5 percent of that company's stock, or to have that share in a market in which he or she has other investments, creating possibilities for conflicts of interest. Then, within those less monopolized firms, media decision making should be insulated as much as possible from the profit concerns of stockholders and advertisers to reduce influence on media content. For example, the FCC could require that all advertisements be the same length, cost a single set fee to run, and be randomly assigned across the various slots and media companies available in the given market.

Nonprofit Media. Nonprofit public channels should be expanded and further freed from political pressure. One need only compare the quality of public affairs broadcasting on PBS in contrast to most commercial stations to note the value of having a healthy public-funded alternative. Beyond what already exists, then, a public wire service and public newspaper chain could be established, structured like PBS and National Public Radio (NPR). However, PBS, NPR, and the new Public Newspaper Network (PNN) need secure government funding insulated from the direct control of elected officials. That could be accomplished by placing these funds in an entitlement budgetary category and putting them in a blind trust for 25 years at a time. In addition, the management of these public media could be chosen by professional journalists' associations.

Direct Public Access. Funding for public-service spots and public-service newspaper advertisements needs to be granted to the widest possible array of interest groups on a random basis. Commercial broadcasters should be obliged to carry them, at various times across the entire broadcasting schedule. And their messages should not be censored, except on the basis of nationally established obscenity guidelines. In addition, the advent of cable television has substantially increased possibilities for popular access. As low-frequency channels proliferate, these should be assigned randomly so that all interest groups have equal opportunites to communicate over these less expensive airwaves.

More extreme would be a constitutional amendment to extend rights to free expression. Assuming that freedom of speech is essentially useless if no one else can be reached, First Amendment protections could be expanded to include a positive right to media access. It would then be up to government and the various media to determine how to comply before being compelled to do so by the courts.

NOTES

1. ABC News—Louis Harris poll, conducted September 1–5, 1979.
2. *New York Times,* August 3, 1977; June 28, 1978.
3. Benjamin I. Page, "Taxes and Inequality: Do the Voters Get What They Want?" unpublished manuscript.
4. Doris Lessing, *The Golden Notebook* (New York: Simon & Schuster, 1962), pp. xvi–xvii.
5. George Bereday and B. B. Stretch, "Political Education in the USA and the USSR," *Comparative Education Review* (June 1963).
6. David Hess and Judith Torney, *The Development of Political Attitudes in Children* (Garden City, N.Y.: Doubleday, 1968), p. 41; *New York Times,* September 23, 1970.

7. Howard Zinn, *A People's History of the United States* (New York: Harper & Row, 1980), chap. 1.

8. Hess and Torney, *Development of Political Attitudes; New York Times*, September 23, 1970.

9. Jonathan Kozol, *The Night Is Dark and I Am Far from Home* (Boston: Houghton Mifflin, 1975), p. 177.

10. David Vogel, "Business's New Class Struggle," *The Nation* (December 15, 1979).

11. *New York Times*, October 9, 1981; Sheila Harty, *Hucksters in the Classroom* (Washington, D.C.: Center for Study of Responsive Law, 1979); Betty Medsger, "The Free Propaganda That Floods the Schools," *Progressive* (December 1976).

12. Thomas Dye, *Who's Running America?* (Englewood Cliffs, N.J.: Prentice-Hall, 1983), chap. 5; Rodney Harrett, *College and University Trustees* (Princeton, N.J.: Educational Testing Service, 1969), p. 65.

13. Phillip Meranto et al., *Guarding the Ivory Tower* (Denver: Lucha, 1985).

14. Examples are numerous and varied. Besides the ones detailed in ibid., Accuracy in Academia formed to secretly monitor the "truthfulness" of what was being taught in American classrooms. Marxist Bertell Ollman was denied the chairmanship of the University of Maryland's Department of Political Science after reactionary members of the state legislature rallied to force school officials to change their minds. Small reactionary groups have acquired virtual censorship power over government textbooks in Texas and English texts in East Tennessee. The list goes on.

15. John Holt, *Freedom and Beyond* (New York: Dutton, 1972), p. 251.

16. John Bradley, *World Geography* (New York: Ginn, 1971), p. 426.

17. *New York Times*, May 4, 1983.

18. Herman Hesse, *Beneath the Wheel* (New York: Farrar, Strauss & Giroux, 1968), p. 54.

19. Quoted in David Hagan, *Capitalism and Schooling*, dissertation, University of Chicago, 1978, p. 251.

20. For example, see San Francisco Board of Education, *Report of the Commission on Manual Training* (San Francisco, March 14, 1894). For a detailed discussion of this entire subject, see Ira Katznelson and Margaret Weir, *Schooling for All: Race, Class, and the Decline of the Democratic Ideal* (New York: Basic Books, 1985).

21. Names have been changed.

22. Samuel Bowles and Herbert Gintis, *Schooling in Capitalist America* (New York: Basic Books, 1976), pp. 135–137.

23. John Holt, *The Underachieving School* (New York: Pitman, 1969), p. 19–20.

24. Holt, *Freedom and Beyond*, p. 255.

25. Rose Hoffman, third-grade teacher, quoted in Studs Terkel, *Working* (New York: Avon, 1974), p. 635.

26. Phil Stallings, welder, quoted in ibid., p. 222.

27. Bowles and Gintis, *Schooling in Capitalist America*, p. 174.

28. Samuel Bowles, "Unequal Education and the Reproduction of the Hierarchical Division of Labor," in Richard Edwards (ed.), *The Capitalist System* (Englewood Cliffs, N.J.: Prentice-Hall, 1972), p. 219.

29. See Chapter 5. Also see Christopher Jencks, *Inequality: A Reassessment of the Effect of Family and Schools in America* (New York: Basic Books, 1972); Richard De Lone, *Small Futures: Children, Inequality, and the Limits of Liberal Reform* (Orlando, Fla.: Harcourt Brace Jovanovich, 1979); report by the Carnegie Council on Children, *Behavior Today* (September 10, 1979).

30. Jencks, *Inequality*.

31. Everett Reimer, *School Is Dead* (Garden City, N.Y.: Doubleday, 1971), p. 19.

32. W. E. B. Du Bois, *Black Reconstruction in America, 1860–1880* (New York: Atheneum, 1971), p. 638. Also see Carter Woodson, *The Education of the Negro prior to 1861* (Washington, D.C.: Associated Publishers, 1919).

33. John Hope Franklin, *From Slavery to Freedom: A History of Negro Americans* (New York: Knopf, 1980), p. 237.
34. Jonathan Kozol, *Death at an Early Age* (Boston: Houghton Mifflin, 1967), p. 147.
35. Ibid., p. 33.
36. Lucius Barker and Jesse McCorry, *Black Americans and the Political System* (Cambridge, Mass.: Winthrop, 1976), p. 97.
37. Robert Green, *The Urban Challenge: Poverty and Race* (Chicago: Follett, 1977), pp. 217–221; *Memphis Commercial Appeal*, November 25, 1988; *New York Times*, December 12, 1988.
38. Franklin, *From Slavery to Freedom*, p. 403. For a more detailed discussion of black educational opportunities, see Horace Mann Bond, *The Education of the Negro in the American Social Order* (Englewood Cliffs, N.J.: Prentice-Hall, 1934); Meyer Weinberg, *A Chance to Learn: A History of Race and Education in the United States* (New York: Cambridge University Press, 1977), chaps. 1–3, 7.
39. *New York Times*, December 15, 1979.
40. Michael Parenti, *Inventing Reality* (New York: St. Martin's Press, 1985), p. 27.
41. Peter Dreier and Steve Weinberg, "Interlocking Directorates," *Columbia Journalism Review* (November-December 1979); Dye, *Who's Running America?* chap. 4.
42. Fred W. Friendly, *Due to Circumstances beyond Our Control* (New York: Random House, 1967), pp. 281–282.
43. Ibid., pp. 271–272.
44. For further indications of just how profitable the mass media have become, see Desmond Smith, "Mining the Golden Spectrum," *The Nation* (May 26, 1979); *New York Times*, December 12, 1977.
45. One of the most developed examples of such delegation, a practice called "barter syndication," is detailed in *New York Times*, January 18, 1986.
46. *New York Times*, December 18, 1976.
47. Quoted in *New York Times*, August 6, 1978.
48. *New York Times Magazine* (April 8, 1979), p. 52.
49. Ben Bagdikian, "Fires, Sex, and Freaks," *New York Times Magazine* (October 10, 1976).
50. For example, see Ron Powers, *The Newscasters* (New York: St. Martin's Press, 1977).
51. *New York Times*, June 26, 1977.
52. *New York Times*, May 20, 1984.
53. John Culhane, "Television Taboos," *New York Times*, February 20, 1977.
54. Parenti, *Inventing Reality*, chap. 5.
55. Ibid., chap. 6.
56. Erik Barnouw, *The Television Writer* (New York: Hill & Wang, 1962), p. 27; Robert Cirino, *Don't Blame the People* (New York: Vintage, 1972), pp. 303–306.
57. Howard Kahane, *Logic and Contemporary Rhetoric* (Belmont, Calif.: Wadsworth, 1980), p. 236.
58. Ralph Miliband, *The State in Capitalist Society* (New York: Basic Books, 1969), p. 238.
59. Ben Bagdikian, *The Media Monopoly* (Boston: Beacon Press, 1983); Herbert Gans, *Deciding What's News* (New York: Vintage, 1979); James Aronson, *The Press and the Cold War* (Boston: Beacon Press, 1970); Parenti, *Inventing Reality*, chap. 2.
60. Edward Epstein, *News from Nowhere* (New York: Vintage, 1973); Timothy Crouse, *The Boys on the Bus* (New York: Ballantine, 1973).
61. Leonard Matthews, quoted in *New York Times*, January 2, 1980.
62. Michael Parenti, *Democracy for the Few* (New York: St. Martin's Press, 1983), p. 193.
63. Tom Wicker, *On Press* (New York: Viking, 1978). Also see Todd Gitlin, "When the Right Talks, TV Listens," *The Nation* (October 15, 1983).
64. Kahane, *Logic and Contemporary Rhetoric*, p. 212.
65. Vogel, "Business's New Class Struggle."

66. William Domhoff, *The Powers That Be* (New York: Vintage, 1979), pp. 183–191; Stuart Ewen, *Captains of Consciousness* (New York: McGraw-Hill, 1976).
67. Bruce Howard, "The Advertising Council," *Ramparts* (December 1974–January 1975).
68. For a summary of the media's socializing role, see Noam Chomsky, "Ideological Conformity," *The Nation* (January 27, 1979).
69. Roger Hatch and Frank Watkins (eds.), *Reverend Jesse L. Jackson: Straight from the Heart* (Philadelphia: Fortress, 1987), p. 318.
70. Hanes Walton, Jr., *Invisible Politics: Black Political Behavior* (Albany: State University of New York Press, 1985), p. 72.
71. Clint Wilson and Felix Gutierrez, *Minorities and the Media* (Beverly Hills, Calif.: Sage, 1985); Hatch and Watkins, *Reverend Jesse L. Jackson*, p. 98; Parenti, *Inventing Reality*, p. 11).
72. *New York Times*, April 12, 1985; March 22, 1988.
73. Jesse Jackson, quoted in Hatch and Watkins, *Reverend Jesse L. Jackson*, p. 319.
74. Ibid.
75. Ibid., p. 296.
76. Kahane, *Logic and Contemporary Rhetoric*, p. 219.
77. William Raspberry, "Politics, Blacks, and the Press," in Richard Lee (ed.), *Politics and the Press* (Washington, D.C.: Acropolis, 1970), pp. 119–128.
78. Carl Rowan, *Just between Us* (New York: Random House, 1974), p. 49.
79. Emma Bowen, quoted in *New York Times*, November 19, 1978.
80. Randall Miller (ed.), *Ethnic Images in American Film and Television* (Philadelphia: Balch Institute, 1978).
81. Hatch and Watkins, *Reverend Jesse L. Jackson*, p. 320.
82. *New York Times*, January 8, 1978.
83. Robert Allen, *Black Awakening in Capitalist America: An Analytical History* (Garden City, N.Y.: Anchor/Doubleday, 1969), p. 182.
84. *The Crisis* (June-July 1985), p. 33.
85. New York Times/CBS poll, reported in *New York Times*, July 18, 1986.
86. William Brink and Lou Harris, *Black and White* (New York: Simon & Schuster, 1967); Peter Goldman, *Report from Black America* (New York: Simon & Schuster, 1970); Milton Morris and Carolyn Cabe, "The Political Socialization of Black Youth," *Public Affairs Bulletin* (May-June 1972); Charles Bullock and Harrell Rodgers, *Black Political Attitudes* (Chicago: Markham, 1972); David Sears and John McConahay, *The Politics of Violence* (Boston: Houghton Mifflin, 1973); Lou Harris, *The Anguish of Change* (New York: Norton, 1974); Milton Morris, *The Politics of Black America* (New York: Harper & Row, 1975), pp. 124–135; Paul Abramson, *The Political Socialization of Black America* (New York: Free Press, 1977); Arthur Miller, "The Institutional Focus of Political Distrust," paper presented at the annual meeting of the American Political Science Association, August 1979.
87. Hatch and Watkins, *Reverend Jesse L. Jackson*, p. 323.
88. Franklin, *From Slavery to Freedom*, p. 412.
89. Ibid., p. 414.
90. Ibid., p. 415.
91. Allan Morrison, "The Crusading Press," in *The Negro Handbook* (Chicago: Johnson, 1966), p. 380.
92. James H. Brewer, "The Futile Trumpet," master's thesis, Virginia State University, 1959; Martin Dann (ed.), *The Black Press, 1827–1890* (New York: Capricorn, 1972); Edwina Mitchell, *The Crusading Black Journalist* (St. Louis: Farmer Press, 1972); Hanes Walton, Jr., Review of Andrew Buri, "Robert L. Vann of the *Pittsburg Courier*," *American Historical Review* (December 1975), p. 1409.
93. Manning Marable, *How Capitalism Underdeveloped Black America* (Boston: South End Press, 1983), p. 197.

94. Franklin, *From Slavery to Freedom*, pp. 237–238.
95. Adolph Reed, Jr., *The Jesse Jackson Phenomenon* (New Haven, Conn.: Yale University Press, 1986), pp. 54–55.
96. Ibid., p. 414. Also see Charles S. Johnson, *Growing Up in the Black Belt* (Washington, D.C.: American Council of Education, 1941); E. Franklin Frazier and C. Eric Lincoln, *The Negro Church in America* (New York: Schocken, 1973).
97. Ibid.; Charles V. Hamilton, *The Black Preacher in American Politics* (New York: Morrow, 1972); Benjamin Mays and Joseph Nicholson, *The Negro's Church* (New York: Arno, 1969); "The National Black Survey, 1972–74," as summarized in Walton, *Invisible Politics*, pp. 47–48; Reed, *Jesse Jackson Phenomenon*, chap. 4; Doug McAdam, *Political Process and the Development of Black Insurgency* (Chicago: University of Chicago Press, 1982), p. 129; Everett Carll Ladd, *Negro Political Leadership in the South* (New York: Atheneum, 1969), p. 239; M. Elaine Burgess, *Negro Leaders in a Southern City* (Chapel Hill: University of North Carolina Press, 1960).
98. M. Kilson, "New Black Political Class," in Joseph Washington (ed.), *Dilemmas of the Black Middle Class* (Philadelphia: University of Pennsylvania Press, 1980), p. 87; Reed, *Jesse Jackson Phenomenon*, chap. 4. For an insightful prediction of such a transformation, see W. E. B. Du Bois, *The Souls of Black Folk* (Chicago: McClung, 1903), pp. 113–114.
99. For example, see Allison Davis et al., *Deep South* (Chicago: University of Chicago Press, 1941).
100. Marable, *How Capitalism Underdeveloped Black America*, chap. 7; "The Failure of the Negro Church," *Messenger* (October 1919), p. 6; V. F. Calverton, "Orthodox Religion: Does It Handicap Negro Progress?" *Messenger* (July 1927), pp. 221–236; LeRoi Jones, *Home* (New York: Morrow, 1966), pp. 94–95, 138–139; Gayraud Wilmore, *Black Religion and Black Radicalism* (Garden City, N.Y.: Anchor/Doubleday, 1973); Harold Cruse, *The Crisis of the Negro Intellectual* (New York: Morrow, 1967), pp. 90, 322; August Meier and Elliott Rudwick, *CORE: A Study in the Civil Rights Movement* (Urbana: University of Illinois Press, 1975), pp. 120, 270–271; Harold Cruse, *Rebellion or Revolution?* (New York: Morrow, 1968), pp. 60–62, 128.
101. Gary T. Marx, "Religion: Opiate or Inspiration of Civil Rights Militancy among Negroes?" *American Sociological Review* (February 1967), pp. 67–69.
102. Numan Bentley, *Massive Resistance* (Baton Rouge: Louisiana State University Press, 1969), pp. 294–301; James Graham Cook, *The Segregationists* (Englewood Cliffs, N.J.: Prentice-Hall, 1962); Martin Luther King, Jr., *Stride toward Freedom*, (New York: Harper & Row, 1958), pp. 34–36. For conflicting views, see Vincent Harding, "Religion and Resistance among Antebellum Negroes, 1800–1860," in August Meier and Elliott Rudwick (eds.), *The Making of Black America*, vol. 2 (New York: Atheneum, 1969); Hart Nelson and Anne Nelson, *The Black Church in the Sixties* (Lexington: University of Kentucky Press, 1975); Joe Feagin, "The Black Church: Inspiration or Opiate?" *Journal of Negro History* (October 1975).
103. For examples of the more militant positions, see C. Eric Lincoln, *The Black Muslims in America* (Boston: Beacon Press, 1973); George Breitman (ed.), *Malcolm X Speaks* (New York: Grove Press, 1965); James Cone, *Black Theology and Black Power* (New York: Harper & Row, 1969); James Cone, *God of the Oppressed* (New York: Harper & Row, 1978); James Cone, *For My People: Black Theology and the Black Church* (Maryknoll, N.Y.: Orbis, 1984); James Cone, *A Black Theology of Liberation* (Maryknoll, N.Y.: Orbis, 1986); James Cone, *Speaking the Truth: Ecumenism, Liberation, and Black Theology* (Grand Rapids, Mich.: Eerdmans, 1986).
104. *New York Times*, November 19, 1978.
105. Holt, *Underachieving School*, p. 34.
106. Jesse Jackson, quoted in Hatch and Watkins, *Reverend Jesse L. Jackson*, pp. 320–321.
107. National Advisory Commission on Civil Disorders, *Report* (New York: Bantam, 1968), p. 389.

PART FOUR

Conclusions

CHAPTER TEN

Shaping the Future

Has the system designed by the Founding Fathers succeeded in protecting American inequality? There is clear evidence that inequality has been preserved and that the political-economic system described in Chapters 5–9 has impeded challenges to it.

On the eve of the Revolutionary War, for example, 10 percent of the local population controlled 40 percent of all taxable assets in Newburyport, Massachusetts. A comparable 10 percent controlled 44 percent of the assets in Albany, New York; 47 percent in New York City; 50 percent in Portsmouth, New Hampshire; 57 percent in Boston; 62 percent in Charleston, South Carolina; and 90 percent in Philadelphia. Twelve persons owned three-fourths of all the land in New York State. Seven persons owned 1.7 million acres in Virginia. Approximately 500 men owned virtually the entire eastern seaboard.[1]

Not much has changed since then. The top 5 percent of American families hold more than two-thirds of all corporate stock and more than one-half of all the money in savings accounts, and 0.2 percent of Americans are paid more than 40 percent of all stock dividends.

Using a revised version of systems theory as its basic empirical framework, we have attempted to examine the relationship between the American political process and the economic process and to analyze the results. We found that the American political and economic systems are intricately intertwined, especially in the postindustrial era. There is a clear-cut economic class structure in the United States, which the American government, educational system, and mass media reinforce in various ways. And this arrangement primarily serves the interests of a small number of white elites.

How has that political economy affected black America? The existing system is inherently conservative and has functioned to lock in a history of individual and institutional racism—legacies of slavery. These political and economic structures must be altered if justice is to be achieved. But the analysis must not end there. Understanding must guide the development of both policy and tactical agendas for transforming the political and economic structures.

The transformation to a new more equitable political economy will not materialize out of thin air. It will only emerge when progressive groups and individuals come together to create it through the application of political power, both within and outside the present system. The first task is to provide a general outline of what is required in order to exercise political power effectively.

In the political pursuit of a more just society, progressive forces must first pool their power resources, such as votes, time, money, and skills. Second, they must understand the existing political-economic system in order to know where to focus their efforts, to know what to demand when victories are won, and to know how to institutionalize those gains so that they can be built on over the long term. Given limited power resources, there is simply little room for inefficiency on the occasions when power opportunities do emerge. Finally, progressive reformers must act.

So far we have drawn on past and present experience to further understanding of the political-economic system. Now it is time to suggest a path of action. I shall clarify the general goal. I shall review and selectively expand the specific structural changes proposed throughout the book. I shall chart a political plan. And I shall assess the prospects for change.

Realize, however, that there are no blueprints for revolutions. They emerge dynamically as groups and individuals react to circumstances and seize moments of political opportunity. Social scientists can only provide guideposts based on their own interpretations of historical trends and current realities.

GENERAL GOAL

As prospective delegates began to mobilize for the 1968 Black Power Conference in Philadelphia, a representative of the Clairol Corporation sent them the following message:

> Forget black militancy and all this foolish talk of revolution! Rely on the American businessman, for it is only he who has the power—and now the will—to promote black "self development."[2]

As indicated at the outset of this book, my primary goal has not been to see more black Americans incorporated into the existing economic mainstream, stripping class inequities of their racial component. Racially proportionate dependence, exploitation, and insecurity do not constitute purpose enough. Instead, the most basic goal is for all American citizens to have maximum control over their own lives, rather than creating a new hierarchical system to replace the old. As a delegate to the 1967 Black Power Conference in Newark put it, "I don't want to be exploited by a black man any more than I want to be exploited by a white man. You've got to change the whole system."[3]

However, by focusing on the reduction of political and economic barriers to this self-determination, I have not lost sight of other important impediments to fundamental change, white racism being the most obvious. As mentioned in the introduction, altering political and economic structures is necessary but not sufficient to achieve the primary goal of racial justice in America. Racist individuals in positions of power will indeed continue to discriminate even in a less hierarchical political economy. Nevertheless, these structural changes will accomplish two important ends. First, they will help clear the way for more equal economic and political opportunity, especially if and when racism diminishes.

Second, they will take some of the sting out of existing racism by forcibly providing more equity for most black Americans. Thus the institutionalization of past racism can be reduced, even if dismantling white racism continues to prove difficult.

PROGRAM

We can no longer rely on pressuring and cajoling political units toward desired actions. We must be in a position to change those political units when they are not responsive.[4]

Political Structures

Chapters 6–9 suggested ways to begin opening the political process so as to facilitate rather than impede fundamental change. Taken together, these alterations promise a considerably more open political process. However, the people actually engaged in the exercise of political power at any particular point in time will have to decide what to "settle for" on the road to such a system.

Judicial Arena. In a nation that prides itself in subscribing ultimately to the rule of law as opposed to the rule of individuals, it is imperative that those fundamental laws and their enforcers be as just as possible from the outset. Toward that end, the following policies were proposed:

1. Positive constitutional rights, such as housing, health care, a job at a livable wage, and an adequate guaranteed annual income for those unable to work
2. Random appointment of all judges, from lists both approved by their peers and weighted to ensure that blacks would have more equal demographic representation on the bench
3. More racially integrated law enforcement agencies, placed under the judicial, as opposed to the executive, branch of government
4. More neighborhood control over choosing, overseeing, and disciplining the police (and other government employees) who implement the law at the street level in residential areas

Electoral Arena. Within the fundamental rights and liberties established and protected in the judicial arena, the American citizenry makes laws that affect how the nation's resources are allocated. This is generally done indirectly by means of a process of representative democracy; however, voters also make law directly at the state and local levels by initiative and referendum. Thus, for the purposes of direct and indirect democracy, it is important to create an electoral mechanism that will be as open and fair as possible. In that pursuit, the following changes were proposed:

1. Increasing voter turnout by relaxing registration laws and possibly even by requiring participation

2. National ballot initiatives
3. Deprivatizing corporate decision making by requiring that workers and other community members be represented on corporate boards of directors, placing more government limitations on corporate decisions, and facilitating worker ownership of the firms in which they work
4. Federal preclearance of all new election laws anywhere in the country
5. Public financing of all electoral campaigns, with supporting constitutional amendments as necessary
6. An end to the purchase of media time and space for campaign advertising, an allocation of free media time and space in its place, and supporting constitutional amendments as necessary
7. A bona fide multiparty system facilitated by using a proportional representation formula for electing representatives, simplified and lenient national standards for petitioning one's candidates onto the ballot, minor-party representatives on the Federal Election Commission, and a relatively equal allocation of public funding and free media time to all established political parties
8. Further opening the party nomination processes by assigning nominating convention delegates strictly by proportional representation (no longer requiring any minimum percentage of a state's primary vote in order to receive delegates) and by affirmative efforts to increase race, sex, and class representation among the delegates
9. A parliamentary system to strengthen political parties and thus help facilitate the passage of legislation outlined in the winning coalition's platforms

Legislative Arena. Even if the electoral arena becomes more open and fair, elected representatives must be able to implement the platforms on which they were elected if representative democracy is to be meaningful. Consequently, the following proposals, besides converting to a parliamentary system, were presented to reduce many of the checks and balances that presently obstruct those opportunities:

1. Standing rules that limit debate in both the House and the Senate
2. Simplified rules that would make it easier for House majorities to extract bills from committees
3. An end to the presidential veto
4. Bureaucrats with policy-related discretion to be assigned randomly outside the area from which they live at the time of their application and rotated periodically
5. Affirmative action efforts that would increase the number of blacks appointed to executive, staff, and bureaucratic positions in federal, state, and local government

6. An expanded federal Justice Department with more leeway to observe and intervene in the local implementation of federal laws
7. Omsbudsmen to serve as liaisons between service recipients and bureau-cratic agencies
8. A strong Legal Aid program to assist all citizens in bringing and fending off lawsuits
9. A strong Consumer Protection Agency to help consumers press their rights in the private marketplace

Information Arena. Lastly, it is quite clear that none of this will come to pass if people are not aware of the problems and alternatives and if the nation's political culture is not broadened to incorporate more egalitarianism. Therefore, the following reforms were suggested in the educational and media processes by which information and culture are transferred:

1. Random selection of school boards and trustees
2. An alteration of school curricula and practices to emphasize both the interrelationship of politics and economics and a more balanced analysis of both American and other nations' systems and histories, as well as rewards for behavioral traits such as creativity, independence, critical analysis, and cooperation
3. A formula by which no school would have less than 90 percent of what the richest school had to spend, subsidized by a progressive income tax on wage earners and their employers
4. More black representation in media decision making, including black commissioners on the Federal Communications Commission, greater affirmative action hiring and promotion efforts in the mass media, and start-up money for black media outlets
5. Significant limits on media ownership, for example, no person being allowed to own more than 5 percent of any medium or to have that share in a market where he or she has other investments
6. The pooling and random assignment of all media advertisements
7. Expansion and further political insulation of publicly funded media outlets
8. Increasing popular access to media by facilitating a broader use of public-service advertisements, as well as more equal access to low-frequency cable channels
9. A First Amendment right to media access

As has been stressed throughout the book, it is critical to address the political and economic systems simultaneously, as they are intricately intertwined. Thus conservative economic structures must also be altered if the inequities described in Chapters 3–5 are to be rectified. The preferred economic component of the new program is less capitalistic and more socialistic in nature—eliminating the dominance of an owning class by much more evenly dispersing the control of capital.

Economic Structures

> "Why are there 40 million poor people in America?" And when you begin to ask
> that question you are raising questions about the economic system, about a
> broader distribution of wealth. When you ask that question, you begin to
> question the capitalistic economy. . . . But one day we must come to see that an
> edifice which produces beggars needs restructuring.[5]

At about the very same time that Martin Luther King, Jr., made this pronounce-
ment, a young delegate to the 1967 Newark Black Power Conference took it a step
further when he stated, "The capitalist system hasn't worked for us in the four
hundred years we've been under it. . . . Capitalism is the most successful system of
enforced exploitation in the world, I agree. It's the latest model of slavery."[6]

Socialists reject the economic system of capitalism. As Manning Marable put
it, "The road to Black liberation must also be a road to socialist revolution."[7]

In general, socialists argue that capitalism generates a small capital-owning
class that possesses the controlling shares of the nation's wealth and power and that
as a consequence, the political and economic systems come to function primarily
in the owners' interests. Robert Allen warns that "simple transference of business
ownership into black hands . . . is in itself no guarantee that this will benefit the
total community. Blacks are capable of exploiting one another just as easily as
whites."[8]

Socialist Alternatives. According to socialists, a new economic system must be
fashioned that will democratize the ownership of capital and thus allow all citizens
to have more control over the political and economic decisions that affect their
lives. Samuel Bowles and Herbert Gintis have described such democratization of
ownership as a precondition to "self-actualization," meaning one's physical,
emotional, aesthetic, cognitive, and spiritual development. They also see it
helping society to gain more justice and democracy, as well as a more rational and
appropriate use of its natural resources. The needs of people would begin to receive
more weight than profits as the central guide to society's economic and political
decisions, for what is good for General Motors is not necessarily good for America
as a whole.[9]

To put it more concretely, a socialist society would be distinguishable first and
foremost by worker control of the means of production. That, however, has come
to mean at least two different things, depending on the analyst. Some put their
emphasis on democratizing the decisions of existing corporations, while others
maintain that the means of production must also be owned either directly or
indirectly by the workers themselves.

Economic Democracy

> We must speak out for racial justice. And we must work for an economic policy
> that takes lives of working people seriously; an economic strategy that encourages
> joint ventures between local governments and local plants, building mutual
> commitments among manufacturers, consumers and communities; for new

strategies that will give workers and local government the technical assistance and financial backing to keep plants open and profitable.[10]

Members of the Congressional Black Caucus and prominent black spokespersons like Coretta Scott King have called for more centralized government planning of the existing American economy, in particular to create full employment.[11] Ralph Nader has proposed what he terms his Corporate Democracy Act, which among other things requires that all corporations be chartered by the federal government, that they be subject to regular independent audits, that the majority of a corporation's board of directors be chosen independently of the stockholders, and that a "community impact analysis" be undertaken and approved should an industrial enterprise intend to expand or relocate. Countries like West Germany, for example, already have "codetermination laws," which mandate worker representation on the boards of large corporations.[12]

In point of fact, however, these are only "left liberal" approaches, as much of the means of production would remain in the hands of the small owning class, at least at the outset. The owners of capital could still exert ultimate influence by the threat to withhold essential investments. The workers, however, would indeed have more control than they do at present.[13]

Socialism. The more traditional position is to socialize ownership of at least the major means of production. As Manning Marable stated:

> Socialism . . . would involve radical changes. . . . The state would assume the ownership of major corporations, and their direction would be left in the hands of those best qualified to make decisions at the point of production, the working class. Socialism would mean the expropriation of wealth from the capitalist class, and the guarantee of employment, decent housing, education, and health care to all citizens.[14]

Among other things, conversion to a socialist economic system would involve most, if not all, of the following:

1. Wage labor would come to an end as such, for there would no longer be a separate capital-owning class. Workers would directly, or at least indirectly, own the companies where they worked and thus work for themselves.
2. With no separate owning class, the extraction of "surplus value" would also come to an end, as the people actually working in the businesses would collectively receive the full market value of what they were producing.
3. The workplace would be democratized in the sense the worker-owners would have far greater control over such decisions as what products they were to produce, where, at what pace, under what conditions, for what wages, and under what kind of management system.
4. The distribution of products would be based more on people's needs, with guaranteed rights to food, shelter, clothing, and medical and social services.

5. There would be a legal obligation to share the undesirable but socially necessary chores, such as street cleaning and waste collection.

6. Without a profit-maximizing capital-owning class continually increasing production and then using advertising to stimulate contrived markets for those products, there would be less production of socially unnecesary goods and thus more time for artistic, athletic, and cultural activities.

7. Some centralized economic planning would be necessary, such as for allocating scarce basic natural resources, coordinating the large state-owned primary industries, and deciding which worker-entrepreneurs get start-up loans to form other businesses. Nevertheless, the planners would be elected more democratically than elected representatives are at present.

8. Finally, the educational system would have to help prepare people for creative work as well as for a more active political life, to help purge them of a variety of social prejudices, and to teach them to structure their personal needs within the requirements of society.[15]

Implementation could include having the federal government employ the power of eminent domain in order to nationalize the most basic major industries, such as steel, autos, and oil. The tax system could be used to dismantle monopolies, as well as to raise money in order to spur and sustain cooperative businesses. A governmental "consumer cooperative fund" already exists and could be significantly expanded.[16]

Socialist Trends. Structural alterations are beginning to appear in the economic system. A number of workers and citizens—white and nonwhite, male and female—have come together to demand, and in some cases achieve, greater control over their lives.

> We must speak out against plant closings that happen without prior notice; against economic royalism while thousands of workers lose their jobs; against factories fleeing to third world countries, where workers' health and safety is ignored and union organizing is forbidden.[17]

Local Content Legislation. Serious congressional discussion and action on "local content" legislation has already begun. Such legislation, for example, requires that a fixed percentage of certain manufactured products be made in the United States if they are to be sold here. At least indirectly, one effect of such legislation would be constraint on the mobility of multinational corporations.[18]

Regulating Plant Closings. To contain corporate mobility more directly, some relatively strong legislation has been proposed in 19 states and the Congress. As discussed in Chapter 7, one of the boldest examples was Oregon's Employment Stability Bill of 1981, which would have required businesses with more than 50 employees (1) to give one year's notice before closing or making any significant layoff, (2) to compensate the community they leave by paying 85 percent of any "adjustment costs," (3) to pay for the relocation of all workers, (4) to pay benefit premiums for one year after closing, and (5) to give the Oregon Bureau of Labor and Industry the first option to buy. Ohio's so-called Schwarzwalder Bill would have required virtually the same thing of its departing firms, but it called for a two-year notice. In addition, at least a half dozen members of Congress have introduced national variants of such legislation, and in 1988 the federal government passed a law that requires 60-day notice before any sizable plant can close.[19]

Eminent Domain. Eminent domain has long been available as a mechanism whereby government could forcibly acquire private property for public use. The property is simply condemned, a "fair market" price is paid to the owner, and the space is then used for whatever public purpose the government has designed. The state of Hawaii even used eminent domain to acquire parts of large family estates so that land would be available for badly needed private housing construction.[20] Thus the legal groundwork would seem to be in place for one of the newest innovations in eminent domain application.

Going a step further, cities have begun to consider the right of eminent domain as a way to prevent large corporations from deserting them. For example, the government of New Bedford, Massachusetts, designed a plan whereby it would condemn a cutting-tools plant, purchase it, and then sell it to an organization that would keep it in New Bedford—another company, a public-private partnership, or a group made up of plant managers and union employees. The Pittsburgh area's Tristate Conference on Steel—a combination of steelworkers, religious leaders, and other residents—designed a plan that included a regional authority that could use eminent domain to allow steelworkers to buy a number of ailing steel mills in the region, modernize the mills, and run them.[21]

Unitary Taxes. Despite considerable corporate opposition, unitary taxation has existed in more than a dozen states. In these states, all of the international profits of multinational corporations are taxed according to the proportion of that corporation represented by the subsidiaries operating within that state. That adds constraints on multinational corporate investment.

Worker Cooperatives. Besides simply constraining the decisions of corporations belonging to the owning class, there are now as many as 200 fully worker-owned cooperative businesses in operation across the land. Such states as Massachusetts and Maine paved the way with important legal revisions. One success story has been the Workers' Owned Sewing Company of Windsor, North Carolina, owned and controlled primarily by black women employees.[22]

Employee Stock Ownership Plans. In addition, some 8,000 employee stock ownership plans (ESOPs) exist, involving some 8 million workers, and more than one-fifth of these firms employ at least 1,000 people. When 10,000 steelworkers in Weirton, West Virginia, agreed in September 1983 to spend $193.9 million to buy their plant, they made the Weirton Works the largest worker-owned enterprise in the United States. Workers have also purchased significant portions of companies as large as Ashland Oil, Colt Industries, Avis, Pan American World Airways, and Chrysler.[23]

Worker Self-management. Another method of gaining at least some control, self-management, is also finding its way onto shop floors. For example, at the General Motors battery plant in Fitzgerald, Georgia, worker-management teams have been choosing their leaders and helping to determine their own budgets, schedules, and proficiency and maintenance standards. They have also had some disciplinary jurisdiction. A New York Stock Exchange survey found that some 14 percent of U.S. companies with more than 100 employees had similar plans, and a government study found that 44 percent of firms with more than 500 employees included their workers in discussions of plant operations. However, a number of analysts warn that many of these changes have been largely cosmetic, with the tougher and more important decisions still remaining in the hands of management.[24]

Control through Unions. Nonetheless, workers are beginning to bargain collectively for even more control. For example, the United Food and Commercial Workers got several meat-packing companies to agree that if they closed a union plant, they would not open a nonunion one for at least five years. The United Rubber Workers got the four largest tire producers to guarantee that if they should shut down a plant, they would give six months' notice and grant full pensions after 25 years of work (or after five years if the worker is over the age of 55), preferential hiring at other plants, and the right to negotiate ways of saving the plant or the method by which it was to be closed. Beyond that, the United Auto Workers and General Motors/Toyota agreed that workers would both participate in corporate decision making as well as have access to corporate financial data and that before any layoffs can occur, salaries of executives and managers must be cut and all outside contract work must be called in. All of this is but a prelude to the kind of worker control that would emerge should workers begin to pool and strategically invest their hundreds of billions of dollars in pension funds.[25]

European Models. Finally, Western European countries provide model legislation for a good deal of this transformation. For example, centralized industrial planning and regulation of plant relocations have existed there for some time. Mondragon, Spain, pioneered worker-owned cooperatives in which employees have direct one-person, one-vote control over corporations, and many other European governments have taken further progressive steps as well. For example, most have been taxing and spending at much higher rates than in the United States in order to provide a more elaborate welfare state, including national health insurance and more extensive mass transportation. In addition, the large majority of public utility companies, as well as rail and air transportation, have been nationalized, as have sizable shares of the manufacturing and banking industries. The Swedes have been pioneering the concept of taxing individuals and corporate profits in order to create a fund with which unions, representing 90 percent of all Sweden's workers, could gradually buy up the nation's corporate stock.

Socialist Dilemmas. There are, however, some obvious challenges here as well. For example, should these socializing efforts come to fuller fruition, critics point to the inefficiencies and repressiveness of virtually all self-styled socialist or communist states.[26] Nevertheless, there are also a number of reasons to believe that an American adaptation would not have to end up that way.

In response to questions concerning efficiency, the American farming industry has been governmentally planned and sustained for years without any glaring problems with inefficiency. Bowles and Gintis have argued that overall American production is actually likely to improve under socialism, given the rationality of centralized planning, the increased size of the work force in a full-employment economy, and such work incentives as full partnership in the firm, more generally meaningful work, and far more leisure time.[27] Even in mixed economies like those in West Germany, Japan, and Scandinavia, far less inequality is tolerated vis-à-vis the United States, yet they remain prosperous.[28] Meanwhile, the more highly collectivized Soviet Union inherited severe underdevelopment and was ravaged by two successive world wars, yet today its largest cities have quick and efficient mass transportation, virtually no poverty or unemployment, and free medical care —even while the USSR remains one of the world's premier military powers.[29]

As for repression, David Mermelstein contends that socialism in the United States would be qualitatively different from that in any other place where it presently exists. The United States is already economically well developed and thus would not require the sacrifices that have been necessary for economic development in most emerging socialist countries. Its people cherish the principles of individual liberty and democracy. And fewer freedom-restricting security measures would be necessary as no hostile capitalistic powers of any real consequence would be threatening its existence.[30]

Nonetheless, socialists are generally quick to admit that they are not promising an overnight utopia. Socialism is viewed as a gradual process, not as an immediate event.[31] Consequently, racism and other social pathologies, for example, will not cease the moment the means of production are finally controlled by the workers, nor will the frustration, anger, despair, self-hatred, and alienation that have built up over many generations disappear with the first dividend check or the first trip to the boardroom. What is promised, however, is considerably more equality and more popular control over the economic and political decisions that affect people's lives. At the very least, socialism would significantly reduce the way in which the inherent inequalities in the present economic system amplify racial discrimination.[32]

STRATEGIES AND TACTICS

> The whole history of the progress of human liberty shows all concessions yet made to her august claims have been of struggle. . . . The struggle may be a moral one; or it may be a physical one; or it may be both moral and physical, but it must be a struggle. Power concedes nothing without a demand. It never did and it never will.[33]

What will be proposed now is a variant of what has come to be called the "rainbow coalition." The central idea is that fundamental political and economic change is not likely to increase significantly and endure until a sizable working coalition is formed from a variety of groups being treated unjustly under the present political economy. Each will have its own particular agenda, but all will have a common interest in altering the political and economic structures discussed throughout this book. The first step will require each of the subgroups to organize among itself so that it understands its own special needs and can enter as a strong functioning component of the coalition. The second step entails forming the coalition itself, with a first goal of establishing a new political and economic arrangement. This multigroup coalition will be encouraged to pursue a multifront strategy, using all available political resources.

Organizing the Black Community. In recent years, a variety of progressive black organizations have existed at both the national and local levels. They have included working- and lower-class groups such as the League of Revolutionary Black Workers (Detroit), the United Brothers (Newark), the Black United Front (District of Columbia), the North City Congress (Philadelphia), the United Front (Boston), the Black United Conference (Denver), and the Black Congress (Los Angeles), culminating in the formation of the National Black United Front in 1981. In addition, there is the Peoples' Alliance, as well as more middle-class groups that could also help organize the black community for the struggle ahead, including the National Bar Association, the Progressive Black Baptist Alliance, and even the Delta Sigma Theta sorority and Alpha Phi Alpha fraternity. Such groups need to continue organizing; and regardless of some major disagreements, they need to bring their memberships together into a loose coalition for the purpose of pursuing structural changes that will allow their members to maximize control over their lives.

A Rainbow Coalition

> I propose to . . . build a new functional Rainbow Coalition of the Rejected spanning lines of color, sex, age, religion, race, region, and national origin. The old minorities—Blacks, Hispanics, women, peace activists, environmentalists, youth, the elderly, small farmers, small businesspersons, poor people, gays, and lesbians—if we remain apart, will continue to be a minority. But, if we come together, the old "minorities" constitute a "new majority."[34]

Although questions have been raised about the viability of Jesse Jackson's "rainbow coalition" movement,[35] the idea remains conceptually attractive. Quite frankly, it appears to be the only long-term vehicle on the horizon, no matter who leads it. Besides the numerical realities, there is a real commonality of interest that can be tapped. Former senator Edward Brooke argued that

> [black] economic interests are clearly aligned with those of the majority of Americans. Inflation, unemployment, inequitable taxation, inadequate health care and housing are not black issues, but issues affecting millions of Americans who suffer the agonies of our economy without ever sharing its abundance.[36]

Manning Marable put it even more strongly when he stated:

> If there is no attempt on the part of white labor to engage in extensive self-criticism, and to construct a common program for struggle against capital with non-whites, the final emancipation of the American working class will be unattainable.[37]

As an example of his point, he noted that the subordinate position of black workers lowers everybody's wages. When blacks are forced to accept less pay just to have a job, this bids down the wage rate in general.[38]

The roots of this movement run deep. The abolitionist, early feminist, and free-soil movements all drew on a diversity of supportive groups. At the turn of the century, the Populist movement in the rural areas and the urban political machines were clear examples of such coalitions at work, despite unequal input and treatment of their various components. And in the early 20th century, the Unemployment Councils and parts of the early labor and black rights movements also drew diverse group support. Yet the specific roots of the present-day effort can be traced rather directly to movements that gathered force in the 1950s and 1960s: black power, feminist, antiwar, environmental, Hispanic, Native American, New Left, and gay.

The challenge has been to link them together in pursuit of mutual interests, and certain issues have facilitated that endeavor. For example, many of these groups joined forces in the 1950s and 1960s to press for passage of the Civil Rights and Voting Rights acts, and Martin Luther King's subsequent Poor People's Campaign was one of the best examples of such an alliance. Thereafter, the neoconservative backlash embodied by the likes of Richard Nixon and Ronald Reagan fueled the fires in the 1970s and 1980s. An increasing number of these groups pulled together to defeat the Supreme Court nominations of archconservatives Harold Carswell, Clement Haynesworth, and Robert Bork and to protest against unemployment, the nuclear arms race, and U.S. foreign policy in South Africa and Central America. Self-proclaimed socialists have been elected to public offices ranging from mayor in Burlington, Vermont, and Santa Monica, California, to president of the International Association of Machinists.

Out of such efforts came progressive multigroup organizations like the Southern Organizing Committee, the Center for Third World Organization, Theology in the Americas, the National Coalition, the All-Peoples' Congress, the North American Farm Alliance, and the People's Institute for Survival and Beyond.[39] Meanwhile, the Rainbow Coalition itself drew 756 delegates to its national unity convention in April 1986, and 1988 presidential candidate Jesse Jackson amassed an electoral coalition that included 4.4 million blacks, 2.1 million whites, and more than 200,000 Hispanics—54 percent of them women.[40]

> Common ground between the Black movement—in both its integrationist and Black nationalist tendencies—and predominantly white progressive movements, is the principle of equality. . . . Equality implies a theory of justice which assumes that all parties within the state should have free access to the state apparatus, can reform existing economic and social institutions, and can enact laws that promote a more humane society.[41]

Clearly, there are many obstacles. For instance, most of these groups are far from internally united and organized and have members who are suspicious of the motives of other groups.[42] Much cultural sensitivity is required. Group interests conflict. White males tend to dominate such coalitions.[43] And, as Melvin King found out in his unsuccessful mayoral bid in Boston, the owning class can employ far more money, and the mass media are conditioned not to take such movements seriously.[44]

Nevertheless, there are advantages. Rather than demanding integration and conformity, for example, the rainbow concept actually encourages diversity. Such coalitions have successfully formed around individual policy issues in the past. And frankly, no more promising vehicle is presently available.

Yet, as Jesse Jackson put it, "Ultimately the poor do not just want friends, they want to be empowered."[45] Where to begin?

[The black community] should not rely on exclusively legal campaigns, nor should it restrict itself to all-out street warfare. Instead it must devise a strategy of calculated confrontation, using a mixture of tactics to fit a variety of contingencies. . . . Tactical innovation should be the order of the day, and anything workable goes . . . from legal struggle, to electoral politics, to direct action campaigns, to force. In short, what is required is a coordinated, multifaceted, multilateral struggle.[46]

A Multifront Strategy. A rainbow coalition can become an ongoing protest organization outside of the context of individual crises. Beyond that, it could organize more traditional political efforts, too. From the Mississippi Freedom Democratic party to the Democratic Socialists of America, the Peoples' Alliance, and the Citizens' Party, a variety of progressive groups have seen the need for working within the system at the same time. Hopefully, a rainbow coalition can serve to unite these efforts.

Litigation. As suggested in Chapter 6, the Bill of Rights and certain federal civil rights and voting rights laws do offer some protection. Thus legal efforts must continue, with the purpose of guaranteeing that hard-won gains from the past are fairly and fully enforced. But much structural change is also needed if new, more positive rights and fuller justice are to be forthcoming. To achieve those structural changes, legislators must be confronted.

Lobbying. Elected and appointed officials must be pressed to enforce existing laws; they must also be pressured to change the political and economic structures themselves. Letters and telegrams must be sent, and phone calls must be made. And the officials must be informed and persuaded on a face-to-face basis wherever possible. Yet only so much can be expected from the elected and appointed products of the present arrangement. More diverse and progressive-thinking individuals have to be placed in legislative and administrative positions—and that can be set in motion through the ballot box.[47]

Voting. Calculated nonvoting can send a message of overall disapproval. Unfortunately, it can also be interpreted as apathy, indifference, or contentment. Thus the low-cost tactic of registering and voting is strongly encouraged. But the only valuable vote is a rationally cast vote, which also requires attentiveness to the campaign process. Within that campaign process, talented progressive-thinking people must seek office, and others of like mind must support their efforts with time and money.

Structural impediments to this pursuit of course exist. Chapter 7 pointed out that existing practices filter out candidates with radically new agendas and that the owning class begins with sizable advantages in its efforts to keep it that way. In addition, many crucial decisions are presently being made outside of government in the private sector.

Economic Power. To exert pressure on private-sector decision makers, employees and consumers can band together to pressure noncooperating businesses. Employees can organize labor unions and demand seats on boards of directors, management input, and employee stock ownership plans, striking if necessary in order to achieve them. In addition, mass protests can be launched. In April 1980, for example, a variety of progressive groups came together across the country in what was called Big Business Day. They marched and spoke out against a number of offensive corporate practices.

As an example of consumer power, although not challenging economic structures as such, Jesse Jackson's Operation PUSH organized an Economic Justice Campaign designed to force private companies to have more black-owned franchises and distributorships, to provide more research money to black colleges, to implement affirmative action policies for hiring and promoting managers, and to use black advertising agencies, black media sources for those ads, black banks, black insurance companies, and black contractors, on a regular basis. In July 1981, for instance, PUSH began a boycott against the Coca-Cola company. Not only were people urged not to purchase Coke products, but a number of grocery stores pulled the products from their shelves, and Coke machines were physically removed from a number of government buildings. In the end, the Coca-Cola Corporation agreed to create 32 black distributorships, to lend nearly $2 million to small entrepreneurs in the black community, and to deposit more money in black-owned banks. Comparable campaigns were launched against Anheuser-Busch, Burger King, Avon, Quaker Oats, General Foods, and the Southland Corporation (owners of 7-Eleven convenience stores).

Direct Action. Besides going outside the traditional political process to place direct pressure on private corporations, direct-action techniques can be directed toward governmental decision makers as well. Martin Luther King, Jr., spoke of the need to create a crisis in order to force a dialogue. Such crisis-creating tactics have taken both legal and illegal forms, ranging from lawful protest assemblies and marches to sit-ins and freedom rides to arson and physical violence.[48] Because the American system craves stability, a host of concessions have been won over the years as the system strove to end such turmoil.

Education. Progressive political education must be institutionalized—particularly in light of the limits of mainstream schooling and the mass media discussed in Chapter 9. Labor unions, for example, have long employed a Committee on Political Education (COPE) to disseminate pertinent political information to their members and help to organize their political forces. Another example is the Center for Popular Economics, run from the University of Massachusetts and providing progressive education and training for labor leaders.[49] Comparable seminars, workshops, and newsletters must be institutionalized at the grass-roots level across the entire population.

By way of summary, Sheila Collins points to the rainbow coalition initiated by Jesse Jackson as a reasonable starting point:

> Jackson's genius lay in linking nonelectoral forms of political mobilization and protest with traditional electoral politics, and in sensing those areas of convergence that could unite the interests of disparate groups around a common program. Although embryonic and fragile, the Rainbow Coalition represents the construction of a new kind of politics appropriate to the historical, cultural realities, and changing socioeconomic context of late twentieth-century America.[50]

POLICY AGENDA

Any one of the political or economic changes summarized at the outset of this chapter would be constructive. However, to build and maintain a mass-based rainbow coalition, some relatively immediate rewards for those who participate must be made apparent. As Charles V. Hamilton has argued, people usually need to see a connection between a political process and a concrete political product before they will contribute their participation.[51] So while the structural changes are being sought for long-term benefits, it is important not to ignore short-term gains, especially in light of the socioeconomic position of many in the coalition.

What to push for first? A full-employment policy could certainly help establish a solid foundation for the political coalition. Putting the unemployed to work building roads, sewers, mass transportation systems, hospitals, housing, and day care centers would address a number of problems at once. The Equal Rights Amendment, a gay rights act, guaranteed annual income, and universal health care would also help. But realistically, most of these are not likely to come about without some structural alterations, such as public financing of electoral campaigns or some reduction of legislative checks and balances on the political side and a viable cooperative bank, regulation of plant closings, and significant federal wealth, gift, and inheritance taxes on the economic front. As a consequence, both short- and long-term changes must be pressed simultaneously.

PROSPECTS

> Blacks are the weather vane for this society. Because of racism, we are in the front and bear the brunt of social and economic deterioration and in the rear of social

and economic development. [But] whatever is happening to blacks today will be happening to whites tomorrow.[52]

Unifying Issues

A number of issues taking shape may begin to unite the nation's non-elite blacks and whites, making them increasingly aware of their common interests in structural change. For example, Chapter 5 spelled out at length the declining socioeconomic position of most of the nation. Let us consider this in human terms.

Terry Hatfield, age 34, lost his job as a shipping department foreman when a Cleveland-area plant closed in 1982. When his unemployment benefits expired, he and his family were in trouble. The last source of income for Terry, his wife Susan, and their two children (ages 4 and 5) was a welfare check of $327 a month. Unable to continue to pay their rent of $300 a month and with their electricity cut off by the utility company for overdue bills, the Hatfields sold what they could and moved into a pair of tents. "It definitely breaks your pride," Terry said. "No one could have told me when the plant closed that I'd still be out of work a year and a half later." And even after the recession started taking its toll on their neighbors, forcing them also to go on welfare and food stamps, the Hatfields still assumed that poverty was somehow the fault of those afflicted. "I used to think, What's their problem?" Susan said. "Now I realize the problem."[53]

Ninety-one-year-old Mattie Schultz lived in San Antonio, Texas, on a combined social security and veteran's benefit check of $233 per month. Too proud to accept public welfare or private charity, Mattie was arrested and jailed in 1979 for shoplifting $15 worth of food to keep from starving. Humiliated, all she could say was that she just wished God would close her eyes.[54]

Howard and Fannie Spears resided in St. Louis. Howard was 93 years old and blind; his wife was 88. Unable to pay $800 in overdue utility bills, their gas was shut off. In the winter, forced to heat their apartment with a small electric heater, ice began to form on their floor and walls. On December 22, 1983, three days before Christmas, Howard froze to death. His wife was taken to the hospital, treated, and then released.[55]

On December 23, 1980, Luther and Audrey Beaver, ages 74 and 63, respectively, were arrested for drug trafficking. As it turned out, they had indeed been selling LSD and marijuana out of their Columbus, Ohio, home in an attempt to supplement their income of $381 monthly from social security. On November 18, 1981, despite doctors' warnings about their health, the two were sentenced to serve from 1 to 10 years in the Ohio state penitentiary.[56]

As more and more examples like these have come to light, the level of consciousness in the United States has begun to rise.

Emerging Consciousness

The discontent of the lower classes, difficult to direct, is relatively easy to document. But both capitalist Lee Iacocca and socialist Howard Zinn agree that fundamental change is not likely to commence until middle-class faith in the current system is shaken. Iacocca said:

It's the middle class that gives us stability and keeps the economy rolling. As long as a guy is making enough money to meet his mortgage payments, eat fairly well, drive a car, send his kids to college, and go out with his wife once a week for dinner and a show, he's satisfied. And if the middle class is content, we'll never have a civil war or a revolution.[57]

Zinn observed:

In a highly developed society, the Establishment cannot survive without the obedience and loyalty of millions of people who are given small rewards to keep the system going. . . . These people—the employed, the somewhat privileged —are drawn into alliance with the elite. They become the guardians of the system, buffers between the upper and lower classes. If they stop obeying, the system falls.[58]

As a result of a history of oppression, many black Americans have become alienated. In 1967, for example, only 14 percent of Newark blacks not involved in that city's ghetto unrest felt that local government could be trusted. The figure was a mere 5 percent for those who participated in the turmoil.[59] Meanwhile, Harris polls indicate that nationwide, the number of alienated blacks has increased from 46 percent at the time of the ghetto disturbances to more than 70 percent in the 1980s—a figure so large that it has to include the majority of the black middle class.[60] Beyond that, blacks trust in government institutions has declined faster than the national average as well.[61]

The only group that is more alienated is lower-class whites. For example, in 1969, when 40 percent of black Americans felt "what I think doesn't count for much anymore," that figure was 60 percent for lower-class whites, and whereas less than a third of all blacks felt that "people in power don't care about us," half the lower-class whites felt that way.[62] Like their black counterparts, these whites saw themselves living in deteriorating housing, attending inferior schools, and being stereotyped in the mass media, yet they did not feel that they were receiving even the limited attention blacks were receiving from the government or from the "limousine liberals."[63]

Tables 10.1 and 10.2 show that such alienation reaches well beyond blacks and the white lower class. The size of the numbers indicates that at least some members of the middle class also seems to feel that they have been left out of a system that is perceived to be functioning primarily to serve the interests of the rich. As a parallel development, many also display a rapidly shrinking amount of confidence in society's major institutions.[64]

Alienation can also be seen in the low rates of voter turnout mentioned in Chapter 7. Americans vote at lower rates than virtually any other functioning democracy in the world, and that rate has actually been declining.[65]

Some attitude and value changes do appear to be emerging out of all this. For one thing, the difference between the way blacks and whites perceive national problems is lessening. For example, a 1986 Gallup poll found blacks and whites agreeing on 6 of the nation's 10 most serious problems, and they were in complete

TABLE 10.1 AMERICAN ALIENATION, 1966–1986

	Percentage of Respondents Agreeing with Statement							
	1966	1971	1972	1973	1977	1980	1983	1986
The rich get richer and the poor get poorer.	45	62	67	76	77	77	79	81
Most people with power try to take advantage of people like yourself.	28	33	43	54	60	66	65	66
What you think doesn't count very much anymore.	37	44	50	61	61	61	62	60
The people running the country don't really care what happens to you.	26	41	48	55	62	49	57	55
You're left out of things going on around you.	9	20	24	29	35	44	48	37
Harris "Alienation Index"	29	40	46	55	59	60	62	60

Source: Adapted from Louis Harris polls, 1966–1986.

TABLE 10.2 CONFIDENCE IN INSTITUTIONS, 1966–1986

	Percentage of Respondents Declaring "A Great Deal of Confidence"*						
	1966	1973	1976	1979	1982	1985	1986
Medicine	73	57	42	30	32	39	33
The military	61	40	23	29	31	32	36
Higher education	61	44	31	33	30	35	34
Major corporations	55	29	21	18	18	17	16
The U.S. Supreme Court	50	33	16	28	25	28	32
The Congress	42	24	9	18	13	26	21
Organized religion	41	36	24	20	20	21	22
The executive branch of government	41	19	11	17	—	19	18
Television news	—	41	28	37	24	23	27
The press	29	30	20	28	14	16	19
Local government	—	28	19	—	—	18	21
State government	—	24	16	—	—	16	19
Law firms	—	24	12	16	—	12	14
Organized labor	22	20	10	10	8	13	11
Advertising agencies	21	—	7	—	—	—	—
The White House	—	18	18	15	20	30	19

Source: Adapted from Louis Harris polls, 1966–1986.
*In response to the question "As far as people in charge of running (READ LIST) are concerned, would you say you have a great deal of confidence, only some confidence, or hardly any confidence at all in them?"

agreement on the top three (unemployment, drug abuse, and the high cost of living).[66]

As for values, rugged individualism seems to be giving way to an increased recognition of people's interdependence, the obsession with private property appears to be giving way to growing concern for the nation's common property, and blind allegiance to the so-called work ethic does not appear to be nearly as strong as it was previously perceived to be.[67] And regarding the ultimate distribution of money and wealth, nearly two-thirds of the American public indicated that they felt such resources "should be more evenly distributed among a larger percentage of the people."[68] Another poll found two-thirds of Americans in favor of employee ownership and control of large corporations and nearly half favoring direct public control of all natural resources.[69]

> As the contradictions of late twentieth-century capitalism deepen, more and more of the white electorate will be tainted with the aversive stain once reserved for blacks and "dirty immigrants." As white feminists, workers, farmers, peace and environmental activists, and gays and lesbians are shunned by the institutions they once gave their loyalty and are branded "un-American" . . . they will begin to accept their place in that "other America" represented by the brightly colored hues of the Rainbow Coalition—a creature half in, half out of the two-party system, part social protest movement, part electoral machine—a political amphibian in the process of evolving.[70]

NOTES

1. Jackson Turner Main, The Social Structure of Revolutionary America (Princeton, N.J.: Princeton University Press, 1965); Sam Bass Warner, The Private City (Philadelphia: University of Pennsylvania Press, 1968).
2. Quoted in Robert Allen, Black Awakening in Capitalist America: An Analytical History (Garden City, N.Y.: Anchor/Doubleday, 1969), p. 164.
3. Ibid., p. 158.
4. Quoted in Francis Broderick and August Meier (eds.), Negro Protest Thought in the Twentieth Century (Indianapolis: Bobbs-Merrill, 1965), p. 425.
5. Martin Luther King, Jr., "The President's Address to the 10th Anniversary Convention of the Southern Christian Leadership Conference (August 16, 1967)," in Robert Scott and Wayne Brockreide (eds.), The Rhetoric of Black Power (New York: Harper & Row, 1969), pp. 161–162. For further discussion of King's socialist leanings, see James Cone, For My People: Black Theology and the Black Church (Maryknoll, N.Y.: Orbis, 1984), p. 96.
6. Quoted in Allen, Black Awakening, p. 159.
7. Manning Marable, How Capitalism Underdeveloped Black America (Boston: South End Press, 1983), p. 256. Also see Phillip Foner (ed.), The Black Panthers Speak (Philadelphia: Lippincott, 1970); W. E. B. Du Bois, "Is Man Free?" Scientific Monthly (May 1948); W. E. B. Du Bois, "There Must Come a Vast Social Change in the United States," National Guardian, July 11, 1951.
8. Allen, Black Awakening, p. 153.
9. Samuel Bowles and Herbert Gintis, "Schooling for a Socialist America," in David Gordon (ed.), Problems in Political Economy (Lexington, Mass.: Heath, 1977), pp. 263–270; Kenneth Dolbeare and Patricia Dolbeare, American Ideologies (Boston: Houghton Mifflin, 1976), chap. 8.

10. Jesse Jackson, quoted in *New York Times,* January 28, 1987.
11. Coretta King and others have advocated this position in organizations like the Full Employment Action Council.
12. *Village Voice,* September 29, 1975.
13. For further development of such "left liberal" approaches, see Gar Alperovitz and Jeff Faux, *Rebuilding America* (New York: Pantheon, 1984); Samuel Bowles et al., *Beyond the Wasteland* (Garden City, N.Y.: Anchor/Doubleday, 1983); J. Morton Davis, *Making America Work Again* (New York: Crown, 1983); Martin Carnoy and Derek Shearer, *Economic Democracy* (Armonk, N.Y.: Sharpe, 1980); Neil Jacoby, *Corporate Power and Social Responsibility* (New York: Macmillan, 1973); David Mahoney, *New York Times,* February 7, 1983; Wassily Leontief, quoted in *New York Times,* April 6, 1983.
14. Marable, *How Capitalism Underdeveloped Black America,* p. 16.
15. See Bowles and Gintis, "Schooling for a Socialist America"; William Tabb, "A Pro-people Policy," in William Tabb and Larry Sawers (eds.), *Marxism and the Metropolis* (New York: Oxford University Press, 1984); William Tabb, "Economic Democracy and Regional Restructuring: An Internalization Perspective," in Larry Sawers and William Tabb (eds.), *Sunbelt/Snowbelt* (New York: Oxford University Press, 1984); Richard Child Hill, "Fiscal Crisis, Austerity Politics, and Alternative Urban Policies," in Tabb and Sawers, *Marxism and the Metropolis;* Bowles, *Beyond the Wasteland.*
16. *New York Times,* June 27, 1982.
17. Quoted in *New York Times,* January 28, 1987.
18. *New York Times,* November 4, 1983; November 11, 1983; February 4, 1984.
19. Bennett Harrison and Barry Bluestone, "The Incidence and Regulation of Plant Closings," in Sawers and Tabb, *Sunbelt/Snowbelt,* pp. 368–402; Tabb, "Pro-peole Urban Policy," p. 371.
20. *New York Times,* June 3, 1984.
21. *New York Times,* June 10, 1984.
22. *New York Times,* April 17, 1984.
23. *New York Times,* January 15, 1984.
24. *New York Times,* June 25, 1980; February 13, 1983; February 23, 1983; January 15, 1984.
25. Jeremy Rifkin and Randy Barber, *The North Will Rise Again: Pensions and Power in the 1980s* (Boston: Beacon Press, 1978). Also see *New York Times,* May 23, 1980.
26. Friedrich Hayek, *The Road to Serfdom* (Chicago: University of Chicago Press, 1944).
27. Bowles and Gintis, "Schooling for a Socialist America."
28. Malcolm Sawyer and Frank Wasserman, "Income Distribution in the OECD Countries," *OECD Economic Outlook* (July 1976), p. 14; Lester Thurow, *Zero-Sum Society* (New York: Basic Books, 1980); Charles Lindbloom, *Politics and Markets* (New York: Basic Books, 1977), chap. 20.
29. Marcus Pohlmann, "Socialism in Soviet Armenia," *National Forum* (Spring 1985).
30. David Mermelstein, "Austerity, Planning, and the Socialist Alternative," in Roger Alcaly and David Mermelstein (eds.), *The Fiscal Crisis of American Cities* (New York: Vintage, 1977), pp. 360–361.
31. Bowles and Gintis, "Schooling for a Socialist America," p. 265.
32. For further references on socialism, see David McLellan, *The Thought of Karl Marx* (New York: Harper & Row, 1971); Shlomo Avineri, *The Social and Political Thought of Karl Marx* (New York: Cambridge University Press, 1969); Robert Tucker (ed.), *The Marx-Engels Reader* (New York: Norton, 1978); Bruce Brown, *Marx, Freud, and the Critique of Everyday Life* (New York: Monthly Review Press, 1973); Michael Harrington, *Socialism* (New York: Saturday Review Press, 1972); David McLellan, *Marxism after Marx* (Boston: Houghton Mifflin, 1979); R. N. Berki, *Socialism* (New York: St. Martin's Press, 1975). For examples of socialist thought as applied by black scholars, see

the later writings of W. E. B. Du Bois, as well as writings of Herbert Aptheker, Robert Allen, Manning Marable, Phillip Foner, and James Cone.

33. Frederick Douglass, quoted in Howard Zinn, *A People's History of the United States* (New York: Harper & Row, 1980), p. 179.

34. Jesse Jackson, quoted in Sheila Collins, *The Rainbow Challenge: The Jackson Campaign and the Future of U.S. Politics* (New York: Monthly Review Press, 1986), p. 83. Also see Melvin King, "The Rainbow Coalition," in Jeffrey Elliott (ed.), *Black Voices in American Politics* (Orlando, Fla.: Harcourt Brace Jovanovich, 1986); Marable, *How Capitalism Underdeveloped Black America*, p. 258; Charles V. Hamilton, "Deracialization: Examination of a Political Strategy," *First World* (March-April 1977).

35. Bob Faw and Nancy Skelton, *Thunder in America* (Austin: Texas Monthly Press, 1986); Adolph Reed, Jr., *The Jesse Jackson Phenomenon* (New Haven, Conn.: Yale University Press, 1986); *New York Times*, December 4, 1987.

36. *Focus* (October 1973), p. 2.

37. Marable, *How Capitalism Underdeveloped Black America*, p. 51.

38. Ibid., chap. 1.

39. Collins, *Rainbow Challenge*, chaps. 2–3. Also see *New York Times*, January 19, 1980; *Guardian* (June 20, 1984), p. 8; Janice Perlman, "Grassrooting the System," *Social Policy* (September-October 1976); John Herbers, "Citizen Activism Gaining in Nation," *New York Times*, May 15, 1982; Bennett Harrison, "Regional Restructuring and Good Business Climates," in Sawers and Tabb, *Sunbelt/Snowbelt*, pp. 88–89; Peter Dreier, "The Tenants' Movement," in Tabb and Sawers (eds.), *Marxism and the Metropolis*, pp. 174–201; William Tabb, "A Pro-people Urban Policy"; Joe Feagin, "Sunbelt Metropolis and Development Capital," in Sawers and Tabb, *Sunbelt/Snowbelt*, pp. 123–124; Frances Fox Piven and Richard Cloward, *The New Class War* (New York: Pantheon, 1982); Dan Luria and Jack Russell, *Rational Reindustrialization* (Detroit: Widgetripper, 1981); Harry Boyte, *The Backyard Revolution* (Philadelphia: Temple University Press, 1980); Dan Georgakas and Marvin Surkin, *Detroit, I Do Mind Dying* (New York: St. Martin's Press, 1975).

40. *New York Times*, June 13, 1988.

41. Marable, *How Capitalism Underdeveloped Black America*, p. 17. Also see W. E. B. Du Bois, *The Education of Black People* (New York: Monthly Review Press, 1973).

42. *New York Times*, January 5, 1984; Collins, *Rainbow Challenge*, chap. 6.

43. Harry Holloway, "Negro Political Strategy," *Social Science Quarterly* (December 1968), pp. 545–546.

44. King, "Rainbow Coalition."

45. Interview in *Playboy* (January 1984), p. 77.

46. Allen, *Black Awakening*, p. 280.

47. Charles V. Hamilton, "Racial, Ethnic, and Social Class Politics and Administration," *Public Administration Review* (October 1972). Also see Stokely Carmichael and Charles V. Hamilton, *Black Power* (New York: Random House, 1967).

48. This author does not advocate the use of violence, especially against other human beings—at least not within a system with as many other avenues available as the present U.S. system.

49. *New York Times*, August 12, 1979.

50. Collins, *Rainbow Challenge*, p. 19.

51. Charles V. Hamilton, "The Patron-Recipient Relationship and Minority Politics in New York City," *Political Science Quarterly* (Summer 1979).

52. Jesse Jackson, quoted in Roger Hatch and Frank Watkins (eds.), *Reverend Jesse L. Jackson: Straight from the Heart* (Philadelphia: Fortress, 1987), pp. 38–39.

53. *Akron Beacon Journal*, June 26, 1983, pp. 1, 7.

54. *New York Times*, July 30, 1979.

55. *Quad City Times*, December 23, 1983, p. 5.

56. *Wooster Daily Record,* November 11, 1981, p. 1.
57. Lee Iacocca, *Iacocca: An Autobiography* (New York: Bantam, 1984), p. 319.
58. Zinn, *People's History,* p. 574.
59. Joe Feagin and Harlan Hahn, *Ghetto Revolts* (New York: Macmillan, 1973), p. 41. For similar findings on the Watts unrest, see David Sears and John McConahay, *The Politics of Violence* (Boston: Houghton Mifflin, 1973)..
60. ABC-Harris survey, March 1980. Also see Milton Morris, *The Politics of Black America* (New York: Harper & Row, 1975), chap. 7; Ada Finifter, "Dimensions of Political Alienation," *American Political Science Review* (June 1970); Sears and McConahay, *Politics of Violence;* William Brink and Lou Harris, *Black and White* (New York: Simon & Schuster, 1967); Peter Goldman, *Report from Black America* (New York: Simon & Schuster, 1970); Lou Harris, *The Anguish of Change* (New York: Norton, 1974); Milton Morris and Carolyn Cabe, "The Political Socialization of Black Youth," *Public Affairs Bulletin* (May-June 1972); Charles Bullock and Harrell Rogers, *Black Political Attitudes* (Chicago: Markham, 1972); Paul Abramson, *The Political Socialization of Black Americans* (New York: Free Press, 1977).
61. Arthur Miller, "Political Issues and Trust in Government," *American Political Science Review* (September 1974).
62. Brink and Harris, *Black and White,* p. 135.
63. Barbara Mikulski, "Who Speaks for Ethnic America?" *New York Times,* September 29, 1970; Pete Hamill, "The Revolt of the White Lower Middle Class," *New York* (April 14, 1969), pp. 26–29; Paul Wilkes, "As the Blacks Move In, the Ethnics Move Out," *New York Times Magazine* (January 24, 1971).
64. Miller, "Political Issues and Trust"; Michael Harrington, *The New American Poverty* (New York: Viking Penguin, 1984), chap. 3; Arthur Levine, *When Dreams and Heroes Died* (San Francisco: Jossey-Bass, 1980); Andrew Levison, "The Rebellion of Blue Collar Youth," *Progressive* (October 1972), pp. 38–42.
65. Murray Levin, *The Alienated Voter* (New York: Holt, Rinehart and Winston, 1960); Donald Warren, *The Radical Center* (South Bend, Ind.: University of Notre Dame Press, 1976); Arthur Hadley, *The Empty Polling Booth* (Englewood Cliffs, N.J.: Prentice-Hall, 1978).
66. Gallup poll for the Joint Center for Policy Studies (1986), cited in National Urban League, *The State of Black America, 1987* (New York: National Urban League, 1987), p. 13.
67. Kenneth Dolbeare, *Democracy at Risk* (New York: Chatham, 1984), p. 34; Daniel Rogers, *New York Times,* April 16, 1980.
68. Gallup poll, December 1984.
69. Collins, *Rainbow Challenge,* p. 55.
70. Ibid., p. 301.

Bibliography

Abramson, Paul. *The Political Socialization of Black America.* New York: Free Press, 1977.

Adamany, David. "Money, Politics, and Democracy: A Review Essay." *American Political Science Review* (March 1977).

Adams, John. *Works.* New York: AMS Press, 1971.

Allen, Robert. *Black Awakening in Capitalist America: An Analytical History.* Garden City, N.Y.: Anchor/Doubleday, 1969.

Almond, Gabriel, and G. Bingham Powell. *Comparative Politics: A Developmental Approach.* Boston: Little, Brown, 1966.

Alperovitz, Gar, and Jeff Faux. *Rebuilding America.* New York: Pantheon, 1984.

Anderson, Charles. *The Political Economy of Social Class.* Englewood Cliffs, N.J.: Prentice-Hall, 1974.

Anderson, Martin. *The Federal Bulldozer.* Cambridge, Mass.: MIT Press, 1964.

Anderson, Stanley. *Ombudsmen for American Government.* Englewood Cliffs, N.J.: Prentice-Hall, 1968.

Aronson, James. *The Press and the Cold War.* Boston: Beacon Press, 1970.

Au Claire, Philip. "Public Attitudes towards Social Welfare Expenditures." *Social Work* (March-April 1984).

Avineri, Shlomo. *The Social and Political Thought of Karl Marx.* New York: Cambridge University Press, 1969.

Bachrach, Peter, and Morton Baratz. "Decisions and Nondecisions: An Analytical Framework." *American Political Science Review* (September 1963).

Bachrach, Peter, and Morton Baratz. "Two Faces of Power." *American Political Science Review* (December 1962).

Bagdikian, Ben. "Fires, Sex, and Freaks." *New York Times Magazine* (October 10, 1976).

Bagdikian, Ben. *The Media Monopoly.* Boston: Beacon Press, 1983.

Balbus, Isaac. "The Concept of Interest in Pluralist and Marxian Analysis." *Politics and Society* (February 1971).

Baldus, David, et al. "Comparative Review of Death Sentences: An Empirical Study of the Georgia Experience." *Journal of Criminal Law and Criminology* (June 1983).

Baran, Paul, and Paul Sweezy. *Monopoly Capital.* New York: Monthly Review Press, 1966.

Barker, Sir Ernest. *Social Contract: Essays by Locke, Hume, and Rousseau.* London: Oxford University Press, 1960.

Barker, Lucius, and Jesse McCorry. *Black Americans and the Political System.* Cambridge, Mass.: Winthrop, 1976.

Barnet, Richard, and Ronald Muller. "The Negative Effects of Multinational Corporations," in David Mermelstein (ed.), *The Economic Crisis Reader.* New York: Random House, 1975.

Barnett, Marguerite Ross. "The Congressional Black Caucus," in Michael B. Preston,

Lenneal J. Henderson, Jr., and Paul L. Puryear (eds.), *The New Black Politics*. White Plains, N.Y.: Longman, 1982.

Barnouw, Erik. *The Television Writer*. New York: Hill & Wang, 1962.

Bates, Timothy. *Black Capitalism*. New York: Praeger, 1973.

Beard, Charles. *An Economic Interpretation of the Constitution*. New York: Macmillan, 1962.

Becker, Theodore, and Vernon Murray. *Government Lawlessness in America*. New York: Oxford University Press, 1971.

Bell, Derrick. *And We Are Not Saved: The Elusive Quest for Racial Reform*. New York: Basic Books, 1987.

Bentley, Arthur. *The Process of Government*. Chicago: University of Chicago Press, 1908.

Bentley, Numan. *Massive Resistance*. Baton Rouge: Louisiana State University Press, 1969.

Bereday, George, and B. B. Stretch. "Political Education in the USA and the USSR." *Comparative Education Review* (June 1963).

Berki, R. N. *Socialism*. New York: St. Martin's Press, 1975.

Berle, Adolph. *The Twentieth Century Capitalist Revolution*. Orlando, Fla.: Harcourt Brace Jovanovich, 1954.

Berle, Adolph, and Gardner Means. *The Modern Corporation and Private Property*. New York: Commerce Clearing House, 1932.

Best, Michael, and William Connolly. *The Politicized Economy*. Lexington, Mass.: Heath, 1982.

Bickel, Alexander. *The Least Dangerous Branch*. Indianapolis: Bobbs-Merrill, 1962.

Black, Randall. *Private Pressure on Public Law: The Legal Career of Justice Thurgood Marshall*. New York: Kennikat, 1973.

Blackwell, James. *The Black Community*. New York: Dodd, Mead, 1975.

Blaustein, Albert, and Robert Zangrando. *Civil Rights and the Black American*. New York: Washington Square Press, 1968.

Bluestone, Barry, and Bennett Harrison. *Capital and Communities*. Washington, D.C.: Progressive Alliance, 1980.

Bluestone, Barry, and Bennett Harrison. *The Deindustrialization of America*. New York: Basic Books, 1982.

Blumberg, Paul. "Another Day, Another $3,000," in Mark J. Green, and Robert Massie, Jr. (eds.), *The Big Business Reader*. New York: Pilgrim Press, 1983.

Bolling, Richard. *House out of Order*. New York: Dutton, 1965.

Bond, Horace Mann. *The Education of the Negro in the American Social Order*. Englewood Cliffs, N.J.: Prentice-Hall, 1934.

Bowles, Samuel. "Unequal Education and the Reproduction of the Hierarchical Division of Labor," in Richard Edwards (ed.), *The Capitalist System*. Englewood Cliffs, N.J.: Prentice-Hall, 1972.

Bowles, Samuel, and Herbert Gintis. "Schooling for a Socialist America," in David Gordon (ed.), *Problems in Political Economy*. Lexington, Mass.: Heath, 1977.

Bowles, Samuel, and Herbert Gintis. *Schooling in Capitalist America*. New York: Basic Books, 1976.

Bowles, Samuel, David Gordon, and Thomas Weisskopf. *Beyond the Wasteland*. Garden City, N.Y.: Anchor/Doubleday, 1983.

Boyte, Harry. *The Backyard Revolution*. Philadelphia: Temple University Press, 1980.

Bradley, John. *World Geography*. New York: Ginn, 1971.

Breitman, George (ed.). *The Last Year of Malcolm X*. New York: Merit, 1967.

Breitman, George (ed.). *Malcolm X Speaks*. New York: Grove Press, 1965.

Brewer, James H. "The Futile Trumpet," master's thesis, Virginia State University, 1959.

Brink, William, and Lou Harris. *Black and White*. New York: Simon & Schuster, 1967.

Broderick, Francis, and August Meier (eds.). *Negro Protest Thought in the Twentieth Century*. Indianapolis: Bobbs-Merrill, 1965.

Brown, Bruce. *Marx, Freud, and the Critique of Everyday Life*. New York: Monthly Review Press, 1973.

Browning, Edgar. "The Trend toward Equality in the Distribution of Net Income." *Southern Economic Journal* (July 1976).

Bullock, Charles, and Harrell Rodgers. *Black Political Attitudes*. Chicago: Markham, 1972.

Burgess, M. Elaine. *Negro Leaders in a Southern City*. Chapel Hill: University of North Carolina Press, 1960.

Burke, Vee. "Cash and Non-cash Benefits for Persons with Limited Income," Congressional Research Service Report No. 85-194. Washington, D.C.: GPO, 1984.

Burnham, Walter. "American Politics in the 1970s: Beyond Party?" in W. N. Chambers and Walter Burnham (eds.), *The American Party System*. New York: Oxford University Press, 1975.

Burnham, Walter. "The Changing Shape of the American Political Universe." *American Political Science Review* (March, 1965).

Burnham, Walter. *Critical Elections and the Mainsprings of American Politics*. New York: Norton, 1970.

Bush, Rod (ed.). *The New Black Vote*. San Francisco: Synthesis Publications, 1984.

Butters, Keith, Lawrence Thompson, and Lynn Bollinger. *Effect of Taxation on Investments by Individuals*. Cambridge, Mass.: Riverside Press, 1953.

Calverton, V. F. "Orthodox Religion: Does It Handicap Negro Progress?" *Messenger* (July 1927).

Carmichael, Stokely, and Charles V. Hamilton. *Black Power*. New York: Random House, 1967.

Carnoy, Martin, and Derek Shearer. *Economic Democracy*. Armonk, N.Y.: Sharpe, 1980.

Chamberlain, Lawrence. *The President, Congress, and Legislation*. New York: Columbia University Press, 1946.

Chambers, Julius. "The Law and Black Americans: Retreat from Civil Rights," in National Urban League, *The State of Black America, 1987*. New York: National Urban League, 1987.

Chicago Tribune Staff. *The American Millstone: An Examination of the Nation's Permanent Underclass*. Chicago: Contemporary Books, 1986.

Chomsky, Noam. "Ideological Conformity." *The Nation* (January 27, 1979).

Cirino, Robert. *Don't Blame the People*. New York: Vintage, 1972.

Clark, Kenneth. *The Dark Ghetto*. New York: Harper & Row, 1965.

Cole, Leonard. *Blacks in Power*. Princeton, N.J.: Princeton University Press, 1976.

Coleman, Richard, and Lee Rainwater. *Social Standing in America, 1978*. New York: Basic Books, 1978.

Coles, Robert, and Jon Erickson. *The Middle Americans*. Boston: Little, Brown, 1971.

Collier, Peter, and David Horowitz. *Rockefellers: An American Dynasty*. New York: Holt, Rinehart and Winston, 1976.

Collins, Sheila. *The Rainbow Challenge: The Jackson Campaign and the Future of American Politics*. New York: Monthly Review Press, 1986.

Common Cause. *Sunset*. Washington, D.C.: Common Cause, 1976.

Cone, James. *Black Theology and Black Power*. New York: Harper & Row, 1969.

Cone, James. *A Black Theology of Liberation.* Maryknoll, N.Y.: Orbis, 1986.

Cone, James. *For My People: Black Theology and the Black Church.* Maryknoll, N.Y.: Orbis, 1984.

Cone, James. *God of the Oppressed.* New York: Harper & Row, 1978.

Cone, James. *Speaking the Truth: Ecumenism, Liberation, and Black Theology.* Grand Rapids, Mich.: Eerdmans, 1986.

Connolly, William. "Appearances and Reality in Politics." *Political Theory* (November 1979).

Converse, Phillip. "The Nature of Belief Systems in Mass Publics," in David Apter (ed.), *Ideology and Discontent.* New York: Free Press, 1964.

Cook, James Graham. *The Segregationists.* Englewood Cliffs, N.J.: Prentice-Hall, 1962.

Crockett, George W., Jr. "The Role of the Black Judge." *Journal of Public Law,* vol. 20 (1971).

Cronin, Thomas. *The State of the Presidency.* Boston: Little, Brown, 1975.

Crouse, Timothy. *The Boys on the Bus.* New York: Ballantine, 1973.

Cruse, Harold. *The Crisis of the Negro Intellectual.* New York: Morrow, 1967.

Cruse, Harold. *Plural but Equal: Blacks and Minorities in America's Plural Society.* New York: Morrow, 1987.

Cruse, Harold. *Rebellion or Revolution?* New York: Morrow, 1968.

Cruse, Harold. "Revolutionary Nationalism and the Afro-American." *Studies on the Left,* 1962.

Culhane, John. "Television Taboos." *New York Times,* February 20, 1977.

Dahl, Robert. *Dilemmas of Pluralist Democracy.* New Haven, Conn.: Yale University Press, 1982.

Dahl, Robert. *Pluralist Democracy in the United States.* Chicago: Rand McNally, 1967.

Dahl, Robert. *Who Governs?* New Haven, Conn.: Yale University Press, 1961.

Dahl, Robert, and Charles Lindbloom. *Politics, Economics, and Welfare.* Chicago: University of Chicago Press, 1976.

Daniel, Johnnie. "Changes in Negro Political Mobilization and Its Relationship to Community Socioeconomic Structure." *Journal of Social and Behavioral Sciences* (Fall 1969).

Daniel, Johnnie. "Negro Political Behavior and Community Political and Socioeconomic Structural Factors." *Social Forces* (March 1968).

Dann, Martin (ed.). *The Black Press, 1827–1890.* New York: Capricorn, 1972.

Davidson, Roger, and Walter Oleszak. *Congress against Itself.* Bloomington: Indiana University Press, 1977.

Davis, Allison, Burleigh Gardner, and Mary Gardner. *Deep South.* Chicago: University of Chicago Press, 1941.

Davis, Frank. *The Economics of Black Community Development.* Chicago: Markham, 1972.

Davis, George, and Glegg Watson. *Black Life in Corporate America: Swimming in the Mainstream.* Garden City, N.Y.: Doubleday, 1985.

Davis, J. Morton. *Making America Work Again.* New York: Crown, 1983.

De Lone, Richard. *Small Futures: Children, Inequality, and the Limits of Liberal Reform.* Orlando, Fla.: Harcourt Brace Jovanovich, 1979.

De Vries, Walter, and Lance Tarrance. *The Ticket-splitter.* Grand Rapids, Mich.: Eerdmans, 1972.

Dolbeare, Kenneth. *Democracy at Risk.* New York: Chatham, 1984.

Dolbeare, Kenneth, and Patricia Dolbeare. *American Ideologies.* Boston: Houghton Mifflin, 1976.

Dolbeare, Kenneth, and Murray Edelman. *American Politics.* Lexington, Mass.: Heath, 1981.

Domhoff, William. *The Powers That Be.* New York: Vintage, 1979.

Domhoff, William. "The Study of State and Ruling Class in Corporate America: New Directions," paper presented at the annual meeting of the American Political Science Association, Washington, D.C., September 1977.

Domhoff, William. *Who Rules America?* Englewood Cliffs, N.J.: Prentice-Hall, 1967.

Dooley, Peter. "The Interlocking Directorate." *American Economic Review* (June 1969).

Downie, Leonard, Jr. *Justice Denied.* New York: Praeger, 1971.

Drake, St. Clair, and Horace Cayton. *Black Metropolis.* Orlando, Fla.: Harcourt Brace Jovanovich, 1945.

Dreier, Peter. "The Tenants' Movement," in William Tabb and Larry Sawers (eds.), *Marxism and the Metropolis.* New York: Oxford University Press, 1984.

Dreier, Peter, and Steve Weinberg. "Interlocking Directorates." *Columbia Journalism Review* (November-December 1979).

Drew, Elizabeth. *Politics and Money.* New York: Macmillan, 1983.

Drucker, Peter. *The Unseen Revolution.* New York: Harper & Row, 1976.

Du Bois, W. E. B. *Black Reconstruction.* New York: Russell, 1935.

Du Bois, W. E. B. *Black Reconstruction in America, 1860–1880.* New York: Atheneum, 1971.

Du Bois, W. E. B. *The Education of Black People.* New York: Monthly Review Press, 1973.

Du Bois, W. E. B. "Is Man Free?" *Scientific Monthly* (May 1948).

Du Bois, W. E. B. *The Souls of Black Folks.* Chicago: McClung, 1903.

Du Bois, W. E. B. "There Must Come a Vast Social Change in the United States." *National Guardian,* July 11, 1951.

Dudar, Helen. "The Price of Blowing the Whistle." *New York Times Magazine* (October 30, 1977).

Dye, Thomas. *The Politics of Equality.* Indianapolis: Bobbs-Merrill, 1971.

Dye, Thomas. *Whos' Running America?* Englewood Cliffs, N.J., Prentice-Hall, 1983.

Easton, David. *A Framework for Political Analysis.* Englewood Cliffs, N.J.: Prentice-Hall, 1965.

Easton, David. *The Political System.* Chicago: University of Chicago Press, 1971.

Easton, David, and K. H. Guddat. *Writings of the Young Karl Marx on Philosophy and Society.* Garden City, N.Y.: Doubleday, 1967.

Eccles, Mary Eisner. "Backers Defend Revised Humphrey-Hawkins Bill." *Congressional Quarterly Weekly Reports* (November 26, 1977).

Edelman, Murray. *The Symbolic Uses of Politics.* Urbana: University of Illinois Press, 1964.

Edsall, Thomas. *The New Politics of Inequality.* New York: Norton, 1984.

Edwards, Helen. *Black Faces in High Places.* Orlando, Fla.: Harcourt Brace Jovanovich, 1971.

Edwards, Richard (ed.). *The Capitalist System.* Englewood Cliffs, N.J.: Prentice-Hall, 1978.

Eldersveld, Samuel. *Political Parties in American Society.* New York: Basic Books, 1982.

Elliot, Jeffrey (ed.). *Black Voices in American Politics.* Orlando, Fla.: Harcourt Brace Jovanovich, 1986.

Epstein, Edward. *News from Nowhere.* New York: Vintage, 1973.

Erickson, Robert, and Norman Luttbeg. *American Public Opinion*. New York: Wiley, 1973.

Ewen, Lynda Ann. *Corporate Power and Urban Crisis in Detroit*. Princeton, N.J.: Princeton University Press, 1978.

Ewen, Stuart. *Captains of Consciousness*. New York: McGraw Hill, 1976.

Fain, Jim. "The Nation Is the Loser." *Memphis Commercial Appeal*, May 23, 1988.

Fainstein, Susan, and Norman Fainstein. *Restructuring the City*. White Plains, N.Y.: Longman, 1983.

Farrand, Max (ed.). *The Records of the Federal Convention of 1787*. New Haven, Conn.: Yale University Press, 1937.

Faw, Bob, and Nancy Skelton. *Thunder in America*. Austin: Texas Monthly Press, 1986.

Feagin, Joe. "The Black Church: Inspiration or Opiate?" *Journal of Negro History* (October 1975).

Feagin, Joe. "Sunbelt Metropolis and Development Capital," in Larry Sawers and William Tabb (eds.), *Sunbelt/Snowbelt*. New York: Oxford University Press, 1984.

Feagin, Joe, and Harlan Hahn. *Ghetto Revolts*. New York: Macmillan, 1973.

Fein, Bruce. *Significant Decisions of the Supreme Court, 1978–1979 Term*. Washington, D.C.: American Enterprise Institute, 1980.

Finifter, Ada. "Dimensions of Political Alienation." *American Political Science Review* (June 1970).

Flaming, Karl. "Black Powerlessness in Policy-making Positions." *Sociological Quarterly* (Winter 1972).

Flanigan, William, and Nancy Zingale. *Political Behavior of the American Electorate*. Boston: Allyn & Bacon, 1978.

Foner, Phillip (ed.). *The Black Panthers Speak*. Philadelphia: Lippincott, 1970.

Ford, Henry Jones. *The Rise and Growth of American Politics*. New York: Macmillan, 1898.

Franklin, John Hope. *From Slavery to Freedom: A History of Negro Americans*. New York: Knopf, 1980.

Fraser, Douglas. *Economic Dislocations: Plant Closings, Plant Relocations, and Plant Conversion*, report prepared for the U.S. Congress, Joint Economic Committee, Washington, D.C., 1979.

Frazier, E. Franklin, and C. Eric Lincoln. *The Negro Church in America*. New York: Schocken, 1973.

Frieden, Bernard, and Marshall Kaplan. *The Politics of Neglect*. Cambridge, Mass.: MIT Press, 1975.

Friedman, Milton. *Capitalism and Freedom*. Chicago: University of Chicago Press, 1962.

Friendly, Fred W. *Due to Circumstances beyond Our Control*. New York: Random House, 1967.

Friesema, Paul. "Black Control of Central Cities: The Hollow Prize." *Journal of the American Institute of Planners* (March 1969).

Froebel, Fowlker, Jurgen Heinrichs, and Otto Kreye. *The New International Division of Labour*. Cambridge: Cambridge University Press, 1980.

Freud, Sigmund. *An Outline of Psycho-analysis*. New York: Norton, 1970.

Galbraith, J. K. *The New Industrial State*. Boston: Houghton Mifflin, 1967.

Gans, Herbert. *Deciding What's News*. New York: Vintage, 1979.

Gans, Herbert. *More Equality*. New York: Pantheon, 1972.

Georgakas, Dan, and Marvin Surkin. *Detroit, I Do Mind Dying*. New York: St. Martin's Press, 1975.

Gilder, George. *Wealth and Poverty.* New York: Basic Books, 1981.

Ginsberg, Benjamin. *The Consequences of Consent.* Reading, Mass.: Addison-Wesley, 1982.

Gitlin, Todd. "When the Right Talks, TV Listens." *The Nation* (October 15, 1983).

Glasgow, Douglas. *The Black Underclass.* San Francisco: Jossey-Bass, 1980.

Glasgow, Douglas. "The Black Underclass in Perspective," in National Urban League, *The State of Black America, 1987.* New York: National Urban League, 1987.

Glen, Maxwell. "Republicans and Democrats Battling to Raise Big Bucks for Vote Drives." *National Journal* (September 1, 1984).

Goings, Kenneth. "The NAACP Comes of Age: The Defeat of Judge John J. Parker," in Winfred B. Moore, Joseph Tripp, and Lyon Tyler (eds.), *Developing Dixie: Modernization in a Traditional Society.* Westport, Conn.: Greenwood Press, 1988.

Goldman, Peter. *Report from Black America.* New York: Simon & Schuster, 1970.

Goldsmith, William. "Bringing the Third World Home," in Larry Sawers and William Tabb (eds.), *Sunbelt/Snowbelt.* New York: Oxford University Press, 1984.

Goodwin, Leonard. *Do the Poor Want to Work?* Washington, D.C.: Brookings Institution, 1972.

Gordon, David (ed.). *Problems in Political Economy.* Lexington, Mass.: Heath, 1977.

Gosnell, Harold. *Machine Politics: Chicago Model.* Chicago: University of Chicago Press, 1934, 1968.

Grantham, Dewey (ed.). *The Political Status of the Negro in the Age of FDR.* Chicago: University of Chicago Press, 1973.

Green, Robert. *The Urban Challenge: Poverty and Race.* Chicago: Follett, 1977.

Greenberg, Edward. *The American Political System.* Boston: Little, Brown, 1983.

Greenberg, Edward. *Capitalism and the American Political Ideal.* New York: Sharpe, 1985.

Greenstein, Fred I. *The American Party System and the American People.* Englewood Cliffs, N.J.: Prentice-Hall, 1970.

Grossman, Joel. *Lawyers and Judges: The ABA and the Politics of Judicial Selection.* New York: Wiley, 1965.

Grossman, Joel, and Stephen Wasby. "The Senate and Supreme Court Nominations: Some Reflections." *Duke Law Journal* (August 1972).

Hadley, Arthur. *The Empty Polling Booth.* Englewood Cliffs, N.J.: Prentice-Hall, 1978.

Hagan, David. *Capitalism and Schooling,* dissertation, University of Chicago, 1978.

Hamill, Pete. "The Revolt of the White Lower Middle Class." *New York* (April 14, 1969).

Hamilton, Charles V. *American Government.* Glenview, Ill.: Scott, Foresman, 1982.

Hamilton, Charles V. *The Bench and the Ballot: Southern Federal Judges and Black Votes.* New York: Oxford University Press, 1973.

Hamilton, Charles V. *The Black Experience in American Politics.* New York: Putnam, 1973.

Hamilton, Charles V. *The Black Preacher in American Politics.* New York: Morrow, 1972.

Hamilton, Charles V. "Conduit Colonialism and Public Policy." *Black World* (October 1972).

Hamilton, Charles V. "Deracialization: Examination of a Political Strategy." *First World* (March-April 1977).

Hamilton, Charles V. "The Patron-Recipient Relationship and Minority Politics in New York City." *Political Science Quarterly* (Summer 1979).

Hamilton, Charles V. "Racial, Ethnic, and Social Class Politics and Administration." *Public Administration Review* (October 1972).

Hamilton, Richard. *Class and Politics in the United States.* New York: Wiley, 1972.

Harding, Vincent. "Religion and Resistance among Antebellum Negroes, 1800–1860," in August Meier and Elliott Rudwick (eds.), *The Making of Black America*, vol. 2. New York: Atheneum, 1969.

Harrett, Rodney. *College and University Trustees*. Princeton, N.J.: Educational Testing Service, 1969.

Harrington, Michael. *The New American Poverty*. New York: Viking Penguin, 1984.

Harrington, Michael. *Socialism*. New York: Saturday Review Press, 1972.

Harris, Abram. *The Negro as Capitalist*. New York: Haskell, 1936.

Harris, Lou. *The Anguish of Change*. New York: Norton, 1974.

Harrison, Bennett. "Regional Restructuring and Good Business Climates," in Larry Sawers and William Tabb (eds.), *Sunbelt/Snowbelt*. New York: Oxford University Press, 1984.

Harrison, Bennett, and Barry Bluestone. "The Incidence and Regulation of Plant Closings," in Larry Sawers and William Tabb (eds.), *Sunbelt/Snowbelt*. New York: Oxford University Press, 1984.

Harty, Sheila. *Hucksters in the Classroom*. Washington, D.C.: Center for Study of Responsive Law, 1979.

Hatch, Roger, and Frank Watkins (eds.). *Reverend Jesse L. Jackson: Straight from the Heart*. Philadelphia: Fortress, 1987.

Hawley, Willis. *Strategy for Effective Desegregation: A Synthesis of Findings*. Nashville, Tenn.: Center for Education and Human Development Policy, 1987.

Hayek, Friedrich. *The Road to Serfdom*. Chicago: University of Chicago Press, 1944.

Hayes, John. *Lonely Fighter*. Secaucus, N.J.: Lyle Stuart, 1979.

Herbers, John. "Citizen Activism Gaining in Nation." *New York Times*, May 15, 1982.

Herman, Edward S. *Corporate Control, Corporate Power*. New York: Cambridge University Press, 1981.

Hess, David, and Judith Torney. *The Development of Political Attitudes in Children*. Garden City, N.Y.: Doubleday, 1968.

Hesse, Herman. *Beneath the Wheel*. New York: Farrar, Strauss & Giroux, 1968.

Hill, Richard Child. "Fiscal Crisis, Austerity Politics, and Alternative Urban Policies," in William Tabb and Larry Sawers (eds.), *Marxism and the Metropolis*. New York: Oxford University Press, 1984.

Hirschorn, Larry. "The Political Economy of Social Services Rationalization," in R. Quinney (ed.), *Capitalist Society*. New York: Dorsey, 1979.

Hofstadter, Richard. *The Idea of a Party System*. Berkeley: University of California Press, 1969.

Holloway, Harry. "Negro Political Strategy." *Social Science Quarterly* (December 1968).

Holt, John. *Freedom and Beyond*. New York: Dutton, 1972.

Holt, John. *The Underachieving School*. New York: Pitman, 1969.

Howard, Bruce. "The Advertising Council." *Ramparts* (December 1974–January 1975).

Howard, Joseph C. "Why We Organize." *Journal of Public Law*, vol. 20 (1971).

Hunter, Marjorie, and Tom Bloom. "The Longest-running Game in Town." *New York Times*, June 24, 1985.

Iacocca, Lee. *Iacocca: An Autobiography*. New York: Bantam, 1984.

Jacob, Herbert. *Justice in America*. Boston: Little, Brown, 1972.

Jacob, Herbert. *Urban Justice*. Englewood Cliffs, N.J.: Prentice-Hall, 1973.

Jacoby, Neil. *Corporate Powers and Social Responsibility*. New York: Macmillan, 1973.

James, Judson. *American Political Parties*. New York: Harper & Row, 1974.

Jencks, Christopher. *Inequality: A Reassessment of the Effect of Family and Schools in America.* New York: Basic Books, 1972.

Jennings, James, and Melvin King. *From Access to Power: Black Politics in Boston.* Cambridge, Mass.: Schenkman, 1986.

Jhabvala, Firdaus. "A Critique of Reformist Solutions to Discrimination," in David Gordon (ed.), *Problems in Political Economy.* Lexington, Mass.: Heath, 1977.

Jhabvala, Firdaus. "The Economic Situation of Black People," in David Gordon (ed.), *Problems in Political Economy.* Lexington, Mass.: Heath, 1977.

Johnson, Charles S. *Growing Up in the Black Belt.* Washington, D.C.: American Council of Education, 1941.

Jones, Charles O. "The Role of the Campaign in Congressional Politics," in M. Kent Jennings and Harmon Ziegler (eds.), *The Electoral Process.* Englewood Cliffs, N.J.: Prentice-Hall, 1966.

Jones, LeRoi. *Home.* New York: Morrow, 1966.

Judd, Dennis. *The Politics of American Cities.* Boston: Little, Brown, 1984.

Kahane, Howard. *Logic and Contemporary Rhetoric.* Belmont, Calif.: Wadsworth, 1980.

Katznelson, Ira, and Mark Kesselman. *The Politics of Power.* Orlando, Fla.: Harcourt Brace Jovanovich, 1987.

Katznelson, Ira, and Margaret Weir. *Schooling for All: Race, Class, and the Decline of the Democratic Ideal.* New York: Basic Books, 1985.

Kaul, Donald. "Over the Coffee." *Des Moines Register,* January 18, 1977.

Keech, William. *The Impact of Negro Voting.* Chicago: Rand McNally, 1968.

Keller, Edmund. "The Impact of Black Mayors on Urban Policy." *Annals of the American Academy of Political and Social Science* (September 1978).

Keller, S. *Beyond the Ruling Class.* New York: Random House, 1963.

Kilson, M. "New Black Political Class," in Joseph Washington (ed.), *Dilemmas of the Black Middle Class.* Philadelphia: University of Pennsylvania Press, 1980.

Kimball, Penn. *The Disconnected.* New York: Columbia University Press, 1972.

King, Arthur (ed.). *The New American Political System.* Washington, D.C.: American Enterprise Institute, 1979.

King, Martin Luther, Jr. "The President's Address to the 10th Anniversary Convention of the Southern Christian Leadership Conference (August 16, 1967)," in Robert Scott and Wayne Brockreide (eds.), *The Rhetoric of Black Power.* New York: Harper & Row, 1969.

King, Martin Luther, Jr. *Stride toward Freedom.* New York: Harper & Row, 1958.

King, Melvin. "The Rainbow Coalition," in Jeffrey Elliott (ed.), *Black Voices in American Politics.* Orlando, Fla.: Harcourt Brace Jovanovich, 1986.

Kleniewski, Nancy. "From Industrial to Corporate City: The Role of Urban Renewal," in William Tabb and Larry Sawers (eds.), *Marxism and the Metropolis.* New York: Oxford University Press, 1978.

Kline, Mary Jo (ed.). *Alexander Hamilton.* New York: Harper & Row, 1973.

Kolko, Gabriel. *The Roots of American Foreign Policy.* Boston: Beacon Press, 1969.

Kolko, Gabriel. *Wealth and Power in America.* New York: Praeger, 1962.

Kornhauser, William. *The Politics of Mass Society.* New York: Free Press, 1959.

Kotz, David. "Finance Capital and Corporate Control," in Richard Edwards (ed.), *The Capitalist System.* Englewood Cliffs, N.J.: Prentice-Hall, 1978.

Kozol, Jonathan. *Death at an Early Age.* Boston: Houghton Mifflin, 1967.

Kozol, Jonathan. *The Night Is Dark and I Am Far from Home*. Boston: Houghton Mifflin, 1975.

Kristol, Irving. *Two Cheers for Capitalism*. New York: Basic Books, 1978.

Ladd, Everett Carll. "The Brittle Mandate." *Political Science Quarterly* (Spring 1981).

Ladd, Everett Carll. *Negro Political Leadership in the South*. New York: Atheneum, 1969.

Ladd, Everett Carll. *Transformations of the American Party System*. New York: Norton, 1978.

Laffer, Arthur, and James Seymour. *The Economics of the Tax Revolt*. Orlando, Fla.: Harcourt Brace Jovanovich, 1979.

Lampman, Robert. *The Share of Top Wealth-holders in National Wealth*. Princeton, N.J.: Princeton University Press, 1962.

Larner, Jeremy. "The Effect of Management Control on the Profits of Large Corporations," in Maurice Zeitlin (ed.), *American Society, Inc.* Chicago: Rand McNally, 1970.

Larson, Calvin. *Crime, Justice, and Society*. Dix Hills, N.Y.: General Hall, 1984.

Latham, Earl. "The Group Basis of Politics." *American Political Science Review* (June 1952).

Lawson, Stephen. *In Pursuit of Power*. New York: Columbia University Press, 1985.

Leggett, John. *Class, Race, and Labor*. New York: Oxford University Press, 1968.

Lessing, Doris. *The Golden Notebook*. New York: Simon & Schuster, 1962.

Levin, Murray. *The Alienated Voter*. New York: Holt, Rinehart and Winston, 1960.

Levine, Arthur. *When Dreams and Heroes Died*. San Francisco: Jossey-Bass, 1980.

Levison, Andrew. "The Rebellion of Blue Collar Youth." *Progressive* (October 1972).

Levison, Andrew. *The Working Class Majority*. Baltimore: Penguin, 1974.

Levy, Frank. "The Vanishing Middle Class and Related Issues." *PS* (Summer 1987).

Lewinsohn, Paul. *Race, Class, and Party*. New York: Grosset & Dunlap, 1965.

Lincoln, C. Eric. *The Black Muslims in America*. Boston: Beacon Press, 1973.

Lindbloom, Charles. *Politics and Markets*. New York: Basic Books, 1977.

Lindbloom, Charles. "The Science of Muddling Through." *Public Administration Review* (Spring 1959).

Lindert, Peter, and Jeffrey Williamson. "Long-Term Trends in American Wealth Inequality," University of Wisconsin's Research Institute on Poverty, Discussion Paper No. 472, 1977.

Lipsitz, Lewis. "On Political Belief: The Grievances of the Poor," in Phillip Green and Sanford Levinson (eds.), *Power and Community*. New York: Pantheon, 1970.

Locke, John, "Second Treatise on Civil Government," in Maurice Cranston (ed.), *Locke on Politics, Religion, and Education*. New York: Collier, 1965.

Lundberg, Ferdinand. *The Rich and the Super-rich*. Secaucus, N.J.: Lyle Stuart, 1968.

Luria, Dan, and Jack Russell. *Rational Reindustrialization*. Detroit: Widgetripper, 1981.

Lynd, Staughton. "Slavery and the Founding Fathers," in Melvin Drimmer (ed.), *Black History: A Reappraisal*. Garden City, N.Y.: Anchor/Doubleday, 1969.

MacPherson, C. B. *The Political Theory of Possessive Individualism*. New York: Oxford University Press, 1973.

Main, Jackson Turner. *The Social Structure of Revolutionary America*. Princeton, N.J.: Princeton University Press, 1965.

Mandel, Ernest. *Late Capitalism*. London: New Left Books, 1975.

Manley, John. "Neo-pluralism." *American Political Science Review* (June 1983).

Mann, Dean E. "The Selection of Federal Political Executives." *American Political Science Review* (March 1964).

Mann, Eric. *Comrade George*. New York: Harper & Row, 1974.

Marable, Manning. *How Capitalism Underdeveloped Black America.* Boston: South End Press, 1983.

Marx, Gary T. "Religion: Opiate or Inspiration of Civil Rights Militancy among Negroes?" *American Sociological Review* (February 1967).

Marx, Karl. "A Contribution to the Critique of Political Economy," in Robert Tucker (ed.), *The Marx-Engels Reader.* New York: Norton, 1978.

Marx, Karl. *Das Kapital,* ed. Frederick Engels. Moscow: Progress Publishers, 1965.

Marx, Karl. *The Grundrisse,* tr. Martin Nicolaus. Baltimore: Penguin, 1973.

Marx, Karl. *The Poverty of Philosophy,* ed. Frederick Engels. Moscow: Progress Publishers, 1966.

Marx, Karl. "Profit of Capital," in J. B. Bottomore (ed.), *Karl Marx: Early Writings.* London: Watts, 1963.

Marx, Karl. *Value, Price, and Profit.* New York: International Publishers, 1935.

Marx, Karl, and Frederick Engels. *Articles from the Nene Rheinische,* tr. S. Rvazanskava, ed. B. Isaacs. Moscow: Progress Publishers, 1964.

Marx, Karl, and Frederick Engels. *The German Ideology,* tr. and ed. S. Rvazanskava. Moscow: Progress Publishers, 1964.

Mason, Edward S. "Corporation." *International Encyclopedia of the Social Sciences,* vol. 3 (1968).

Matthews, Donald. *The Social Background of Political Decision-makers.* New York: Random House, 1955.

Matthews, Donald. *U.S. Senators and Their World.* Chapel Hill: University of North Carolina Press, 1960.

Mays, Benjamin, and Joseph Nicholson. *The Negro's Church.* New York: Arno, 1969.

McAdam, Doug. *Political Process and the Development of Black Insurgency.* Chicago: University of Chicago Press, 1982.

McGahey, Richard. "Industrial Policy." *Review of Black Political Economy* (Summer-Fall 1984).

McLellan, David. *Marxism after Marx.* Boston: Houghton Mifflin, 1979.

McLellan, David. *The Thought of Karl Marx.* New York: Harper & Row, 1971.

McMurtry, John. *The Structure of Marx's World View.* Princeton, N.J.: Princeton University Press, 1978.

Medsger, Betty. "The Free Propaganda That Floods the Schools." *Progressive* (December 1976).

Meier, August, and Elliott Rudwick. *CORE: A Study in the Civil Rights Movement.* Urbana: University of Illinois Press, 1975.

Melman, Seymour. *Profits without Production.* New York: Knopf, 1983.

Menchik, Paul. *Conference on Research in Income and Wealth.* New York: National Bureau of Economic Research, 1979.

Meranto, Phillip, Oneida Meranto, and Matthew Lippman. *Guarding the Ivory Tower.* Denver: Lucha, 1985.

Mermelstein, David. "Austerity, Planning, and the Socialist Alternative," in Roger Alcaly and David Mermelstein (eds.), *The Fiscal Crisis of the American Cities.* New York: Vintage, 1977.

Meyers, M. (ed.). *The Mind of the Founder.* Indianapolis: Bobbs-Merrill, 1973.

Michaels, Marguerite. "Why Congressmen Want Out." *Parade* (November 5, 1978).

Mikulski, Barbara. "Who Speaks for Ethnic America?" *New York Times,* September 29, 1970.

Milbraith, Lester, and M. L. Goel. *Political Participation*. Chicago: Rand McNally, 1977.

Miliband, Ralph. *The State in Capitalist Society*. New York: Basic Books, 1969.

Miller, Arthur. "The Institutional Focus of Political Distrust," paper presented at the annual meeting of the American Political Science Association, August 1979.

Miller, Arthur. "Political Issues and Trust in Government." *American Political Science Review* (September 1974).

Miller, Randall (ed.). *Ethnic Images in American Film and Television*. Philadelphia: Balch Institute, 1978.

Miller, Warren, and Donald Stokes. "Constituency Influence in Congress." *American Political Science Review* (March 1963).

Miller, Warren, and Arthur Miller. *American National Election Studies Data Sourcebook, 1952–1978*. Ann Arbor, Mich.: ICPSR, 1979.

Mills, C. Wright. *The Power Elite*. New York: Oxford University Press, 1956.

Mintz, Beth, and Michael Schwartz. "The Structure of Power in American Business," paper presented at the annual meeting of the American Political Science Association, Washington, D.C., September 1977.

Mitchell, Edwina. *The Crusading Black Journalist*. St. Louis: Farmer Press, 1972.

Monroe, Sylvester, and Peter Goldman. *Brothers*. New York: Newsweek/William Morrow, 1988.

Morgan, James N. "Panel Study on Income Dynamics," dissertation, University of Michigan, 1977.

Morris, Milton. *The Politics of Black America*. New York: Harper & Row, 1975.

Morris, Milton, and Carolyn Cabe. "The Political Socialization of Black Youth." *Public Affairs Bulletin* (May-June 1972).

Morrison, Allan. "The Crusading Press," in *The Negro Handbook*. Chicago: Johnson, 1966.

Morrison, Samuel. *The Oxford History of the American People*. New York: Oxford University Press, 1965.

Nagel, Stuart. "Disparities in Criminal Procedure." *UCLA Law Review* (August 1967).

National Commission on Urban Problems. *Building the American City*. New York: Praeger, 1969.

National Urban League. *Full Employment as a National Goal*. New York: National Urban League, 1974.

National Urban League. *The State of Black America, 1987*. New York: National Urban Leaque, 1987.

Nelson, Hart, and Anne Nelson. *The Black Church in the Sixties*. Lexington: University of Kentucky Press, 1975.

Newton, Kenneth. "Feeble Governments and Private Power," in Louis Masotti and Robert Lineberry (eds.), *The New Urban Politics*. Cambridge, Mass.: Ballinger, 1976.

O'Connor, James. *The Fiscal Crisis of the State*. New York: St. Martin's Press, 1973.

O'Connor, James. "Who Rules the Corporations?" *Socialist Revolution* (February 1971).

O'Loughlin, John. "Racial Gerrymandering," in Michael B. Preston, Lenneal J. Henderson, Jr., and Paul L. Puryear (eds.), *The New Black Politics*. White Plains, N.Y.: Longman, 1982.

Orfield, Gary. *Congressional Power*. Orlando, Fla.: Harcourt Brace Jovanovich, 1975.

Page, Benjamin I. "Taxes and Inequality: Do the Voters Get What They Want?" unpublished manuscript.

Parenti, Michael. *Democracy for the Few*. New York: St. Martin's Press, 1983.

Parenti, Michael. *Inventing Reality*. New York: St. Martin's Press, 1985.

Parenti, Michael. "Power and Pluralism." *Journal of Politics* (August 1970).

Parsons, Talcott. "A Revised Analytical Approach to the Theory of Social Stratification," in R. Bendix and S. M. Lipset (eds.), *Class, Status, and Power.* New York: Free Press, 1953.

Pechman, Joseph. *Who Paid the Taxes, 1966–1985?* Washington, D.C.: Brookings Institute, 1985.

Perkins, Dexter. *Charles Evans Hughes.* Boston: Little, Brown, 1956.

Perlman, Janice. "Grassrooting the System." *Social Policy* (September-October 1976).

Peterson, Paul. *City Limits.* Chicago: University of Chicago Press, 1981.

Piven, Frances Fox, and Richard Cloward. *The New Class War.* New York: Pantheon, 1982.

Piven, Frances Fox, and Richard Cloward. *Regulating the Poor.* New York: Vintage, 1971.

Pohlmann, Marcus. "The Electoral Impact of Partisanship and Incumbency Reconsidered." *Urban Affairs Quarterly* (June 1978).

Pohlmann, Marcus. *Political Power in the Postindustrial City.* Millwood, N.Y.: Associated Faculties Press, 1986.

Pohlmann, Marcus. "Socialism in Soviet Armenia." *National Forum* (Spring 1985).

Polsby, Nelson. *Community Power and Political Theory.* New Haven, Conn.: Yale University Press, 1980.

Powers, Ron. *The Newscasters.* New York: St. Martin's Press, 1977.

Ranney, Austin. *Curing the Mischief of Faction.* Berkeley: University of California Press, 1975.

Ransom, Roger, and Richard Sutch. *One Kind of Freedom.* Cambridge: Cambridge University Press, 1977.

Raspberry, William. "Politics, Blacks, and the Press," in Richard Lee (ed.), *Politics and the Press.* Washington, D.C.: Acropolis, 1970.

Record, Wilson. *The Negro and the Communist Party.* New York: Atheneum, 1971.

Record, Wilson. *Race and Radicalism.* Ithaca, N.Y.: Cornell University Press, 1964.

Redman, Eric. *The Dance of Legislation.* New York: Simon & Schuster, 1973.

Reed, Adolph, Jr. *The Jesse Jackson Phenomenon.* New Haven, Conn.: Yale University Press, 1986.

Reich, Michael. "The Development of the U.S. Labor Force," in Richard Edwards (ed.), *The Capitalist System.* Englewood Cliffs, N.J., Prentice-Hall, 1978.

Reid, Samuel. *The New Industrial Order.* New York: McGraw-Hill, 1976.

Reimer, Everett. *School Is Dead.* Garden City, N.Y. Doubleday, 1971.

Reiselbach, Leroy. *Congressional Politics.* New York: McGraw-Hill, 1973.

Re Pass, David. "Issue Salience and Voter Choice." *American Political Science Review* (June 1971).

Rifkin, Jeremy, and Randy Barber. *The North Will Rise Again: Pensions and Power in the 1980s.* Boston: Beacon Press, 1978.

Rossiter, Clinton. *Conservatism in America.* New York: Vintage, 1962.

Rossiter, Clinton (ed.). *The Federalist Papers.* New York: New American Library, 1961.

Rossiter, Clinton. *Parties and Politics in America.* Ithaca, N.Y.: Cornell University Press, 1960.

Rovetch, Emily (ed.). *Like It Is.* New York: Dutton, 1981.

Rowan, Carl. *Just between Us.* New York: Random House, 1974.

Ruskay, Joseph, "Tax Reform: The Loopholes Still with Us." *The Nation* (March 22, 1971).

Salamon, Lester. "Protest, Politics, and Modernization in the American South," doctoral dissertation, Harvard University, 1971.

Salamon, Lester, and Stephen Van Evera. "Fear, Apathy, and Discrimination." *American Political Science Review* (December 1973).

Samuelson, Paul, and William Nordhaus. *Economics.* New York: McGraw-Hill, 1985.

Sawyer, Malcolm, and Frank Wasserman. "Income Distribution in the OECD Countries." *OECD Economic Outlook* (July 1976).

Schattschneider, E. E. *Party Government.* New York: Holt, Rinehart and Winston, 1942.

Schattschneider, E. E. *The Semi-Sovereign People.* New York: Holt, Rinehart and Winston, 1960.

Scherer, Frederic. *Industrial Market Structure and Economic Performance.* Chicago: Rand McNally, 1980.

Schlozman, Kay Lehman, and John Tierney. *Organized Interests and American Democracy.* New York: Harper & Row, 1985.

Schuman, Howard, Charlotte Steeh, and Lawrence Bobo. *Racial Attitudes in America.* Cambridge, Mass.: Harvard University Press, 1985.

Schumpeter, Joseph. *Capitalism, Socialism, and Democracy.* New York: Harper & Row, 1950.

Schwartz, Herman. *Packing the Courts: The Conservative Campaign to Rewrite the Constitution.* New York: Scribner, 1988.

Sears, David, and John McConahay. *The Politics of Violence.* Boston: Houghton Mifflin, 1973.

Sheehan, Robert. "Proprietors in the World of Big Business." *Fortune* (June 15, 1967).

Sherman, Howard. *Radical Political Economy.* New York: Basic Books, 1972.

Shostak, Arthur. *Blue Collar.* New York: Random House, 1969.

Sickels, Robert. "Dragons, Baconstrips, and Dumbbells: Who's Afraid of Reapportionment?" *Yale Law Journal* (July 1966).

Sinkler, George. *The Racial Attitudes of American Presidents.* Garden City, N.Y.: Doubleday, 1972.

Smith, Adam. *The Wealth of Nations.* New York: Modern Library, 1969. Originally published 1776.

Smith, Bob. *They Closed Our Schools.* Chapel Hill: University of North Carolina Press, 1965.

Smith, Desmond. "Mining the Golden Spectrum." *The Nation* (May 26, 1979).

Smith, James D., and Staunton K. Calvert. "Estimating the Wealth of Top Wealth-holders from Estate Tax Returns." *Proceedings of the American Statistical Association* (1965)

Smith, James D., and Stephen D. Franklin. "The Concentration of Wealth, 1922–1969." *American Economic Review* (May 1974).

Smith, James D., and Finis Welch. *Closing the Gap.* Santa Monica, Calif.: Rand, 1986.

Smith, Michael D. "Social Background and Role Perception of Black Judges," paper presented at the annual meeting of the American Political Science Association, New Orleans, September 1973.

St. Angelo, Douglas, and Paul Puryear. "Fear, Apathy, and Other Dimensions of Black Voting," in Michael B. Preston, Lenneal J. Henderson, Jr., and Paul L. Puryear (eds.), *The New Black Politics,* White Plains, N.Y.: Longman, 1982.

Stanley, David, Dean Mann, and Jameson Doig. *Men Who Govern.* Washington, D.C.: Brookings Institute, 1969.

Steele, Lewis M. "Nine Men in Black Who Think White." *New York Times,* October 13, 1968.

Sternleib, George, and James Hughes. *Income and Jobs: USA*. New Brunswick, N.J.: Center for Urban Policy Research, 1984.

Stone, Chuck. *Black Political Power in America*. Indianapolis: Bobbs-Merrill, 1964.

Storper, Michael, and Richard Walker. "The Spatial Division of Labor," in Larry Sawers and William Tabb (eds.), *Sunbelt/Snowbelt*. New York: Oxford University Press, 1984.

Swinton, David. "Economic Status of Blacks, 1986," in National Urban League, *State of Black America, 1987*. New York: National Urban League, 1987.

Szatmary, David. *Shays' Rebellion: The Making of an Agrarian Insurrection*. Amherst: University of Massachusetts Press, 1980.

Tabb, William. "Economic Democracy and Regional Restructuring: An Internationalization Perspective," in Larry Sawers and William Tabb (eds.), *Sunbelt/Snowbelt*. New York: Oxford University Press, 1984.

Tabb, William. "A Pro-people Urban Policy," in William Tabb and Larry Sawers (eds.), *Marxism and the Metropolis*. New York: Oxford University Press, 1984.

Tabb, William, and Larry Sawers (eds.), *Marxism and the Metropolis*. New York: Oxford University Press, 1978.

Terkel, Studs. *Division Street: America*. New York: Pantheon, 1967.

Terkel, Studs. *Working*. New York: Avon, 1974.

Thompson, Gayle B. "Pension Coverage and Benefits: Findings from the Retirement History Society," U.S. Department of Health, Education and Welfare, Social Security Administration. *Social Security Bulletin* (February 1978).

Thurow, Lester. *Generating Inequality*. New York: Basic Books, 1975.

Thurow, Lester. *Zero-Sum Society*. New York: Basic Books, 1980.

Tolchin, Martin, and Susan Tolchin. *Buying into America*. New York: Times Books, 1987.

Truman, David B. *The Governmental Process: Political Interests and Public Opinion*. New York: Knopf, 1971.

Tucker, Robert C. (ed.). *The Marx-Engels Reader*. New York: Norton, 1978.

Tufte, Edward. "The Relationship between Seats and Votes in Two-Party Systems." *American Political Science Review* (June 1973).

Turner, Julius. *Party and Constituency: Pressures on Congress*. Baltimore: Johns Hopkins Press, 1970.

van den Berghe, Pierre L. *Race and Racism*. New York: Wiley, 1967.

Verba, Sidney, and Norman Nie. *Participation in America*. New York: Harper & Row, 1972.

Vernon, Raymond. *Storm over the Multinationals*. Cambridge, Mass.: Harvard University Press, 1977.

Villarejo, D. "Stock Ownership and the Control of Corporations." *New University Thought* (Fall 1961, Winter 1962).

Vines, Kenneth. "Federal District Judges and Race Relations Cases in the South." *Journal of Politics* (May 1964).

Vivian, C. T. *Black Power and the American Myth*. Philadelphia: Fortress, 1970.

Vogel, David. "Business's New Class Struggle." *The Nation* (December 15, 1979).

Walsh, Joan. "Police Brutality Divides Milwaukee." *In These Times* (September 9, 1981).

Walton, Hanes, Jr. *Black Political Parties*. New York: Free Press, 1972.

Walton, Hanes, Jr. *Invisible Politics: Black Political Behavior*. Albany, N.Y.: State University of New York Press, 1985.

Walton, Hanes, Jr. Review of Andrew Buri, "Robert L. Vann of the *Pittsburg Courier*." *American Historical Review* (December 1975).

Wanninski, Jude. *The Way the World Works*. New York: Basic Books, 1978.

Ware, Gilbert (ed.). *From the Black Bar: Voices for Equal Justice*. New York: Putnam, 1976.

Warner, Sam Bass. *The Private City*. Philadelphia: University of Pennsylvania Press, 1968.

Warren, Donald. *The Radical Center*. South Bend, Ind.: University of Notre Dame Press, 1976.

Watson, Sharon. "Do Mayors Matter?" paper presented at the annual meeting of the American Political Science Association, Washington, D.C., August 1980.

Weinberg, Meyer. *A Chance to Learn: A History of Race and Education in the United States*. New York: Cambridge University Press, 1977.

Weinstein, James. *The Decline of American Socialism*. New York: Monthly Review Press, 1967.

Wicker, Tom. *On Press*. New York: Viking, 1978.

Wildavsky, Aaron. *The Politics of the Budgetary Process*. Boston: Little, Brown, 1974.

Wilkes, Paul. "As the Blacks Move In, the Ethnics Move Out." *New York Times Magazine* (January 24, 1971).

Williams, Henry. *Black Response to the American Left, 1917–1920*. Princeton, N.J.: Princeton University Press, 1973.

Willie, Charles V. "The Future of School Desegregation," in National Urban League, *The State of Black America, 1987*. New York: National Urban League, 1987.

Wilmore, Gayraud. *Black Religion and Black Radicalism*. Garden City, N.Y.: Anchor/Doubleday, 1973.

Wilson, Clint, and Felix Gutierrez. *Minorities and the Media*. Beverly Hills, Calif.: Sage, 1985.

Wilson, James Q. *Negro Politics*. New York: Free Press, 1965.

Wilson, William J. *The Declining Significance of Race*. Chicago: University of Chicago Press, 1980.

Wilson, William J. *The Truly Disadvantaged*. Chicago: University of Chicago Press, 1987.

Wirt, Frederick. *Politics of Southern Equality*. Hawthorne, N.Y.: Aldine, 1970.

Wolfinger, Raymond, and Steven Rosenstone. "The Effect of Registration Laws on Voter Turnout." *American Political Science Review* (March 1978).

Wolman, Harold, and Norman Thomas. "Black Interests, Black Groups and Black Influence in the Federal Political Process." *Journal of Politics* (November 1970).

Woodson, Carter. *The Education of the Negro prior to 1861*. Washington, D.C.: Associated Publishers, 1919.

Wright, Erik. "Race, Class, and Income Inequality." *American Journal of Sociology* (May 1978).

Zeitlin, Maurice. "Corporate Ownership and Control." *American Journal of Sociology*, (March 1974).

Zilg, Gerald. *Du Pont: Behind the Nylon Curtain*. Englewood Cliffs, N.J.: Prentice-Hall, 1974.

Zinn, Howard. *A People's History of the United States*. New York: Harper & Row, 1980.

Index